Reflections of Nero

Reflections of Nero

culture, history & representation

edited by

Jaś Elsner & Jamie Masters

Duckworth

First published in 1994 by
Gerald Duckworth & Co. Ltd.
The Old Piano Factory
48 Hoxton Square, London N1 6PB
Tel: 071 729 5986
Fax: 071 729 0015

© 1994 by Jaś Elsner and Jamie Masters

All rights reserved. No part of this publication
may be reproduced, stored in a retrieval system, or
transmitted, in any form or by any means, electronic,
mechanical, photocopying, recording or otherwise,
without the prior permission of the publisher.

A catalogue record for this book is available
from the British Library

ISBN 0 7156 2479 2

Picture credits

Plates 1 and 2: courtesy of the USC Film and Television Library;
plates 4 and 5: courtesy of the British Film Institute, copyright
Turner Entertainment Co., all rights reserved; plates 6-11:
courtesy of the Trustees of the British Museum. The editors
are grateful to the Classics Faculty, University of Cambridge,
for funding the illustrations.

Typeset by Ray Davies
Printed in Great Britain by
Redwood Books Trowbridge

Contents

List of contributors	vii
List of plates	viii
Introduction *Jaś Elsner & Jamie Masters*	1

Part I. The representation of Nero

1. Make like Nero! The appeal of a cinematic emperor *Maria Wyke*	11
2. Nero in Tacitus and Nero in Tacitism: the historian's craft *Joan-Pau Rubiés*	29
3. The *inventio* of Nero: Suetonius *Tamsyn Barton*	48

Part II. Tropes of history

4. The tyrant at table *Justin Goddard*	67
5. Beware of imitations: theatre and the subversion of imperial identity *Catharine Edwards*	83
6. Nero at play? The emperor's Grecian odyssey *Susan E. Alcock*	98
7. Constructing decadence: the representation of Nero as imperial builder *Jaś Elsner*	112

Part III. Tropes of literature

8. Persius and the decoction of Nero *Emily Gowers*	131
9. Deceiving the reader: the political mission of Lucan *Bellum Civile* 7 *Jamie Masters*	151
10. Nero, Seneca and Stoicism in the *Octavia* *Gareth Williams*	178
11. Seneca's *Thyestes* and the morality of tragic *furor* *Alessandro Schiesaro*	196
12. Educating Nero: a reading of Seneca's *Moral Epistles* *Yun Lee Too*	211
13. Famous last words: authorship and death in the *Satyricon* and Neronian Rome *Catherine Connors*	225
Index	237

Contributors

Susan E. Alcock is assistant professor of Classical Archaeology and Classics, University of Michigan, Ann Arbor.

Tamsyn Barton was lately research fellow, Newnham College, Cambridge.

Catherine Connors is assistant professor in the Department of Classics, University of Washington, Seattle.

Catharine Edwards is lecturer in Ancient History and Latin Literature at the University of Bristol.

Jaś Elsner is lecturer in Classical Art at the Courtauld Institute, London University.

Justin Goddard is teaching fellow at Royal Holloway and Bedford New College, London.

Emily Gowers is lecturer in Latin Literature at University College, London.

Jamie Masters was lately research fellow, Clare College, Cambridge.

Joan-Pau Rubiés is research fellow, Queens' College, Cambridge and the European University Institute in Florence.

Alessandro Schiesaro is assistant professor of Classics, Princeton University.

Yun Lee Too is research fellow, Gonville and Caius College, Cambridge.

Gareth Williams is assistant professor of Latin, Columbia University, New York.

Maria Wyke is lecturer in Latin Literature in the University of Reading.

Plates

between pages 120 and 121

1. Sample advertisement for Munsingwear rayon boxer shorts, from the campaign book for *Quo Vadis* (1951).

2. Sample poster advertising the reissue of *The Sign of the Cross*, from the campaign book of 1944.

3. Cecil B. DeMille directs the filming of *The Sign of the Cross* (1932).

4. Nero shows his court plans for rebuilding Rome, from *Quo Vadis* (1951).

5. Nero plays as Rome burns in *Quo Vadis* (1951).

6. Neronian coin showing the Ara Pacis.

7. Neronian coin showing Nero's arch.

8. Neronian coin showing the harbour at Ostia.

9. Neronian coin showing the closure of the gates of the Temple of Janus Geminus.

10. Neronian coin showing the Macellum Magnum.

11. Neronian coin showing the Temple of Vesta.

Introduction

Jaś Elsner & Jamie Masters

Once upon a time Nero took it into his head that he wished to give birth to a child, and so he called in his physicians and prevailed upon them to give him a magic potion which would cause him to become pregnant. This they did, and in due course he gave birth, out of his mouth, to a toad ...

Kaiserchronik, twelfth century[1]

Nero therefore ordered his mother to be brought before him, for he was living in concubinage with her, and he also sent for his doctors and ordered them to kill his mother, for the desire and will had come to him to see the secrets of his mother's belly and how a child formed in the womb ... And when they opened her belly, the emperor looked at the inside of the womb and saw in it seven little compartments each adapted for a human form and prepared for a seventh child. Then he was filled with great indignation and said 'I came out of such a place!' And he let down his breeches and relieved himself into the belly of his mother ...

Jean d'Outremeuse, fourteenth century[2]

Augustus dominates our vision of the Roman principate. In our time he has been the subject not only of extensive detailed studies, but also of outstanding synthetic accounts which have brought together literary, archaeological, art-historical and historiographic discussions into an interconnecting cultural history of early imperial Rome.[3] But modern historiography, so dedicated to teasing out the complex issues of the birth of the principate, somehow tires at the monotony of succeeding emperors, each (at least in the first century AD) an increasingly flawed copy of the original paradigm. And thus, for all the good work that has been done on the literature, art, archaeology and history of the Neronian regime, little attempt has been made as yet to bring all these aspects together into a cultural history, or within the purview of a single volume.[4] Nero, like many interesting post-Augustan Roman emperors (Tiberius, Domitian, or Hadrian, for example) falls victim to the misfortune of not being Augustus.

But there is more to it than that. The problem of Neronian history in particular lies in the issue of credibility. The essentially positive picture we have of Augustus is – even in our sources – sufficiently *ambivalent* for us to find it plausible in a world where nothing is ever black and white. The traditional picture we have of Nero is, by contrast, impossibly crude. The historical sources constantly revile him: he is depicted as a monster of lust, a tyrant, an egomaniac, a murderer, an incompetent, indeed, in every way the antithesis of the ideal

Roman statesman; and he is granted only so many virtues as will throw his vices into sharper relief. However attractive this may be as a story[5] – and it does, undeniably, have its appeal – it is hard in the end to *believe* that any historical figure could have been so uniformly depraved, or any era so hopelessly steeped in crime and sycophancy. Unreliable as the sources for Augustus may be, they are at least inconsistent: the scope of the problem is definable, and we know where to begin. But modern historians of the Neronian regime are faced with a bewildering unanimity of hostile evidence in which they can put little faith; and their task is the essentially negative one of choosing how much *not* to believe. Though some controls are possible, and a few facts can be tested against, say, archaeological evidence, by and large if historians want to challenge the hostility of the sources, they must venture out on their own, unsupported, with no objective way of knowing how far they can go.

For scholars brought up on the primacy of source material, the idea of simply disregarding the evidence is, frankly, unpalatable; and even in our time, when the need for a more sympathetic reappraisal of Nero has been fully recognised, the portrait of the monster as handed down to us by Tacitus and Suetonius is still widely influential. Caution, it would seem, is the rule; and there is nothing to be gained from rejecting the ancient tradition outright if the underlying truth can be teased out with delicacy, circumspection and taste. Miriam Griffin's volume on Nero (to take an important recent example) has just those virtues; and as an exercise in the judicious dissection of bias, exaggeration and cliché, it could hardly be bettered.[6] She continually searches for a plausible middle ground between polemical positions, explodes old misconceptions, recognises virtues where the ancients saw only vices; and if in her account Nero still emerges more or less as a bloody tyrant, he has at least been given a fair trial. And yet, for all that, some dissatisfaction must remain: a suspicion that the whole project is *too* judicious, that the very nature of the exercise has compelled Griffin to accept a good proportion of lies and distortions simply because there are so many of them.

This weakness is inherent in the discipline of ancient history. The sources may lie, but without the sources we are nothing. In our desire to separate the facts from the invention we must fall back on weakly defended (and usually unstated) claims about human nature and ancient standards of plausibility; assume that Tacitus, for instance, was – for all his bias – at least a man of honour, a man determined to tell the truth as he saw it; that Suetonius was enough of a scholar to be relatively objective in his presentation of data; that neither would have lied when the events they were writing about were so recent in the consciousness of their age. Such claims are familiar; but none of them, save on a casual level, is entirely compelling. And indeed, even to assume that the sources had access to the 'facts' is a desperate move – as if facts were absolute entities which could be objectively 'known'.

For most of us, such profound distrust of the evidence, of the facts, of the very basis on which we write history, may appear unacceptably cynical. In the case of Nero, however, such radical questioning is entirely apposite; and it does not take much to imagine a way of telling Nero's story which would demonstrate just how precarious is our reliance on standard historical methods. We present here, by way of example, just such a story: it does not, let it be said, represent a summation of any position we have reached in the volume as a whole, though it has been influenced by some of the contributions. It begins by disregarding an axiom:

Imagine Nero, then, not as the omnipotent boy-king who squanders his power on debauchery. See him instead as a strangely powerless figure, a pawn in other people's political games; see the principate itself not as the Augustan edifice so long-established that no one had the heart or guts to tear it down, but as an institution continually on edge, whose meaning evolved and re-evolved year to year as power was drained away and re-asserted. The emperor's court stands to gain by keeping him just powerful enough to be valuable to it, but not so powerful as to get in its way. But the court is united only in ensuring that the boy-puppet remains on the throne; its factions are in constant strife using any and every means to preserve their power, from Senecan philosophy and Thrasean morality to murder. At any time the emperor's 'allies' might be displaced by a new group whose offer to the emperor for his support is the prize (they hope, the illusion) of greater imperial autonomy. In an extreme case the emperor himself might be displaced by a candidate who is more willing to compromise. An unstable situation at best.

At the beginning of Nero's story, before Claudius died, the principal characters who stood to gain were, let us say, Seneca, Burrus, Agrippina and Pallas: the group who put Nero on the throne and hoped to keep him firmly under their thumbs. If it was this group that assassinated Claudius and cleared the way for Nero, so much the better for our narrative; if Claudius died of natural causes, the timing was precisely right: Nero at the age of seventeen was nearly old enough to compare with the Octavian who had won the battle of Philippi at nineteen; and young enough for his supporters to act plausibly as a regency. Moreover, Britannicus, Claudius' natural son and backed by a different faction in the Claudian court, was at thirteen years old just too young to wear the purple. The regency began united; united in despatching the leaders of the old court (like Claudius' freedman Narcissus) in the same direction as the old emperor. Britannicus, the alternative emperor, was held as a threat over Nero himself, to keep the young Caesar in his place. Then Britannicus enacted his father's end, perishing at dinner. The regency evolved, split, collapsed as the various participants – including Nero himself – strove for ascendancy: within five years Agrippina was dead, the first victim, perhaps, of the regime's murderous internal divisiveness; within eight, Burrus and Pallas were dead, Octavia was dead, Seneca had tactfully withdrawn from public life, with only three more years to live before he too fell to the daggers of ruthless pragmatism. Tigellinus had emerged as the new imperial right-hand man, riding into power on a programme of personal loyalty to Nero (to whom he owed his command in the urban militia), and a promise to give the emperor what he wanted. A promise which, of course, was hardly kept, even if it temporarily gave Nero some room for manoeuvre. And so on ...

If we take this picture of seething court politics at all seriously, if, that is, we see the Neronian regime as a tense battle between rival factions around the idea of the *princeps*, then this must have a profound effect on the way we receive the 'facts'. For on the one hand it is clear that much of the anti-Neronian myth handed down to us by the likes of Tacitus and Suetonius is constructed in the wake of Nero's fall and the senatorial *damnatio memoriae* (the public condemnation of his memory). Nero's chroniclers are likely to be biassed, to exaggerate, they have every reason to condemn, because after its demise there is only one story left to be told about an overthrown regime. But on the other hand, even in Nero's own lifetime, the 'facts' of the regime will, at the very root, have been subject to bias, exaggeration and mythmaking in the intense theatre of cut-and-thrust political manoeuvre. Nero acted on stage, wrote poems and sung, held banquets, competed in the games, built buildings. These things presumably happened, but even as they happened they were subsumed into myth, as competing factions strove to interpret them to their own advantage. It was not so much what the facts meant as what they could be made to mean; and they could be made to mean many things, because there were many competing cultural narratives to appeal to. To give a lavish banquet was to figure in a myth of luxurious decadence, or of fatherly social responsibility, or of canny public munificence; to act on stage was to participate in a narrative of moral irresponsibility and lack of dignity, or of social change and redefinition, or of enlightened encouragement of the arts. No one controlled these interpretations; everyone fought for them, for to control the meaning was to control the act. The interpretations, as much as the acts themselves, were the terms of the struggle. And that is the reality on which historiography built. So let the story continue:

Nero is unable to act on his own. His intimates, his family, the senate, are prepared to help him only so far as they help themselves. He can be encouraged to experiment, say, with his cultural activities because in the end they are harmless and can be interpreted as infantile caprice. It is, further, in everyone's interest to represent Nero as an autocrat, because he has no real power; he can be made solely responsible for his 'mistakes', and gets no credit for the cunning, compromise and behind-the-scenes manoeuvring that allow the system to function apparently in spite of him. Nero, for his part, must make the best of what little power he has; must struggle to enunciate it, define it, expand it. What his court is happy to write off as indulgence in his own idiosyncrasies is in fact (let us surmise) a conscious policy of exploiting hitherto untapped sources of popularity; when Nero sings or builds baths or races chariots, he is, in part, turning his back on the senatorial ethic and trying to find a power-base in the people's love for him – in the hope that a well-loved emperor might earn the respect of the ruling class.

It might have gone either way. Nero's populist policy was, it appears, remarkably successful (and his positive reputation survived for a surprisingly long time in popular tradition); but in the end he had been too imaginative for his own good. Perhaps the very vehemence with which he was condemned at the end of his reign is an indication of just how nearly he succeeded in portraying himself as the glorious culmination of the Julio-Claudian dynasty – cultured, generous and magnificent – against all attempts to represent him as an incompetent egomaniac with a taste for arson and matricide. They had tried to control him; they had nearly failed; and their revenge was crushing.

In an imaginary scenario such as this, our written sources would count for very little: they would reflect only the victorious misrepresentation of Nero's reign, as Seneca's *Apocolocyntosis* reflects the Neronian misrepresentation of Claudius. Such a retelling of Nero's story would obviously be very difficult to derive by traditional scholarly methods, and, indeed, is more the province of the historical novelist. And yet some such willingness to disregard axioms is necessary if we are to free ourselves from the tyranny of the uniformly biassed source material. Otherwise, Neronian history has gone as far down the road of scholarly discretion as the old slanders will allow.

For all that, political history at least has been good at presenting us with interesting new perspectives. But the very real advances made by historians have, regrettably, been slow in filtering down to other disciplines; and a worrying amount of scholarship still works with a static picture of Nero the monster as a backdrop to studies of the culture. If Nero and his age were somehow morally degenerate, the unargued assumption is that moral degeneracy inevitably produced decadent art. But if we begin from the arts and writings themselves, we find a body of work that is innovative and experimental, grandiose in intention and in execution; whose bold exuberance is anything but the baroque death-throes of an age of madness. To judge them decadent is to prejudge, and can only reflect a prior belief in Nero's wickedness.

★

This book was born in an attempt to re-examine the problem of believing the image of Nero. All the contributors to the volume have been willing to question the foundations of the Neronian myth. They have responded in different ways to this challenge. Some wholly reject the ancient portrait: after reading Tamsyn Barton's paper, it is hard to take a word of Suetonius at face value; similarly, Yun Lee Too and Jamie Masters start from a position of profound scepticism and even go on to examine new Neros, new Senecas. Some, like Susan E. Alcock, Justin Goddard, and Jaś Elsner, have subjected the ancient account to a revisionist critique, but have still found some of its foundations sufficiently reliable to derive aspects of the history of Nero from it. Others, like Maria Wyke, Catharine Edwards and Joan-Pau Rubiés, have explored the process of image-making – looking at how different periods (including Nero's own time) have created different and even contradictory paradigms from the ancient story. Others, Emily Gowers, Alessandro Schiesaro, Gareth Williams and Catherine Connors, have turned to the literature of Nero's own time and immediately after, to put the spotlight on the cultural crucible in which images and models of the principate in the second half of the first century AD were forged.

Explicitly, then, we present an analysis of Nero which moves from the representation in later history of the wickedest of all emperors to the way in which the tropes and terms of Nero's wickedness were created in his own lifetime by the literature of his age. Our own culture inevitably views Nero through the lens of Hollywood farce and Renaissance rhetoric, but, we suggest, the language out of which the Neronian myth has been constructed is in many respects remarkably Neronian. While the model for Nero's character is that created by Suetonius and Tacitus, much of the material for that model was generated by the complex strategies of Neronian self-fashioning, and by the fabrication of court identities during his reign.

Part I explores representations of Nero. As both Wyke and Rubiés imply, the post-Classical reflections of the emperor are tinged with his Christian portrait as persecutor; the monster provided a paradigm for any number of polemical ends: Machiavellian, anti-Machiavellian, royalist, republican, humanist, liberal, pro-fascist, anti-fascist. As Barton demonstrates, this image was already rhetorically generated (with a persuasive orator's regard for the telling detail before the factual or even the plausible) in Suetonius' punchy Hadrianic account. Before these representations lay the powerful portrait of Tacitus, a moral picture of declining Rome in which every most cynical interpretation of the 'facts' was made to carry its full weight in a brilliantly, incrementally, negative and polemical history.

The chapters of Part II attempt to reflect upon some of the bases of these 'facts'. They address the themes of Neronian vice not just because the crimes are the most accessible elements in Nero's biography, but because they are the test-case and evidence upon which the overall portrait of monster and debauchee is based. In part, the essays of Alcock, Elsner and Goddard have a revisionist bent in exploring what plausible actions, concerns and motivations may lie beneath Nero's reported frolics in Greece, his outrageous buildings and his habits of feasting. To some extent there are convincing political motives in an emperor publicly wooing the populace of Rome at the centre of the empire and the populations of the periphery in provinces like Greece. But any such pragmatic intentions were already caught up in a pattern of public gestures and interpretations in Nero's own time. As Edwards argues, Nero was himself implicated in his own representation, was at least in part responsible for fostering the image which would outlive his death. The cruel tyrant, the actor, the ambitious builder, the traveller, the sybarite, the pervert – these were all tropes in Roman culture before Nero's own time and they were tropes in which – to whatever extent, in whatever way and with whatever reasons – every emperor might participate.

To explore more deeply the cultural clichés out of which identity, self-presentation and the public image of the *princeps* (not to say history itself) were fashioned in the age of Nero, we have to turn to its literature. The chapters of Part III, taken as a group, show some aspects of the competing positions and themes of Neronian culture as they were generated, and above all the basic ambiguity of what should serve as a final model or arbiter of decorum.

Williams, writing on the *Octavia*, a play probably produced in early Flavian times which directly addresses the history of Nero, shows how the image of the monster was already established in full Roman tragic dress almost as soon as its subject was dead. Schiesaro explores the complexity and ambiguity of Neronian tragedy, addressing the plays of Seneca which formed the model for the *Octavia*. He shows how difficult it was to read Seneca's drama straightforwardly, how tragedy both challenged the audience to make moral assumptions and then challenged the moral basis of such assumptions. Schiesaro's Senecan world is one where the audience not only contemplates but is morally implicated in the dramas it voyeuristically watches. For Too, pedagogy itself, the very basis upon which Seneca's career as imperial tutor, Stoic philosopher and tragedian to the nation is predicated, is itself at stake in the philosopher's moral epistles. This late work shows Seneca questioning the consistency and credibility of his own actions, of philosophic language itself. Above all, these letters imply an indeterminate and shifting persona, a self-fashioned but not entirely consistent identity in the writer.

Gowers presents a fantasia on themes by Persius. Her paper interweaves echo, allusion and wordplay, anecdote and quotidiana to evoke an impression of a Neronian 'cultural unconscious'. Her particular choice of images of immaturity and overripeness, precocity and distillation equips us with motifs by which to approach the imaginative frame of the age. Connors, similarly, expands on the theme of death, likening the tropes of dying in Petronius to other literary and historical deaths. Together these chapters suggest how the discourse of history and 'real life' is imbued with the language of art and borrows from a satiric literature which professes to distort reality. The 'real world' was itself imagined, reflected, interpreted, through the anamorphic tropes of its culture. But in a world where the topsy-turvy is the normative mode of literary expression, we must beware of taking any text at face value. Masters shows that Lucan's 'anti-Neronian' epic can be read as a flagrant attempt to mean the positive while dressed in the robes of the negative, to sail with the wind of political favour while steering most strongly against it. In reconstructing visions of the recent past, Lucan was driven by an unrestrained imperative to *transgress*.

There is more to all of this than just youthful impetuosity: it is the expression of the spirit of a culture, which finds itself impelled to slaughter the sacred cows of the Augustan settlement in the name of exuberant self-definition. Because there were no limits, no culturally established sense of where the experiment with the arts and the realities of a principate should end, Neronian culture exploded in a glorious and ultimately rejected orgy of transgressive experimentation. The result was excessive texts like the *Satyricon* and the *Bellum Civile*, excessive arts like the *Domus Aurea*, and excessive acts like the liberation of Greece.

For all its diversity, this volume was conceived from the start as a collaborative effort. Proposals for papers, once submitted, were collected and circulated to all the contributors; early versions of the papers were presented and discussed at a Neronian seminar in Cambridge in December 1991; and finally this introduction was passed on to the contributors for comment and correction. There were, of course, many points of disagreement at each of these stages; but while we cannot claim to have hammered out a unified view, we can, at least, be sure that what differences remain are the result of individual policy rather than carelessness. For the editors, the process has been highly stimulating; this book, we hope, will be equally so.

It remains to note our thanks: the Faculty of Classics in Cambridge not only helped us by providing facilities for our Neronian seminar, but has also generously supported the costs of the illustrations for this volume.

Notes

1. As retold in Frazer (1971) p. 215.
2. See Walter (1957) p. 264.
3. One thinks particularly of Paul Zanker's (1988) synthesis of history and archaeology, and of the two excellent multidisciplinary collections of essays edited by Winkes (1985), and Raaflaub & Toher (1990).
4. Valiant exceptions include Croisille and Fauchère (1982) and Sullivan (1985).
5. It retains its attraction for Rudich (1993), for whom Nero emerges as an early Stalin.
6. Griffin (1984).

Bibliography

Croisille, J. -M. and Fauchère, P.M. (1982), *Neronia 1977*, Clermont Ferrand.
Frazer, R.M. (1971), 'Nero the Singing Animal', *Arethusa* 4, pp. 215-18.
Griffin, M.T. (1984), *Nero: the end of a dynasty*, London.
Raaflaub, K. and Toher, M. (eds.) (1990), *Between republic and empire: interpretations of Augustus and his principate*, Berkeley.
Rudich, V. (1993), *Political dissidence under Nero: the price of dissimulation*, London.
Sullivan, J.P. (1985), *Literature and politics in the age of Nero*, Ithaca and London.
Walter, G. (1957), *Nero*, London.
Winkes, R. (1985), *The age of Augustus*, Louvain.
Zanker, P. (1988), *The power of images in the age of Augustus*, Ann Arbor.

Part I

The Representation of Nero

1

Make like Nero! The appeal of a cinematic emperor*

Maria Wyke

Nero was the instrument of considerable commercial success in 1951, as the result of his portrayal by Peter Ustinov in the Hollywood epic *Quo Vadis*. American markets were saturated with publicity for the film and with a host of merchandising and advertising tie-ins. The MGM campaign book distributed to cinema managers in the United States, for example, contained a sample advertisement for Munsingwear rayon boxer shorts which appealed to its potential customers with the intriguing caption 'Make like Nero in … Quo Vadis shorts'. Beside the caption was drawn the figure of a man wearing a wreath and happily playing a fiddle, suitably attired in a vest and a pair of shorts from one of the company's 'eight fiery patterns blazing with colour' (see Plate 1). Nero had become a symbol of luxury and the pleasures of consumerism for 1950s America.

By the 1950s, large numbers of people received their first or even principal vision of Nero through such representations of the emperor in popular cinema and other associated mass media. The purpose of this chapter is to explore the genesis and evolution of that cinematic Nero, who reached ever-increasing audiences and gradually became embedded in the popular imagination of our century.[1] An exploration of this, perhaps the most widely disseminated and pervasive set of representations of Nero, will reveal the specific place of the cinematic industry in a narrative tradition unbroken from antiquity – a tradition which constantly rewrote Nero to suit new technologies for his narration and new historical contexts within which to interpret his reign.

The origin of the Hollywood vision of Nero lies in a nineteenth-century popular tradition of historical novels which, composed in opposition to contemporary religious scepticism, described a conflict between Christian and pagan ideals set in the ambience of the Roman empire.[2] Nero, in particular, was the subject of Henryk Sienkiewicz's historical novel *Quo Vadis?*, which was initially serialized between 1894 and 1896 in the *Gazeta Polska* (in the original Polish), and subsequently achieved vast international success in numerous translations.[3] Within nineteenth-century conventions for the composition of historical novels, Sienkiewicz was able to seek authority for his representation of the Neronian age not only in his claimed reliance on ancient historiography such as that of Tacitus and Suetonius, but also in contemporary histories of antiquity and even in the Polish novelistic tradition itself. In particular, he described Ernest Renan's

History of the Origins of Christianity, published in 1873, as an historical document of capital importance for the reconstruction of the Neronian age.[4] The historical novelist depended not just on supposed primary sources, but also on their most recent literary mediations to authenticate the 'realities' of the ancient world he depicted.[5]

The fourth volume of Renan's history, on which Sienkiewicz so heavily relied for his own characterisation of Nero, was pointedly entitled 'The Antichrist'. For Renan himself reiterated not the pagan assessments of Nero, but his incorporation into early Christian eschatalogical literature. A number of pagan sources had reported rumours circulating soon after AD 68 that Nero had not died but fled East shortly to return at the head of a Parthian army. The Revelation to John, dated variously to the late 60s or 90s AD, appears to have adapted these rumours to construct the myth of a resurrected Rome, personified in its emperor, as a satanic opponent of and counterpart to the resurrected Christ. By the end of the first century, some Christian writers had integrated this apocalyptic vision with that of an Antichrist who would establish a reign of terror on earth before the second coming of Christ. Although no specific mention is made in Revelation of Nero or an Antichrist, for several centuries the legend of Nero seems to have been identified with that of the Antichrist by some Christian apologists, and both Nero and Antichrist with 'the Beast' of Revelation 13.[6] Thus Commodianus states explicitly, 'for us Nero is the Antichrist',[7] and Victorinus of Petau, in his commentary on Revelation, speaks of Nero as the Beast and the Antichrist.[8] The identification seems to have been shortlived, since there is little evidence for it beyond the fifth century,[9] and by then many writers such as Lactantius, Sulpicius Severus and Augustine had already distanced themselves from it or expressed misgivings about its validity.[10]

In the late nineteenth century, however, Renan reaffirmed the identification. Arguing that the *Apocalypse* was 'the book of Nero', he constructed his history of Nero's reign as an illumination of the apocalyptic theme. The history of Nero's fall became a narrative of the struggle between Christianity and the imperial power of Rome, between Christ and Antichrist, between Nero and the martyrs Peter and Paul.[11] So Sienkiewicz's romantic novel began towards the end of Nero's reign and followed the love story of a pagan soldier Marcus Vinicius and his Christian beloved Lygia, the progress of whose love is blessed by Peter, Christ's Vicar in Rome, but endangered by the Antichrist Nero. After the initiation of the fire at Rome (which, in the novel, is revealed to be unquestionably Nero's responsibility), the emperor's persecutions include sending the girl into the arena to be gored by a bull in one of his many morbid spectacles. Her giant protector Ursus, however, rescues her, and Vinicius appeals to the sympathy of the spectators to help overthrow the emperor. The novel ends, not with the lovers' happy prospects, but with a description of Nero's death and the foretelling of the eventual triumph of Peter's Church at Rome.

Sienkiewicz further embellished his novel with legends of martyrdom ultimately derived from the early Church fathers. The title of his work refers to one such legend in which Peter encounters a vision of Christ approaching him along the Appian way as he flees from the persecutions at Rome to safety. When Peter asks, 'Quo vadis, Domine?' ('Whither goest thou, Lord?'), he receives the reply,

'Now that thou art abandoning my people, I am going to Rome – there to be crucified for a second time.' So Peter turns back to face an ultimately glorious death.[12] The restatement of such legends (within the novelistic framework) as authentic events of Nero's reign held an immediate and enormous appeal for their nineteenth-century readers. In the same year as the novel's first publication in an Italian translation, in 1899, the Roman Catholic Church felt compelled by its enormously favourable reception to hold a conference in the Church of Saint Ambrogio at Genoa in which the clergy could debate the relative merits of *Quo Vadis?* as a serious Christian apology.[13]

Popular interest in the novel was further stimulated by the excavations which were being conducted on a massive scale in the city of Rome in this same period, from 1870 to 1914.[14] Reports by the archaeologists De Rossi and Lanciani, published in both scholarly volumes and newspaper articles, stimulated widespread interest in their attempts to support the theological doctrine that both Peter and Paul had been martyred at Rome at some point in Nero's reign. Surveying the current excavations in the catacombs and recently discovered Christian inscriptions, the archaeologists stated their support for many of the legends of martyrdom to be found in Christian writers from the second century onward, writers such as Clement, Tertullian and Eusebius.[15] As late as 1913, their arguments continued to be aired, when for example George Edmundson preached the eight Bampton lectures at the University of Oxford on the subject of 'The Church in Rome in the first century'. In this series of sermons, he drew on the work of Lanciani and De Rossi to declare that the presence and execution of Peter and Paul at Rome towards the end of Nero's reign were now facts of Christian history 'practically outside controversy'.[16] It is conceivable that the additional sympathy he expressed for the *Quo Vadis?* legend[17] may have arisen as a result of its apparent authentication by the archaeologist Marucchi in his scholarly introduction to an Italian translation of Sienkiewicz's novel published in 1900,[18] and the legend's visual portrayal in the cinematic adaptations of Sienkiewicz's novel which followed shortly thereafter.

Significantly, by the time the cinematic tradition for Nero had already developed, Sienkiewicz's narrative of Nero's fall and Christianity's triumph was being interpreted by some commentators as not just a Christian apology but also a patriotic manifesto for more contemporary concerns. Although *Quo Vadis?* is his only novel to be set outside Poland, its two entirely fictional main characters – Lygia and Ursus – are made to originate from an area of northern Europe which later, it was supposed, became Poland. The innocent child and her giant defender came to be understood as representing respectively Poland and the Polish people. The people, embodied in the shape of Ursus, then rescue their martyred country from the horns of the terrible beast that is Poland's foreign oppressors, namely Germany, Russia and Austria. The downfall of Nero, the novel's other 'Beast', operates as a symbol of the possibilities of popular vindication against the tyrannies exercised by the empires of the nineteenth century.[19] And in Petronius, who is given a central role in the novel as bold commentator on and critic of the habits of his emperor, might be seen a parallel for Sienkiewicz himself[20] – the nineteenth-century author's fears of artistic censorship and repression being expressed through the hounding and final suicide of the ancient novelist in the narrative's interior. The novel's allegorical strategies were then implemented more forcefully in the cinematic reconstructions of Nero as a representation of present as well as past histories.

The novelistic myth of Nero the Antichrist, the orgiastic reveller, burner of Rome, first persecutor of the Christians, and symbol of tyranny overthrown by populist force, achieved a unique diffusion for a nineteenth-century literary work. Soon after its publication, *Quo Vadis?* became a world bestseller, and in 1905 its author received the Nobel prize for literature. By 1933 more than a hundred translations of the novel had been published in many languages. Its apocalyptic theme inspired operas and was adapted for the stage, where it obtained long runs in the first years of this century at, for example, the Teatro Manzoni in Rome.[21] So popular did this religious fable become that the names of the novel's ancient heroes were even given to French racehorses,[22] and so instructive did it seem that it was for many years on lists of books recommended to American college students.[23]

Just six years after publication, *Quo Vadis?* was also seized on by the fledging cinematic industry, and in 1901 Pathé studios in Paris produced a one-reel short in which a selection of scenes from the novel were represented in the form of fairly static tableaux.[24] The literary tradition of the historical novel had great importance for the new film medium, for its popularity guaranteed directors an audience for their productions.[25] The representational strategies of cinema borrowed additionally from a much broader repertoire of nineteenth-century aesthetic forms than the novel, drawing also on theatrical codes and the visual arts in its pursuit of authenticity and equal authority as a mode of 'high' culture.[26] Thus in 1912 Enrico Guazzoni of the Cines Company in Rome produced what was by now the third cinematic adaptation of *Quo Vadis?* with the unusual length of eight reels (approximately two hours), thereby allowing for a storyline that could do justice to the complexities of the novelistic narrative, at the same time giving his audiences a cultural artefact that lasted as long as a play or an opera.[27] In the design of the mise-en-scène where gladiators salute Nero in the royal box at the arena, Guazzoni appears to have been influenced by paintings such as Jean-Luc Gérôme's 'Ave Caesar, morituri te salutant' (1859), 'Pollice Verso' (1872), or 'The Christian Martyrs' (1883). Audiences are said to have clapped every time they recognised the representation in film of such neo-classical paintings as these.[28] Two years later, while the film was still in circulation in Italy, its status as an artefact of 'high' culture was conveniently reinforced when a new edition of Sienkiewicz's novel was published in Milan illustrated with stills drawn from Guazzoni's production.[29] Simultaneously the cinematic Nero had achieved the status of both literary and visual art.

In its recourse to contemporary cultural artefacts as authentication for the translation of ancient history onto the screen, cinema effectively established the nineteenth-century constructions of the Neronian age as the canonic narratives for Nero's popular dissemination in the twentieth century. The differing technologies and economic practices of the cinematic industry, however, inevitably reshaped the Nero of the nineteenth-century tradition into a new emperor for a new medium.[30] Now yet another layer of mediation further concealed the original Nero from his twentieth-century cinematic spectator.

Historical film-making of the silent era exploited the new technologies of the cinema to adapt the subject-matter and grandiose register of nineteenth-century historiographic expression into a language accessible to a much broader and often less literate audience.[31] In the 1912 version of *Quo Vadis?* the visual and aural potentials of cinema were fully exploited as the arena became a focal point for the development of a new Neronian narrative. The film here drew additional inspiration from more popular institutions of the nineteenth century – equestrian shows and circus spectacles. Barnum's circus, for example, had some twenty years earlier toured Europe and the United States with a show entitled 'Nero or the destruction of Rome', the centrepiece of which comprised the restaging of gladiatorial combats and chariot races, the slaughter of Christians and the announcement of a revolt by Galba, all within the confines of a reconstructed Circus Maximus.[32]

The arena sequences of *Quo Vadis?* (1912) departed from the conventions of theatre in numerous ways.[33] The use of a auditorium built in depth on a vast open-air film studio broke the bounds of theatrical space with its confines of painted backdrops and a proscenium stage. The new emphasis on Nero's reign as *spectacle* was achieved by the employment of vast numbers of extras to play the slaughtered Christians and the Roman witnesses to their martyrdom. The whole sequence was enhanced by the specifically cinematic techniques of expansive long shots and pans around the crowd. The sympathies of the cinematic spectator were directed towards the Christians by the exploitation of point-of-view shots as they are led into the arena to the accompaniment, at the Italian première of the film, of a chorus of fifty singers from the churches of Rome.[34] The film's audience found that it too was face-to-face with the lions. The fire of Rome and the visitation of Christ also became highlights of the new narrative of Nero as the cinematic spectator became witness to the use of real flames and saw divine visions, both achieved through the special effect of superimposition. The new technologies for representing Nero as spectacular arsonist and mass murderer against whom the disciple Peter has to be encouraged to fight by Christ himself were met with considerable enthusiasm by the film's Italian and American reviewers and acclaimed with the critical rhetoric of 'realism'.[35] The fire, the gladiatorial combats, the chariot races, the massacres, Christ and the Antichrist, all seemed to come alive on the screen and thus further authenticate the new cinematic history of the emperor.

Guazzoni's 1912 version of *Quo Vadis?* became an enormous international success. In London, its première was held at the Royal Albert Hall in the presence of King George V. In New York, it was the first film ever to play in a Broadway theatre usually devoted to the 'legitimate' stage, where it ran for twenty-two weeks. In Rome, the première was held at the Teatro Costanzi in the presence of ambassadors, politicians and literati, and it remained in circulation in Italy until the end of the First World War. Each opening was described in all the respective daily newspapers, and the relatively new publications dedicated to cinema, such as *The Motion Picture World*, filled page after page with details of these events.[36] This new mediation of the Roman world immediately achieved a level of popularity to match that of the novelistic Nero.[37]

The institutions of cinema changed the relationship between historical narrative and audience, and consequently reinforced Nero's role as contemporary cultural symbol.[38] As the artistic product of many contributors rather than a single author, and as a commercial product in need of a vast audience to recoup the expense of manufacturing the pleasures of a spectacle, the silent historical film was a social document in which early twentieth-century society reconstructed the past and, using the pretext of the past, appealed to its audiences through a recognition of the present.[39] The practice of cinema-going brought huge audiences out of their homes and thus rendered their experience of historical reconstruction a more public event than the private reading of a novel.[40] The technologies of cinema spectacle accommodated masses of people on the screen before whom, or even for whom, the central characters of the narrative acted. Through these crowds of extras, mass audiences were able to visualise on the screen their own collectivity and gain a stake in the action. Historical films therefore became ideal vehicles for representing a nation's sense of its own identity.[41]

Silent Italian cinema, in particular, was constantly preoccupied with its own historical past and with the concept of Romanità.[42] The historical figures who were projected onto the screen became metaphors for the contemporary Italian body politic.[43] The release of the film *Quo Vadis?* coincided with a period of rampant nationalism in Italy, generated by the recent conquest of Tripolitania in the war with Turkey of 1911-12 and stimulated constantly in the lead up to Italy's participation in the First World War.[44] Shortly before the period in which the film was distributed, the archaeologist Lanciani, in a speech at the opening of the *Mostra Archeologia* held at the Baths of Diocletian during the Great Exhibition of 1911, expressed clearly the nationalistic agenda behind Italian displays of the Roman past. For Laniciani, the *Mostra* ought to form the basis of a future museum of the Roman empire 'where Italian youth may seek inspiration for all those virtues which rendered Rome, morally as well as materially, the mistress of the world'.[45] Italian cinema then became a site for the popularisation of this Roman imperial ideal, most notably in the film *Cabiria* of 1913-14 which, set in the period of the Punic Wars, represented a unified Roman community under the leadership of the morally upright Scipio winning victory over a decadent and disorganised Carthage.[46] The Neronian myth, however, clearly did not provide an appropriate site on which to explore the moral and political cohesiveness of modern Italy in successful confrontation with external opponents. Instead the film *Quo Vadis?* appears to have used Nero's fall as a metaphor for the possible outcome of the new state's own internal dissensions.

A curious scene occurs in the course of Guazzoni's film which seems to have warned its Italian spectators to look carefully for correspondences between the cinematic fable of the Neronian age and the condition of Italy in the first decades of the twentieth century. As in Sienkiewicz's novel, the Roman soldier Vinicius is converted to Christianity through his love for the innocent girl Lygia. When in the film, however, he kneels alongside Lygia in a humble Christian house to be blessed by Peter, a symbol attached to the room's back curtain is revealed framed centrally on the cinematic screen – it seems to be an axe and sickle arranged in what would become a very familar design in this century.

Quo Vadis? appears to offer itself as an ancient allegory for the conflicts between church and secular state in early modern Italy. Since the unification of Italy in the nineteenth century, the Vatican had refused to recognise the secular state's existence — the *risorgimento* was an anti-clerical movement. Towards the turn of the century the Liberal government had banned a large number of Catholic and Socialist organizations, and had arrested and imprisoned many of their supporters. By 1912, the role of Catholics and Socialists in Italy's national life had become a central preoccupation.[47] Through the film's simple symbolic code, its spectators were being asked to equate the Christians of the Neronian age with those groups (Catholics, peasants, Socialists) who had been persecuted by the Liberal government. Peter speaks for the Church, Nero for the secular government under whose authority the new persecutions had been taking place. In the spectacular climax to the film, the giant Ursus then wrests the innocent girl who is Catholic Italy from the clutches of the beast who is the secular kingdom. The cinematic depiction of Nero's subsequent downfall points to its contemporary value as a precedent and parallel for current claims to the realization of liberty through the populist movement of Catholic Socialism.[48]

The cinematic practice of employing Romanità as an instrument for the exploration of modern Italy's national identity meant the effective demise of the Neronian fable as Italian film spectacle under the years of Fascist rule. After the commercial failure of another Italian remake of the *Quo Vadis?* narrative in 1924,[49] and with the advent from 1925 of an official Fascist cultural policy,[50] Nero effectively ceased to be reconstructed as cinema spectacle in Italy. After Mussolini's rise to power in 1922, the myth of Romanità was appropriated gradually for his own political rhetoric. By the 1930s, the ideological connotations of Romanità had become both more pronounced and more oppressive, the *fascio littorio* had become the official symbol of the Fascist party and the supposedly Roman salute and marching step had been introduced into party ritual and mass demonstrations.[51] The Neronian narrative was not an appropriate paradigm for the regime. It was redolent neither of national unity nor of rightful dominion over foreign peoples, but of dictatorship, persecution, internal discord and dissent. And the body of the emperor when viewed on the screen could only act as a metaphor at best of luxury, at worst of moral decay.

The sequence of opening intertitles for the *Quo Vadis?* of 1924 demonstrates the difficulty that would have been attached to rewriting the cinematic Nero within the terms of the new regime. The first intertitle would have been appropriate enough: 'Rome was capital of the world. Its eagles and standards, planted by the victorious legions, marked the boundaries of the known world.' But the second and third intertitles were not: 'To Rome flowed ... the vices and virtues of all the world./ Symbol of that mixture of power and corruption, beauty and sin, was a man, an emperor – Nero.' Unsurprisingly, Augustus and Scipio Africanus became the Roman heroes of the Fascist regime and its ancient legitimators. In 1937, Rome's history was put on display at the *Mostra Augustea della Romanità*, where the exhibition's spatial rhetoric gave the reign of Augustus centrality and Fascism finality, as the inevitable heir and outcome of that earlier, supposedly benevolent, dictatorship.[52] Similarly, immediately after the conquest of Ethiopia in 1935, the Fascist government helped procure considerable investment capital for the production of the spectacular historical film *Scipione Africano*, in which the hero is seen to lead a unified, rural and warlike Rome to victory in Africa. The cinematic construction of Scipio's character rehearsed the model for the perfect Fascist citizen,[53] and his designed analogy with Mussolini was both exploited by the *Duce* himself and recognised by the film's audience. Much publicity was given by the regime to Mussolini's visit to the film set where the cast, dressed in togas, hailed him as if Scipio incarnate[54] and an edition of the cinema journal *Bianco e Nero* for August 1939 printed interviews with children, the introduction to which concluded: 'For the children Scipio is not the Roman hero, he is Mussolini ... The analogy becomes identity.'[55]

Only one Nero entered film distribution in Italy after 1925 and before Mussolini's fall, and that Nero belonged to a different artistic tradition from that of film spectacle. From 1917, before the establishment of the Fascist regime, the comedian Ettore Petrolini began to include among his numerous sketches performed on the Italian stage a parody of the Neronian court which was full of humorous anachronisms. Dressed in the guise of both Nero and clown – wearing a wreath, a red nose and baggy pants – Petrolini sets light to Rome with a box of matches and explains to firemen on the telephone that he wants to rebuild Rome in fortified cement.[56] The act clearly originated as a parody of the Italian rhetoric of Romanità, including all its manifestations in the literary, theatrical and cinematic versions of the *Quo Vadis?* narrative.[57] Petrolini continued to perform this sketch in Italian theatres throughout the 1920s, and in 1930 a film of one of his performances was released throughout the country. The film's title, *Nerone*, gave the parody of Romanità pride of place in the actor's comic anthology.

It is still the subject of some controversy whether the *Nerone* which Petrolini played in the 1920s had become a subversive critique of dictatorship under Fascism, for Petrolini (in person) expressed his admiration for Mussolini and received awards from the regime, while Mussolini himself was a great admirer of the comedian. On one occasion, the *Duce* is said to have covered his face laughing when the Petrolinian Nero produced a speech reminiscent of one of his own. At the very least, the comic sketch gave theatre audiences of the 1920s a momentary licence to laugh at the enduring posturings of Romanità, and perhaps even served the interests of the regime at the time by parading before the Italian public Fascism's apparent broadmindedness.[58] However, by the time the Petrolinian Nero passed beyond the confines of Italian comic theatre on to the cinema screen in 1930, the dangers of its incompatibility with the official rhetoric of the regime were openly recognised. On the release of the film *Nerone*, the *Giornale d'Italia* claimed indignantly that it was intolerable to display this sort of Nero – a Nero in rags, part despicable, part foolish – to the world at large.[59]

After the Second World War, the Italian film industry did not again invest considerable capital in the production of spectacular Neros for mass, international audiences. It was only as late as 1985, at a time when television had taken over from cinema as the new medium for expensive historical productions, that Rai television co-produced a colossal, Felliniesque remake of *Quo Vadis?* as a six-hour mini-series. In the intervening sixty years, the Italian cinematic Nero had only resurfaced in small-scale ventures, cheap parodies, or the so-called 'sexy' genre, designed for release in the less prestigious movie theatres. From the

1930s, Neronian film spectacle became the sole prerogative of Hollywood[60] and yet another Neronian narrative was constructed to suit the requirements of a different cinematic system and another continent's history.

The earliest versions of the Neronian fable produced by the American film industry were largely based on adaptations of Sienkiewicz's novel or other similar nineteenth-century narratives. When Paramount released Cecil B. DeMille's *The Sign of the Cross* around Christmas 1932, it was already the studio's second version of a Wilson Barrett play[61] in which the prefect of Rome, Marcus Superbus, is torn between loyalty to his depraved emperor and love for the pure Christian girl Mercia. DeMille's Neronian narrative for 1930s America begins when Rome has already been burning for three days and ends not with the successful rescue of Mercia from Nero's arena and its political and religious consequences for the history of the city, but with the soldier's conversion to Christianity and his personal salvation through martyrdom in the arena by his beloved's side. The film's climatic sequence symbolically pitches a Nero dwarfed by the huge sculpture of an eagle with outstretched wings (which sits above his throne in the arena's royal box) against the two lovers who walk up the steps of their dungeon to death swathed in brilliant light that, conveniently, falls on them in the shape of a cross. In the absence of a Petronius or a Peter, the Americanised Neronian fable is thus focussed even more exclusively on the arena as the site of spectacular conflict between the eagle and the cross, empire and individual, tyranny and religious devotion.

The rhetoric of historical accuracy – such as references to the employment of a huge research team – was a constant component of the publicity campaigns for DeMille's historical epics, none the less there was also always an American quality to his cinematic reconstructions of antiquity.[62] The cinematic technology of sound, for example, was now applied for the first time to an American spectacular film, thereby assisting the process of establishing in the film's audience a national alignment that differed substantially from that constructed for Italian audiences of earlier Neronian spectacles. The heroic protagonist Marcus speaks in the American cadences of the actor Fredric March, the hated emperor in the English accent of the actor Charles Laughton. When, early in the film, the Christians are observed to be propagating the view that the meek shall inherit what belongs to the mighty, the audience is prepared for a spiritual salvation that will reap rich historical rewards – another glorious American revolution, where the mighty are to be identified with the rulers of the British Empire, the meek with the American rebels against that colonial rule.[63] The narrative of early Italian cinema is rewritten to render Nero the embodiment of essentially *foreign* evils against which a modern American crusade is still to be fought. The eagle signifies an oppression and moral decadence which is quintessentially foreign, the cross a freedom and innocence which is quintessentially American. Americanism is thus associated with the dogmas of Christianity and gifted with the endorsement of God.[64]

How DeMille's Nero could be read as a cultural symbol of the evil against which modern-day America fights was made explicit on the film's reissue in 1944. At the time of the Allied campaign in Italy, Paramount saw the possible appeal and commercial potential of a rerelease of *The Sign of the Cross*, and began preparations to add a costly new prologue to the film outlining its additional, suddenly acquired, relevance. Through the technologies and practices specific to the cinematic industry, the studio was able swiftly both to disclose and to extend their Nero's engagement with developments in contemporary history. In the specially filmed prologue, two American army chaplains, one Catholic and one Protestant, are on board an aeroplane whose mission is to drop propaganda leaflets on Rome about the merits of the Allied invasion. They explain to the pilot and turret-gunner the history of the city. The prologue concludes 'Nero thought he was master of the world. He cared no more for the lives of others than Hitler does ... ' and, as the plane turns back, the clouds of anti-aircraft smoke which fill the screen dissolve to be replaced by the smoke of the ancient city burning under Nero's orders, accompanied by the sounds of the emperor's demonic laughter. Through the addition of a prologue, and the technique of dissolve, the ancient besieged city becomes the clear counterpart of the modern occupation.[65]

When, soon after the production of the new prologue, Rome fell to the Allies, Paramount rushed this revised *The Sign of the Cross* for early marketing[66] and distributed to cinema managers a campaign book which was able to extend even further the rhetoric of the film's engagement with the rapidly changing events of the war. Within the campaign book, a sample poster had superimposed over scenes of Neronian debauchery the bold caption, 'You've added a glorious chapter, lads, to the greatest story ever told!', and above the caption was positioned a group of Allied bombers formed in the shape of a cross (see Plate 2). In the face of such bold strategies for establishing the significance of the film, it comes as no surprise that *Variety* for 24 August 1944 recognised that, in the terms of the reissue, 'the early Christians gave their lives like American soldiers are giving theirs today for the sake of tolerance and freedom'. The array of signifying practices with which cinema can swiftly manipulate its audiences' readings of film narrative gave the historical film, and its Nero, great elasticity as a metaphor for modern times.[67]

Notwithstanding the moralising metaphors to which Paramount drew such heavy attention, DeMille's Neronian narrative was also produced as a selfconscious demonstration of cinema's virtuosity in the creation of spectacle.[68] In the final arena sequence, the spectator is regaled with a vast array of gladiators, wrestlers and boxers, elephants, bears, tigers and bulls, combats between a girl and a gorilla, amazons and pygmies, before ultimately reaching the display of Christian piety before hungry lions. *The Sign of the Cross* is a slice of cinematic showmanship, in which the luxurious palaces, the pomp, the exotic costumes, the erotic display of female flesh – the film's so-called 'production values' – all belong to the oppressors.[69] During the era of the American depression, when *The Sign of the Cross* was originally made, cinema became a showcase for the display of commodities.[70] DeMille translated the basis for extravagant display to ancient Rome and coated the appeal of American consumerism with a legitimating layer of religious uplift.[71] Seduced by the pleasures of the display of excess, the film subverted its own inspirational message.[72] The consequent ambivalence of Nero as moral metaphor is disclosed by the strategies of the campaign book for the 1944 reissue, which encourages cinema managers to sell the film's religious element to church-goers, its historical element to schools, but its *spectacle* – 'the glitter, the excitement, the thrills which characterised Rome at the height of her power and the depth of her depravity' – to the masses.

The conflict of interests appears to have been partially resolved in the figure of the film director himself. He is the external constructor of the film's internal spectacle but whereas the ancient Nero directed scenes of horror, the modern Nero's spectacles are more benign. In a lengthy article by Dorothy Donnell which appeared in the *Motion Picture Magazine* of November 1932, DeMille takes on the role of a new, beneficent Nero. He puts Hollywood's 'extras', unemployed since the beginning of the Depression, back to work. Vestal virgins and gladiators, the article continues, now order malted milks and ham sandwiches in the studio cafeteria, and DeMille tries to spare the destitute among his cast when he chooses those who must appear in only a single scene. Articles such as this, and the publication of illustrative photographs drawing attention to the process of *creating* the ancient world as cinema (see Plate 3), disclose Hollywood's use of the film spectacle as yet a further metaphor – this time for the Hollywood industry itself.[73] Once again the rhetoric of the Neronian fable is changed to suit new historical contexts and new selfconscious cinematic practices. Hollywood films become the modern arena for spectacle, and their directors new, heroic Neros.

From the late 1930s, MGM planned the production of what was to become the last film to date to address the Neronian myth in spectacular style, namely Mervyn LeRoy's remake of *Quo Vadis?*, which was finally released in 1951. It too appealed to its audiences as a multi-faceted and somewhat contradictory metaphor for contemporary America and, specifically, America's own film industry. At a cost of over $7 million, this colossal Technicolor production none the less achieved considerable commercial success and eight Oscar nominations.[74] Its rhetoric for historical authentication was remarkably extravagant, thus imparting to the film's social action an apparent ideological authority[75] – studio publicity drew attention in particular to one of the film's contributors, Hugh Gray, as an Oxford man, educated in classics, knowledgable in both Greek and Latin, whose research for the film was claimed to originate in the study of Juvenal, Suetonius, Ovid, Petronius and Tacitus, and now filled many notebooks which would be generously donated to the University of Rome (or, alternatively, the UCLA library) upon completion of production.[76]

As with *The Sign of the Cross*, the Hollywood studio practice of releasing pre- and post-production information for the press, often reproduced verbatim in newspaper and magazine articles, effectively prepared audiences to see the cinematic Nero as a reflection on the triumphs of contemporary America. As early as April 1943, for example, an MGM newsletter described its forthcoming historical spectacle as 'never more timely'. For it was said to deal with the beginning of Christianity and 'an oppression that threatened its destruction through Nero, the despotic, brutal, ruthless Hitler of his day'. Within *Quo Vadis* itself, national alignments were effected using the conventions of sound initiated by DeMille's *Sign*. The film's producer Sam Zimbalist had the script of *Quo Vadis* rewritten in order to present the storyline clearly from the point of view of the film's hero,[77] played by the American actor Robert Taylor, while the villain, played by Peter Ustinov, again speaks with an English accent now familiarly signifying *foreign* autocracy. The cinematic narrative then replays America's past and most recent contributions to the overthrow of European dictatorships. Similarly, those who in 1951 observed the paraphernalia of imperial rule that clutter the screen portrayal of Nero – the spread eagles, for example, which adorn his monuments, his throne, even his clothing – could not fail to recall Mussolini's own use of such potent images of Romanità, including the decoration of one of his caps with a spread eagle (see Plate 5). For during the war, cinema-goers, both in Europe and the United States, had become familiar with the Fascist appropriation of Romanità through newsreel footage and documentaries concerning the *Duce* and his spectacles of popular consent.[78] Thus, according to one contemporary film critic, it was a special pleasure for the Italian spectators of *Quo Vadis* to enjoy identifying the crowds massed beneath Nero's balcony with those who had recently filled the Piazza Venezia.[79]

In the self-reflexive publicity that MGM manufactured in the American press, the Hollywood studio itself was treated literally or figuratively as a conquering hero. Both the film script and the Italian studios in which *Quo Vadis* was made were represented in the manner of disputed territories wrested by the American cinematic industry from the clutches of the Italian dictator. Mussolini was reported as having offered Metro in 1938 a significant sum for the film rights to the *Quo Vadis?* novel which the studio patriotically refused.[80] Much was made of the circumstances of the film's production at the Cinecittà studios in Rome which, it was noted, were originally built by Mussolini as a threat to the world dominance of Hollywood.[81] The production notes MGM distributed on the release of *Quo Vadis* in 1951 were replete with military analogies: the marshalling of the thousands of people involved in the film-making process were claimed to be 'as complex a problem of logistics as has ever faced a general in the field', while the construction of the film's spectacular sequences was claimed to have merited 'as much attention to detail as a modern army might employ for a full scale land or sea invasion'. Newspaper articles concerning the first American film to be produced in Italy since the war, with resonant titles like 'Americans in Rome',[82] constantly reinforced the studio's own attempt to establish a relationship between Hollywood film production and America's wartime military successes.

The voiceover which introduces the 1951 *Quo Vadis* sets out Nero as the Antichrist of the apocalyptic tradition who is countered and defeated by Christ and his representatives on earth. Cinematographically, the spectator witnesses the eagle of the Roman legionaries being overwhelmed by the superimposition of the cross. The wording of the voiceover, however, with its talk of AD 64 as a period in history when 'the individual is at the mercy of the state, murder replaces justice, and rulers surrender their subjects to bondage', exposes the connotative and ideological richness of the, by now, highly conventionalised Neros of the American cinematic tradition.[83] For the voice is authoritatively American and its terms take on the resonance of the Cold War era.[84] On 12 March 1947, President Truman formally launched the anti-Communist crusade with an address to Congress in which he depicted a far-reaching struggle between 'free' and 'totalitarian' ways of life, and argued that 'it must be the policy of the United

States to support free peoples who are resisting attempted subjugation ...'.⁸⁵ The year of the production of *Quo Vadis*, 1950, also saw the full flowering of the anti-Communist crusade in America in which religion took on a patriotic significance. Only a few years later, President Eisenhower would declare that the 'recognition of the Supreme Being is the first, the most basic expression of Americanism' and fundamentalist Protestant sects would portray the Cold War in apocalyptic terms, assimilating Stalin to the Antichrist.⁸⁶

The studio publicity for *Quo Vadis* brought out more explicitly this additional facet of MGM's Nero as contemporary cultural symbol of a pagan Stalinism that, in its cinematic translation, is overwhelmingly defeated. The 1951 campaign book contained an announcement that the world could well use the message of *Quo Vadis* 'in the dark days that seem to be threatening us', that its storyline 'cries out a creed of non-violence and a just resistance to godless aggression'. The community relations department of the Motion Picture Association of America took up the studio's clarion call by mailing to appropriate community leaders a letter which argued that, by giving the impression of revulsion against a dictatorship which denies personal security to everyone and precludes the freedom to worship one's deity, *Quo Vadis* teaches a great lesson from the past that is equally greatly needed in the present.⁸⁷ Such Cold War didacticism rehearsed within the institution of cinema was evidently effective for, according to the *Gazeta Wyborcza* of 31 May 1991, the film was treated as a threatening weapon of enemy ideology by the communist rulers of Eastern Europe, where its screening was out of the question for decades.⁸⁸

In the figure of Petronius, however, *Quo Vadis* attached a slight qualification to this essentially conformist position and revealed further the use to which the cinematic Nero was put for Hollywood's own obsessive self-presentation. In 1947 the House committee for un-American activities had initiated an investigation into the political makeup of the motion picture industry itself. Ten screen-writers and directors who refused to discuss their political beliefs and affiliations were sentenced to a year in prison.⁸⁹ The hounding and suicide of the writer Petronius within the film's narrative seems then to recall and criticise the witch-hunts against Hollywood undertaken during the McCarthy era.⁹⁰ The film's hidden agenda, to vindicate the institution of Hollywood cinema itself, was abetted by the rhetoric of its production details. Everywhere MGM disseminated representations of itself as having contributed in some small way to America's Marshall Plan for the restoration of Europe's post-war economies. The stacking up of details of the film's vast expense in the process of creating spectacle, its manufacture of thousands of costumes, sandals, helmets and goblets, its construction of costly sets such as the reconstructions of Nero's palace and the Circus Maximus, the employment of thousands of extras at the Cinecittà studios, all became images of the Hollywood industry's generosity to Italy's dispossessed. The campaign book boasted that food from the reconstructed Neronian banquet scenes were subsequently distributed to five relief agencies for poor Italian children. Following in the tradition of DeMille's beneficent Nero, *Quo Vadis* was greeted by the *Hollywood Reporter* for 25 May 1950 as having 'breathed new fire into the economic life of Italy'.⁹¹ Nero the mad architect of a new Rome (see Plate 4) becomes Hollywood the lavish architect of ancient Roman sets and generous provider for the modern, reconstructed city.

The introduction to this volume refers to the 'temptation' to recreate our own 'Neros' from out of the reflections put at our disposal by the ancient historiographers. This history of the cinematic reconstructions of Nero demonstrates that the film industry is a graphic example of an institution that, despite its exploitation of the rhetoric of authenticity, did not resist the temptation, but, on the contrary, put that temptation to good use and was singularly successful in so doing. The cultural force of Hollywood, in particular, disseminated into the popular imagination of this century the myth of Nero as a myth of the industry's own spectacular, if temporary, excess.[92] The appeal of Nero to the cinematic industry was that on screen he could embody the pleasures of cinematic spectacle itself. In the case of its final Nero, Hollywood sold to a mass audience its self-absorbed vision through an enormous array of advertising and promotional strategies.[93] Designs associated with *Quo Vadis* were used to sell to the American consumer everything from raincoats, sports shirts, wallpaper, tablecloths, slippers, pyjamas, jewellery, tie clips and, of course, Munsingwear rayon boxer shorts. If those advertisements called on the consumer to 'Make like Nero!', it was the Hollywood cinematic industry above all that answered the call.

Notes

* Most of the films discussed in this paper are available for viewing at the British Film Institute, London. The British Academy, the British School at Rome and the Wingate Foundation generously provided me with research funding to examine archive material held at the University of Southern California, Los Angeles, and at the Cineteca Nazionale, Rome. I would like to express my great thanks to Giancarlo Concetti of Cineteca for all his patient and painstaking assistance in my research on the Italian film industry and, most notably, for introducing me to the Petrolinian Nero. Ned Comstock of the USC Film and Television library gave me considerable help in sifting through the archive's clipping files and campaign manuals, and in tracking down the illustrations.

1. As recently as August 1992, English television's Channel 4 broadcast a repeat of the six-hour TV mini-series *Quo Vadis?*, which first appeared on television screens in 1985 and starred Klaus Maria Brandauer in the role of Nero.
2. Highet (1949) p. 462 and p. 464, and cf. Lednicki (1960) p. 55.
3. D'Amico (1946) p. 119.
4. In a letter of 1901, cited in Lednicki (1960) p. 55.
5. For Sienkiewicz's sources cf. Giergielwicz (1968) pp. 127-8 and d'Amico (1946) p. 120. In addition see Walter (1957) pp. 268-9 for an extensive list of the huge numbers of tragedies, operas, ballets and pantomimes that had already been produced on the subject of Nero from the sixteenth century onwards.
6. For the Nero legend, Revelation and the myth of the Antichrist see Walter (1957) pp. 257-62; Lawrence (1978) p. 54; Gwyn (1991) pp. 452-3; Jenks (1991) pp. 240-53.
7. *Carmen de duobus populis* v.933, in McGinn (1979) pp. 22-3.
8. 18.10, for which see Lawrence (1978) pp. 60-3.
9. Gwyn (1991) pp. 452-3.
10. Cited in Lawrence (1978) pp. 60-3.

11. See Walter (1957) p. 261 and Jenks (1991) pp. 252-3.
12. From Hogarth's translation (1989) p. 424.
13. D'Amico (1946) pp. 121-2.
14. Barber (1990) p. 392.
15. For more recent discussions of the evidence for the martyrdoms of Peter and Paul, see Sordi (1983) pp. 23-37 and Frend (1984) p. 109.
16. Edmundson (1913) pp. 47-51 and p. 118, citing G. B. de Rossi *Roma sotterranea cristiana* (1864-1877), de Rossi *Inscriptiones Christianae* (1861-1888), and R. Lanciani *Pagan and Christian Rome* (1892).
17. Edmundson (1913) pp. 151-3.
18. See Marucchi's historical preface to the translation by E. Salvadori (1900, Rome).
19. See d'Amico (1946) p. 125; Damiani (1946) pp. 15-22; Highet (1949) pp. 462-3; Hogarth (1989) pp. v-vii.
20. Sienkiewicz's sympathetic treatment of Petronius was observed as early as a review by George McDermot in *The Catholic World* for February 1898, cited in Giergielwicz (1968) p. 131.
21. For the success of Sienkiewicz's novel see Begey (1946) pp. 77-9; d'Amico (1946) pp. 121-2; Calendoli (1967) p. 69.
22. Lednicki (1960) p. 11.
23. Giergielwicz (1968) p. 145.
24. Cary (1974) p. 6; Elley (1984) p. 124.
25. De Vincenti (1988) pp. 9-10; Elley (1984) p. 124.
26. Lindgren (1963) p. 17; Farassino (1983) p. 29; Hay (1987) p. 11 and p. 168.
27. Bernadini (1982) pp. 146-51; Elley (1984) p. 124.
28. According to Cary (1974) p. 7 and see also p. 102.
29. The edition was published in 1914 by Fratelli Treves. See Bernadini (1982) p. 149.
30. Compare, more generally, Staiger (1986) p. 97.
31. Hay (1987) p. 168.
32. Verdone (1963); Farassino (1983) p. 30; De Vincenti (1988) p. 14.
33. Cary (1974) p. 7; Elley (1984) p. 124. See more generally on silent epics Lindgren (1963) p. 17.
34. Bernadini (1982) p. 150.
35. Turconi (1963) pp. 48-9 and cf. Bernardini (1982) p. 15 and Brunetta (1979) pp. 142-3 on reviews of the earlier film *Nerone* (1909).
36. Cary (1974) pp. 6-7; Liehm (1984) p. 9; Bernadini (1982) pp. 149-50; Martinelli (1983) p. 9; Elley (1984) p. 124.
37. cf. De Vincenti (1988) p. 12 on filmic versions of the ancient world.
38. cf. Hay (1987) pp. 12-13.
39. Gori (1988) pp. 10-11, commenting on the work of the film historian Pierre Sorlin.
40. Hay (1987) pp. 12-13.
41. Hay (1987) pp. 12-13 and pp. 151-2.
42. Brunetta (1979) p. 146; Bernadini (1983) pp. 20-1.
43. Dalle Vacche (1992) pp. 3-4.
44. Dalle Vacche (1992) p. 29.
45. Cited in Cubberley (1988) pp. xi-xii.
46. De Vincenti (1988) pp. 25-6.
47. See the relevant chapters of Mack-Smith (1959).
48. See especially Cammarota (1987) pp. 15-16.
49. Another *Quo Vadis?* was made by Georg Jacoby and Gabriellino D'Annunzio for

the *Unione Cinematografica Italiana* in 1924. For its poor reception by both critics and the general public see Chiti and Quargnolo (1957).

50. Braun (1990) p. 351.
51. Braun (1990) pp. 344-50.
52. Braun (1990) p. 345 and pp. 350-1.
53. Dalle Vacche (1992) p. 25.
54. Hay (1987) p. 158.
55. Giuseppe Bottai, *Bianco e Nero* 3.8 July-August 1939. My thanks are due to Luisa Quartermaine for allowing me to read a draft of her article on 'Mussolini's imperial vision', in which she discusses Bottai's comments. On the film, see also Hay (1987) pp. 155-61; Gori (1988) pp. 19-25; Dalle Vacche (1992) pp. 25-56.
56. For a transcript of the sketch, see Angelini (1984) pp. 103-18.
57. Angelini (1984) p. 2 and p. 18; Petrocchi (1984) p. 181; Calò (1989) p. 133.
58. Calò (1989) pp. 134-5; Angelini (1984) p. 17.
59. *Giornale d'Italia* 14 November 1930, cited in Angelini (1984) p. 19. On the modern controversy surrounding the political agenda of the Petrolinian Nero see also Brunetta (1979) p. 473.
60. cf. Cary (1974) p. 103.
61. Solomon (1978) p. 138.
62. Hirsch (1978) p. 18.
63. See Wood (1975) pp. 183-5 on such strategies in American epics in general.
64. Higashi (1985) p. 33.
65. Hirsch (1978) p. 62.
66. See the comments in *Variety* for 16 August 1944.
67. cf. Gili (1979) p. 133.
68. As Hirsch (1978) p. 13 on epic films in general.
69. Wood (1975) pp. 183-5.
70. Higashi (1985) p. 23 and cf. p. 30 and pp. 71-2.
71. Higashi (1985) p. 33 and pp. 36-7.
72. cf. Hirsch (1978) p. 72 more generally.
73. Wood (1975) p. 173.
74. Cary (1974) p. 105.
75. As Hay (1987) pp. 178-80 on Italian cinema under Fascism.
76. See the studio press releases reproduced in the campaign book for the distribution of *Quo Vadis* in 1951, and their often verbatim reappearance in newspaper articles such as those in the *Los Angeles Times* of 22 May 1949 and the *New Yorker* of 10 July 1950. According to the rhetoric of 'authenticity' in which the 1951 *Quo Vadis* was publicised, the film's title did not include a question mark since such punctuation was not an ancient phenomenon.
77. According to a report in the *New York Times* for 7 May 1950.
78. See, for example, Hay (1982) p. 222 and the still from a LUCE documentary on Mussolini reproduced on p. 227.
79. Noted briefly by Giulio Cesare Castello in *Cinema* (1953) 105 p. 151.
80. According to the *New York Times* for 7 May 1950.
81. In the *Los Angeles Times* for 22 May 1949.
82. *New York Times* 14 May 1950.
83. cf. Hay (1987) p. 155.
84. For the Cold War rhetoric of the 1951 *Quo Vadis*, compare Elley (1984) pp. 125-6.
85. Cited in Wittner (1974) p. 34.
86. Wittner (1974) p. 123.
87. The letter is signed by Arthur H. DeBra and dated 28 November 1951. It can be found in the MGM archives at the University of Southern California.

88. I am most grateful to Laura Gibbs-Wichrowska for providing me with a copy and a translation of this newspaper article.
89. Wittner (1974) p. 91.
90. As Elley (1984) p. 125. A similar reading of the film at the time of its release is suggested by a review in *Newsweek* for 19 November 1951 where Petronius is equated with the journalist Walter Lipmann who was critical of McCarthy's position.
91. Compare the similar remarks of the producer himself quoted in the *Daily News* of 12 December 1950.
92. Space does not permit a discussion of why the American cinematic tradition of a spectacular Nero appears to have ended in the 1950s. Explanations might range from the decline of cinema audiences with the advent of television, the notorious commercial failure of ill-managed spectacles like *Cleopatra*, to the erosion of classical education in American schools.
93. Cary (1974) p. 105.

Bibliography

Angelini F. (ed.) (1984), *Petrolini: la maschera e la storia*, Rome.
Barber R. (1990), 'Classical art: discovery, research and presentation, 1890-1930', in (eds.) Cowling and Mundy, pp. 391-411.
Begey M.B. (1946), 'La fortuna di Enrico Sienkiewicz in Italia', in *Nel centenario di Enrico Sienkiewicz* (Rome), pp. 75-83.
Bernardini A. (1982), *Cinema muto italiano: arte, divismo e mercato 1910-1914*, Rome.
—————— (1983), 'Il primo boom del cinema italiano (1911-1920)', in (eds.) D. Turconi and A. Sacchi, *Bianconero rosso e verde* (Florence), pp. 13-27.
Braun E. (1990), 'Political rhetoric and poetic irony: the uses of classicism in the art of Fascist Italy', in (eds.) Cowling and Mundy, pp. 345-58.
Brunetta G.P. (1979), *Storia del cinema italiano 1895-1945*, Rome.
Calendoli G. (1967), '*Cabiria* e il film della *Romanità*' in *Materiali per una storia del cinema italiano* (Parma), pp. 61-108.
Calò A.M. (1989), *Ettore Petrolini*, Florence.
Cammarota M.D. (1987), *Il cinema peplum*, Rome.
Cary J. (1974), *Spectacular! The story of epic films*, London.
Chiti R. and Quargnolo M. (1957), 'La malinconica storia dell'U.C.I.', *Bianco e Nero* 18.7 pp. 21-35.
Cowling E. and Mundy J. (eds.) (1990), *On classic ground: Picasso, Léger, de Chirico and the new classicism 1910-1930*, London.
Cubberley A.L. (ed.) (1988), *Rodolfo Lanciani: notes from Rome*, British School at Rome.
Dalle Vacche A. (1992), *The body in the mirror: shapes of history in Italian cinema*, Princeton.
Damiani E. (1946), 'Henryk Sienkiewicz', in *Nel centenario di Enrico Sienkiewicz* (Rome), pp. 15-22.
D'Amico M. (1946), 'Il *Quo Vadis?*', in *Nel centenario di Enrico Sienkiewicz* (Rome), pp. 117-27.
De Vincenti G. (1988), 'Il kolossal storico-romano nell'immaginario del primo Novecento', *Bianco e Nero* 49.1 pp. 7-26.
Edmundson G. (1913), *The Church in Rome in the first century: an examination of various controverted questions relating to its history, chronology, literature and traditions*, London.
Elley D. (1984), *The epic film: myth and history*, London.
Farassino A. (1983), 'Anatomia del cinema muscolare', in (eds.) Farassino and Sanguineti, pp. 29-49.
Farassino A. and Sanguineti T. (eds.) (1983), *Gli uomini forti*, Milan.

Frend W.H.C. (1984), *The rise of Christianity*, London.
Giergielewicz M. (1968), *Henryk Sienkiewicz*, New York.
Gili J.A. (1979), 'Film storico e film in costume', in (ed.) R. Redi *Cinema italiano sotto il fascismo*, (Venice) pp. 129-44.
Gori G.M. (1988), *Patria diva: la storia d'Italia nei film ventennio*, Florence.
Gwyn W.B. (1991), 'Cruel Nero: the concept of the tyrant and the image of Nero in western political thought', *History of Political Thought* 12.3 pp. 421-55.
Hay J. (1987), *Popular film culture in Fascist Italy: the passing of the rex*, Bloomington.
Higashi S. (1985), *Cecil B. DeMille: a guide to references and resources*, Boston.
Highet, G. (1949), *The classical tradition: Greek and Roman influences on western literature*, Oxford.
Hirsch F. (1978), *The Hollywood epic*, New Jersey.
Hogarth C.J. (1989), *Quo Vadis?* (Continental Classics translation of H. Sienkiewicz's novel), Gloucester.
Jenks G.C. (1991), *The origins and early development of the Antichrist myth*, Berlin.
Lawrence J.M. (1978), 'Nero *Redivivus*', *Fides et Historia* 11.1 pp. 54-66.
Lednicki, W. (1960), *Henryk Sienkiewicz: a retrospective synthesis*, Hague.
Liehm M. (1984), *Passion and defiance: film in Italy from 1942 to the present*, California.
Lindgren E. (1963), '1908-1914: the years of the industrial revolution', *Bianco e Nero* 1/2 pp. 14-19.
Martinelli V. (1983), 'Lasciate fare a noi, siamo forti', in (eds.) Farassino and Sanguineti, pp. 9-11.
Mack-Smith D. (1959), *Italy*, Ann Arbor.
McGinn B. (1979), *Visions of the end: apocalyptic traditions in the middle ages*, New York.
Petrocchi G. (1984), 'Nerone mancato centurione', in (ed.) Angelini, pp. 173-82.
Solomon J. (1978), *The ancient world in the cinema*, New York.
Sordi M. (1983), *The Christians and the Roman Empire*, London.
Staiger J. (1986), 'Mass-produced photoplays: economic and signifying practices in the first years of Hollywood', in (ed.) P. Kerr *The Hollywood industry* (London), pp. 97-119.
Turconi D. (1963), 'I film storici italiani e la critica americana dal 1910 alla fine del muto', *Bianco e Nero* 1/2 pp. 40-54.
Verdone M. (1963), 'Preistoria del film storico', *Bianco e Nero* 1/2 pp. 20-5.
Walter G. (1957), *Nero*, London.
Wood M. (1975), *America in the Movies, or 'Santa Maria, it had slipped my mind'*, London.
Wittner L.S. (1974), *Cold War America: from Hiroshima to Watergate*, New York.

2

Nero in Tacitus and Nero in Tacitism: the historian's craft

Joan-Pau Rubiés

Agricola understood well the times of Nero, when to be passive was to be wise.[1]

The modern image of Nero is almost entirely based on what a few ancient historians wrote, and among these Tacitus has traditionally been considered to hold a special place as a reliable source. To illustrate this, few modern authorities on Tacitus are as significant as the influential (and massive) study by Ronald Syme:

> Not much need be said about the personality of Nero, no item where the credit and veracity of Cornelius Tacitus can be seriously impugned. He wrote of times within the reach of memory or of reliable testimony. What has been transmitted by Suetonius and by Cassius Dio shows a remarkable concordance (...) The concordance has been ascribed to the influence of a single dominant source, used by all three. A better explanation serves: the portrayal of Nero corresponds in large measure with the facts.[2]

In the following pages I will attempt to create a perspective from which to qualify this statement. My aim is not simply to refute Syme. Rather, I will seek to present a different kind of approach in which we are made aware of multiple layers of interpretation between Nero, Tacitus and us.

There was a medieval Nero which stood as model of moral depravity in the prince, an image which was mainly based on Suetonius' account, although it was also transmitted by the fifth-century historian Paulus Orosius.[3] These authors characterised Nero with a list of his vices,[4] but quite early the emphasis of medieval writers fell on *cruelty*, which was identified as a distinctive mark of Nero's tyranny in Isidor of Seville and Boethius. By the thirteenth century, the influential encyclopaedist Brunetto Latini could merely define 'a Nero' as 'cruelty and madness'.[5] This medieval tradition had a Christian dimension, in particular through Tertullian's view of Nero as the first great persecutor. The moral language was nevertheless already in Suetonius' detailed account.

The development of an image of Nero as a tyrant throughout the Renaissance must be associated not just with the changing historical circumstances, but also with the substantial contribution of Tacitus' narrative, which had been neglected until the fifteenth century. The impact of the recovery of Tacitus was so strong that it actually generated a distinctive 'Tacitist' movement.[6] An analysis of Nero in Tacitism, as opposed to both Nero in the Middle Ages and Nero in Tacitus, helps measure not only the contribution of Tacitus' rhetorical technique, but also the extent to which Europeans developed his themes for original purposes related to specific circumstances. The obvious conclusion is that the continuity between Tacitus' Nero and the Tacitist Nero has little to do with the factual validity of the ancient historian's account, stressed by Syme. On the contrary, it responds to a long-term continuity in the understanding of history as a rhetorical exercise with a moralising tendency at its core – a continuity only questioned by the modern historiographical ideal, echoed by Syme, of an empirical truth independent from any morality.

*

The interest of the Renaissance in Tacitus contrasts with obvious neglect of the Middle Ages. While Virgil, Cicero, Sallust, Seneca, Suetonius and Ovid had something to add to the Latin Christian tradition, Tacitus clearly did not. He did not seem to fill any lacunae, and he was not easy to turn into a Christian moralist (like, let us say, Seneca). But after his manuscripts were recovered and published by fifteenth-century Italian humanists, his influence began to grow quite steadily until the seventeenth century. He provided a source of inspiration for two genres that belonged quite typically to the culture of the Renaissance: a secularised political history, and a secularised political thought. He thus became a privileged model both for historians and for political commentators. The former imitated his tone and style, while the latter sought in history maxims and examples for practical politics (as opposed to abstract theorising or any morality based on a theological tradition). Not surprisingly, Tacitism was associated with Machiavellianism, confused with it, and attacked (in particular by pious scholars) because of it. But Tacitism was also occasionally presented as part of a Neo-Senecan revival, and even served to buttress a discourse against despotism.[7] One of the reasons why Tacitus was not copied and read in the Middle Ages is because his portrait of the Roman emperors was not a glorification of divine grace. Tacitus is too sceptical about the sacredness of power. In his view, 'the gods are indifferent to our tranquillity, but eager for our punishment'.[8] On the other hand, his harsh criticism of moral corruption was not based on a Christian standpoint, but rather the opposite, on a specifically anti-Christian and anti-oriental Roman morality. Therefore, Tacitus' works could be used neither as a model for an idealised morality, 'a mirror for princes', nor as a conventional source for radical apocalyptic thinking.

When in the early fifteenth century some Italian humanists sought and published Tacitus' works, those who were most impressed developed an argument against tyranny which considered the qualities of liberty as intrinsically superior to those of empire. Leonardo Bruni created this tradition when he used the first words of the *Histories* to argue that when a Republic became a monarchy, intellectual and artistic freedom declined. At the time, in 1403, the Republic of Florence to which he belonged had successfully (and narrowly) escaped the expansionist tendencies of Giangaleazzo Visconti, the Duke of Milan. There were thus moral reasons for resisting his tyranny. Some humanists in the courts of Milan and Ferrara, naturally committed to the praise of principalities, retorted a few years later that great writers – specially Vergil – had flourished under Caesar and Augustus. The Florentine Poggio Bracciolini, one of the key figures in the recovery of the Tacitus manuscripts, answered back (in 1436) that all the great writers of the early empire had actually been born in the late years of the Republic.[9]

Bruni and Poggio therefore placed Tacitus' texts within a novel debate, concerning the effects of the organisation of political power on civil societies. Inevitably, it was not those intent on writing eulogies of princes, but rather those concerned with re-defining the relationship between morality and politics in secular terms, who thereafter found Tacitus a source of inspiration. It is significant that most fifteenth-century humanist historians, who imitated Cicero and Livy, did not develop an understanding of political conflict and injustice that went beyond the occasional denunciation of the passions of particular human beings. While history was primarily interpreted in conventional moralistic terms – in a providentialist framework rather than through the study of the effects of laws and institutions on human psychology – Tacitean themes were neglected together with his style.[10]

It was several decades after Bruni and Poggio, in the early sixteenth century, that a more 'realist' approach became relevant again, when both Machiavelli and Guicciardini tried to come to terms with the success of ambitious princes – from France and Spain – against the divided powers of Italy. Machiavelli's use of Tacitus is secondary, mainly as a critic of degenerate republics and monarchies.[11] However, the concerns he expressed – about political failure and success in rational human terms – were those that drove later writers to seek political wisdom in Tacitus, especially since the writings of Machiavelli had themselves been often forbidden as pernicious reading. Guicciardini's influence was less pointed, but his understanding of Tacitus as the key source on the nature of tyranny was pervasive.

Machiavelli and Guicciardini wrote from an Italian (and, more specifically, Florentine) standpoint, and yet they succeeded in formulating a new understanding of history and politics that became influential in the rest of Europe. While Italy in the sixteenth century had to adapt to foreign rule, the issue concerning many other countries had much to do with the more general question of the nature of power under the rule of princes. Europe was not a mere collection of absolute monarchies, but rather it was based on traditions of self-government which equally involved cities and aristocracies. This European idea of self-government, parallel to the Roman idea of *libertas*, could express itself in the language of contractual constitutions based on feudal privileges, or more radically follow the models of republican regimes. But in any case 'liberty' was a preoccupation that connected with classical themes. As the progress of the Reformation shattered the theological consensus on which such issues had been discussed in the past, more secularised ways of thinking were adopted both by defenders of the power of princes and those who defended constitutional arrangements. Tacitus' historical writings became a favourite source as the sixteenth century advanced, spreading from Italy to France and the Netherlands, and then enjoyed particular success in Venice and England.

The complexity of Tacitus' analysis allowed different people to learn different things from it – thus the popularity of Tacitean themes from the end of the sixteenth century did not amount to a single coherent political philosophy. Tacitus was certainly used to spread ideas of 'reason of state', so that attitudes which were conventionally defined as short of Christian moral ideals could in fact be defended as virtuous in the name of political realism. Tacitus' characters could also be presented by anti-Machiavellian writers as deserving their tragic fates because of their many crimes. Finally, one of the most pervasive uses of Tacitus consisted of seeking some kind of Stoic consolation against tyrannical power in the figures of Seneca and others who virtuously accepted death, a use inspired by two famous editors of Tacitus, the Milanese Andrea Alciato (1517) and the Dutch Justus Lipsius (1574).

It is perhaps Guicciardini's statement, written in 1530 as part of a collection of personal maxims, which best expresses what Renaissance Tacitism was about: 'Tacitus teaches very well to those who are under a tyranny how to live and govern themselves with prudence, in the same way that he teaches tyrants how to sustain their tyranny'.[12] The assumption behind that statement was the perceived link between history and the teaching of politics.[13] 'Tacitism' in fact was the result of various genres based on Tacitus' works: critical editions and translations of the Latin original, collections of maxims extracted from the text, and political commentaries or digressions which constituted a form of 'creative reading'.[14] To these we may add political histories of European affairs which imitated Tacitus, and plays whose characters and, occasionally, themes, were taken from Tacitus.

As we saw, a detailed account of Nero was available in the Middle Ages through Suetonius.[15] More generally, since his image as a cruel emperor was a commonplace among poets, philosophers and historians, it also became part of the mental world of Christian writers like Tertullian and Augustine, who could draw on him as a kind of negative moral example: men could be worse than beasts. Tacitus' account of Nero was however the most thoughtful and detailed, and became very influential during the Renaissance, contributing to a fresh assessment of the emperor. While the fundamental figure of the monstrous and dissolute tyrant remained constant, the moral language in which this was analysed changed significantly from one author to another. One remarkable instance of a non-Tacitist Renaissance Nero is provided by the fifteenth-century Neo-platonist Marsilio Ficino, who characterised *humanitas* as an inverted image of cruelty:

> Why are boys more cruel than old men, madmen more cruel than the sane, stupid men more than the clever? Because the former are, so to speak, less human than the others. Hence those who are more cruel are called inhuman and brutish (...) Nero was not a man, I would say, but a monster in a man's skin. For if he had really been a man, he would have loved all men as members of the same body'.[16]

The definition of inhumanity could not have been more emphatic: children, idiots, the insane – that is to say, Nero. Ficino's Neoplatonic idea of universal *humanitas* was of course based on his own anthropological concerns: 'all individual men, formed by one idea in the same image, are one man'[17] – which is why failing to love each other was a betrayal of nature.

Perhaps nothing reveals better the extent to which a critical assessment of Nero was a moral option that the unexpected and provocative *Neronis Encomium* published in 1562 by a most untypical Renaissance polymath, the Italian doctor Gerolamo Cardano (1501-1576).[18] Cardano's systematic defence of Nero as an ideal emperor, an 'optimus princeps' who has been misjudged by history, is unique. Against contemporary opinions, which tended to see this apology of Nero as a mere rhetorical fiction,[19] and beyond the psychological interpretations of modern biographers, who have tended to explain Cardano's originality in terms of his hypochondriac and self-obsessed personality,[20] it is possible to see the *Encomium* as exposing some of the tensions in Renaissance moral and political thought.

Erasmus had been one of the most influential humanists to exploit the possibilities of Lucianesque satire when he wrote the *Moriae encomium* to redefine Christian virtue through the negative mirror of that which was not proper wisdom. Nero stood for Cardano as an obvious figure if he wanted to discuss in a similar fashion what princely virtue was not about – that is, by writing not simply a treatise on the good prince, but more radically an illustration of the limitations of conventional wisdom.[21] Thus the arguments employed in the *Encomium* pointed towards some kind of moral relativism, entirely consistent with Cardano's general mistrust of the human world of laws, as opposed to the much more reliable world of natural phenomena.[22] The faults for which Nero had been criticised, argued Cardano, could be found in other emperors usually praised by the same authors.[23] Tacitus was in fact a biased historian, and his judgment inevitably coloured by the interests of a senatorial class whose behaviour was as morally questionable as that of any of the emperors.[24] Even Thrasea, Tacitus' model of ethical dignity, was pointed out by Cardano as morally at fault. On the other hand, Nero's political intentions were defined as good, and his alleged 'crimes' legitimate. Nero was, unlike other princes, consistent with the values that demanded that he should care for the oppressed masses, to the point that he was brave enough to threaten the interests of the selfish Roman elite.

Cardano did not question Tacitus' accuracy as much as his judgment. Neither was Cardano fully consistent in his appreciation of Nero. In his other works, in particular in his astrological researches (which he believed, as part of the natural sciences, to be much more reliable than a piece of human historical rhetoric) Nero appeared as the traditional monster of wickedness.[25] What Cardano was really targeting had little to do with Nero, even less with Tacitus. It was the relativity of human opinions, the power of rhetoric, and the fact that moral and historical judgments were related to political ones.

The two main approaches to Nero that dominated in the Renaissance were of course more conventional. Even though the influence of Tacitus was evident, neither was purely Tacitean. The first theme is more properly described as Neo-Senecan, insofar as Nero was not opposed to a Roman ideal of public virtue as much as to a Christianised Stoicism. This is the Nero that figured prominently in seventeenth-century plays and operas, often as a tyrant who failed to observe reason and, instead, followed his lusty passions. It was this indulgence of a corrupt nature that led him, from his position of supreme power, to become a monster.²⁶ So, in Busenello's *L'incoronazione di Poppea* (1643) the triumph of Nero's love against all political considerations is shown to be futile – because love is here mere lust.²⁷

The second Neronian theme can be best defined as Machiavellian. I will concentrate on one remarkable example: in 1591 Henry Savile, a humanist-trained Oxford scholar at the service of the English court, translated the *Histories* and the *Agricola* but felt the need to add an initial section entitled *The ende of Nero and beginning of Galba* which was, in fact, an invented conclusion for the *Annals*.²⁸ One of the central figures of that section is of course Nero, whose loss of power is described. But Savile did not merely extract the material from Plutarch, Cassius Dio and Suetonius. He also addressed the politics of the English court. The terms in which this political interpretation was expressed were Machiavellian, and in that sense European, rather than ancient Roman.

Savile sets his own agenda when he writes the speech of Julius Vindex to his troops: principalities are 'the best, short of a commonwealth' – and, for that reason, intolerable when princes become tyrants. The cause of rebellion is publicised, only rhetorically, as a declaration 'in favour of mankind against that monster of nature [Nero]'.²⁹ In fact, what dooms Nero's reaction is the combination of vice with lack of political skill. The writer's two key concerns are thus the nature of Nero's tyranny and the quality of the rebellion of Julius Vindex. It has recently been argued that these two elements can be best related to the specific circumstances of the relationship between the second Earl of Essex, alias 'Julius Vindex', and Queen Elizabeth, possibly 'the tyrant'.³⁰ Savile presents the obscure Vindex as 'a man in the course of his action more vertuous then fortunate'³¹ – in this way suggesting that Essex may well be both virtuous and fortunate (eventually, in 1601, he was not). The speech of Julius Vindex, in which he praised principalities but also encouraged rebellion against tyrants, acquires new meaning: even though Essex does not deny his love for Queen Elizabeth (to whom in fact Savile dedicates the work), the legitimacy of her reign is open to question. It all depends on whether she is perceived to be tyrannical. Nero, in fact, was 'not of Virtue sufficient to upholde his vices by might'. Thus Nero is not just another tyrant: he is a tyrant who deserved to be unseated, and who was indeed unseated, because of a lack of political virtue. Nero is not only a man of private vices, but more dangerously a man of public vices. This reads very much like Tacitus; however, it is not the loss of the love of his subjects, but rather of their fear, that which finally causes Nero's unprecedented fall. These terms of analysis are purely Machiavellian.³²

Savile's veiled Republicanism found a reply from a younger colleague, the Catholic Edmund Bolton.³³ His *Nero Caesar, or Monarchie depraved* (1624) combined methodological eclecticism with the most strict political conservatism.³⁴ In his full biography of Nero he did not reject Tacitus' account, but used it in order to develop his own thesis: 'No prince is so bad as not to make monarchie seeme the best forme of Government.' Openly quoting Savile, Bolton saw no difficulty in using Tacitus to reach the opposite conclusion: 'that sacred monarckie could preserve the people of Rome from finall ruine, notwithstanding all the prophanations, blasphemies, and scandals of tyranous excesses, wherewith NERO defiled and defamed it, is the wonder which no other forme of government could performe.'[35] Bolton's reaction only serves to underline that the Nero of the Tacitists was now a card in the European game of politics.

In fact the tradition of reading Tacitus as an anti-despotic writer took root in England in the seventeenth century, from the 'Essex circle' to which Henry Savile, Ben Jonson and Francis Bacon belonged, up to the whig historiography after the glorious revolution – in particular, with Thomas Gordon's discourses on *The works of Tacitus* (1728). The quite obvious political circumstances of this tradition need not detain us here. The fact is that this Tacitist tradition eventually connected with the anti-despotic literature of the French Revolution. Tacitus was hardly a Republican, even less a revolutionary, but he was easily made into one.[36]

*

The distance between the Nero of Tacitism and the Nero of Tacitus can be best measured by looking back at the ancient historian. Tacitus was a child during Nero's reign, and wrote his main historical works under Trajan, at the beginning of the second century AD. He belonged to an earlier generation than his contemporary Suetonius, whose imperial biographies were probably written at the beginning of Hadrian's reign (after AD 117). He is also much earlier than the third-century Greek writer Dio Cassius, whose discussion of Nero we only have as an epitome by the Byzantine monk Xiphilinus in the eleventh century. However, the special position occupied by Tacitus among the ancient historians of the Roman principate has little to do with his position as an eyewitness, or his access to sources. It has been quite clearly established that Suetonius and Dio Cassius had independent access to similar narratives to those used by Tacitus.[37] Concerning these sources we only have a few names: the elder Pliny, Cluvius Rufus, and Fabius Rusticus. Rather, what sets Tacitus apart is the way he projects himself as a critical writer who rejects both flattery and hatred, as well as the rhetorical elaboration of hazy hearsay;[38] Tacitus is also distinguished by the claim that he will unlock the deep causes of events, and by the gravity with which he treats the theme of moral corruption under tyranny.[39] All these, rather than the unrestrained palace gossip of both Suetonius and Dio Cassius, are congenial to the modern understanding of historical scholarship.

The great paradox concerning Tacitus is that almost all commentators agree on the fact that his success as a historian is a result of his supreme skill as a rhetorician.[40] How can Tacitus be both the supreme rhetorician and the reliable source has hardly been explained.[41] While I agree entirely with the traditional appreciation of Tacitus' style as an intense 'dry wit' targeting political futility,[42] it is also possible to think further about the exact implications of his literary exercise. In particular, it is necessary to relate our attitudes as modern readers with his intentions as a rhetorician, because a fundamental gap separates his moral world from ours – and, if anything, Tacitus was a moralist. His portrait of Nero was not just the portrait of a particular man in power, it was the image of a tyrant, and more precisely, the image of a tyrant in the Roman tradition of public morality.[43] And yet, what Tacitus thought about this Roman tradition was quite personal, and cannot be easily reduced to a facile dilemma between republic and empire. This is where modern assumptions need to be checked.

I therefore want to argue that the modern historians' attempt to reconstruct an empirical record on the basis of Tacitus, so as to find something like 'the real Nero', distorts the conventions and intentions of ancient historiography, and of Tacitus in particular.[44] Moreover, this attempt is only likely to perpetuate the kind of rhetorical effect intended by Tacitus. That is to say that modern scholars, while attempting to separate facts from interpretation, only reproduce a watered-down version of the interpretations of ancient historians. And yet, as we have seen, there exist in our tradition many possibilities for active engagement with Tacitus' rhetoric. In the case of Nero, for instance, this opens the possibility of alternative metaphors concerning our understanding of public and private virtue.

Tacitus introduces his *Annals* with a short reflection on the nature of the Roman principate at the height of the rule of Augustus:

> Actium had been won before the younger men were born. Even most of the older generation had come into a world of civil wars. Practically no one had seen truly Republican Government. The country had been transformed, and there was nothing left of the fine old Roman character. Political equality was a thing of the past; all eyes watched for imperial commands.[45]

The *Annals*, which carry on from the death of Augustus to a detailed account of the reigns of Tiberius, Gaius Caligula, Claudius and Nero, constitute an exploration of the development of this seed of corruption. They are thus about the long-term cost of the peace of Augustus. Nero's reign was particularly significant because it marked the end of this distinct period in the history of Rome – the end of the Julio-Claudian dynasty that had established and consolidated the principate (31 BC – AD 68).

The organisation of the narrative is, superficially at least, chronological, in a Roman tradition of annalistic writing whose most famous representative was perhaps Livy. Tacitus, unlike earlier Latin historians who had been greatly influenced by Greek historiographical models, could rely almost exclusively on the tradition established by authors like Livy and Sallust. Inspired, in particular, by Sallustian themes and style, Tacitus' works were written from a Roman standpoint and within a Roman tradition, and in fact were devoted to a particular idea of a Roman *ethos*. As a man of his own times, however, Tacitus was concerned with the moral implications of the consolidation of the principate. This concern, unprecedented in Roman historiography, was in his case also deeply personal, and prompted an original response that challenged traditional uses of historiography:

> Now that Rome has virtually been transformed into an autocracy, the investigation and record of these [apparently unimportant and trivial] events may prove useful. Indeed, it is from these studies – from the experience of others – that most men learn to distinguish right and wrong, advantage and disadvantage. So these accounts have their uses. But they are distasteful. What interests and stimulates

readers is a geographical description, the changing of fortune of a battle, the glorious death of a commander. My themes are on the other hand cruel orders, unremitting accusations, treacherous friendships, innocent men ruined – a conspicuously monotonous glut of downfalls with its monotonous causes.[46]

More precisely, the narrative was distinctly marked by the relationship between empire and liberty (*principatum ac libertatem*)[47] as understood by someone who identified himself quite narrowly with the senatorial class and its cultural tradition – to the detriment of the common people of Rome. A fickle mob, mercenary armies, peripheral provinces, uncivilised barbarians, and even disturbing unassimilated groups like the Jews and the Christians, play an increasing (and yet unwelcome) role as the Roman aristocratic tradition of public virtues progressively disintegrates. It was the corruption of this tradition under the principate that really concerned Tacitus.[48] The *Annals* are, above all, an analysis of this process, with both style and theme reminiscent of Sallust, who had written on the moral and political crisis of the late republic. But while Tacitus had learnt from Sallust that the very growth and success of the republic had brought about social tensions and the corruption of traditional morals, he also knew (from personal experience) that concentration of authority may have created stability, but did not interrupt the degradation of political life. The principate had soon developed into a tyranny.[49]

Roman citizens could now only pray for good emperors and fear bad ones, but they could no longer use senatorial power in order to maintain the virtues that had made Rome powerful. On the contrary, the nature of the principate inevitably created a continuous degradation of the senatorial class. But since Tacitus did not believe in popular participation in politics, nor in a mixed constitution ('easier to applaud than to achieve, and if achieved not long-lasting'),[50] he could only hope that some good citizens would survive the catastrophe. In fact, his interpretations consistently express a bitter disappointment with the Roman oligarchy, the only human group for which he really cared (and he does not really seem to mean anything else when, occasionally, he refers to 'the voice of the people' or 'the conscience of mankind').[51] Whenever Tacitus mentions the noble action of a woman, or the powerful influence of an ex-slave, he implies that this situation is somehow unnatural, and uses the example to deride the senatorial class. The long catalogue of Nero's scandalous behaviour and crimes also takes a similar turn:

> Every reader about that epoch, in my own work or others, can assume that the gods were thanked every time the Emperor ordered a banishment or murder; and, conversely, that happenings once regarded joyfully were now treated as national disasters. Nevertheless, when any senatorial decree reaches new depths of sycophancy or abasement, I will not leave it unrecorded.[52]

In this context, the year-by-year analysis of conquest, rebellion and punishment is less meaningful than the emperor-by-emperor analysis of the degradation of Roman public life. Nero, at the end of the dynasty, could only be the extreme example of moral corruption and tyranny. 'Remember Nero', says Galba in the *Histories* to his appointed successor, 'who prided himself on being the heir of a long line of Caesars. It was not Vindex with his undefended province, nor I with one legion, who dislodged this incubus from the shoulders of Rome. His own monstrous excesses and life of pleasure did so, though there was no precedent at that time for the condemnation of an emperor'.[53] Galba's speech, with its vision of a good emperor is of course invented by Tacitus. The historian, whose skill consisted of arranging and rewriting his sources in a personal way, found in Nero all the qualities that threatened the tradition of Roman morality to which he was committed. Nero lacked, more than any of his predecessors, that sense of public duty which made emperors tolerable. Not that Nero did not have any appeal – but he appealed to the mob, and to the Greeks, rather than to the senatorial class. In Tacitus' account, the worst consequences of Nero's rule were not his personal crimes and vices, but rather the stain they placed on public office, and more specifically the bad example they set for the very senatorial class that should learn to be virtuous.[54]

Therefore, when finally Nero fell – and he was the first emperor to fall through provincial rebellion – the people, 'who in the course of fourteen years under Nero had come to like the vices of emperors no less than they had once feared their virtues'[55] no longer approved of a rather austere but old-fashioned candidate whose family went back to the days of the Republic, like Galba. Galba was murdered a few weeks after he reached Rome, a murder that gave way to the 'year of the four emperors' (AD 69). The process of degradation that culminated in Nero meant that the very principate which had been established in order to save the Roman empire from internal faction and civil war was now a weak institution. And the figure of the emperor was a meaningful expression of the paradox of political life: nothing outside the empire matched the values and power of Rome, nothing inside the empire matched the centrality of its capital city, and yet this city was no longer ruled by its prominent families and in accordance with traditional values. Rather, it was ruled by a prince whose vicious personal life was the more despicable because it determined the flavour and direction of the life of the community.

A key to the understanding of Tacitus' *Annals* and *Histories* lies in the discordant note represented by his *Agricola*, a minor work written several years earlier (AD 98) under Domitian (who was, of all the tyrants whom Tacitus had to serve, the one most often compared to Nero).[56] The *Agricola* was a biographical eulogy. The reason why Agricola is presented as an example of virtuous moderation is not simply because he was Tacitus' father-in-law. More interestingly, Agricola stood for all those things generally missing in the later historical works, the possibility of virtue and service to the state (the *res publica*) even under tyrants (when the true republican regime was no longer a possibility, but only a matter for nostalgia): 'Let those whose way is to admire only what is forbidden learn from him [Agricola] that great men can live even under bad rulers.'[57] It is this ideal, hidden under the general pessimism of his other works, what makes sense of Tacitus as a historian – since he was also a man who succeeded in his career under the principate.[58]

Tacitus' Nero is not just the Nero of Tacitus' sources, even less 'the real Nero' of a purely factual account. He is, above all, a particular manifestation of the anti-Agricola. Tacitus, who had of course an idea of truth in history, was able to read previous sources critically and probably found a tradition in which experience and hearsay had already been coloured by praise, blame and moralising. But Tacitus' idea of historical writing was not the search for a purely factual account, and his technique did not consist of checking statements, nor creating antiquarian contexts for their interpretation. Tacitus chose and arranged material which was often already in the form of a historical narrative, and then rewrote it with a personal rhetorical skill appropriate to his particular moral vein. The Nero that emerges is not just the negation of a conception of imperial office based on the Roman values of public service – more dramatically, it represents its ultimate degradation:

> Older men, who spent their leisure in making comparisons with the past, noted that Nero was the first ruler to need borrowed eloquence. The dictator Julius Caesar had rivalled the greatest orators, Augustus spoke with imperial fluency and spontaneity. Tiberius was a master at weighing out his words – he could express his thoughts forcibly, or he could be deliberately obscure. Even Gaius' mental disorders had not weakened his vigorous speech; Claudius' oratory, too, was graceful enough, provided it was prepared. But from early boyhood Nero's mind, though lively, directed itself to other things – carving, painting, singing, and riding. Sometimes, too, he wrote verses, and thereby showed that he possessed the rudiments of culture.[59]

Not being able to practise rhetoric in a political context automatically placed Nero in a category outside that of a responsible citizen who could hold a public office, no matter how skilful an artist he may be. This was Tacitus' view. It can be speculated whether this observation had been made by 'older men' or was just the historian's invention – it does not occur in either Suetonius or Dio Cassius. But it is typically Tacitean, and it has a flavour remarkably different from Suetonius' more frivolous (and equally dubious) remark that 'His tutor Seneca hid the works of the early rhetoricians from him, intending to be admired himself as long as possible. So Nero turned his hand to poetry ... .'[60]

There are various characters in the *Annals* who achieve virtuous service to the republic despite Nero's disorders and crimes. It would be a temptation to identify Seneca, the young emperor's teacher and adviser, as the centre of a so-called 'Stoic-Republican opposition'. This identification, however, misrepresents Tacitus, who understands liberty as self-government, and therefore never supports the view that philosophers should be kings. Although his Seneca is spared the direct criticism of double-standards hinted at by Suetonius and Dio Cassius, the extent to which his influence corrects Nero's vicious tendencies is nevertheless limited. That is, Seneca does restrain Nero on several occasions, but not everything beneficial should be credited to him (as for instance Fabius Rusticus, one of Tacitus' sources and a friend of the philosopher, is accused of having done in his now lost account).[61] In some ways Seneca's achievement is hollow: 'Nero pledged himself to clemency in numerous speeches; Seneca put them into his mouth, to display his own talent or demonstrate his high-minded guidance.'[62] But Nero's clemency is never portrayed to be consistent. A crucial moment of the narrative is the assassination of Agrippina, the powerful mother of the emperor – after which crime Nero lost all vestige of moral restraint.[63]

Tacitus clearly implies that Seneca somehow approved of this assassination, and even composed a clumsy letter for the senate in which Nero, trying to make up a justification, only incriminated himself.[64]

Figures other than the philosopher become prominent during Nero's reign who are closer to Tacitus' idea of virtue: Domitius Corbulo, the successful military leader whose glory Nero appropriates, and Paetus Thrasea, who consistently refuses to endorse flattery of tyranny (and walks out of the senate because he does not want to condone Agrippina's death). Like Seneca, Corbulo and Thrasea are murdered at the instigation of Nero – but their innocence and virtue are more conspicuous. Thrasea does not receive the full approval of Tacitus, since by his walkout he 'endangered himself without bringing general freedom any nearer'.[65] But the more prudent Corbulo easily evokes the image of Agricola.[66]

It is in fact this succession of innocent deaths that distinguishes the final pages of the *Annals* that we have. And (as in the *Histories*) the 'style' of each death is crucial.[67] Through its historical degradation *libertas* has been reduced to this single last instance, a remnant of senatorial power in which the virtue of the Roman nobility can still be expressed. A dignified death may then be recorded by the historian so that, perhaps as an answer to the crimes of the emperors and the weakness of the citizens, it will remain in the memory of posterity:

> This slavish passivity, this torrent of wasted bloodshed far from active service, wearies, depresses, and paralyses the mind. The only indulgence I would ask the reader for the inglorious victims is that he should forebear to censure them. For the fault was not theirs. The cause was rather heaven's anger with Rome (...) let us at least make this concession to the reputation of famous men: just as in the manner of their burial they are distinguished from the common herd, so when their deaths are mentioned let each receive his separate, permanent record.[68]

*

So far it has become apparent that Tacitus' Nero is a literary figure, rather than the casual result of impartial historical reconstruction. It is for instance during the description of the emperor's premeditated murders and unconventional behaviour that Tacitus develops his dramatic skills more fully. The condemnation of Nero as the representative of a corrupt Roman morality was not invented by Tacitus, who inherited the theme, together with the historical material, from a dominant tradition of senatorial writers – Pliny the Elder and Piny the Younger are both testimonies of this.[69] Such a tradition – common also to Suetonius and Dio Cassius – did not do full justice to the popularity that the emperor seems to have enjoyed during his life. To be more precise, if anything can be said about the tradition we have received, it is that it tends to make Nero's portrait increasingly lurid as new accounts supersede old ones. Dio Cassius is more condemnatory than Suetonius, who was already more extreme than Tacitus.[70] This tendency was picked up by the later European tradition, so that (as we saw) from the Middle Ages, and with a new emphasis after the Renaissance, Nero became the archetypical figure of a vicious tyrant in dramatic literature, historiography and even political thought.

A final reflection must consider our own readings of Tacitus. Because Tacitus has become so much part of a classical canon, it has been too strong a temptation to 'read back' onto him modern ideas about what a historian is supposed to do. Not that Tacitus is a particularly appropriate model for the aims of modern historians: in the eighteenth century Voltaire explained that Tacitus taught him little concerning Roman laws, manners and institutions – in fact, much less than Titus Livy – and in the nineteenth century Friedrich Leo defined him as a good poet, rather than a good historian.[71] But a significant number of modern historians beginning with Edward Gibbon and ending with Ronald Syme have been inspired by Tacitus, perhaps because they could identify with the plight of his pseudo-republican aristocratic virtues.[72] And since the modern historian is meant to produce a positivistic factual account, all too easily Tacitus has been treated as if he intended to do the same. I wish now to return to the paradox I outlined above: while admiring Tacitus for his rhetorical skill, modern scholars have only paraphrased his 'factual account' of Nero;[73] while claiming to separate reality from legend, they have easily deluded themselves into swallowing Tacitus' overall rhetoric. All too easily they have called 'facts' what cannot be retrieved outside the framework of a Roman rhetorical tradition. In this tradition, oriented towards a range of moral concerns quite different from our own, *inventio* played a role that no modern historian would be ready to accept.

Of course Tacitus' account can be criticised from the wider empirical perspective provided by modern scholarship. Already Gibbon, eighteenth-century antiquarian and reader of travel accounts as much as the inheritor of Renaissance historiography, was on the way to doing that. But when Ronald Syme in our century rests his monumental interpretation of Tacitus on a long series of highly speculative correlations, and the equally suspicious assumption that Tacitus was a factual researcher who 'does not need to be vindicated for accuracy', the only lasting conclusion that can be critically accepted is that Syme writes as much like Tacitus as he can justify.[74]

If projecting back modern concerns is a danger, getting caught in traditional readings is another possibility of which we should be aware. We do relate not only to Tacitus as historian, but also to Tacitism as a tradition. Thus Nero easily becomes the timeless tyrant, and Seneca the timeless example of stoic virtue. As late as 1969 T.A. Dorey remarked that 'Tacitus is of particular interest to our own times. He poses the question of what is the correct course of action for an individual member of society living under tyranny – a question that is relevant whether the tyranny is that of a single military despot, a foreign power, or a machine-dominated system of technology.'[75] The philosophy of this particular passage takes us straight back to Renaissance Tacitism, even though the references are twentieth-century. It is as if the readings appropriate at the time of Elizabeth I were only a variation of eternal readings of Tacitus naturally retrievable today.

If anything, this brief history of Nero in Tacitism makes it quite clear that various readings of the same texts have changed and made sense in different contexts. In the Middle Ages Tacitus and his concern with the moral corruption of the Roman empire may as well have been completely obliterated. Christian emperors waiting for eternal judgment could not, in principle, be analysed as tyrants. Even Dante saw in a new Roman monarch the solution of all political problems. But the development of European society came up with a completely different attitude after the fifteenth century, thus beginning a process to whose complexity I cannot do full justice here. By the time of Gibbon, Tacitism had superseded Tacitus, because the terms of the equation between empire and liberty had radically changed. The European system of a balance of powers meant that while the political imperialism of a universal monarchy could be kept in check, the new forms of commercial expansionism were not perceived as despotic.[76] The political experience of the Renaissance stood between Gibbon and Tacitus as Tacitus stands between Nero and us – and Gibbon between Syme and Tacitus. Today we may still wish to construct a Nero, but we cannot use Tacitus to make our Nero unless we also construct a Tacitus. Confronting Tacitus' Nero as a rhetorical construction is simply admitting that we are also trying to construct ourselves.

Notes

1. *Agricola*, 6. I have used the Loeb editions of the works of Tacitus (1925-37, 1970), but I quote according to the published translations of the *Annals* by M. Grant (1977) and the *Histories* by K. Wellesley (1964). Whenever I translate I only give a traditional reference. Besides the editors, I would like to thank various people who pointed at useful material: David Armitage, Tamsyn Barton, Warren Boutcher, Catherine Edwards and Peter Miller.

2. R. Syme (1958) I, p. 437. On Tacitus as a source for Nero's reign see also Warmington 1981, pp. 3-7.

3. See Gwyn (1991), p. 436. Gwyn's article is extremely useful, albeit that it reflects little on the rhetorical qualities of Tacitus' account and its influence after the Renaissance.

4. In particular *petulantia, libido, luxuria, avaritia* and *crudelitas*.

5. Gwyn (1991), p. 442.

6. For Renaissance Tacitism in general see Burke 1969; Momigliano 1947 and 1990; Schellhase 1976; A now classic study that inspired much of the modern scholarship is Toffanin 1921.

7. In general terms, we may define *Machiavellianism* as an understanding of politics based on the analysis of human psychology in history, to the point of questioning the validity of a conventional religious morality as a basis for political decisions, because the useful is not the same as the honest and (in particular for a ruler) it is often necessary to be unjust. Sixteenth-century Machiavellianism was often criticised because of its 'immoral secularism'. The Neo-Senecan revival, strong since the end of the sixteenth century, focused on the ideal of a steadfast, rational moral attitude as against the changing world of human passions. It was therefore easily made compatible with Christian traditions, even though it also made some concessions to trying to combine the useful with the honest. We could say that Machiavellian virtue taught how to seize fortune, while Neostoic virtue emphasised how to resist it.

8. *Histories* I,3; (1986) p. 23.

9. See Schellhase 1976, pp. 17-25, following the now classic argument of Hans Baron (1966).

10. The rather more successful reception of the *Germania* in late-fifteenth-century Germany, for patriotic reasons, does not of course affect this argument.

11. Schellhase 1976, pp. 82-3.

12. F. Guicciardini (1977), p.109 (series C, 18).

13. Guicciardini did not think that ancient historians could teach modern people everything, and was emphatic that different circumstances made Roman situations different from those of his own times; and yet he also believed that there was a general theme running through Tacitus' writings which had a universal relevance for the understanding of politics. On the one hand, the things of the human world were so varied that it was dangerous to generalise, and each case required special judgement (ibid. p. 106: C, 6). Experience, on the other hand, had taught many nations to draw similar conclusions from similar situations (ibid. p. 108: C, 12). The combination of particularism and recurrent patterns constituted a 'realist' approach to human history. This 'science of politics', later in the century known as 'reason of state', was the fundamental departure of the Renaissance.

14. Remarkable 'Tacitist' writers were Carolus Paschalius (1581), Justus Lipsius (1581), Annibale Scoto (1589), Scipione Ammirato (1594), Traiano Boccalini (before 1613) and Alamos de Barrientos (1614). Justus Lipsius, the famous NeoSenecan writer and editor of Tacitus, was crucial in making the Roman historian popular late in the sixteenth century, but his approach was very limited: he tried to extract from the Roman historian a lesson of virtuous 'constantia', not a political lesson. See Momigliano 1947. I am not entirely convinced by various scholars who try to amalgamate Seneca and Tacitus as a combined influence. See for instance Salmon 1989.

15. Gwyn (1991), pp. 450-4.

16. Ficino (1975), pp. 100-1, 'De humanitate'.

17. ibid.

18. On Cardano's life see *Dizionario Biografico Italiano*, XIX, pp. 758-63. In English Morley 1854 is probably still the best. On the *Neronis Encomium* see Cavalli 1887 and Solís 1988.

19. For instance the English historian Edmund Bolton thought in 1624 that Cardano's *Encomium* was merely 'a fiction, and a toy' written in order to display the author's 'wonderful wit' (Bolton 1624, p. 204). But in modern times, W.B. Gwyn repeats: 'in short, a clever rhetorical exercise' (1991, p. 441).

20. As a young student Cardano 'perversely advocated the opinions that were most distasteful to his company'. Morley (1854), I p. 64.

21. It has been suggested that Cardano was inspired by Lucian (Morley 1854, I p. 303). Lucian's *Phalaris*, a rhetorical defence of the ruler of Agrigento who was Nero's main rival as the foremost example of a cruel tyrant, must have been Cardano's closest model. But of course, the existence of a classical precedent is insufficient the explain such untypical work in the Renaissance.

22. See A. Ingegno (1980), pp. 184-208. See also Siraisi (1991), p. 583.

23. Throughout his argument Cardano targets various 'good' Emperors: Nerva, Trajan, Julius Caesar, even Augustus.

24. 'For Tacitus was an priest who worshipped idols, and a man of the utmost ambition and wickedness, if you wish to deduce his life from his works.' Cardano (1640), p. 3.

25. Morley 1854, p. 303. Also in Cardano's *De consolatione libri tres* (1542).

26. Some famous examples: In Italy, Busenello's *L'incoronazione di Poppea* (premiere 1643), which was the libretto for an opera attributed to Monteverdi; in France, l'Hermite's *Mort de Sénéque* (premiere 1644) and Racine's *Britannicus* (premiere 1669); In England and in Germany, Tom May (1628) and Casper von Lohenstein (1665) wrote plays on Agrippina, Nero's mother.

27. See Fenlon and Miller (1992). P. Miller firmly sets the libretto – first printed in Naples in 1651 – in a seventeenth-century Venetian 'Tacitean' context (pp. 11-20).

28. Savile (1591).

29. ibid. p. 2.

30. I am here indebted to Womersley 1991.

31. Savile (1591) p. 6.

32. Of course, Elizabeth found in Savile's text more than a threat to her legitimacy: she could learn the 'political virtue' that would enable her to secure the fear of her subjects.

33. On Edmund Bolton see *Dictionary of National Biography*, II, 787-9 (Thompson Cooper). Bolton's manuscripts concerning research on Nero, together with notes on Tiberius (for a history he did not complete), are to be found in B.L. Harleian ms. 6521. Evidence of his link with Savile is that in the latter's 1618 edition of Latin historians, there was printed as a prefix Bolton's 'Hypercritica, or a rule of judgment for writing or reading our histories'.

34. Bolton was a protégé of the Duke of Buckingham, and had distinguished himself by trying to convince king James to set up an aristocratic royal academy in which poor lay gentlemen in need for a job like himself would prepare an index to censor the translation of secular works into English.

35. Bolton (1624), p. 69.

36. Tacitus' influence persisted despite the decline of the conventional Tacitism of the Renaissance political commentaries, and clerical attacks only stirred anti-religious writers to seek in Tacitus an alternative model to the traditional legitimation of Christian principalities. It was nevertheless an influence that by 1700 had lost much of its centrality as a major model of political thinking. As Guicciardini had earlier intimated, it was self-defeating to seek for generalisations based on empirical material exclusively in a historian of the Roman empire, however penetrating a writer. Thus 'Tacitism can be seen as no more than a transition between moralised politics and scientific politics' (Burke 1969, p. 168.)

37. Warmington 1981, p. 3.

38. While partisanship was, in Tacitus' opinion, particularly obvious among the historians of the principate (*Histories* I, 1; also *Annals* I, 1), the reference to Livy as 'eloquentissimi' is somehow opposed to Tacitus' own 'rerum fide tradentur': 'where earlier writers embellished with rhetoric things not yet researched, this is a faithful account' (*Agricola* 10).

39. *Histories* I, 1-4.

40. See for instance F. Goodyear (1982).

41. For instance, Warmington (1981, pp. 1-9) recognises the biased character of Tacitus' works and the fact that his sources are mainly derivative, but then, in the rest of his book, goes on to distinguish facts from misstatements in order to construct an image of Nero fundamentally based on Tacitus. The same paradox appears in M. Grant ed. (1977, pp. 16-20). In a more subtle piece of work, Goodyear (1982, p. 643) agrees with various modern scholars – including Ronald Martin in *Tacitus* (1981) – in defining Tacitus' content as inseparable from his style. This is convincing, but somehow a tautology: it is the modern ideal of scientific objectivity that inevitably creates a problem of definition. When, after much pain, the scholar reaches the conclusion that in ancient historiography rhetoric is inseparable from factual account, one senses that this should have never been a problem. But modern historians have not always recognised that their concern with expanding the empirical field with a critical attitude towards sources and interpretations does not dissolve the rhetorical and moral dimensions of their exercise.

42. I borrow the characterisation from P. Plass (1988).

43. The extent to which there is a rhetorical tyrant in Roman historiography has long been established. See Dunkle 1971.

44. As A.J. Woodman has noted, even though modern history is *also* rhetorical, in particular after the so-called revival of narrative, the modern distinction between literature and history crucially affects the relationship between the 'rhetorical' and the

'scientific' within historiography. To be more precise, the use of *inventio* by ancient historians allows Tacitus to write about 'what could or might have happened' in ways that (let us say) Steven Runciman would have had to reject. I would like to argue that in all cases these different views of historical truth are ultimately dependent on moral considerations. For instance, Syme thought that Tacitus was thoroughly reliable because he provided a criticism of autocracy at the time of the growth of Nazism: Woodman (1988), pp. 197-212.

45. *Annals* I, 3-4; (1977) p. 33.
46. ibid. IV, 33; p. 173.
47. *Agricola*, 3.
48. It would be wrong to think that Tacitus simply stood for liberty against Empire. In his account of barbarians like the Germans or the Britons, the idea of liberty is dramatically portrayed as freedom from Roman rule, and the fight for liberty as a rational choice. Liberty is however also associated with lack of civilisation, unpleasant living conditions, peripherality and ultimate military defeat, none of which Tacitus wished to commend. The straightforward morality that Tacitus admired in the Germans (most remarkably in *Germania*, 11-27) was simply the traditional morality that the Romans had lost. In fact, Tacitus never solves the paradox that he identifies: civilization ('humanitas') is slavery ('servitus'), *Agricola*, 21.
49. Tacitus' experience of terror under Domitian, expressed in particular in his *Agricola*, seems to have coloured his assessment of imperial power in earlier times.
50. *Annals* IV, 33.
51. 'vocem populi Romani et libertatem senatus et conscientiam generis humani' (*Agricola*, 2).
52. *Annals* XIV, 64; (1977) p. 343.
53. *Histories* I, 16; (1986) p. 32.
54. This becomes particularly clear in the account of Nero's more enthusiastic initiatives, such as the Youth Games: 'Promiscuity and degradation throve. Roman morals had long become impure, but never was there so favourable an environment for debauchery as among this filthy crowd.' *Annals* XIV, 15; (1977) p. 321.
55. *Histories* I, 5; (1986) p. 24.
56. 'Nero after all withdrew his eyes, nor contemplated the crimes he authorised. Under Domitian it was no small part of our sufferings that we saw him and were seen by him.' *Agricola*, 45; (1970) p. 111.
57. ibid. 42; p. 107.
58. Almost everything concerning Tacitus' origins is a matter of speculation, but we have a clear image of his respectable position in the senatorial class, in particular through the *Agricola* and the letters of the younger Pliny.
59. *Annals* XIII, 3; (1977) p. 285.
60. Suetonius: 'Nero', 52; (1979), p. 244.
61. *Annals* XIII, 20.
62. ibid. XIII, 11; (1977) p. 288.
63. ibid. XIV, 13.
64. ibid. XIV, 11.
65. ibid. XIV, 12; (1977) p. 318.
66. Tacitus' account of Corbulo's death would have belonged to the missing part of the *Annals*, but there are various references to it in the *Histories* (see for instance II, 76).
67. See C.M. Connors, *Laborat Carmen in fine: authorship and death in the Satyricon and in Neronian Rome*, in this volume. This insight is also the basis for a famous piece by Roland Barthes (1972: 99-102).
68. *Annals* XVI, 16; (1977) p. 388. In the *Histories* also the dramatic events of AD 69 serve to show that, while under a 'reign of terror (...) the reward of virtue was inevitable

death', some good moral lessons could be also learnt. Among these, 'distinguished men driven to suicide faced the last agony with unflinching courage, and there were death-scenes not inferior to those held up to our admiration in the history of early Rome'. *Histories* I,3; (1986) pp. 22-3.

69. Elder Pliny, *Nat. Hist.* bk VII, viii 45-6 etc. Also Younger Pliny, *Let.* III, 5 to Baebius Macer.

70. See T. Barton, *Suetonius: Neronian vice*, in this volume.

71. I follow Momigliano 1990, pp. 126-31.

72. Gibbon praised Tacitus for his philosophical method: 'Tacitus employs the force of rhetoric only to display the connection between the links that form the chain of events, and to instruct the reader by sensible and profound reflections' (quoted in Burrow 1985, p. 23). However, what Gibbon found really compelling was the kind of analysis that hinted at the triumph of barbarism and religion over civilization. And of course, Gibbon's concern for civilization was related to his concern with eighteenth-century Europe. His main conclusion was that the barbarians would not return because European civilisation was no despotism, the fatal flaw of Tacitus' Rome. This conclusion was in fact the inheritance of Renaissance political thought: Tacitism had superseded Tacitus.

73. A case in point is R. Martin. In 1969 he dissected Tacitus according to his 'Sallustian', 'Livian' and 'Ciceronian' stylistic moments (see R. Martin, 'Tacitus and his predecessors', in Dorey (ed.) 1969, pp. 117-47). In his 1981 *Tacitus*, even after repeating that Tacitus is not merely a factual historian but also a rhetorician whose political concerns fall within a specific senatorial tradition, he goes on to paraphrase the *Annals* as a factual narrative told, perhaps, with particular emphasis and techniques.

74. Syme 1958 I, p. 378.

75. Dorey (1969), p. xi.

76. See Pocock 1977.

Bibliography

Baron, H. (1966), *The crisis of the early Italian Renaissance: civic humanism and republican liberty in an age of classicism and tyranny*, Princeton.

Barthes, R. (1972), 'Tacitus and the funerary baroque', *Critical essays*, translated by R. Howard, Illinois.

Bolton, E. (1624), *Nero Caesar, or Monarchie depraved*. London.

Burke, P. (1969), 'Tacitism', in T.A. Dorey (ed.) *Tacitus*. London.

Burrow, J.W. (1985), *Gibbon*, Oxford.

Cardano, G. (1640), *Neronis Encomium*, Amsterdam.

Cavalli, F. (1887), 'G.C. e il suo Encomio di Nerone', in *Atti del R. Istituto Veneto*.

Dorey, T.A. (ed.) (1969) *Tacitus*.

Dunkle, J.R. (1971), 'The rhetorical tyrant in Roman historiography: Sallust, Livy and Tacitus', *Classical World* 65: 12-20.

Fenlon, I. and Miller, P. (1992), *The song of the soul: understanding Poppea*, London.

Ficino, M. (1975), *The letters of Marsilio Ficino*, I, London.

Goodyear, F. (1982), 'History and biography: Tacitus', in *The Cambridge History of Classical Literature*, II, pp. 642-55.

Guicciardini, F. (1977), *Ricordi*, ed. by M. Fubini, Milan.

Gwyn, W.G. (1991), 'Cruel Nero: the concept of the tyrant and the image of Nero in western political thought', *History of Political Thought* XII (3).

Ingegno, A. (1980), *Sagio sulla filosofia di Cardano*. Firenze.

Momigliano, A. (1947), 'The first political commentary on Tacitus', *Journal of Roman Studies* 37: 91-101.

——— (1990), 'Tacitus and the Tacitist tradition', in *The classical foundations of modern historiography*, California.
Morley, H. (1854), *Life of Gerolamo Cardano*, 2 vols., London.
Plass, P. (1988), *Wit and the writing of history*. London.
Pocock, J.G.A. (1977), 'Between Machiavelli and Hume: Gibbon as civic humanist and philosophical historian', in *Edward Gibbon and the decline and fall of the Roman Empire*, ed. G.W. Bowersock et al., London.
Salmon, J. (1989), 'Stoicism and Roman example: Seneca and Tacitus in Jacobean England', *Journal of the History of Ideas* 50: 199-225.
Savile, H. (1591), *The ende of Nero and beginning of Galba*, followed by *Fower bookes of the histories of Cornelius Tacitus. The life of Agricola*.
Schellhase, K.S. (1976), *Tacitus in Renaissance political thought*, Chicago.
Siraisi, N.G. (1991), 'Girolamo Cardano and the art of medical narrative', *Journal of the History of Ideas* 52: 581-602.
Solís, J. (1988), 'El *Neronis Encomium* de Cardano', in J.M. Candau et al. (eds.) *La imagen de la realeza en la antigüedad*, Madrid, pp. 241-54.
Suetonius (1979), *The twelve Caesars*, translated by R. Graves, revised by M. Grant, Harmondsworth.
Syme, R. (1958), *Tacitus*, 2 vols., Oxford.
Tacitus (1925-37), *The Histories* and *The Annals*, translated by C.H. Moore and J. Jackson respectively, 4 vols, London.
——— (1970), *Agricola. Germania. Dialogus*, translated by M. Hutton et al. Loeb Classical Library, London (revised edition).
——— (1977), *The Annals of Imperial Rome*, translated by M. Grant, Harmondsworth (revised edition).
——— (1986), *The Histories*, translated by K. Wellesley, Harmondsworth (revised edition).
Toffanin, G. (1921), *Machiavelli e il 'Tacitismo', la 'politica storica' al tempo della Contrariforma*, Padua.
Warmington, B.H. (1981), *Nero: reality and legend*, London.
Womersley, D. (1991), 'Sir Henry Savile's translation of Tacitus and the political interpretation of Elizabethan texts', *Review of English Studies* 167: 313-42.
Woodman, A.J. (1988), *Rhetoric in classical historiography*. Portland.

3

The *inventio* of Nero: Suetonius[1]

Tamsyn Barton

Some recent work has attempted to rehabilitate Suetonius, to save him from charges of failure to be a good historian[2] or a fine writer;[3] in short he has been forgiven for not being Tacitus. He is no longer a mere compiler of sources or a slavish imitator of Alexandrian models:[4] some attention has even been paid to his skills of composition.[5] One influential view rehabilitating Suetonius as author of his own text is that which revives him as a political actor; Suetonius was the spokesman for a political faction headed by Septicius Clarus, the dedicatee of his *Lives*: the *Lives* were partly involved in his downfall.[6] So Cizek argued (1977, 189-92), adapting Della Corte's depiction of Suetonius as spokesman for the *equites*.

Though this approach had the merit of emphasising the political importance of the official posts held by Suetonius, the thesis finds less favour when more recent research has cast doubt on the vision of Roman politics implicit in the model. Furthermore these scholars are writing against the grain of the tradition in taking Suetonius as a spokesman for anything. The tradition portraying him as an apolitical source-compiler has remained remarkably tenacious. Recent assessments have revived the old categorisation of the biographer as above all a scholar and an antiquarian. From Leo onwards, the label of scholar has justified condemnation of his literary abilities.[7] For Dalmasso he is an impassively frigid writer, suffering from an impotence of style, such as one would expect from a circumscribed academic, unable to look up from his books.[8] Wallace-Hadrill, though more appreciative of the extent to which Suetonius has made deliberate choices in his writing, still sees his style as merely 'the businesslike style of the ancient scholar': 'He is mundane: has no poetry, no pathos, no persuasion, no epigram' (1983, 19).

Pliny's description of Suetonius as a *scholasticus* (*Epist.* 1.24.4) has done much to encourage this view,[9] but the term actually refers to a student preparing for practice at the bar in the *schola*, or rhetorical school.[10] Suetonius did indeed try his abilities at the courts (Plin. *Epist.* 1.18); he was trained in the arts of oratory. This chapter examines Suetonius as a rhetorician and debunks the myth of scholarly objectivity along with its less favourable version, which allows Suetonius objectivity as an accidental result of his inability to control his material. The myth of scholarly objectivity is based on anachronistic notions of intellectual life in the ancient world. Suetonius was certainly a scholar, but this did not imply that he remained a recluse with his head buried in an archive: ancient notions of learning were bound up with rhetorical competition. It is a mark of the successful construction of his *ethos*, or rhetorical persona, in rhetorical theory, that modern scholars have read him as innocent of persuasion.

Suetonius' avoidance of chronology in favour of lists of qualities and examples is seen as unhelpful to historians, and lacking the qualities appealing to literary critics. Historians like Gascou are unhappy at the anti-historical nature of the arrangement, involving unnecessary repetition, superficiality and a failure to examine causation properly, while Norden set the tone for critical discussion of Suetonian style with the laconic remark: 'Sueton schreibt farblos.'[11] Wardman compares him unfavourably with Plutarch, who does use a chronological framework in his *Lives*. This is seen to allow room for discussion of character-development, and explanation for inconsistencies of character. Plutarch's *Lives* are linked to an explicit moral programme: of improvement by impressing on his readers the importance of political *arete*, excellence. His moral studies are linked to Greek philosophical theories of virtue and human nature. It is perhaps the contrast with Plutarch which has led to the conclusion that Suetonius had no views at all.[12]

This view can only be taken because Suetonius has concealed the vehemence of his allegations with his apparently dry enumeration of vices and virtues, with the masking of his authorial presence in the text so as to give the impression of objectivity. The impression is given that he leaves the reader to pass judgment on each emperor on the basis of a neutral set of data, according to our notions of scholarship. 'Without enthusiasm or indignation, he recounts the vices and virtues of his Caesars with the indifference of one who watches life and the world and amuses himself at the spectacle', observed Dalmazzo in 1906; in 1980 nothing has changed for Ektor: 'Suetonius does not distort the facts. The absence of artistic concerns, of generalisations or dubious interpretations helps the clarity of the writing. His deliberate intent is to hold to objective reality.'[13] His lack of art and his objectivity are contrasted with Tacitus, who used the same sources: 'He bases his work on authentic actions and quotations, in contrast to Tacitus who rearranges the words and even the thoughts of characters.'[14]

The absence of an explicit ethical programme has not only led to the views that Suetonius has no views and is objective; some scholars are also suspicious of Suetonius' interest in vice. Funaioli saw him as 'soiling the purple of the emperors'.[15] Wardman, who contrasts Suetonius with Plutarch, cannot see that Suetonius offers any real incentive to virtue; indeed he inspires rather too much curiosity about vice (1974, 145). The scholar thus becomes a dirty old man, and he is not even given the credit for creative fantasies: 'It is as though Suetonius were a writer of pornography whose deficiencies of imagination were helped out by an encyclopaedic knowledge of the exact medical terms' (1974, 145). Carney allows Suetonius fantasies, but of a rather unoriginal nature: according to him, Suetonius was an authoritarian personality preoccupied with sexual fantasies and the penis. His psychoanalysis is only a development of the attitude prevalent as a result of Suetonius' style: Suetonius' text is so unadorned, so transparent, that one can see straight through it to the man himself.[16] But the text is far from transparent in my reading – it is hard to see through the woven threads of rhetorical topoi to anything beyond.

Attempts to reconstruct Suetonius' sources have failed to offer much precise information, except that he, Tacitus and Plutarch clearly drew on at least one common source, imaginatively christened *Ignotus* (unknown).[17] Clearly the lost *Histories* of Pliny the Elder, and the works of Cluvius Rufus and Fabius Rusticus, to whom Tacitus refers, are likely to have been important literary sources. The extent to which Suetonius used primary material has also been much debated; however, De Coninck casts great doubt on the old notion that he used the archives to which he had access as a result of his positions in the imperial household, or even senatorial records, but rather relied on literary sources.[18] At any rate, the literary sources on Nero were not uniformly hostile: Josephus mentions the work of historians who favoured him (*A.J.* 20.153).[19] The Flavians certainly encouraged an anti-Neronian line as part of their own ideological programme,[20] but could hardly have suppressed all alternative versions. Suetonius had choices to make.

It is important to remember that the lists of *exempla* of virtues and vices seen as so colourless by Norden are there to support a case. Nero is condemned by the evidence marshalled against him by Suetonius the *scholasticus* according to rhetorical rules. The influence of rhetoric on Suetonius' *divisiones*, announcements of topics in order, and his arrangements *per species* (by rubric)[21] have often been noted.[22] It has also been remarked in passing that literary antecedents to the *Lives* include epideictic rhetoric, in particular encomium,[23] though this is seen as more relevant to Plutarch.[24] It is indeed important to set the *Lives* in the context of imperial panegyric: Pliny's *Panegyricus* is merely the sole survivor of what must have been a constant outpouring of encomia of the living emperor, as Wallace-Hadrill reminds us.[25] However, little attention has been given to the relevance of a tradition of invective. This is partly because ancient rhetorical theory was much less specific about blame than praise, usually confining discussion of the *psogos* (speech of censure) to explaining it as the opposite of encomium.[26] For Quintilian, invective was rather undignified, and should be used sparingly by the ideal orator (*Inst.* 3.7.19ff.). However, an idea of the topoi can be found by working out the opposite of categories of the encomium, and looking at specific examples. Suetonius himself wrote a treatise on terms of abuse in Greek, which has been preserved in fragmentary form, and edited by Taillardat. It is clear from this that he was familiar with literary invective.

The detailed examples of the qualities Suetonius discusses are far from colourless, *pace* Norden. Scholars have frequently noted the preponderance of detail that characterises his writing. It is perhaps the detail which convinces above all. In the recent case in which Judge Clarence Thomas was accused of sexual harassment in Washington, the details such as the pubic hair and the Coke can were regarded as the most convincing elements in Anita Hill's testimony.[27] Detail creates what the New Rhetoricians call 'presence', what the ancients would call *enargeia* (vivid description).[28] Yet there was licence for the orator to make *inventio* (the power of discovering all means of persuading by speech) into invention in the rhetorical handbooks. Quintilian declares that there is nothing wrong with telling untruths in pursuit of justice; even a philosopher is at times permitted to tell a lie. If the power of hatred, influence, power and false witness is destroyed, there is little scope for eloquence (*Inst.* 2.17.26). Discussing false *expositiones*

3. The inventio of Nero

(statements of facts), he is equally frank: '... We must take care, first that our fiction is within the bounds of possibility, secondly that it is consistent with the persons, dates, and places involved and thirdly that it presents a character and sequences that are not beyond belief ...' (*Inst.* 4.2.89). He is specific about the importance of *enargeia*:

> I am complaining that a man has been murdered. Shall I not bring before my eyes all the circumstances which it is reasonable to imagine must have occurred in such a connexion? Shall I not see the assassin burst suddenly from his hiding-place, the victim tremble, cry for help, beg for mercy, or turn to run? Shall I not see the fatal blow delivered and the stricken body fall? Will not the blood, the deathly pallor, the groan of agony, the death-rattle, be indelibly impressed upon my mind? From such impressions arises *enargeia* ... (*Inst.* 6.2.31)

Here there is a licence to invent circumstances as well as to embroider on the basis of a simple initial datum.[29] The 'wealth of circumstantial detail was largely, or completely fictitious', observes Nisbet on Republican invective (1961, 196). Tales of drunken debauches were favoured: Quintilian furnishes a vivid example in Caelius' portrayal of Antony's arousal from a drunken stupor amidst the remains of the night's debauch as the enemy approaches. 'Could you find anything more plausible in imagination, more vehement in censure or more vivid in description?', he exclaims in delight (*Inst.* 4.2.123-4). The example of the portrayal of Cicero as a boy, handling the dirty washing in his father's laundry in the invective Dio Cassius puts in the mouth of Fufius Calenus is a fine instance.[30] Cicero himself always reacts either indignantly or dismissively to the slander of others, of course.[31] There is little doubt that the rules of the game involved constant shifting of the goalposts.

The encomium began with a recital of the glorious ancestry of its subject.[32] The invective thus did the opposite.[33] Süss details the theme of the inglorious occupations and activities of the forebears of the opponents of the Attic orators, a theme continuing to the Roman period. Where the ancestors were too well known, if they were distinguished, the *Rhetoric to Herennius* advises contrasting the subject unfavourably with them (3.13). Suetonius, who is dealing with people usually of well-known and distinguished family, uses the ancestors to set the tone for the *Life* to follow. Thus with Nero, he says that many of Nero's vices were probably inherited from his ancestors, and that he made a ghastly caricature of his ancestor's virtues (1.2). There is a similar matching in the case of Tiberius, whose virtues are balanced with his vices: his ancestors did distinguished service and grave injuries to the Roman state (2). In the case of Nero, many of the themes of his life are foreshadowed by his ancestors: not only examples of cruelty, arrogance, extravagance and rudeness, but even specific incidents, like the attempt at suicide which failed through cowardice (2.3), or the putting of equestrians and matrons of rank on the stage (4.1).

In Quintilian's example of encomium Achilles' birth is attended by the prophecy that he will be greater than his father. Nero's horoscope, however, looked ominous, while his father replied to congratulations with the remark that any child of his and Agrippina's was bound to be detestable and a public danger

(6.1). Similarly, Tiberius is supposed to have remarked that Caligula's advent portended his own death and the ruin of everyone else (11).

The reference to Nero's early youth in the charge of a dancer and a barber (6.3) clearly owes much to a tradition of invective,[34] and is paralleled by the throwaway remark that Domitian spent a poverty-stricken and degraded youth without even any silver on the family table, circumstances entirely excluded from the *Lives* of the virtuous Vespasian and Titus. Cicero's youth spent naked and dealing with excrement-covered clothes is the extreme version of this topos (see n. 30).

Suetonius makes a clear *divisio* between the first part of his *Life of Nero* and the second, as he does for Caligula and Domitian. Here he separates the unexceptionable from the *probra* and *scelera* (shameful and evil).[35] For all three, it is assumed that any earlier virtuous acts were a parade (*ostentatio*). In fact, Nero gave signs of cruelty from youth (7.1). In the case of Tiberius, there is an equally abrupt division, immediately after his arrival in Capri.[36] But Tiberius is allowed real virtues.[37]

The first section on Nero is thus cast retrospectively by Suetonius in the light of a description of his good points. However, most positive remarks are undercut. Apart from further ill-omens or references to the future, we hear that Seneca dreamt that his pupil was really Caligula, which was borne out by the early signs of his cruel disposition. Nero tried to convince Claudius that Britannicus was not his son and testified against the aunt who had brought him up (7.1). Here is the first appearance of another favourite theme of invective: the ill-treatment of one's family.[38] On this theme Suetonius is deliberately ironic. Thus Nero's accession begins with appropriate filial behaviour. Claudius is given a lavish funeral, eulogised and deified (9.1). This reference to deification looks forward to Nero's joke, which in Suetonius' account proves his complicity in the murder of Claudius by means of poisoned mushrooms, that mushrooms are the food of the gods (33.1). Similarly there is a reference to the future in Suetonius' description of Nero's filial behaviour to his mother. On the day of his accession the password for the Guard is 'The Best of Mothers'; Agrippina and her son often rode out together in her litter (9.3). This looks forward to 28.6, where the proof of Nero's incest with his mother is the stains on his clothes every time he went with his mother in her litter![39] Caligula's early good behaviour towards his family is similarly the subject of sardonic humour.[40] A further striking example of this ironising technique comes in the discussion of Nero's building-projects: here the biographer picks out his construction of platforms specifically to fight fires! (16.1, ctr. 38.3)

But the real venom appears after the *divisio*. From 20-5, the first *exempla* of the *probra* appear: Nero's musical and charioteering exploits and his public performances in Italy and Greece. The accounts of his public appearances on stage, singing and playing the lyre, and singing in tragedies, are filled with incidental details drawing attention to the inversions of Nero's farcical world.[41] Here Suetonius goes beyond the usual traditions of invective. The emperor enters the competition for heralds, when in the Attic and Roman traditions of invective, a herald is one of the low occupations suggested for the enemy's ancestors.[42] In Republican Rome, mere association with actors and dancers was a usual accusation, and eccentric dress enough to bring disgrace, while here the emperor becomes one of them. It is notable that Caligula is the only other emperor treated to this theme, though in his case it is relatively undeveloped.[43]

In chs. 26-38 the *scelera* are subdivided, with each illustrated by anecdotes: 26-7 *petulantia* (insolence), 28-9 *libido* (lustfulness), 30-1 *luxuria* (extravagance), 32: *avaritia* (greed), 33-8, further subdivided: *saevitia* (cruelty). Nero's night-time raids, illustrations of his *petulantia*, can be paralleled in accusations made or rebutted in Cicero's speeches: he has to defend Caelius against the charge that he attacked matrons on their way home from a dinner-party (*Cael.* 20). Nero's profligacy and rapacity (30-2), themes found also in the *Lives* of Tiberius, Caligula and Domitian, are paralleled by Cicero's attacks on Antony and Verres.[44]

Nero also followed good Verrine precedent in robbing various temples of their treasures,[45] melting down the gold and silver images, including the Penates (guardian-deities of the State: 32.4). The accusation that someone is a temple-robber is so common that the (second/third-century) author of a rhetorical textbook ('Hermogenes') uses it as an illustration of the commonplace:

> Once agreed that so-and-so is a temple-robber, there are many and various ways of developing this theme: e.g ... beginning with small offences, he went on to this one last, so that you have before you in the same person a thief, a house-breaker and an adulterer. It is called commonplace because it is applicable to every temple-robber ...[46]

This accusation is related to the charge of irreligion (56.1). In the cameo-accounts of the irreligious acts of the tyrant-emperors, there is a kind of surreal humour in the incongruities. Nero despised all religious cults except that of Atargatis, and showed that one day he had changed his mind even about her, by urinating on her statue. Tiberius too is accused of lack of regard for the gods (69), but in his case there is a perverted twist: he is accused of hardly waiting to finish a sacrifice before sexually assaulting the acolyte and the sacred trumpeter. Meanwhile in the case of Caligula, himself described as a *prodigium* (prodigy), the insults are more violent and excessive: he interrupted a sacrifice to hit a ceremonial official with a mallet (32.3), replaced the heads of gods' statues with his own, and threatened Capitoline Jupiter. The only god he took seriously was himself.

Krenkel has examined the erotica in Suetonius, and has realised that they are topoi, rather than to be taken at face value, though he sees the biographer as promulgating gossip along with fact without reflection, as part of a mindless collection of facts (65). He is right to observe that the sexual misdeeds of Nero are based on a standard format; however they are carefully worked up in a crescendo from all-night drinking sessions in the lowest company to the marriage with Doryphorus.

Let us take a brief glance at the antecedents. In the Attic orators, the usual accusations are of debauchery of citizen women, adultery, being a *kinaidos* (passive homosexual, or effeminate) and self-prostitution.[47] For Republican Rome Gonfroy (1978) provides a useful compendium of examples, of which I cite a few. Accusations included naked dancing (*Cat.* 2.23), the seduction of young boys (*Cat.* 2.4), adultery (Caesar was every woman's husband, every man's wife, according to the Elder Curio: Suet. *Jul.* 52), accusations of making one's house a brothel (*Verr.* 2.3.3.6) and self-prostitution (Antony: *Phil.* 2.18.44, cf. Suet. *Jul.* 49.1). Effeminacy is a recurrent theme. A whole town was kept occupied in making women's clothes for Verres (4.103), Catiline's friends wear feminine tunics and veils (2.22), and Clodius the clothes of an Oriental effeminate (*Har. Resp.* 2.44), thus, naturally, he served the desires of others. Just so did Cicero allude to the *leitmotiv* of invective against Caesar traced to Licinius Calvus, Dolabella and Curio the Elder and to his soldiers at his triumph, accusing him of being deflowered by King Nicomedes of Bithynia.[48] Catiline is referred to as the husband of Gabinius (*Senat.* 12), and Curio is described as making an honest woman of the courtesan Mark Antony (*Phil.* 2.44; cf. 50). Cicero committed incest with his daughter (Ps.-Sallust: *In Cic.* 2.2, Dio Cass. 46.18.6), and Clodius with his sisters (*Har. Resp.* 5.9, *Pis.* 28, *Cael.* 32 etc.) Clodius also debauched the sacred beds of the Bona Dea (*Har. Resp.* 3.4; 5.8; 7.13), and if he achieves his ends, Vestals will be raped (*Cat.* 4.12). Such accusations become tableaux in Suetonius, according to the oratorical goal of *enargeia*, and are worked up in hyperbolic style.

Nero not only had prostitutes and dancing-girls to his luxurious dinner-parties, but arranged for noblewomen 'madams' to solicit his custom in temporary brothels along the shore when he was revelling on a boat (27.2-3). Not satisfied with seducing free-born boys and matrons, Nero raped a Vestal Virgin and married Sporus in the guise of a bride in the presence of the whole court, having castrated him (28.1).[49] He certainly wanted to commit incest with his mother, even if he may have failed to do so (28.5). (Here it seems that Suetonius has selected the worst version, without mentioning alternatives: *nemo dubitavit* – no one had any doubt.)[50] Sadistic pleasures were also a feature: dressed in the skins of wild animals, he attacked the genitals of men and women tied to stakes, and was then given sexual relief by his freedman Doryphorus. The climax of this crescendo comes with Doryphorus' marriage to him as bride – on the wedding-night he imitated the screams and moans of a girl being deflowered (29.1). Here was the ultimate inversion, with the First Citizen submitting (in a slave's role) to an ex-slave, and literally acting the woman's part.

Of the emperors, Caligula's antics are again most similar to Nero's, beginning with adultery (12.2), then taking the bride away for the *ius primae noctis*, even sending for the consular governor's wife (25.2). In a classic tyrant-tableau, he is portrayed as choosing from other men's wives as if at a slave-market, discussing their performance afterwards, and if necessary forcing divorces on them (36.1). As well, of course, he was said to have committed incest with his sisters (24.1-3). He was accused of having played active and passive sexual roles with Marcus Lepidus, Valerius Catullus, Mnester the actor, and various foreign hostages (36.1).

The description of Tiberius' sexual mores might prove wearisome; suffice it to say that paedophilia is the basic theme (42-4), though he also lusted after women (45.1).[51] The full list of erotica in Suetonius is set out and discussed in Krenkel (1980): it is clear that variations on the basic topoi can be used to individualise each emperor to a degree.

3. The inventio of Nero

Few would be amazed by Krenkel's conclusion that the erotica in Suetonius arise from political invective, but it may be more controversial to suggest that the famous instances of Nero's cruelty should be set in this light. His cruelty is illustrated first of all by his treatment of his family, a theme common from the Attic orators onwards, as already mentioned. Caligula is given similar treatment.[52] As with Nero, insults become murders (see n. 40). Here Suetonius begins with Nero's immediate family and works outwards through other relatives and friends until he comes to the Great Fire, which affected all the inhabitants of Rome.[53] In this latter case Suetonius has again chosen the worst version. Tacitus merely records that there was disagreement as to whether Nero was responsible,[54] while Suetonius not only asserts as the climax of his account of Nero's cruelty: 'But Nero showed no greater mercy to the common people, or to the walls of the fatherland ... he brazenly set fire to the city', but adds a host of details to back this up, typically according the most trivial reasons for Nero's action.[55]

However, to return to the immediate family, let us look at the charge-sheet. '*Parricidia et caedes a Claudio exorsus est.*' Claudius 'was the first victim of Nero's murderous career (though he may not have been actually responsible for the poisoning of his adoptive father ...)' (33.1). Here Suetonius has definitely chosen the version which sets Nero in the worst light, even contradicting his account in the *Life of Claudius* (44.2-3) where Agrippina is made solely responsible. It is notable that the official version probably survives in the *Apocolocyntosis* ascribed to Seneca, where the Goddess Fever seems responsible for Claudius' death. Josephus describes the poisoning as only a hypothesis of some people (*A.J.* 20.8.1).[56] We shall return to this subject shortly.

Meanwhile, Nero's step-brother Britannicus follows his father at the second poisoning attempt (33.2-3), while Agrippina survives three attempts at poison, discovers the collapsing ceiling, and swims to safety from the collapsible boat before succumbing to a dagger.[57] His aunt Domitia is poisoned to fulfil immediately her affectionate wish that she should be presented with his coming-of-age beard before she passes on (34.5), and Octavia is executed (35.1). 'There was no family relationship which Nero did not criminally abuse ...' He also executes his step-sister Antonia and Aulus Plautius, after sexually assaulting him, has his step-son drowned, and banishes his foster-mother's son.

Caster (1938, 79-93), in a discussion of Lucian's treatment of his opponents, examines the rhetorical tradition of invective: 'the most revolting accusations ... arise from pure and simple commonplaces in invective ... the ancient audience would have been astonished had the enemies of the polemicist not been prostituted or assassinated' (88). The themes of *diabolê* (slander): murder, attempted murder, theft, depraved morals and lack of culture, were all taught in the rhetorical schools, as were methods of refuting slander (*apoluesthai tas diabolas*).[58]

Murder of one's parents was obviously the logical extreme of the theme of unfilial behaviour, and therefore much rarer than accusations of murders in general. False accusations of parricide were actionable in Attic law (along with parent-beating and cowardice in battle), but, like the other two accusations, are nevertheless found (Lysias 10). The themes were developed in Greece under the Roman Empire, and are prominent in sophistic quarrels. It is noteworthy that murder of members of one's family is usually in the list of typical accusations parodied by Lucian: at the banquet of philosophers the climactic counter-accusation is that Clitodemos sold Crito poison to kill his father (*Conv.* 32), while Timocles, furious at being rejected by Damis, accuses him in his long list of insults of having strangled his brother (*Zeus Trag.* 50). In Lucian's most sustained piece of invective, he not only accuses Peregrinos of having strangled his father, but also adds verisimilitude by saying that he was thrown into prison for it (*Per.* 10ff.).

Parricide is a frequent theme in imperial declamations (see Pseudo-Quintilian *Decl.* 1; 2; 17), usually spiced up with other elements, including the ubiquitous stepmother. Apart from these fantasies, the number of references to the crime have led several scholars to take seriously Seneca's remark in the *De Clementia* (1.23), that parricide has become common.[59]

Let us take a look at the speeches of the Late Republic for parallels. Cicero's first speech was a defence of Roscius of Ameria on a charge of parricide, which seems to have been made by those who took advantage of the Sullan proscriptions in order to gain his father's property, while Plutarch reports another defence and an accusation of parricide on Cicero's part (48.1; 26.7). In the extant defence Cicero naturally emphasises the rarity and extreme seriousness of the crime, yet a reference in the *De Inventione* suggests that it might be thrown in as simply an extra accusation on the part of the prosecution. Here he refers to an indictment alleging parricide, when at the trial, while other crimes were proved by testimony, the charge of parricide was barely mentioned (2.19.58).[60]

But the most interesting speech extant is the *Pro Cluentio*, which shows the extent to which accusations of murders of one's family might go. In this speech Cicero defends Cluentius against the charges that he has poisoned one Vibius Capax for money, attempted to poison his opponent Oppianicus, killing one Balbutius by mistake, and has poisoned Oppianicus' father. The prosecution focussed on accusing Cluentius of having bribed the judges to convict Oppianicus senior of various crimes. Cicero thus allows himself full rein in depicting Oppianicus senior in the blackest colours, with a very confusing account of his dealings with his relatives. According to the orator he arranged the death of his brother-in-law (who had been enslaved in war), organised the proscription and death of three others, murdered a man to marry his wife, and murdered his sons to please her, murdered another wife by poison, killed his brother and sister-in-law and the baby in her womb, bribed another wife to abort so that she could marry him and finished with his mother-in-law. Like members of the imperial household, he employed a trusted doctor for the purpose. What are we to make of this incredible list of crimes?[61] Quintilian, in a passage where he admits that rhetoric sometimes substitutes falsehood for truth, tells us that Cicero boasted of throwing dust in the eyes of the jury in this speech.[62]

There is another piece of evidence to suggest that murder of family members was an accusation which may have been thrown out quite casually in the course of invective, and it comes from a text which illustrates very neatly the way in which Nero's crimes conform to topoi of the *psogos* or *vituperatio*, as well as casting light on an aspect of Suetonius' possible development of the traditional topos of the evil appearance, so I conclude with a brief discussion of it.

The physiognomical treatise of Suetonius' contemporary, the rhetor Polemo of

3. The inventio of Nero

Laodicea, might seem an unlikely place for parallels to Suetonius. (In this treatise the rhetor set out the rules of interpreting bodily features as signs of character.) However, Suetonius' knowledge of physiognomical tenets is illustrated by his treatise on terms of abuse mentioned earlier, which includes terms from physiognomics, as has been noted by Couissin (1953) and Evans (1969). Both these writers note the implications for the characters of emperors of the detailed physical descriptions in the *Lives*. They do not discuss Nero. Bradley (1978, 282ff.), who has looked at the treatises in relation to the details in Suetonius' *Life of Nero*, remains cautious about accepting the influence of physiognomics, but once it is realised that inconsistency of signs is to be accepted, his arguments are not decisive. The extant treatises do allow reconstruction of a physiognomical portrait which is consistent with the rest of Suetonius' account.[63]

There are good qualities as well as bad, but the bad predominate, as is the case with Nero's life. Physiognomists like the anonymous Latin author advise a careful weighing up of contradictory signs to arrive at a conclusion. First, his *statura prope iusta* (he was about the right size): moderate physical proportions connote sensitivity and a capacity to accomplish goals (*Phgn.* 813b, 30-5) as well as being implicitly lauded throughout the Corpus. Also, his *subflavus* (blondish) hair indicates good qualities, a sign of culture and aestheticism, or even good character if it is thick (Polemo F.1.250, 13-17; Anon. §14). However, his body was *maculosus* (mottled) a characteristic of the panther, the epitome of evil feminine qualities in physiognomical theory (*Phgn.* 810a, 6-9). Furthermore, his weak eyes are a sign of cowardice (*Phgn.* 807b, 8, and his thick neck of strength, insensitivity and temper (*Phgn.* 807b, 26, 811a, 1-2), irascibility and ignorance (Anon §53; 93), or strength of mind, but timidity of body (Polemo F.1.220, 11-12), while his fat stomach is a sign of licence or deceitfulness (Polemo F.1.210, 7-12), of insensitivity, drunkenness, and intemperance (Anon. §64; §93) or debauchery (ibid. §112, cf. Adam. F.1.361, 5-362, 2, Ps.-Pol. 361, 16-362, 10). Finally, his spindly legs betray an evil disposition, like monkeys (*Phgn.* 810b, 3-5), feminine cowardice and lack of spirit (Polemo F.1.194, 10; 270, 17, Anon. §91), lustfulness (§112) or intemperance (§71). As in the case of most of the other emperors, most of the traits described find suitable interpretations in the physiognomical texts, if not all. Since we have only a small part of the physiognomical Corpus, it is possible that Suetonius may have been entirely influenced by the physiognomists in his choice of physical characteristics, though that is certainly not proven. It does however seem likely enough that his interests played a part in his descriptions, rather than a blind love of detail. His physical descriptions contrast strikingly with Plutarch's, and Plutarch seems to offer a deliberately anti-physiognomical perspective, as has recently been argued (Sassi forthcoming)

In Polemo's text, unlike those of the other physiognomists which have survived, there are many cameo 'lives' in the guise of illustrations of the principles of the art of reading the body. Polemo starts with the body to show that the character is worthy of praise or blame; in fact he elevates his friends (including Hadrian, who is praised for his eyes), and destroys his rivals through their bodies. In a sense it is the Suetonian procedure in reverse; where Suetonius' long biographies include a brief description of physique which seems designed to invite physiognomical interpretation backing up the character-depiction, Polemo's long treatise includes brief biographies to illustrate physiognomical theory.

These two sorts of biographies are based on the same *topoi*. This is unsurprising once one realises that the main purpose of physiognomics for Polemo, as I have argued elsewhere (Barton forthcoming), is as a weapon of invective against his political enemies. The topoi of invective are remarkably limited. One of Polemo's cameo lives, for instance, bears striking resemblances to the Suetonian Nero (F.1.126-32). An unknown Lydian(?) is accused of poisoning his father, trying and failing to drown his mother at sea and committing a variety of sexual crimes with adolescents and women. Furthermore, he is violent (a creator of carnage), cruel, irreligious, and cursed by the gods. At points, in Polemo's cameos, the sort of circumstantial detail found in Suetonius is provided.

Here is clearly a procedure in which *inventio* becomes invention in a manner taken for granted by Cicero and Quintilian. Such generosity with the truth was doubtless equally acceptable to the elaborators of the hostile tradition on Nero from Pliny, Cluvius Rufus and Fabius Rusticus to Suetonius himself. Clearly the acceptability of this sort of elaboration on standard lines poses problems for historians hoping to extract kernels of truth from Suetonius. The tradition should not be taken on trust.

Some have attempted to exonerate Nero of his crimes. Dawson (1964), for instance, proposes that the official account of Agrippina's death is more plausible than the muddled and inconsistent comic opera plots of Tacitus and Suetonius, arguing that Agrippina was in fact plotting against Nero with Otho. In his view the matricide story derives from Nero's own portrayal of the role of Orestes, in his own mask, as the account of his contemplation and handling of the corpse derives from the model of Oedipus and Jocasta.[64] According to Dawson, the basis of these accounts was then circulated for propaganda purposes; Suetonius gives examples of such lampoons (39.2). Furthermore, a recent contribution to the *Classical Quarterly*, Grimm-Samuel's 'On the mushroom that deified the Emperor Claudius', has attempted to prove that the symptoms suffered by Claudius show that he died, in the manner of a whole dinner-party described by Pliny (*Nat. Hist.* 22.47), because he mistook the death-cap or *amanita phalloides* for the edible *amanita caesarea*!

However, I do not propose to use these alternative accounts as the starting-point of an argument to whitewash Nero; if I were to insist that every word of Suetonius is a complete fabrication on the grounds that the 'facts' reported have literary precedents, I should be joining one side in the famous literature versus real life debate, which I would prefer to avoid. Literature and real life, after all, are not opposites. Rather, I hope that, by examining the parallels in extant invective to Suetonius' account of Nero's life, I have gone some way towards showing what kind of enterprise was involved, and how that might shape contemporary reaction. I see the world of invective as a world of 'virtual reality', where illusion creates substance. Above all, as with games in virtual reality, plausible and well-constructed invective was there to be enjoyed, as both Quintilian and 'Hermogenes' imply.[65] I would hope that historians will plunder his works for evidence with the same caution, and perhaps read them with the same literary appreciation, as those of rhetoricians such as Cicero and Polemo.

Notes

1. I would like to acknowledge the bibliographical assistance I have received, essential for a worker in an unfamiliar field, in particular from Justin Goddard, Alessandro Schiesaro and Catharine Edwards.
2. Wallace-Hadrill 1983.
3. Lounsbury 1987.
4. Steidle 1963.
5. Mouchova 1968; Croisille 1969/1970.
6. According to 'Spartianus' (*SHA Hadr.*, 11.3), Suetonius was dismissed because he had behaved with less than the necessary decorum to the Empress.
7. cf. Funaioli 1949, 178-9, 'But he is not a real writer. He is a scholar.'
8. '... la fredezza e l'impassibilità del narratore ... devono spesso dependere da impotenza artistica piu che da deliberato proposito ... nè fu uomo da spinger lo sguardo tropp'oltre la cerchia dei suoi studi e delle sue ricerche' (809; 823).
9. See e.g. Syme 1980, 111.
10. Thus Baldwin 1983, 147. Wallace-Hadrill 1983, see below. Plin. *Epist.* 2.3.5, Quint. *Inst.* 12.11.16, Tac. *Dial.* 35: cf. Lounsbury 1987. Also generally, a declaimer: Suet. *Rh.* 6. Only in late sources does it mean a learned man (Veg. Mul. 4, pr. 2, Hier. *Vir.* 99).
11. 'Suetonius' style is colourless', 1909, 387, n.1.
12. Paratore 1959. Unfortunately, only two of Plutarch's *Lives of the Caesars* survive in any form, so that comparison of like with like is difficult. For Paratore, Suetonius is a mere man in the street, 'with all the narrow-mindedness of those funny people' (!); he has no political, religious or philosophical views.
13. Ektor 1980, 326.
14. Gascou (1984, 677ff.) does realise however that Suetonius' objectivity is assumed, that the search for balance between good and evil, the appearance of scientific detachment, the impassive enumeration of facts and the impeturbable style are all deliberate, and do not prevent him from having a parti-pris.
15. *RE* IV A, 1, col. 619.
16. cf. Lounsbury 1987, 5.
17. Syme 1980, 105; 110.
18. cf. Della Corte 1967, 168.
19. 'For many historians have written the story of Nero, of whom some, because they were well-treated by him, have out of gratitude been careless of truth, while others from hatred and enmity towards him have so shamelessly and recklessly revelled in falsehoods as to merit censure', tr. L.H. Feldman. Agrippina's *Commentarii* were certainly used by Tacitus (*Ann.* 4.53.3)
20. Gagé 1952.
21. Suetonius announces in the *Life of Augustus* (9): 'Instead of keeping chronological order, I use subject-headings' (*neque per tempora sed per species*).
22. Townend 1967, 85.
23. Della Corte 1967, 77-90, Townend 1967, 82, Wallace-Hadrill 1983, 144.
24. Stuart 1928, Steidle 1951, 129-33, Wardman 1974. The scholarly tide has turned against Leo's (1901) thesis that Suetonius followed a tradition of Alexandrian biography; now Suetonius' originality in writing *Lives* of emperors is stressed. The only precedent cited in Townend (1967, 81) is Phaenias of Eresus, who wrote on the tyrants of Sicily.
25. Wallace-Hadrill 1983, 145.

26. Ar. *Rhet.* 1.9. 1368a, 33-7, Aphthonius, p. 27, 17-18, Theon 2, p. 112, 17-18 (both Spengel), *Auct. ad Her.* 3.6.10; 14.

27. *Time* magazine, 28 October 1991, p. 32. 'As Anita Hill poured forth her lurid tale of porn flicks and Coke cans, some [Bush] aides even suspected she was telling the truth.' The aides attempted to show the origin of the pubic hair in literature rather than in life: 'A Justice Department lawyer had recently read "The Exorcist" ... and recalled a reference to pubic hair floating in gin ...' (ibid.)

28. Perelman and Olbrechts-Tyteca 1969 (1958), Dion. Hal. *Lys.* 7, Quint. *Inst.* 4.2.63; 6.2.32; 8.3.61.

29. Cicero: *De Orat.* 2.240-1 has Crassus recommend similar vividness in fabrication. 'Hermogenes' also allows that the orator will speak falsely, but not even on the basis of a plea like Quintilian's that it is in a just cause, but simply on the grounds that it does the audience good to hear what he has to say (*Rh. Gr.* VI, pp. 435, 4-6 (Rabe))

30. 46.4.3-5.1: Cicero's father was a fuller, who traded in grapes and olives, and made a living from wash-tubs. Daily and nightly he defiled himself with the foulest filth. Cicero grew up naked among naked companions, collecting clothes stained with sheep-dung, pig-manure and human excrement.

31. *Mur.* 11-13; *Planc.* 12.30; *Cael.* 3.6, *Dom.* 35.93.

32. Topoi of encomia, for instance: 'Hermogenes': Progymnasmata: *Rh. Gr.* VI, pp. 15, 18-17, 2 (Rabe): main divisions – race and city, family, events at birth, upbringing, education, bodily and mental qualities, accomplishments, actions, external blessings, length of life, manner of death, number of children. Cf., for similar lists, 'Menander Rhetor' (Russell and Wilson), Aphthonius (Progymnasmata: *Rh. Gr.* X, 21, 12-22, 10 (Rabe), Theon and Quintilian *Inst.* 3.7.12.

33. Topoi of *vituperatio* specifically mentioned by Quintilian include the dubious parentage, the ominous omens at birth, poverty, evils of appearance, the terrible institutions founded (*Inst.* 3.7.19ff.).

34. Upbringing: Süss 1910, 246. Cic. *Mur.* 13, *Red. Sen.* 13. Cf. Quint. *Inst.* 11.3.89.

35. Nero: '*Haec partim nulla reprehensione, partim etiam non mediocri laude digna in unum contuli, ut secernerem a probris et sceleribus eius, de quibus dehinc dicam*' (19.3: I have separated this catalogue of Nero's less atrocious acts – some forgiveable, some even praiseworthy – from the others; but I must begin to list his follies and crimes). Caligula: '*Hactenus quasi de principe, reliqua ut de monstro narranda sunt*' (21: So much for Caligula [as if he were] Emperor; the rest of this history must deal with Caligula the Monster). Domitian: '*Sed neque in clementiae neque in abstinentiae tenore permansit, et tamen aliquanto celerius ad saevitiam descivit quam ad cupiditatem*' (10: His good-will and self-restraint were not, however, destined to continue long, and the cruel streak in him soon appeared). All translations adapted from Robert Graves (1957).

36. Here he lets all affairs of state slide. As soon as he is out of public view, he succumbs to all the vicious passions which he had long tried unsuccessfully to hide.

37. Suetonius believes that Augustus weighed the good qualities against the bad, and decided that the good tipped the scale (21.3).

38. Süss 1910, 250-1.

39. Gascou notes this latter connection (1984, 370), but only as an example of the anti-historical constraints of Suetonius' rhetorical schema.

40. Caligula does the same for Tiberius as Nero for Claudius, and organises the reburial and remembrance of his mother and brothers, honours his father Germanicus and Livia posthumously, and his uncle Claudius and grandmother Antonia, while adopting his co-heir Tiberius Gemellus (15). We have already heard that Caligula was responsible for murdering Tiberius (12). But soon we gather that he probably poisoned Antonia (and then showed so little respect that he sat in his dining-room and watched the pyre burn), that he had Tiberius Gemellus executed and that he forced his father-in-

law Marcus Silanus to cut his throat with a razor (23). He committed adulterous incest with his sisters, one before he came of age. The two who did not die were allowed to sleep with his favourites, and then exiled on the grounds of adulterous plotting (24). He caused the death of his cousin Ptolemy of Mauretania.

41. It is a world where an emperor lives in fear of the judges of a singing-competition, where an ex-consul announces song-titles in public, where Roman magistrates offer the emperor money to appear in their public shows, where an emperor's reputation depends not on his dealing with urgent problems in Rome, but on his performance in a musical competition.

42. *Adv. Leoch.* 44.4, Cic. *Pis.* 62 (Süss 1910, 248). Cf. Dio Chrys. *Or.* 7.114.

43. Caligula too showed a passion for theatrical dancing and singing, from his early youth, made appearances as a Thracian gladiator, singer, dancer and chariot-driver, supported tragic actors at public performances, and was to make his stage-début on the day of his death (11; 54).

44. *Phil.* 1.7.17f.; 2.27.66ff.; 37.93; 39.101; 41.104 etc. *Verr.* 1.1.2; 14.40; 2.1.12.32f.; 17.44ff.; 2.2.74.183ff.; 2.3.3.6f. etc., cf. *Prov. Cons.* 11.

45. *Verr.* 2.1.4.10; 17.45ff.; 2.3.3.6.

46. pp. 11, 21-12, 5; 13, 23-14, 1 (Rabe), tr. T. Burgess.

47. Süss 1910, 249-50.

48. Suet. *Jul.* 49.1-4. Cf. on the youth of Augustus: Sextus Pompey jeered at his effeminacy, Mark Antony alleged that he was Caesar's *pathicus* (passive partner), and his brother Lucius added that he also sold his favours to Aulus Hirtius for 3,000 gold pieces, and that he used to soften his leg-hair with red-hot walnut-shells.

49. Here the story leads up to a joke against Nero 'still going the rounds' – 'the course of history would have been better if Nero's father had married such a wife!'

50. See Tac. *Ann.* 14.2 and Dio Cassius 61.11.3-4 for doubts as to whether incest took place, and whether Nero or Agrippina instigated the adultery. Most authors and general rumour supported Cluvius Rufus' version, that Agrippina offered herself several times to Nero, but Acte dissuaded him. Fabius Rusticus claimed that it was Nero's idea, but that Acte dissuaded him. Cf. Gascou (1984, 441-2).

51. The only remarkable feature of the Tiberian erotica is one case where it can be seen that a harmless episode in Pliny, where Parrhasios' picture of Atalanta and Meleager features (*Nat. Hist.* 35.70), has been used to add to the depiction of the emperor as dirty old man; it was an obscene picture which the emperor took with delight for his bedroom (44). See Gascou 1984, 439-40.

52. He would fly into a rage if anyone mentioned his grandfather Agrippa, and cancelled the annual commemorations of his victories, blackened Augustus' name by claiming that he had been born of an incestuous union of Augustus and Julia, called his great-grandmother Livia a she-Ulysses, of low-birth, and insulted his grandmother Antonia (23.1-2).

53. In the case of Caligula there is a movement from Macro and Ennia, who helped him to become emperor, through Senators and *equites* to the general populace, whom he let go hungry (26), but then cruelty, insults and murders of all ranks are considered in no order at all, mirroring the indiscriminate nature of Caligula's cruelty (27-30). He wished all Romans had only one neck (30). Suetonius also begins with Tiberius' actions against his family (50-4). It begins with his attempt to betray his brother, and ends with the miserable deaths of his grandsons. Suetonius then moves on to the men of his *consilium*, his Greek favourites, a man in a crowd, an *eques*, victims of *maiestas* trials, a fisherman, a guardsman and so on in no order. He used to envy Priam for having outlived his entire family. Only Domitian, of the tyrants, is restricted to insulting his family. His murders and rapacity are described in no particular order.

54. *Ann.* 15.38.1: *Sequitur clades, forte an dolo principis incertum (nam utrumque auctores prodidere).*

55. 38.1: he burned Rome because he thought it was ugly, while the fire he acclaimed as 'beautiful'. He sang his song of the sack of Troy as it burned, looted the ruins and bled provincials and citizens white for contributions to a fund for relief of the effects of the fire.

56. Gascou discusses the conflicting reconstructions of Claudius' death in detail (1984, 281-91).

57. 34.1-4. Here again there is an amalgamation of a variety of traditions, and the official version of her death (Tac. *Ann.* 14.10-11) is not even mentioned.

58. Caster 1938, 84, Süss 1910, 245. Murder: Süss 250-1. See e.g. Demosthenes accused of the murder of Nicodemos (*Against Timarchos* 170), of being an accomplice *Embassy* 148, *Lysias* 14.27. In the *Against Alcibiades* attributed to Hyperides, Alcibiades is accused of plotting the death of his brother-in-law Callias (15). Alcibiades' son is accused, in passing, of throwing his friends into the sea, between accusations of pederasty and incest, an accusation not mentioned again. Cf. Plut. *Mor.* 1086E, Lucian parodies such accusations, people will say you are an adulterer or poisoner: *Merc. Cond.* 40

59. Veyne 1978, Thomas 1981.

60. Here the accusation of parricide, since it formed part of the list of official charges signed by the proscutor, was in fact used to jump the queue of cases.

61. Kirby 1990, the first full-length study of the speech, mentions the similarity of the cast-list with the characters of the *Pro Caelio*, whose connections with comedy have been noted, except that the *meretrix* here becomes the *noverca*.

62. *Inst.* 2.17.19. Cicero defends the deviation from the truth necessary in defending the guilty (*De Off.* 2.14.51)

63. Not all the passages Bradley cites are relevant: *Phgn.* 810b, 8-10 refers to the existence of flesh above the hips (a masculine feature) rather than to a prominent stomach, for instance. It is hard to be sure of precise matching in several of the passages cited.

64. Or of Agave and Pentheus in another version of the theory (Baldwin 1979).

65. Quintilian: *Inst.* 4.2.123-4 (see p. 51), 'Hermogenes', see n. 29. I am indebted to Andrew Laird, who in an unpublished paper used the term 'virtual reality' to describe epic.

Bibliography

The physiognomical treatises are cited according to Foerster's Teubner edition (F.), except for the Anonymous Latin author, which follows André's more recent Budé edition, and the Peripatetic treatise, which is cited according to the Loeb edition: Aristotle, *Minor Works*.

Baldwin, B. (1979) 'Nero and his mother's corpse', *Mnemosyne* 32 pp. 380-1.
——— (1983) *Suetonius.* Amsterdam.
Barton, T.S. (forthcoming) 'Voir, savoir, pouvoir: physiognomics in the second century C.E.', in J.I. Porter (ed.) *Constructions of the classical body.* Ann Arbor.
Bradley, K.R. (1978) *Suetonius' Life of Nero: an historical commentary*, Collection Latomus 157, Brussels.
Carney, T.F. (1968) 'How Suetonius' Lives reflect on Hadrian', *Proceedings of the African Classical Association* 11 pp. 7-24.
Caster, M. (1938) *Études sur Alexandre le faux prophète de Lucien*, Paris.
Cizek, E. (1977): *Structures et idéologie dans 'Les Vies des Douze Césars' de Suétone*, Bucharest and Paris.

Croisille, J.-M. (1969/70) 'L'Art de la composition chez Suétone', *Ann. Ist. Stud. Stor.* 2 pp. 73-87
Couissin, J. (1953) 'Suétone physiognomiste dans "Les Vies des XII Césars" ', *R.E.L.* 31 pp. 234-56.
Dawson, H. (1964) 'Whatever happened to Lady Agrippina?', *C.J.* 64 pp. 253-67.
De Coninck, L. (1983) *Suetonius en de archivalia*, Koninklijke Academie voor Wetenschappen, Letteren en Schone Kunsten van Belgie, Klasse der Letteren, Jaargang 45 pp. 104ff. (with French summary).
Della Corte, F. (1967) *Suetonio, eques Romanus*, Firenze (1st ed. 1958).
Dalmasso (1905/6) 'Un seguace di Quintiliano ... ', *Att. Ac. Sc. Tor.* 41 pp. 805-25.
Ektor, J. (1980) L'impassibilité et l'objectivité de Suétone', *Les Études Classiques*, 48 pp. 317-26.
Evans, E. (1969) 'Physiognomics in the ancient world', *Memoirs of the American Philosophical Society* N.S. 69.5, pp. 56ff.
Funaioli, G. (1949) 'I Cesari di Suetonio', in *Studi di letteratura antica. Spiriti e forme, figure e problemi delle letterature classiche*, II. 2 pp. 147-79.
Gagé, J. (1952) 'Vespasien et le mémoire de Galba', *Révue des Études Anciennes* 54 pp. 290ff.
Gascou, J. (1984) *Suétone historien*, Rome.
Gonfroy, F. (1978) 'Homosexualité et idéologie esclavagiste chez Cicéron', *Dialogues d'histoire ancienne* 4 pp. 219-65.
Grimm-Samuel, V. (1991) 'On the mushroom that deified the Emperor Claudius', *C.Q.* 41 pp. 178-82.
Kirby, J.T. (1990) *The Rhetoric of Cicero's Pro Cluentio*, Amsterdam.
Krenkel, W.A. (1980) 'Sex und politische Biographie', *Wiss. Zeitschr. der Wilhelm-Pieck-Univ. Rostock 29, Gesells.-u. Sprachwiss. Reihe, Heft 5* pp. 65-76.
Leo, F. (1901) *Die griechisch-römische Biographie nach ihrer literarischen Form*, Leipzig.
Lounsbury, R. (1987) *The Arts of Suetonius*, New York.
Mouchova, B. (1968) *Studie zu Biographien Suetons*, Acta Univ. Carolinae; Phil. et Hist. Monogr. xxii, Praha.
Nisbet, R.G.M. (1961) 'The "In Pisonem" as an invective', Appendix vi to his ed. of Cicero's 'In L. Calpurnium Pisonem Oratio', Oxford.
Norden, E. (1909) *Die Antike Kunstprosa vom VI. Jahrhundert v. Chr. bis in die neue Zeit der Renaissance*, 2nd ed. vol. 1, Berlin.
Paratore, E. (1959) 'Claude et Néron chez Suétone', *Riv. Cult. Class. Med.* 1 pp. 326-41.
Perelman, C. and Olbrechts-Tyteca, L. (1969) *The New Rhetoric: a treatise on argumentation*, tr. J. Wilkinson and P. Weaver of Paris 1958, Notre Dame.
Sassi, M. (forthcoming) 'Plutarco antifisiognomico, ovvero: del dominio della passione'.
Steidle, W. (1951) *Sueton und die antike Biographie* (Zetemata 1, München 1951, repr. 1963).
Stuart, D.R. (1928) *Epochs of Greek and Roman biography*, Berkeley.
Süss, W. (1910) *Ethos*, Leipzig.
Taillardat, J. (1967) *Suétone: 'Peri blasphemion', 'Peri paidion' (extraits byzantins)*, Paris.
Thomas, Y. (1981) '*Parricidium* I. Le père, la famille et la cité', *M.E.F.R.A.* 93 pp. 643-714.
Townend, G.B. (1967) 'Suetonius and his influence', in *Latin Biography*, ed. T.A. Dorey, pp. 79-111.
Wallace-Hadrill, A. (1983) *Suetonius: the scholar and his Caesars*, London.
Wardman, A.E. (1967) 'Description of personal appearance in Plutarch and Suetonius: the use of statues as evidence', *C.Q.* 17, pp. 414-20.
——— (1974) *Plutarch's Lives*, London.
Veyne, P. (1978) 'La famille et l'amour sous l'Haut-Empire romain', *Annales E.S.C.* pp. 33ff.

Part II

Tropes of History

4

The tyrant at table*

Justin Goddard

> Gradually Nero's vices gained the upper hand: he no longer tried to laugh them off, or hide, or deny them, but openly broke into more serious crimes. His feasts now lasted from noon till midnight, with an occasional break for diving into a warm bath, or if it were summer, into snow-cooled water.[1]

> Agrippina's passion to retain power carried her so far that at midday, the time when food and drink were beginning to raise Nero's temperature, she several times appeared before her inebriated son all decked out and ready for incest.[2]

Like most of the tyrannical emperors of the first century AD, Nero is regularly depicted as a glutton and a drunkard, by critics both ancient and modern. As with all his other desires, the story goes, the emperor indulged a passion for eating and drinking which he had developed as a young man. Accounts critical of Nero's indulgence appear in all the major historical sources. According to Dio Cassius, his tutors Seneca and Burrus were themselves more interested in playing the role of emperor and holding onto the reigns of power, and therefore did nothing to restrain the young prince. Dio detects a change in the emperor which he measures by his altered attitude to eating, drinking and sexual affairs: where once he had been 'comparatively moderate', he later descended into further indulgence, in open emulation of his predecessor Gaius Caligula.[3] Suetonius similarly makes Nero's taste for prolonged banquets mark the turning-point of his career, the moment at which the vices began to outweigh the few imperial virtues.[4]

Tacitus uses the emperor's banquets, his *convivia*, most artfully, as the setting for the greater crimes, and a backdrop against which to depict the monstrosities of Nero's reign. The incest with his mother Agrippina begins with the drunken Nero being approached while dining; it is after an evening's carousal that he first contemplates her murder; the tragedy of senators forced to suicide is heightened by the description of their final meals, taken among friends; and it is at the dinner-table that Nero commits his first great crime, the poisoning of Britannicus.[5] Tacitus juxtaposes the awful excesses of the floating banquet organised for the emperor by Tigellinus with the great fire of Rome: the perversions and degradations of the nocturnal banquet are purged by the conflagration which destroys the city in the subsequent chapter.[6]

Some modern commentators on Nero have embraced wholeheartedly the judgement of their ancient predecessors: 'in spite of the requirements of vocal and athletic training', Grant concludes, 'he did spend a tremendous amount of time reclining at meals and banquets, sometimes from noon ... continuously until midnight.'[7] The fact of Nero's gluttony is readily accepted, an inevitable part of the image of the tyrant: 'although young, he had become heavy and fat'; 'everyone drank a good deal. Nero and Otho were accustomed to this, Agrippina was not.'[8]

Yet Nero's feasting, however gross or excessive, has always been treated as of secondary importance, a commonplace and less revealing vice than the emperor's more particular iniquities. The emperor's first passion, and the focus of most criticism both ancient and modern, was acting. 'It is with the stage, the circus and the arena that Nero's amusements were mostly concerned.'[9] This judgment reflects the opinion of the ancients, for whom Nero was primarily the actor-king.[10] Tales of debauchery and gluttony have therefore been considered only as supporting vices, everyday elements in the stereotypical image of the self-obsessed tyrant. Though they lend credibility to the portrait of Nero as a man dedicated solely to the satisfaction of his desires they have, it has been assumed, nothing more to tell us about the way in which the Principate of Nero was reckoned by ancient writers, nor do they shed any light on the nature and aims of the emperor himself.

This account of Nero's feasting does justice neither to the ancient sources nor to the emperor himself. The ways in which great men ate and drank were considered vital indicators of character in ancient Rome. Each of Suetonius' *Lives of the Caesars* refers to the subject's eating and drinking, sometimes in a specially allocated section.[11] Dio incorporates details of imperial banquets and private dinner-parties into the history of each emperor's reign.[12] The importance attached to eating and drinking by imperial commentators is perhaps best illustrated by Pliny the Younger's description of Trajan's *convivia* in his *Panegyric*: he cites the hospitality and openness of the emperor's table as proof of his superiority to his predecessor Domitian, who by contrast watched and criticised his guests' indulgence before returning to 'secret gluttony and private excesses'.[13]

The criticisms of Neronian feasting need therefore to be examined in more detail and considered alongside other descriptions of imperial banqueting, so that a proper evaluation of the Neronian evidence may be made. The first section of this chapter will look at these descriptions and show that extravagance and profusion, in due measure, were vital qualities regularly attributed to the great emperors; by contrast, an emperor who refrained from indulgence left himself open to accusations of hypocrisy and miserliness unbecoming in the ruler of the world. Lavish banquets operated as vehicles for the display of the emperor's virtues, opportunities for the emperor to reveal to his subjects how he exemplified the necessary qualities of the good ruler. A measure of indulgence was justified by the virtues which the feast promoted. In being extravagant, therefore, and in entertaining frequently, Nero was doing no more than follow the example set by his predecessors.

The second part of this chapter examines the Roman criticism of Neronian feasting. The accusations reveal how it was that, according to the imperial commentators, Nero failed to promote any virtues through his feasting: there was no justification for his extravagance and luxury. Quite the opposite: Nero's feasting represented the very antithesis of that of the good emperor, since it promoted not virtue but vice.

In the third part I suggest some reasons why Nero might have acted as he is alleged to have done. Such an attempt may run counter to some of the other work in this volume, with its rightful emphasis on the difficulty of studying the 'real' Nero, of separating the historical character from the literary and rhetorical images. Nevertheless, if we are to make some sense of Nero as an emperor, it may be useful to speculate on the behaviour which provoked the unflattering criticism.

The importance of extravagance

1. Public banquets

Emperors did not lack public celebrations on which to feast the people of Rome. The number of festivals and holidays increased significantly in the Principate. New celebrations were added to mark events associated specifically with the new regime – Julius Caesar and Augustus both instituted new games, as did Livia in Augustus' honour. Games involved feasts: inside the theatre or the circus, the emperor distributed food and drink to the senators, the equestrians and to men and women alike. In addition, public *convivia* were organised throughout the city on the evenings of festivals. Banquets were also held in the emperor's honour, marking the day of his accession or the imperial birthday. Some emperors even gave games at whim, just to satisfy their populace.[14]

On such occasions the emperor was expected to be magnificent, and to display his generosity and the benefits of imperial government – to the upper orders, with their privileged status, and to the ordinary men and women, who were offered a brief opportunity to share in the life of the rich and the great. Statius, a poet at Domitian's court, writes in extravagant praise of his emperor's bounty, describing a feast given to the assembled guests at the Saturnalian games:

> Another multitude [of slaves], handsome and well-dressed, makes its way along the rows. Some carry baskets of bread and white napkins and more luxurious food; others serve intoxicating wine in abundant measure ... Come now, Antiquity, compare with ours the age of primaeval Jove and the times of gold: less generously then the vintage flowed, not thus did the harvest anticipate the sluggish year. One table serves every class, children, women, people, equestrians and senators ... everyone, rich or poor, boasts himself the emperor's guest. Amid such excitements and novel luxuries the pleasure of the scene flies by.[15]

Statius revels in the luxury, in the profusion of food and drink which is the direct benefit of the emperor's bounty. The produce of the luxurious East – damsons from Damascus, dates from Palestine, figs from Asia Minor – make up the hors-d'oeuvre, literally showered over the guests in such profusion that Nature herself cannot compete. Even Jupiter himself was unable to outdo Domitian, the new Jove: the god might send tempests to destroy the crops, but the emperor could, and did, make up for this.[16] Statius praises the emperor's lack of restraint, his magnificence. In the past, in the age of Jupiter, men had had to be content with comparatively little, to practise frugality. But now that Domitian ruled, there was no longer a need for such restraint.

The emperor's very attendance at this feast proclaimed his virtue. By graciously deigning to be present and to eat and drink alongside his subjects, Domitian displayed his *comitas*, his affability, the positive virtue of condescending to associate so closely with the mass of his people.[17] Domitian's example promotes a sense of unity among his subjects, according to Statius. As guests at the emperor's banquet, all the orders became the beneficiaries of the emperor's great generosity, when 'freedom has loosed the bonds of awe'.[18] This theme is particularly appropriate to this poem, which celebrates the emperor's Saturnalian games, when lack of restraint was the rule and the inhibitions born of respect were temporarily cast aside. Domitian's extravagance thus served a variety of ends, demonstrating his generosity and affability and fostering the welfare and the unity of the Roman people in all their orders, drawn together by their collective enjoyment of the advantages of imperial rule.

Such extravagance was not confined to Domitian, despite his well-known fondness for self-glorification.[19] Augustus too, and even Vespasian, an emperor sometimes despised for his meanness, are known to have hosted and attended extravagant public banquets.[20] Here too the emphasis was placed upon the resulting unity of the people as the emperor's subjects: by special dispensation of the senate, unmarried men and women were permitted to attend Augustus' birthday banquet, and Augustus himself allowed those who had been expelled from the senate to continue dining with the order, a special indication of the emperor's clemency.[21] Even Gaius feasted the senate, the equestrians and their wives and children extravagantly, and twice.[22]

The generosity and equality of such feasts were, of course, hierarchical. Suetonius makes it clear that even when being extravagant to all his people, Domitian was singling out the upper orders for greater prestige: the senators and equestrians received hampers (*panaria*), the people smaller baskets (*sportellae*).[23] Even greater attention was paid to social distinction at the public feasts celebrated in Augustus' Principate. Here the guests were separated by location as well as by fare: the senate and the emperor dined on the Capitol, the rest of the people elsewhere. And when Tiberius celebrated his triumph in 7 BC, the women were entertained separately by Livia and Julia, and not on the Capitol.[24] Public feasts celebrated not only the unity but also the hierarchical structure of Roman society, each man and woman entertained as their status demanded.

Such a brief survey cannot do justice to the many and diverse public banquets hosted and attended by the emperors. In particular, it cannot examine the different approaches and concerns of individual emperors when dining in public. But it will be sufficient to demonstrate the use made of extravagant public banquets for the display of imperial virtues. Extravagance was essential to a show of liberality and generosity, to demonstrate that the great benefits of imperial rule were being shared amongst the emperor's subjects. His commensality, in sharing with his people in their feasts, encouraged a feeling of unity and enabled the emperor to display his *comitas*, his readiness to associate with his subjects and to be seen as a fellow citizen and not as a tyrant. Reserved seating and extra portions ensured that the upper orders received the honour commensurate with their standing in society, and were assured of the emperor's respect for them and their continuing well-being.

2. 'Private' dinners

Even when the emperor dined 'privately', within the walls of his own palace, extravagance still seems to have been the norm. Here too, the virtues of generosity, hospitality and respect for the social hierarchy were celebrated. To describe the formal meals taken at the imperial residence as 'private' is hardly appropriate, as Statius' glowing praise of Domitian's palatial banqueting-hall makes clear:

> An edifice august, huge, magnificent, not with a hundred columns but with as many as would support heaven and the gods ... so huge expands the pile, and the reach of the far-flung hall, more unhampered than a plain, embracing beneath its shelter a vast expanse of air, and only lesser than its lord.[25]

Such a meal, in such a hall, with guests seated at more than a thousand tables, can hardly be called 'private'. So great was Domitian's bounty that Ceres and Bacchus themselves struggled to serve so much to so many.[26] But even if exceptional, Domitian's banquet was not without precedent. Claudius often gave extravagant *convivia* for up to six hundred guests, Otho invited eighty senators to dine with him in the imperial palace.[27] The emphasis is once more upon the emperor's luxury and his willingness to invite his people, and in particular the élite, to dine with him.

Dinners in the imperial palace served not only as an expression of the emperor's bounty, but also as a means of fostering good relations with the upper orders. By inviting members of the élite alone to dine with him, and feasting them in the lavish fashion which befitted their exalted status, the emperor was making a display of the high esteem in which he held his senatorial colleagues and other leading citizens. He could present himself not as a monarch among subjects but as a fellow member of the ruling class, emphasising not what distanced him from his guests but what united them.

Augustus, it was claimed, never invited a freedman to his table, presumably as a mark of respect for his free guests.[28] Tiberius received the consuls at his door and escorted them out at the end of the meal, just as he always rose to greet them in the senate.[29] Claudius, Vespasian and Hadrian did not confine their displays of friendship to the palace, but made a point of dining at the homes of senators and other friends, and visiting them when they were sick. Trajan would even appear unannounced, having dismissed his armed escort, to demonstrate the faith he put in his host.[30]

This does not imply that there were no restraints set upon the imperial standard of eating and drinking, and that any amount of indulgence could be justified. There is no praise, only savage criticism, for the excesses of Vitellius: 'he banqueted three and often four times a day, namely morning, noon, afternoon and evening – the last meal being mainly a drinking bout – and survived the ordeal well enough by taking frequent emetics.'[31] Suetonius denounces the effort and extravagance which went into satisfying Vitellius' sacrilegious appetite. There are no benefits, no positive results arising from his feasts: they were shared neither by the people at large nor by the upper orders, but were intended only to satisfy the emperor's gluttony.

But extravagant living was an accepted part of the emperor's existence. As the ruler of the world, the *princeps* was expected to behave in a magnificent manner, and therefore to entertain his subjects, both in private and in public, in lavish style. For the ordinary inhabitants of Rome, this meant huge feasts laid out in the city to which they were invited, and which were also attended by the leading citizens and the emperor himself. For the upper orders, the senators, equestrians and their wives, it entailed invitations to dine in style at the emperor's table or the opportunity to entertain the emperor in person.

This support for indulgence and extravagance was, at least outwardly, at odds with Roman moral thinking, which lauded the virtues of frugality and simplicity, and condemned luxury vigorously, especially in eating and drinking. The emperor, occupying a special place in Roman society, operated according to different rules: his authority rested, at least partially, upon making a display of certain particular virtues which justified his pre-eminence. Lavish banquets gave him an occasion for the exhibition of some of these virtues. At grand public events he displayed his concern for his people, his readiness to associate with them and his generosity in sharing the riches of imperial rule. On more private occasions the emperor used banquets to cultivate good relations with the élite, advertising his respect for them by inviting them to dinner and treating them with great respect.

Nero's failing

The extravagance attributed to Nero's feasts, however, does him no credit at all. There is no praise for his indulgence and no credit for his dinners as serving the interests of the state and promoting good relations with his people or his élite. Instead, the writers condemn Nero's feasts as harming, rather than promoting, the interests of the state. They result in the neglect of good government, causing the alienation of the élite and disharmony amongst the orders.

The accounts of Nero's private feasting concentrate first upon the emperor's neglect of his duties – the amount of time spent in feasting, its dominance of the working day, his prolonged drunkenness, and the evil consequences which result, notably to sleep with Agrippina, and then to kill her. The emperor's culinary invention, the *decocta Neronis* is an example of this negligence, water boiled and then cooled by being plunged into snow; it is, as Grant points out, 'neither gross nor alcoholic'.[32] Instead it represents a waste of time, an elaborate process destined to achieve nothing, beginning with plain water and ending with plain water.

The climax to Suetonius' life of the emperor provides the most elegant example of this topic. As news of Galba's revolt against him becomes ever more threatening, Nero responds not with positive action but with futile gestures, many of them expressed through eating and drinking. On first hearing the reports he makes no attempt to alter his life of luxury and indolence, but 'on the contrary,

4. The tyrant at table

he celebrated whatever good news came in from the provinces with the most lavish banquets imaginable'.[33] As reports grew worse, Nero planned to salvage the situation by poisoning the entire senate at a banquet, 'and when a dispatch bringing the news that the other armies, too, had revolted was brought into him at dinner, he tore it up, pushed over the table and sent smashing to the ground his two Homeric cups'.[34]

Suetonius uses the images of Nero's feasting to exemplify the emperor's inability to act, his incompetence and his irresponsibility. As Bradley comments, Suetonius' narrative technique is 'deflationary', employing personal details to discredit the emperor, showing his inappropriate reactions and reminding us of the flaws in his character.[35] It is only when forced to flee from the palace that the gravity and the hopelessness of his situation become clear to Nero himself: forced to drink water scooped up from a country pool with his bare hands, he ironically declares 'this is the *decocta Neronis*' — not snow-cooled boiling water but dirty rain-water.[36] Nero's eating and drinking are the subject of Suetonius' hostile comments because they fail to promote the imperial virtues, serving instead to prevent good government, by distracting Nero from any real or beneficial activity and channelling his reaction into vain gesturing.

Far more telling, however, is a second focus of criticism which dominates the accounts of Nero's private dining, and explains the hostility of the members of the élite who wrote the history of his life. This concerns Nero's failure to use the *convivia* as a vehicle for promoting good relations with the upper orders.

Virtuous emperors used the opportunity afforded by private banquets to dine with their élite friends, to demonstrate their openness and generosity, and to express their essential unity as fellow citizens of Rome and senators. Nero, however, is credited with employing such occasions to establish and to consolidate the *gulf* between himself and the élite. Like Gaius, Nero used his dinner invitations as a way of stealing his guests' wives. Otho boasted too long of his wife's affection and her beauty: he was sent off to Lusitania as governor, and his wife, Poppaea Sabina, became Nero's mistress, before becoming his second wife.[37] At other times, Nero simply excluded members of the élite from his dinners altogether, choosing instead to dine in the company of poets. Tacitus introduces the episode as further proof of the emperor's infatuation with the arts, following on from his public performances:

> He affected also a zeal for poetry and gathered a group of associates with some faculty for versification but not yet such as to have yet attracted remark. These, after dining, sat with him ... even to the teachers of philosophy he accorded a little time, after dinner, in order to amuse himself by the wrangling which attended the exposition of their conflicting dogmas.[38]

Here again the critical focus is directed less at the extravagance of Nero's table than upon the emperor's failure to use his dinners to satisfy the demands of the élite. Rather than reclining with close friends, with senators and equestrians, Nero preferred philosophers and poets — and unknown ones, too. It was not simply the fact of being neglected in favour of these artists which would have troubled or enraged the élite. This in itself, of course, marked a failure on the emperor's part, in not making a display of being simply the first senator, engaged in the normal exchange of hospitality and invitations which formed a vital part of the social life of the upper classes.

There was also a political significance in being invited to the imperial dinner-table. Here the emperor could, if he so chose, encourage freedom of speech and listen to advice from his colleagues.[39] The hostile reaction of members of the élite denied access to the emperor's table can be judged from anecdotes told about the emperor Marcus Aurelius. He records in his *Meditations* that he disliked luxury and that he had learned from his adoptive father Pius to allow his friends not to attend his *convivia*. But what the philosopher Marcus saw as admirable frugality, his friends interpreted as imperial disdain, and a preference for his courtiers. Deprived of their ability to meet, converse with and advise the emperor, it was assumed that he was supporting the palace-dwellers against the interests of the traditional élite.[40] Without access to the emperor's *convivia*, the élite were less able to have a say in the government of the state.

But dining with the emperor, according to his critics, could be more destructive than this. For Britannicus, of course, it meant death. It could also mean financial ruin. Suetonius bemoans the fate of two individuals who were forced to spend 4,000,000 sesterces on feeding Nero. The sum is huge, but the size of the figure is not without significance. Four million sesterces was ten times the property qualification necessary for holding the equestrian census in Rome. Suetonius' implication is that entertaining *this* emperor did not advance the hosts' prospects, but instead cost them their status in society ten times over.[41]

In eating out, just as when he dined within the palace, Nero was credited either with ignoring or with harming his élite. Like Claudius, Nero was accused of frequenting the Roman public eating-houses, the *popinae* – indeed, he spent all of his time there, if Dio is to be believed. Yet where Claudius was motivated by simple and somewhat innocent greed, the stories are told of Nero in order to demonstrate the poor relations which existed between *princeps* and élite.

> As soon as night fell he would snatch a hat or a cap and make the rounds of the taverns, or prowl the streets in search of mischief ... one of his games was to attack men on their way home from dinner, stab them if they offered resistance and then drop their bodies down the sewers ... Once he was beaten almost to death by a senator whose wife he molested.[42]

Dio comments upon the double-standards of an emperor who spent his whole life in taverns and then passed legislation to restrict the food and drink which they were allowed to sell. The emperor is revealed as a hypocrite, regulating others while indulging himself.[43] But his main focus, and that of Suetonius, is on the fact that the emperor lowered himself, that he dressed like a common man or even a freedman, in order to frequent the taverns. *Popinae* in Rome were synonymous with low-living, proverbially the haunts of prostitutes, gladiators, pimps and thieves.[44] The taverns were themselves often the object of legal restrictions, along with those who ran and frequented them. Nero, once again, is the object of élite criticism precisely because he chooses to eat and drink not with the upper orders but with the common people. And he goes further: using his disguised drinking-bouts he launches attacks upon senators and others, 'as

4. The tyrant at table

they returned home', presumably from the very dinners which Nero refused to attend. The unfortunate senator who fought back suffered for his spirit: having realised the identity of his assailant, the senator promptly apologised, and was then forced to suicide, 'his apology being interpreted as a slur'.[45]

The criticisms of Nero's private eating and drinking, whether at home or abroad, do not rely solely upon the luxury or the quantity of the emperor's appetite. An emperor who entertained the élite lavishly and ate and drank alongside them won praise, not reproach. Nero, however, was blamed for his failure to use his extravagant entertainments to satisfy other requirements. In the first place, his eating and drinking constituted a distraction from his duties as *princeps*. His efforts and attention, his responses to crises, are focused upon eating and drinking and not upon action. Secondly, and more importantly, eating and drinking are the means through which Nero expresses, or is accused of expressing, his contempt for senators and equestrians, those men whom a good emperor would treat as his peers. Nero did not invite them to his palace – or if he did, it was to poison them. He dined out with them, and thereby destroyed their wealth, or else he ate and drank with common criminals and assaulted them as they returned home from their dinners.

Nero's public feasts attracted similar criticisms, the sources castigating the emperor for using extravagant banquets as a means of attacking the élite, for showing his attachment to the commons and not to senators and equestrians. One such banquet took place in the theatre, flooded for the occasion, and is described by both Tacitus and Dio.[46] The occasion became celebrated in antiquity, and is cited by Tacitus as a typical example of the banquets hosted by the emperor during his Principate: 'Nero himself tried to give the impression that Rome was his favourite abode. He gave feasts in public places as if the whole city were his own home. But the most prodigal and notorious banquet was given by Tigellinus. To avoid repetitious accounts of extravagance, I shall describe it, as a model of its kind.' Tacitus continues to describe the sexual depravity of the occasion, the oarsmen arranged 'according to age and vice', brothels erected for the prostitution of noble ladies. The description culminates in Nero's marriage to a favourite Greek man, before the city of Rome is mercifully purified by the great fire in the next chapter.[47] The most striking feature of the description is that there is no mention of food and drink. We know that this is a great feast – Tacitus states this three times, using the words *epulae* and *convivium*. Yet there is no catalogue of extravagant foods or excesses of wine, and the inevitable conclusion is that the principal focus of Tacitus' criticism lies elsewhere. For a more detailed description we must turn to Dio:

> In the centre of the lake there had first been lowered the great wooden casks used for holding wine, and on top of these, planks had been fastened, while round about this platform taverns and booths had been erected. Thus Nero and Tigellinus and their fellow banqueters occupied the centre, where they held their feast on purple rugs and soft cushions, while all the rest made merry in the taverns. They would also enter the brothels and without let or hindrance have intercourse with any of the women who were seated there, among whom were the most beautiful and distinguished of the city, both slaves and free, courtesans and virgins and married women, and there were not merely of the common people but also of the very

noblest families, both girls and grown women. Every man had the privilege of enjoying whichever one he wished, as the women were not allowed to refuse anyone. Consequently, indiscriminate rabble as the throng was, they not only drank freely but also wantoned riotously; and now a slave would debauch his mistress in the presence of his master, and now a gladiator would debauch a girl of noble family before the eyes of her father.[48]

There is drunkenness and feasting a-plenty in Dio's account, but it is the *inversion* of status, the domination of the masses over the élite, which attracts criticism from the moralising historians. It is not Nero's provision of food and drink, but his allocation of it, which provokes the moralists' censure. In neither account are the senators and equestrians recipients of food and drink, let alone of privileged position or fare. Nero, Tigellinus and their friends feast, and so do the common rabble: luxury is provided for them, and the feast offers them the opportunity to do as they please. The whole banquet represents the antithesis of the spectacle of Domitian's praised by Statius. Disharmony, rather than unity, is fostered, as fights break out between those involved, and men are killed and women suffocated in the mêlée. Hierarchy is not upheld, but subverted, as noblemen become pimps to the prostitution of their wives, and gladiators and slaves feast and act like their masters. All takes place under the gaze of, and with the tacit approval of Nero and Tigellinus, who watch from the safety of the middle of the lake.

The senate's tyrant

Suetonius, Dio and Tacitus reflect the concerns and criticisms of the aristocracy of Rome. For them, Nero's feasts represented the antithesis of all that a good emperor ought to do. It was not simply luxury or extravagance they condemned, for these were accepted features of imperial rule, which were praiseworthy when they advanced the interests of the élite.[49] Nero, however, excluded senators and equestrians from his feasts, or inflicted violence upon them there. In their place, Nero entertained unknown poets and imbibed with common criminals: he hosted banquets at which the common people of Rome ate and drank to excess, and at which the élite were forced to exchange places with their slaves, their gladiators and their whores.

The accusations and exaggerations made by the élite commentators concerning Nero's eating and drinking reflect, I believe, a desire on Nero's part to win popularity not with senators and other members of the upper orders but with the common people of Rome. Veyne has argued that the élite and the urban plebs should be seen as potential rivals, competing for first place in the emperor's attention. The emperor could not be the darling of the people and, at the same time, give the senate the respect which they believed their status demanded. 'Unfortunately,' he continues, 'the senate's conception of its dignity ruled out that of the plebs. An emperor who conformed to their political ideal would be content with making himself popular; only a tyrant would court the plebs by heaping public festivities upon it like flowers ... The senate did not like tyrants, who tended to prefer the plebs to them.' Nero, he suggests, is just such an emperor, 'tyrant to the senate but popular with the plebs of Rome alone'.[50]

4. The tyrant at table

Yavetz attributes to Nero exactly this sort of desire for popular affection at the expense of the support of the senate, crediting him with a wish to become 'an absolute and popular ruler *par excellence*, his entire behaviour expressive of *levitas popularis*'. In support of this, he cites Suetonius' criticism of the emperor, that he was 'carried away by a craze for popularity and .. was jealous of all who in any way stirred the feelings of the mob'.[51]

This account of Nero's policy is consistent with the descriptions of the emperor's eating and drinking. The public feasts, and the more private occasions upon which the emperor dined, reflected the emperor's overwhelming desire to win popular affection and, if necessary, to alienate and even to humiliate the élite. My starting point here is Nero's frequenting of public taverns in the city of Rome. Nero went, according to our sources, dressed like a common man, *hôs kai idiôtês*, or like a freedman, according to Suetonius.[52] He visited the *popinae* and wandered the streets of the city, meeting and eating and drinking with the ordinary poeple of the city.

Such stories of rulers who dress up like their subjects are familiar enough in history; Burke cites many examples, including several English kings, and traces the tale back at least as far as the *Arabian Nights*. In these folktales a king dresses up to walk incognito among his subjects, often among criminals, but always with the best interests of his citizens in mind. Sometimes it is to check upon the administration of justice and the efficiency of his officers, sometimes simply to find out the truth of what is really said about him and to experience criticism, as a change from the flattery of his court: or it is simply to live and share the lives of the humblest of his subjects.[53]

But without exception the tales are told of popular kings, kings who have a genuine concern for the welfare of their people. A similar story is even told of the great Augustus who, according to Dio, dressed up once a year as a beggar and solicited gifts from the ordinary people. Suetonius adds further that Augustus used to enjoy watching the street-fighting, 'slogging matches between untrained roughs in narrow city alleys', which he presumably did incognito.[54] Such stories must have been common in Rome, told of emperors who cut through the imperial ceremony and fraternised directly with their ordinary subjects. Nero's is, so far as I know, the only example of the story being told, or retold, with a hostile purpose, where the ruler uses his disguise to attack his subjects and to steal from them, rather than to benefit them.[55]

It is possible, therefore, that the criticisms of Suetonius and Dio have as their origin stories originally portraying Nero as a popular monarch, the emperor who had the best interests of his ordinary subjects at heart, and who went amongst them to share their pleasures and to experience their lives. This would be consistent with the legends which claimed that Nero was still alive, waiting for the right moment to return to rule.[56] Burke notes that the story of the ruler who is not really dead is another type of the 'ruler as popular hero' story, told of kings who will return to free their people from their oppressors, and restore justice.[57] This popular tradition about Nero may have been distorted by the élite writers who saw, and did not appreciate, the prospect of an emperor so much at home with the common people, so ready to be seen on good terms with them.

If it is correct that the origin of these criticisms lies in popular tales of Nero's fondness for his people, then we may be justified in looking for a similar explanation of the emperor's floating banquet. The accounts of immorality and perversion might result from an original banquet or banquets at which the emperor intended to demonstrate to the masses that they, and not the élite, were his chief concern.

Such an interpretation is at least not denied by Tacitus' narrative. It is true that Tacitus thought of the banquet as the apogee of Neronian vice, but this may not prevent him from revealing the emperor's true intentions. Significantly, Tacitus attributes the decision to stage the feast to Nero's passion for popularity, his desire to please the people of Rome at all costs. The emperor intended, we are told, to travel to his Eastern provinces, and to Egypt in particular, but having announced his plans, he had a change of heart and decided to remain in his capital:

> His patriotism came before everything, he asserted; he had seen the people's sad faces and heard their private lamentations about the extensive travels he planned – even his brief absences they found unendurable, being accustomed (he added) to derive comfort in life's misfortunes with the sight of their emperor. Just as in private relationships nearest are dearest, he said, so to him the inhabitants of Rome came first: he must obey their appeal to stay! The people liked such protestations. They loved their amusements.[58]

Although Tacitus cynically links this to the people's overriding concern for the corn-supply, we need not see this as their only reason.[59] The natural consequence of Nero's decision to remain in Rome is the magnificent feast with which he rewards his adoring masses. The senators and leading men, Tacitus avers, were not so sure of the benefits of having the emperor so close at hand, but the people had no such doubts. The image of Nero as an emperor who listens and responds to his citizens' concerns, already suggested by the tales of Nero in disguise, is further enhanced by this account.

But the people required more than a feast: they wanted the emperor's personal involvement. Nero had to be seen to feast, and to enjoy himself alongside his people. And this necessitated the abandonment of the Augustan style of public meals, which separated the upper orders from the masses, and which gave the former privileged portions. Nero wanted to make the people his personal guests. Tacitus' subsequent comment, that the emperor 'gave feasts in public places as if the whole city were his own home' may appear initially to be simply a criticism of his encroaching on the public space of the city, much as the Domus Aurea would be criticised for monopolising so much of the centre of the city.[60] However, it is more likely that it reflects Nero's desire to appear to invite the commons into his house, to make them his private guests. Of course, such a huge banquet could not have taken place in the imperial palace, although the extensive grounds of the Domus Aurea may later have afforded just such an opportunity. Instead, Nero used the city as his private house, and invited the people to take the place of the upper orders at his personal invitation.

A comment of Dio's suggests, moreover, that Nero's own indulgence was aimed precisely at increasing his popularity with his people, at the expense of the élite. Having previously only practised his passions – his feasts, his drinking, and his amours – in private, he was urged to ignore the restraints of his guardians:

' "Do you not know that you are Caesar, and that you have authority over them rather than they over you?" ... Finally he lost all shame, dashed to the ground and trampled underfoot all precepts ... and as he was applauded for this by the crowd and received many compliments from them, he devoted himself to this course unsparingly.'[61] While in Greece, Nero could not bear to be out of sight of his public even when between performances, and so dined in the theatre orchestra, visible to the audience.[62] Nero's indulgence, his public feasting and drinking, were the response to the applause of the people, part of his policy of winning popular appeal. They also represented, for Dio, the emperor's rejection of his élite advisers, and his self-assertion as a Caesar able to do exactly as he pleased.

Conclusion

Conventional views of Nero have tended to interpret the emperor's self-indulgent eating and drinking as just another aspect of his general immorality, and one which was secondary in importance to his more notorious crimes. Nero is seen as a man bent only on pleasing himself, by setting fire to Rome, in building his huge palace in Rome, and by feasting as he pleased. But this interpretation, as I have argued, is inconsistent with what we know of the standards by which emperors were judged in ancient Rome. Extravagance was expected of an emperor, and only criticised when it failed to serve the interests of the state and, in particular, that of the ruling élite.

Nero did not employ his feasts, according to his Roman critics, to express the good relations which existed between himself and the upper orders of society, nor to establish harmony amongst his subjects. Instead, the descriptions of Nero's eating and drinking present him as a man with no concern for these virtues, who neglected the business of government for his personal satisfaction. Accordingly, the public feasts and private dinners and the emperor's nocturnal excursions are credited with causing precisely the opposite vices to those virtues: the breakdown of good relations with the élite, the inversion of proper status between the different orders of his subjects, and an escalation of public immorality.

These criticisms of Nero, however, naturally reflect the concerns and preoccupations of the élite whose creation they were. Nero is accused of failing to satisfy the demands which they made of an emperor, in particular by not maintaining the semblance of power-sharing and respect which Augustus had built up. It may reasonably be argued that the real Nero is eternally lost to us, hidden by the distorting rhetoric of his chroniclers who took against him. But this pessimism may not be necessary. Individual accounts of Nero's activities support an alternative view of the Principate, that Nero lost the support of the élite as a consequence of winning the favour of the populace. Like most emperors after Augustus, he could not satisfy both masters. Nero's greatest mistake, in the end, was his failure to please those who would write the record of his reign.

Notes

* I would like to thank Peter Garnsey and Christopher Kelly for reading and commenting on an earlier version of this chapter.

1. Suet. *Nero* 27.
2. Tac. *Ann.* 14.2.
3. Dio 61.4.3.
4. Suet. *Nero* 27, quoted above. Suetonius similarly marks a turning-point in the career of Tiberius: 'But having found seclusion at last, and no longer feeling himself under public scrutiny, he rapidly succumbed to all the vicious passions which he had tried, not very successfully, to disguise ... Even as a young officer he was a hardened drinker ... ' *Tib.* 42
5. Agrippina *Ann.* 14.2; murder ib. 13.20; Britannicus ib. 13.16; senators ib. 15.69 and 16.19. The first death of the new principate also takes place at the dinner-table, the murder of Silanus, though Tacitus suggests that this was done without Nero's knowledge: *Ann.* 13.1. It is through the poisoning of Claudius' food that Nero becomes emperor (*Ann.* 12.67).
6. *Ann.* 15.37-8.
7. Grant (1970) 188 and 193.
8. Walter (1957) 144 and 92.
9. Bishop (1964) 123; Cizek (1982) 16 comments on the image of Nero as a 'monstre criminal, fou sanguinaire, mettant à mort les siens et le feu à Rome, sa capitale, par pur plaisir'.
10. Suet. *Nero* 52-4, Eutropius, 7.14.
11. For example, *Aug.* 74-7, *Tib.* 42, *Dom.* 21.
12. See below n. 14.
13. Plin. *Pan.* 49.6.
14. Thus for example, Dio 54.26.2, 54.30.5, 55.2.4, 55.8, 58.22.2, 59.7.1, 59.11.3 etc. Games given on a whim, Suet. *Gai.* 18.
15. Stat. *Silv.* 1.6.28-52.
16. East 9-20, Jupiter and Nature 21-7.
17. On *comitas* see Wallace-Hadrill (1982) 42.
18. Stat. *Silv.* 1.6.45; see D'Arms (1990) 308-10.
19. See Garzetti (1974) 269ff.
20. On Augustus, see n. 14 above: on Vespasian, Suet. *Ves.* 19.
21. Suet. *Aug.* 35.
22. id. *Gai.* 17, Dio 59.7.1 and 59.11.3.
23. Suet. *Dom.* 5 with D'Arms (1990) 309.
24. Dio 54.26.2, 55.2.4, 55.8.2, 55.12.5: Augustus' concern for the maintenance of distinctions between the orders at these feasts is matched by the division of seating he ordered for the games. See Suet. *Aug.* 44.
25. *Silv.* 4.2.18ff. For the problems of applying the public-private distinction to Archaic Greek symposia and the sacrificial meals, see Schmitt-Pantell (1990). As D'Arms (1990) points out, similar problems exist in distinguishing between the 'public' and 'private' meals hosted by the princeps.
26. ib. 4.2.34-5.
27. Suet. *Claud.* 32; Plu. *Otho* 3.
28. Suet. *Aug.* 74.
29. Dio 57.11.3, Suet. *Tib.* 29.

4. The tyrant at table

30. Claudius Dio 60.12.1; Vespasian id. 66.10.6; Trajan id. 68.7.3; Hadrian *HA Had.* 9.
31. Suet. *Vit.* 13.
32. Grant (1970) 193.
33. *Nero* 42.
34. ib. 47.
35. Bradley (1978) 242.
36. Suet. *Nero* 48, Plin. *Nat. Hist.* 31.40 and Dio 63.28.5.
37. Tac. *Ann.* 15.46; Gaius: Suet. *Gai.* 36.
38. Tac. *Ann.* 14.16.
39. Brunt (1975) 24.
40. Condemnation of luxury *Med.* 1.17.3, 5.12, 9.2, 12.2, learning from father to excuse friends from dining, 1.16.2; adverse comment *HA Marcus Aurelius* 29.
41. Multiples of 400,000 sesterces are very common in this kind of criticism: see Sen. *Ep.* 95.41; Suet. *Vit.* 13. Tiberius' prize for a food contest is 200,000 sesterces, the qualification for jury service (*Tib.* 42.2); an invitation to a meal with Gaius, doubtless in the hope of advancing himself politically, cost one man 400,000 sesterces (*Gai.* 39); compare also Lucullus' extravagance, which is calculated at 50,000 drachmae, or about 200,000 sesterces (Plu. *Luc.* 41.7). Juvenal also calculates the loss incurred by a glutton at 400,000 sesterces, before he lost his status and had to enrol as a gladiator (11.19-20).
42. *Nero* 26; cf. Dio 61.8.1 and 62.14.2.
43. The same accusation is made of Tiberius: Suet. *Tib.* 42.
44. Kleberg (1957) 89ff. Cf. Cic. *Phil.* 2.77 and *Pis.* 13.
45. *Ann.* 13.25.1. Dio tells a slightly different version of the same story, 61.9.3.
46. Suetonius, perhaps in a confusion of sources, refers to a banquet held in the Campus Martius specially drained for the purpose. He attributes the subsequent prostitution of noble women to the emperor's cruises down the coast from Rome.
47. *Ann.* 15.37.
48. Dio 62.15.1-6.
49. Plin. *Pan.* 49.5.
50. Veyne (1990) 406-7.
51. Yavetz (1969) 124; Suet. *Nero* 53.
52. Dio 61.8.1, Suet. *Nero* 26.
53. Burke (1988) 152.
54. Suet. *Aug.* 45 and Dio 54.35.3.
55. There is one parallel to the story of Nero's attacking ordinary people: the sultan Mehmet, while contemplating the siege of Constantinople in 1452, used to dress as a common soldier and wander the streets of Adrianople in order to escape his court and contemplate his strategy. He gave orders that anyone who saw through his disguise and recognised him should be killed, but this was not his purpose in dressing up. See Runciman (1965) 73.
56. Suet. *Nero* 57 and Tac. *Hist.* 2.8. Charlesworth (1950) 74 argues that the existence of such stories are 'good evidence for a strong *desiderium* felt by that section of people which believes in the return'. The stories originate in the East, although according to Suetonius there was some popular feeling for Nero after his death in Rome too.
57. Burke (1978) 152.
58. Tac. *Ann.* 15.36.
59. See Yavetz (1969) 126.
60. Stambaugh (1988) 70 and Veyne (1990) 383.
61. Dio 61.4.5 – 61.5.2.
62. Suet. *Nero* 20.

Bibliography

Bishop, J. (1964) *Nero, the man and the legend*, London.
Bradley, K.R. (1978) 'Suetonius' *Life of Nero*: an historical commentary', *Collection Latomus* 157, Brussels.
Brunt, P. (1975) 'Stoicism and the Principate', *PBSR* XLIII pp. 7-35.
Burke, P. (1978) *Popular culture in early modern Europe*, London.
Cizek, E. (1982) *Néron*, Paris.
Charlesworth, M.P. (1950) 'Nero: some aspects', *JRS* XL pp. 69-76.
D'Arms, J.H. (1990) 'The Roman convivium and the idea of equality' in Murray, O. (ed.) *Sympotica: a symposium on the Symposion*, Oxford.
Garzetti, A. (1974) *From Tiberius to the Antonines*, London.
Grant, M. (1970) *Nero*, London.
Kleberg, T. (1957) *Hôtels, restaurants et cabarets dans l'antiquité romain*, Uppsala.
Runciman, S. (1965) *The fall of Constantinople 1453*, Cambridge.
Schmitt Pantell, P. (1990) 'Sacrificial meal and *symposion*: two models of civic institutions in the Archaic city?' in Murray, O. (ed.) *Sympotica: a symposium on the Symposion*, Oxford.
Stambaugh, J.E. (1988) *The ancient Roman city*, Baltimore.
Wallace-Hadrill, A. (1982) 'Civilis Princeps: between citizen and king', *JRS* LXXII pp. 32-48.
Walter, G. (1957) *Nero*, London.
Veyne, P. (1990) *Bread and circuses*, London.
Yavetz, Z. (1969) *Plebs and princeps*, Oxford.

5

Beware of imitations: theatre and the subversion of imperial identity[1]

Catharine Edwards

The younger Pliny, praising the emperor Trajan, contrasts his exemplary rule with that of his predecessors. Among these, one of the most outrageous for his transgression of codes of imperial propriety is the emperor Nero, whom Pliny described as *imperator scaenicus*, 'an actor emperor' (*Paneg.* 46.4). For Romans this was a horrible oxymoron, a concept so riven with contradiction it was almost unthinkable. The qualities that emperors were supposed to exhibit, ideally to a greater degree than all other Romans, the qualities of *gravitas, dignitas, fides, virtus*, were ones that actors, more than any other Romans, conspicuously lacked.

I shall begin my study of Nero as actor-emperor with a brief exploration of some of the associations of acting in ancient Rome.[2] Actors and the theatre were regarded as despicable but also glamorous. The shame associated with acting may seem to us bizarre; the glamour at first sight more comprehensible. I want to suggest that the glamour of Roman actors was intimately connected with their shamefulness. This will, I hope, help to explain the attraction of the theatre for a Roman emperor, while, at the same time, suggesting why Nero's interest in the stage might have been seen as highly problematic by members of the Roman elite. I want to argue, too, that the particular associations of acting made theatrical performance an especially apt emblem for representations of the transgressive nature of Neronian rule.

Actors

Actors are often used by Roman authors as paradigms of the low. Seneca, writing in the time of Nero, observes:

> I often find the following example useful, for I think that none expresses more effectively the drama of human life, in which we are assigned the parts we play so badly. There is the man who stalks upon the stage in padded dress, throws back his head and says: 'I am Lord of the Argives ... ' And who is this fellow? He is just a slave; his ration is five measures of grain and five denarii ... The same applies to those dandies whom you see riding in litters above the heads of men and above the crowd; their happiness is merely put on, like an actor's mask. Tear it off and you will despise them. (*Ep.* 80.7)

We are all actors, Seneca suggests[3] – an idea by no means confined to Roman texts. This simile can work for Seneca's argument because there is a contrast between the mean life of an actor and the glorious roles he temporarily assumes. Acting was good to think with because there was this contrast, this distinction. I shall come back to some of these implications of Seneca's simile later. For the moment, I want to emphasise the role of the actor as a conspicuous symbol of the low.

The status of actors was marked out as low even in Roman law. Like gladiators, prostitutes (and some other categories of person such as procurers and the trainers of gladiators) actors were designated as *infames*, a term which may be translated as 'without reputation'.[4] If they were Roman citizens (many, though not all, actors were slaves or non-citizen free), actors were not permitted to stand for election as magistrates or even to vote.[5] They were limited in their capacity to represent others in the praetor's court.[6] Under the Augustan marriage legislation, actresses were forbidden to marry freeborn Romans.[7] The protection from corporal punishment, which under the republic and early principate was one of the hallmarks of Roman citizenship, was not extended to actors, who could be subjected to flogging by magistrates.[8] To a certain extent, these disabilities applied to all those branded as *infames*, but several legal and other texts single out actors for special mention.

Why were actors denied the rights of other Roman citizens? The rationale for this may, I suspect, be found in Roman ideas of the dignity required of the citizen's body. For the bodies of actors, like those of gladiators and prostitutes, were seen as lacking dignity. They were paraded on stage for financial gain. They served the pleasures of others. And just as actors (along with gladiators and prostitutes) resembled slaves in their lack of control over their own bodies, so they were assimilated to slaves by the law.[9] Thus they were relegated to the bottom rung of the hierarchy of Roman citizens, categorised alongside soldiers dishonourably dismissed, bigamists and men convicted of fraud and calumny. How could one trust the word of those who sold their own bodies?

Actors, moreover, actually sold their speech. They lied for a living. When Cicero discusses the ways in which an honourable Roman may legitimately earn money, he counts as most disgraceful any kind of trading, on the grounds that traders only make a profit from misrepresentation, *vanitas* (*De off*. 1.150). And what were actors engaged in if not misrepresentation? Seneca remarks with disapproval that actors can feign every emotion (*Ep*. 11.7). In the theatre they were applauded for pretending to be what they were not. Such dangerous abilities were incompatible with the quality of *fides* – good faith – so highly prized by respectable Romans.[10] Numerous anecdotes emphasise the untrustworthiness of actors.[11]

One might see this association between the theatre and misrepresentation as a feature of attitudes to acting in many societies (and actors are often the objects of suspicion), but particular considerations affected attitudes to acting in Rome. In Roman law, speech had a vital performative force. Certain processes took effect as a consequence of the uttering of particular verbal *formulae*. Florence Dupont has emphasised the implications of this for Roman views of acting.[12]

5. Beware of imitations

The words of the actor were *leves, vani* – 'empty', 'hollow' – without any effects. They were the antithesis of the weighty sentences uttered in the praetor's court.

There are other reasons why the spoken word may be seen as carrying a particular weight in ancient Rome. Official public speaking was reserved for Romans whose power was sanctioned as legitimate by the possession of office. The privilege of speaking in a public meeting was strictly circumscribed. Even under the republic, Claude Nicolet has suggested, it was very rare for men who were not magistrates to speak in public debate.[13] And yet actors, persons with no official standing, no *auctoritas*, spoke in public and were listened to by thousands.

Most Romans who held public office had trained as orators – a profession associated with respectability, dignity and public service. Yet there were similarities between the actor and the orator. The legal process, in which orators played leading roles, often resembled a public spectacle.[14] Cicero observes that in addition to various other qualities, an orator must have *vox tragoedorum, gestus paene summorum actorum*, 'the voice of an actor of tragedies, the delivery almost of the greatest of actors' (*De orat.* 1.128). Later in the same work, he describes orators as: *veritatis ipsius actores*, 'the players who act real life' (3.214). But the idea that respectable Roman orators were, in a sense, actors was a dangerous one. The resemblance between actors and orators seems to have disconcerted the latter. Cicero and, later, Quintilian, in their treatises on the art of public-speaking, repeatedly advise the would-be orator to avoid gestures which might be associated with the theatre.[15] If social and political order was to be maintained, it was essential that the status of actors should be clearly distinguished from that of men whose words carried proper weight and authority.[16]

But the legal disabilities which excluded actors from participation in legitimate political rituals only made their ability to command huge audiences the more disturbing. And they served, also, to enhance the association of actors with political licence. According to Tacitus, the emperor Tiberius expelled actors from Italy because plays had become the focus for political disturbance (*Ann.* 4.14). Such expulsions occurred under both republic and principate.[17] Cicero and other authors tell of incidents at the theatre where the words spoken by actors were interpreted by the actors themselves or by the audience or by both as having a particular contemporary meaning. Cicero writes of the actor Diphilus' mockery of Pompey:

ludis Apollinaribus Diphilus tragoedus in nostrum Pompeium petulanter invectus est: 'nostra miseria tu es magnus' miliens coactus est dicere ...

[At the games of Apollo, the actor Diphilus set on poor old Pompey quite brutally: 'By our sufferings art thou great.' There were thousands of encores ...] (*Ad Att.* 39.3)

A lowly entertainer with a foreign name had the power to make all Rome hiss the great Pompey.[18]

Actors, then, were dangerous, persons without provenance, disguised, who nevertheless had the right to speak before the Roman people. Partly for this reason, I think, Roman texts regularly express profound ambivalence towards acting and the theatre. This ambivalence is manifested in the attribution of various other characteristics to the theatre, which was often represented as an institution foreign to Rome. Some texts emphasise its Etruscan origins,[19] while others stress the influence of Greek traditions on Roman theatre.[20] The 'otherness' of actors was also emphasised by their association with the feminine. Moralists complained at male actors playing female roles.[21] Juvenal, for instance, is contemptuous of the skills of a Greek actor, remarking that one might think he even had female genitals (3.95-7).[22] The gestures used in theatrical performances are often described as feminine.[23] The theatre was sometimes presented as undermining the manhood even of its audience. Valerius Maximus, writing in the time of Tiberius, notes that the building of a permanent theatre was banned in 154 BC, on the grounds that it was a threat to the *virilitas propria Romanae gentis nota* – 'the famous virility particular to the Roman people'.[24] For performers especially, acting was incompatible with *virtus*, manly virtue, military courage, a distinctively Roman quality.[25] Roman texts represent acting as the inverse of fighting.[26] This antithesis was reflected and reinforced in the law: actors were not permitted to be soldiers in the Roman army (Livy 7.2.8), while capital punishment was prescribed for soldiers who appeared on stage (*Dig.* 48.19.14). Acting, then, was seen as incompatible with virtually anything that was admirable in a Roman citizen.

Acting emperor

The glamour of acting was no doubt partly a consequence of its association with the forbidden. Acting was seen as politically, and also sexually, licentious. It was perhaps this association with licence – as well as the public renown enjoyed by leading actors – which exercised a fascination over upper-class Romans. Successful actors, such as Roscius and Aesopus in the time of Cicero, are said to have become friends of Roman senators (Macrob. *Sat.* 3.14.11-14).[27] Indeed, many leading Romans are alleged to have fallen in love with actors.[28] Guardians of the social order seem to have been disturbed by this mingling of elite Romans and stage performers. According to Tacitus, the emperor Tiberius banned senators and equites from consorting with actors (*Ann.*1.77).

Some members of the elite were reputedly compelled to appear on stage (and in the arena) as a public humiliation by earlier emperors, as well as by Nero himself.[29] Tacitus writes of Nero's youth games in AD 59 that he induced indigent members of noble families to participate by offering them money. This might look like simple bribery – *nisi quod merces ab eo qui iubere potest vim necessitatis adfert*, 'but the money of one who may resort to force can itself be compelling' (*Ann.* 14.14). Some elite Romans, however, seem to have chosen to perform as actors and gladiators, actively embracing the humiliation such activities brought.[30] Nero's own stage appearances can be seen as, in a sense, the culmination of a fashion rather than a peculiar aberration. But the emperor's acting had a particular significance.

The rest of this chapter will explore representations of Nero as an actor, before moving on to look at the role of acting as a metaphor for other aspects of his life. Acting plays an important part in ancient narratives of Nero's rule; the authors of these narratives present acting as wholly inappropriate in a Roman emperor. The modern reader may be tempted to ask how far this insistence on Nero's passion for acting should be regarded as hostile misrepresentation of an emperor unpopular for other reasons. In support of this view, one might note the suspicious resemblance between the theatrical interests attributed to Nero and the alleged activities of several other 'bad' emperors. Caligula too (Nero's maternal uncle) is said to have planned to appear on stage as an actor (though he was assassinated before this could take place).[31] He is also alleged to have played the role of pimp (another of the professions stigmatised in Roman law), providing elite women and children for the sexual gratification of the people of Rome.[32] Later, the emperor Commodus is said to have been assassinated when he planned to be inaugurated as consul for AD 193 dressed as a gladiator.[33]

Representations of one emperor can only begin to make sense in the context of the stories told about his predecessors and successors. There are particular rhetorical conventions for describing 'bad' (and 'good') rulers. 'Bad' emperors are inevitably portrayed as seducing well-born women and boys, spending extraordinary sums of money on recherché pleasures and murdering innocent senators – as well as taking on the roles of the most degraded Roman citizens. But emperors themselves should not be seen as passive victims of stereotyping. Of course, the particular motives of any individual ruler are impossible to fathom but it is, I think, helpful to regard emperors in general as responding to and intervening in (whether consciously or unconsciously) the complex of discourses in which imperial power was made sense of, challenged and reinforced. Suetonius, for instance, suggests that in building a bridge over the Bay of Naples the emperor Caligula was vying with Xerxes, the paradigmatic tyrant (*Calig.* 19). Caligula may be seen as trying to demonstrate his own power by appealing to a facet of 'tyrannical' behaviour with a well-established place in the literary tradition. 'Rhetoric' and 'reality' are inseparable.

Emperors groped for the terms in which to express their power. Some were more successful at choosing a vocabulary which appealed to the elite writers who monopolised Roman historiography. Others found such definitions constraining.[34] Nero is supposed to have observed that no emperor had yet realised the extent of his power (*quid sibi liceret*) – a remark which Suetonius specifically links with his disregard for the senate (Suet. *Nero* 37.3). Nero, in becoming an actor, took on a role which seemed as far removed as possible from that of emperor (at least emperor as understood by the senatorial elite). The man who should have been the noblest of all the Romans aligned himself with the most ignoble. The emperor, by appearing as actor, showed he could transcend the rules that ordered the rest of Roman society, demonstrated his power to turn the social order upside-down – a dangerous trick for one situated at the apex of the social hierarchy.

Henderson describes Nero (or at least the Tacitean Nero) as a 'Self-inventing Tyrant who plays with identity as transgression'.[35] Nero may be seen as attempting to find new discursive strategies for representing imperial power, in part by exploiting the association of the theatre with the extremes of licence. But, especially in the light of his ignominious end (not to mention the subsequent appropriation of the purple by a family quite unrelated to the Julio-Claudians), this transgression offered itself as an easy victim for reinscription as a counter-*exemplum* in prescriptive tracts on imperial behaviour, such as Suetonius' Lives and Pliny's *Panegyricus*. The story of Nero could be used as a cautionary tale to demonstrate precisely that an emperor was not at liberty to do *quid sibi liceret* – or at least not when it involved challenging the self-definition of the Roman upper classes.

The younger Pliny represents acting as one of the most appalling of Nero's excesses. Other Roman writers express similar sentiments. Juvenal in his eighth satire (which focuses on the transgressions of assorted scions of noble Roman families) sees the frightful example of Nero's stage appearances – *citharoedo principe* – as almost excusing other aristocratic Romans who perform as comedians and gladiators (8.198-9). He goes on to describe the full horror of the emperor's theatrical performances. Nero, observes Juvenal, is a matricide like Orestes, but Orestes did not murder his sister or his wife, Orestes did not poison his relatives and:

> ..... in scena numquam cantavit Orestes,
> Troica non scripsit. quid enim Verginius armis
> debuit ulcisci magis aut cum Vindice Galba,
> quod Nero tam saeva crudaque tyrannide fecit?
> haec opera atque hae sunt generosi principis artes,
> gaudentis foedo peregrina ad pulpita cantu
> prostitui Graiaeque apium meruisse coronae.
> maiorum effigies habeant insignia vocis,
> ante pedes Domiti longum tu pone Thyestae
> syrma vel Antigones seu personam Melanippes,
> et de marmoreo citharam suspende colosso.

[Orestes never sang on the stage; he never wrote an epic on the Trojan war. For what, of all the deeds of Nero's cruel and bloody rule, deserved revenge more by Verginius and by Galba, with his associate Vindex? These were the achievements, these the talents of our noble ruler, who took pleasure in making an exhibition of his vile voice for foreign audiences and winning Greek parsley wreaths. Let the images of his ancestors be decked with his singing prizes, make offerings of the robe he wore as Thyestes or Antigone or his Melanippe mask and hang his harp on his marble colossus.] (*Juv.* 8.220-30)

The satirist equates the murder of members of one's family with appearing on stage – satiric bathos, perhaps, but a suggestion of the central place of such accusations in attacks on Nero.[36]

Acting plays a crucial part in the hostile pictures of Nero composed by Tacitus, Suetonius and Dio. They present his passion for acting as initially controlled but gradually given freer rein. The emperor's devotion to the stage was such, according to these accounts, that, in AD 59, he instituted youth games in which he himself allegedly participated.[37] These seem to have had a small and select audience of young equestrians. Since participation in private competitions was not, it seems, a source of disgrace, their private nature is rather played down by Tacitus who presents this as the beginning of Nero's theatrical career, observing *ratusque dedecus molliri si pluris foedasset*, 'he thought his own shame would be lessened if he induced others to share it'.[38] In the next year, AD 60, we are told, Nero established a public festival, the Neronia, on the Greek model, though he did not appear personally in these shows.[39] Tacitus concedes that there was no scandal associated with this round of games. They were merely a prelude.

Nero's first appearance on the public stage was in Naples, Tacitus and Suetonius relate (a 'foreign' location slightly mitigating the horror of imperial participation in such an unRoman activity).[40] But disaster followed, for the theatre collapsed immediately afterwards. It was on the occasion of the second Neronia, in AD 65, that Nero appeared on stage in Rome in public – *publicum flagitium*, 'a public scandal', in Tacitus' words, which anyone who was not innured to the corruption of the city found intolerable (*Ann.* 16.4-5). To make matters worse, the emperor's star turn, according to Suetonius, was singing a female role, that of Niobe (*Nero* 21). Tacitus presents this occasion, too, as culminating in disaster when many members of the crowd were crushed to death. An actor-emperor meant catastrophe.[41]

After this, in AD 66, the emperor decided to compete in the great games of Greece.[42] Suetonius represents Nero as playing the part of an ordinary competitor, scrupulous to observe all the rules, lest he be disqualified – an absurdity, for he would be awarded the prize no matter what his performance (*Nero* 23-4).[43] This trip to Greece is the occasion for a tirade from Dio who scornfully attacks Nero's competition in the games in general, the climax of his invective focusing specifically on acting:

> But why lament these acts of his alone, when he also elevated himself on the high-soled buskins only to fall from the throne, and in putting on the mask, threw off the dignity of his imperial power, to beg dressed up as a runaway slave, to be led as a blind man, to be heavy with child, to be a madman or to wander an outcast – he usually played the roles of Oedipus, Thyestes, Heracles, Alcmeon or Orestes. (63.9.4)

For Dio acting and ruling were incompatible, indeed antithetical.[44]

The parade of role-playing on the part of the emperor raised troubling questions about the authenticity of all the players in the political game. An actor-emperor was also problematic in view of the particular virtues emperors were supposed to exhibit.[45] What was expected of a good emperor emerges clearly from the younger Pliny's approving description of the bearing of the emperor Trajan, as the latter addresses the senate:

> quae enim gravitas sententiarum, quam inadfectata veritas verborum, quae adseveratio in voce, quae adfirmatio in vultu, quanta in oculis habitu gestu, toto denique corpore fides!

> [Consider the weightiness of his sentiments, the straightforward candour of his words, the assurance in his voice, the decisiveness in his visage, the sincerity of his gaze, his stance, his gestures, indeed of his entire person!] (*Paneg.* 67.1)

Trajan is outstanding for his *gravitas, veritas, fides*. Such qualities at once inspired trust in Roman citizens. Here at last was an emperor whose words might be believed by members of the senate.[46]

These particular qualities, so very desirable in an emperor, were ones which the profession of acting could only ever simulate. Actors manifestly lacked *gravitas, veritas* and *fides*. The theatre's parodic evocation of public oratory only served to underline the emperor's failure to do his duty. Though able to compose a poem on the fall of Troy, Nero was, remarks Tacitus, the first emperor to have his speeches to the senate written for him by someone else (*Ann*. 13.3).[47]

Emperors are also frequently praised by ancient authors for their involvement with their armies. Pliny, for instance, asserts that Trajan knows by name practically every man in the numerous units with which he has served (*Paneg*. 13-15). But, if we are to believe ancient accounts, Nero's only use for soldiers was as an audience for his theatrical performances (Tac. *Ann*. 14.15; 15.31). On one occasion, we are told, Nero decided not to address his troops in person out of concern to preserve his voice for singing contests (Suet. *Nero* 25).[48] Worse, his passion for the theatre led him to mock Roman military traditions. When Vindex rebelled in Gaul, Nero was not enthusiastic about leading forces against him, according to Suetonius, but he eventually decided to take an army of concubines, dressed up as Amazons. Suetonius remarks: 'In preparing for his campaign his first concern was to choose a waggon to transport his stage props' (*Nero* 44).

Dio contrasts the military achievements in Greece of republican generals and of Agrippa and Augustus with Nero's grotesque attempts to achieve distinction in the Greek games (62.8.2).[49] If the project was conceived as a serious attempt to place artistic achievements on a par with military ones (as Morford suggests), it was read as a hideous mockery of Roman tradition.[50] There was an element of the spectacular in many of the rituals of Roman public life, as indicated above. But respectable Romans did not like to be reminded of the theatricality of their most serious institutions.[51] On returning from his victories in the Greek games, Nero devised his greatest insult to the Roman military tradition by parodying the ritual of the triumph, normally reserved for the most successful of generals (Suet. *Nero* 25).[52] Wearing a triumphator's robe, decorated with gold stars, he rode in the chariot Augustus had used in his own triumph. On his head, Nero wore not the triumphant general's laurels but the Olympian olive crown and he made his way not to the temple of Jupiter Optimus Maximus but to that of Apollo, god of the arts.[53]

The shameful associations of acting are repeatedly stressed in these accounts of Nero's behaviour. Acting, as was noted above, was viewed by Romans as an especially Greek activity, an association emphasised several times in the Suetonian and Tacitean narratives of Nero's rule.[54] Tacitus refers to the emperor's *studiis externis*, 'unRoman enthusiasms' (*Ann*. 14.20), while Suetonius makes Nero claim it is only the Greeks who appreciate him (Nero 22.3). Nero was seen as having other theatrical qualities. His gender was uncertain. Dio makes the British queen Boudicca mock Nero for his effeminacy, as evidenced by his 'singing, lyre-playing and beautification of his person' (62.6.3). He played the role of Niobe to perfection, Suetonius observes with disapproval, and was also distinguished for his performance as Canace in labour (Suet. *Nero* 21).[55] Some of his performances were altogether too convincing. On one occasion, Suetonius alleges, his freedman Doryphorus played the groom and Nero the bride, 'going so far as to imitate the cries and lamentations of a maiden being deflowered' (Suet. *Nero* 29).[56] Roman virtues were abandoned. The emperor, *imperator*, was supposed to be the symbol of military prowess, but Nero was the inverse of a successful soldier.[57]

In the hands of an actor-emperor, Roman values were distorted. Illusion, unreality, theatre were all that Nero took seriously. His penchant for wandering around Rome in disguise is mentioned in all three of the principal accounts of his reign.[58] In Dio's version, Nero did not take exception to being beaten up by those whom he had offended in the street but became angry when he later received a letter of apology from a senator, Julius Montanus, who recognised him; his ability to disguise himself had been called into question. By the end of his reign his stage performances were the only thing that mattered to him. Suetonius writes: 'There was nothing he so much resented [of the acts of the rebel Vindex] as the taunt that he was a wretched lyre-player' (*Nero* 41.1).

The emperor's stage appearances disrupted the distinction between appearance and reality. When appearing on stage:

> tragoedias quoque cantavit personatus heroum deorumque, item heroidum ac dearum, personis effectis ad similitudinem oris sui ac feminae, prout quamque diligeret.
>
> [He also wore a mask and sang tragedies in the character of gods and heroes and even of heroines and goddesses, having the masks made so that they resembled him or else whatever woman he was in love with at the time.] (Suet. *Nero* 21.3)[59]

The mask represented the face behind it. The emperor acted himself. A young soldier in the audience was said to have been so confused that he failed to comprehend the dramatic conventions. He mistook illusion for reality and: 'seeing the emperor bound with chains, as the play [*The frenzy of Hercules*] required, rushed forward to render assistance.'[60] There were some conventions even an emperor (especially an emperor?) could not transcend.

Rome itself under Nero's rule became nothing but a stage set. Some of the special effects were particularly impressive. According to Suetonius, Nero treated the devastating fire of Rome as an occasion for a unique theatrical performance: 'Viewing the conflagration from the tower of Maecenas and exulting, as he said, "in the beauty of the flames", he sang the whole of the "sack of Ilium" in his usual stage costume' (*Nero* 38).[61] This was the disastrous culmination of Nero's rule.[62] For elite historians, acting – associated with the foreign, the female and the fake, with licence bearable so long as only lowly persons enjoyed it, but intolerable in the hands of an emperor – summed up Nero's offences.

Acting as metaphor

Acting, role-playing, dissembling are central metaphors in ancient representations of Nero. In the narratives of Tacitus, Suetonius and Dio, acting takes over other areas of Nero's life. He is an actor off-stage as well as on, always playing a role – but never the right one. Suetonius represents Nero as a hardened dissembler whose vices are gradually unmasked in the course of his rule. Dissembling plays a larger role in Tacitus' analysis of the principate, which he characterises as rendering all appearances deceptive. Numerous parallels have been noted between Tacitus' portrayals of Tiberius and of Nero.[63] While the Tacitean Tiberius is notable for his dissimulation, his successor Nero takes this further by making a public exhibition of pretending to be what he is not.[64]

Neronian rule causes everyone to dissemble. This common side-effect of autocracy is given an added twist when the autocrat himself parades his taste for role-playing. Authenticity, veracity became dangerous. Dio observes that no one was willing to tell Nero the truth about his own behaviour (61.14). Both Dio and Suetonius allege that when the emperor was performing on stage, members of the audience, since there was no other way they would be allowed out of the theatre, had to feign death (63.15). In Tacitus' account, failure to dissemble could be really fatal. Britannicus, son of the emperor Claudius, dies because he speaks the truth to Nero. Or rather, when he is supposed to humiliate himself by singing a drunken song (thus, like Nero, making a public exhibition of himself), he instead uses the opportunity to recount his own misfortunes (*Ann.* 13.15). Other members of the imperial family are able to postpone their ends only through dissembling. By the time of the death of Britannicus, his sister Octavia, *quamvis rudibus annis, dolorem caritatem, omnis adfectus abscondere didicerat* – 'despite her youth, had already learned to conceal sorrow, affection, all emotions' (Tac. *Ann.* 13.16).[65]

The emperor's mother, Agrippina, is also disconcerted by this demonstration of his willingness to kill a relative. Gradually the relationship between mother and son becomes entirely a matter of dissembling. As Betensky remarks, 'everything is now ... staged'.[66] Nero decides to get rid of his mother. Even here, he seeks inspiration from the theatre, which was, according to Dio, the source for the idea of the collapsible ship (61.12.2). To lull her into a sense of security, he puts on a show of filial affection (*Ann.* 14.4) This attempt fails, for when the ship collapses, another woman pretends to be Agrippina, in the naive hope that she will be rescued sooner. When the false Agrippina is killed, the real one keeps silent and escapes. Tacitus' Agrippina decides that the only way to survive is to pretend not to be aware that this was an attempt on her life (Tac. *Ann.* 14.6 – *solum insidiarum remedium esse si non intellegerentur* 'the plot could only be countered by feigning ignorance of it').[67] Nero now stages the incrimination of Agrippina's freedman, throwing a dagger down at his feet and accusing him of trying to murder the emperor (*Ann.* 14.7 – *scaenam ultro criminis parat*, 'he took the initiative by contriving a stage effect to support the charge'). The culmination of all this is Agrippina's theatrical death – a small act of revenge on the part of his mother against her actor-emperor son?[68] The Roman people feigned gladness at Nero's deliverance from his mother's alleged plot. Nero's pretence was different, observes Tacitus (*Ann.* 14.9). He chose to counterfeit sorrow for his mother's death.[69] The removal of Agrippina is presented as paving the way for Nero's theatrical interests to be given full rein. In the Neronian books of the *Annals*, as Betensky remarks, 'gesture comes to be more and more at variance with feeling, and role becomes what one acts rather than what one is. In the end, Nero's skilled performances in tawdry productions bring about the last act in his family's genuine tragedy at Rome.'[70]

Under an actor-emperor, appearance and reality were confused, categories collapsed.[71] The relationship between sign and meaning was irredeemably corrupted. There was no longer any contrast between theatre and real life. We unmask the actor playing the emperor and find the same face underneath. Seneca's theatrical simile explodes, as there ceases to be a distinction between the actor and the role he plays. Perhaps rather the roles of theatre and real life were reversed. The theatre, where appearances ought to be deceptive, was the only place the emperor really was the emperor, while, everywhere else, appearances had become quite unreliable, as the emperor roamed about his own city in disguise. This carnivalesque surrender of imperial identity left the imperial persona available for appropriation by others. In subsequent years, it seems, there was a proliferation of false Neros.[72]

Only in his last hours did Nero play himself, writes Dio – 'Such was the drama fate had now prepared for him. Thus he no longer played the role of other matricides and beggars but rather his own' (63.28.4-5). By then, though, it was too late, for he had himself become a character from a play. Earlier emperors flirted with theatricality; on his death bed, Augustus is said to have asked his friends 'whether it seemed to them that he had played the comedy of life fitly' – *ecquid iis videretur mimum vitae commode transegisse* (Suet. *Aug.* 99.1). Yet if some of his predecessors had recognised Roman political life as a theatrical performance, they stuck to a single role – that of Caesar. That was the only role Nero could not play.[73]

Notes

1. I would like to thank participants in the Cambridge Neronia of December 1991 and the Cambridge Ancient History Seminar in January 1992 for numerous helpful suggestions, and also my colleague Thomas Wiedemann who kindly read and commented on an earlier version of this piece. Thanks are also due to the editors of this volume for helping me to clarify some important points.

2. For a more detailed discussion of Roman attitudes to acting and the theatre, see Edwards 1993, chapter 3.

3. cf. Sen. *Ep.* 76.31.

4. On *infamia* in general see Greenidge 1894. For a more detailed discussion of the legal position of actors, gladiators and prostitutes, see Edwards forthcoming.

5. Actors (and other performers in public spectacles) were not permitted to stand for magistracies, according to Tertullian (*De spect.* 22), writing in the second century AD (the ban on actors and others who followed infamous professions from standing for local magistracies in the *lex Iulia municipalis* (*CIL* I 593) suggests they were already banned from standing from state magistracies in the time of Julius Caesar). Livy (7.2.12) refers

to the exclusion of actors from the tribes (which functioned as voting units) in a discussion of the theatre in the fourth century BC. Cf. Dupont 1977, 64 & 1985, 95-8.

6. cf. *Dig.* 3.2.1.

7. This seems to be the implication of Ulpian frag. 13 and *Dig.* 23.2.44.7. The *Gnomon of the idios logos* (30, 32) suggests that these rules only apply to *ingenui* above a certain census rating. It seems certainly to have been the case that senators and their descendants were not permitted to marry actresses or the daughters of actors or actresses.

8. cf. Suet. *Aug.* 45; Tac. *Ann.* 1.77; Paul *Sent.* 5.26. For a discussion of the significance of corporal punishment in ancient Rome, see Saller 1991, esp. 151-5.

9. For a more detailed version of this argument, see Edwards forthcoming.

10. cf. e.g. Cic. *De off.* 1.23 on the importance of *fides*.

11. e.g. Livy 24.24.2-3; Tac. *Dial.* 10.5. Cf. Dupont 1977.

12. Dupont 1977 and 1985, 97.

13. Nicolet 1980, 286.

14. cf. Pliny *Ep.* 6.33.3-4.

15. Cic. *De orat.* 3.220; Quint. *Inst.* 1.8.3; 1.11.1-3; 6.3.29; 6.3.47. For a detailed discussion of the parallels between the practice of actors and that of orators in ancient Rome, see Graf 1991.

16. cf. Dupont 1985, 31-4.

17. e.g. Cassiodorus *ad ann.* 639 (115 BC); Suet. *Nero* 16.2; Suet. *Dom.* 7.1 (actors banned from performing in public).

18. Similar incidents are described by Cicero elsewhere (e.g. *Pro Sest.* 118, 120-3; *Ad Att.* 357.2). Suetonius relates parallel stories from the principate (e.g. *Calig.* 30.2, *Nero* 39.3).

19. e.g. Livy 7.2.3-4; Val. Max. 2.4.2; Tac. *Ann.* 14.20; Tert. *De spect.* 5.2; Augustine, *De civ. dei* 3.17.

20. e.g. Hor. *Ep.* 2.1.156-67; Suet. *Gramm.* 1.

21. cf. e.g. Tert. *De spect.* 17.

22. Though actors might boast of their skills in this respect. Cf. e.g. the epitaph of the actor Vitalis which celebrates his ability to imitate female gestures (*Anth. lat.* 487a).

23. Pliny *Paneg.* 46.5,54.1; Quint. *Inst.* 1.10.31; Tac. *Ann.* 15.1; Tert. *De spect.* 10; Lactantius *Divin. inst.* 6.20.

24. cf. the contrast Pliny draws between the inspiring gladiatorial games provided by Trajan and the decadent theatrical shows put on by Domitian which were of a kind *quod animos virorum molliret et frangeret* – 'to soften and emasculate the spirits of men' (*Paneg.* 33).

25. On the actor's lack of *virtus*, see too Dupont 1985, 100-1. For *virtus* as a distinguishing Roman characteristic, see e.g. Nepos *Han.* 1.1; Pliny *NH* 7.130.

26. Livy describes the theatre as *nova res bellicoso populo* (7.2.) Ovid refers to *ludi scaenici* as offerings unsuitable for Mars, the god of war (*Fasti* 5.595-8).

27. Though Cicero, not surprisingly, asserted that Roscius was by no means a typical actor (*Pro Rosc. com.* 17, *Pro Quinct.* 78).

28. e.g. Sulla (Plut. *Sulla* 3.3), Maecenas (Tac. *Ann.* 1.54), Trajan (Dio 68.10.2).

29. Juvenal (8.193), Tacitus (*Ann.* 14.14-15), Suetonius (*Nero* 11) and Dio (61.19) discuss the appearance of members of the elite on stage in response to Nero's pressure. Such incidents are also alleged to have occured under Julius Caesar and other emperors. Cf. Suet. *Jul.* 39.1, Dio 60.7. For a discussion of appearances by members of the elite on stage and in the arena (both voluntarily and under pressure) in the early principate, see Levick 1983.

30. cf. e.g. Juv. 8.183-210, Dio 53.31; 55.10.11, Suet. *Nero* 4. There are numerous references to legislation which ostensibly aimed at preventing members of the elite from humiliating themselves in this manner (discussed by Levick 1983).

31. Suet. *Cal.* 54. He is also said to have appeared as a Thracian gladiator, a charioteer, singer and dancer.
32. Caligula – Suet. *Cal.* 41.1; Dio 59.28.9. Similar stories are told about Nero. Cf. Tac. *Ann.* 15.37; Suet. *Nero* 12, 27; Dio 62.15.2-3.
33. Herodian 1.14-17; Dio 72.19-22. See Wiedemann 1992, 178 for a discussion of examples of other emperors practising as gladiators. So long as this was done in private, it is not presented as deserving criticism.
34. Alternatively one might see them as pursuing the favour of a different sector of the Roman people. Participation in public spectacles was often linked by elite writers with courting the favour of the plebs. Tacitus emphasises the appeal of Nero's interest in public spectacles: *mox ultro vocari populus Romanus laudibusque extollere, ut est vulgus cupiens voluptatum et, si eodem princeps trahat, laetum.* 'Soon the Roman people were even invited and they heaped praise on him, for such is the nature of the mob, eager for entertainment and happy if the emperor shares their tastes' (*Ann.* 14.14). Cf. *Ann.* 16.4., *Hist.* 1.4. On this subject see Yavetz 1967, 62-7, 103-29. Manning (1975) also argues that Nero's stage appearances were a deliberate attempt to cultivate the favour of the plebs.
35. Henderson 1989, 191.
36. According to Tacitus, one of the soldiers involved in the Pisonian conspiracy, when his complicity was discovered, confronted Nero, saying that he had been loyal until the emperor was revealed as a parricide, matricide and actor (Tac. *Ann.* 15.67). A similar remark is attributed to a conspirator by Dio (62.24.2). See Woodman (1993) for an elegant exposition of Tacitus' presentation of the Pisonian conspiracy as a failed dramatic performance – an ironically suitable attack on an actor-emperor.
37. Tac. *Ann.* 14.14-15; Suet. *Nero* 11; Dio 61.19. The Iuvenalia of 64 are referred to by Tacitus at *Ann.*15.33.
38. See Morford (1985, 2018-24) who emphasises the importance of Augustan precedents for establishing games.
39. Tac. *Ann.* 14.20-21; Suet. *Nero* 12.
40. *Ann.* 15.33. Cf. *Suet.* 20.
41. Thomas Wiedemann has suggested to me that it is hardly coincidental that Nero's theatrical exploits are alleged to have alienated public opinion just when the effects of the great fire would have been turning the public against him.
42. Tacitus suggests he had planned to visit Greece earlier (*Ann.*15.33-5). This has been doubted by some modern scholars (cf. Griffin 1984, 161). For a discussion of the chronological order in which the games occurred, see Griffin 1984, 162.
43. cf. Tacitus' description of Nero's scrupulous obedience of performer's etiquette when he first appeared in Rome (*Ann.*16.4)
44. An incompatibility also implied in the speech Dio attributes to the rebel Vindex (63.22.4-6).
45. On the emperor's military role, see Campbell 1984. For the importance of his public speaking, see Millar 1977, 203-7.
46. What qualities, one wonders, would a panegyric of Nero (or Caligula) have selected for special mention?
47. cf. Dio 61.3.1 – who says the same about his speech to the praetorian guard.
48. On the importance attached to imperial addresses to the troops, see Campbell 1984, 69-88.
49. Though elsewhere Dio compares the devastation wrought by Nero's progress through Greece to the consequences of warfare (63.11).
50. For a sympathetic reading of Nero's activities, see Morford 1985, 2024-6.
51. cf. Dupont (1985, 39) on the omnispresence of the spectacular in Roman public life and the anxieties aroused when different sorts of spectacles are confused.

52. cf. Dio 63.20, who relates that Nero proceeded to play the lyre and act in a tragedy in his own triumphal games. Nero's triumph is discussed by Morford (1985). Caligula too is alleged to have made preparations for a fake triumph. According to Suetonius (*Cal.* 47), he selected the tallest of the Gallic soldiers in his army and told them to dye their hair red and grow it long so that they could play the part of captive Germans in his triumphal procession. But at least Caligula's efforts could be seen as an acknowledgement (if somewhat misguided) of the importance of military achievement. Not so Nero's 'triumph'.

53. On the route of Nero's triumphal procession see Makin 1921.

54. Though not in Dio, unsurprisingly.

55. cf. Dio 63.9.4, 63.10.2-3.

56. According to Tacitus, Nero 'married' Pythagoras (*Ann.* 15.37). Elsewhere, Suetonius relates that Nero had Sporus castrated and married him, this time playing the male role (*Nero* 28). In Dio's version of this story (63.13), it is Sporus' resemblance to Poppaea which prompts Nero to have him castrated.

57. One of the Pisonian conspirators, encouraging Piso to strike, is made to remark by Tacitus: *etiam fortis viros subitis terreri, nedum ille scaenicus* – 'When even strong men are frightened by unexpected attacks, that actor will be even more so' (*Ann.* 15.59).

58. Tac. *Ann.* 13.23; Suet. *Nero* 26; Dio 61.9. Cf. Frazer 1966, 18.

59. cf. Dio 62.9.5.

60. cf. Dio 62.10.3. We might note too that again the sensibilities of soldiers are presented as a key indicator of the consequences of the emperor's behaviour.

61. cf. Tac. *Ann.* 15.39.

62. cf. Croisille who describes singing while Rome burns as 'l'apogée des crimes, peut-être, mais en même temps un des plus grands spectacles concevables avec comme protagoniste Néron, l'acteur-roi' (1969/70, 85).

63. e.g. the openings of the two reigns, *Ann.* 1.6 and 13.1. Cf. Walker 1952, 70 and Henderson 1989, 179-80.

64. For Tiberius' dissimulation, see e.g. *Ann.* 1.11.

65. cf. Henderson 1989, 189.

66. Betensky 1978, 420.

67. Another instance is Seneca who, in Tacitus' narrative, pretends to wish for retirement, while Nero pretends he still needs his assistance (14.56). Seneca has to pretend to be grateful. On the interaction between Nero and Agrippina, as well as his dealings with other characters, see Betensky (1978).

68. Dawson (1968) sees Tacitus' representation of Nero's plot against his mother as fiction modelled on the story of Orestes and Clytemnestra, while Baldwin (1979) argues for seeing the scene as Nero's allusion to the *Bacchae*. Plass remarks of these interpretations: 'In the first case, the story is false and material for malicious wit about Nero the actor; in the second it is true and a mad gesture by Nero the actor' (1988, 10-11). See too the comments by Henderson (1989, 190). Frazer (1966) suggests that Nero's alleged plot to have his step-son drowned while fishing was also a theatrical allusion, here to the story of Nauplius, whose son dies under similar circumstances.

69. cf. Nero's feigned mourning for his adoptive father Claudius, poisoned by Agrippina, alleges Tacitus, to secure her son's succession (*Ann.* 13.3).

70. Betensky 1978, 419.

71. cf. Henderson 1989.

72. cf. Tac. *Hist.* 1.2; 2.8; Dio 66.19.3.

73. cf. Dio 63.22.11 – Nero could not even preserve the *schema* 'image', of sovereignty.

Bibliography

Baldwin, B. 'Nero and his mother's corpse' *Mnemosyne* 32 (1979) 380-1.
Betensky, A. 'Neronian style, Tacitean content: the use of ambiguous confrontation in the *Annals*' *Latomus* 37 (1978) 419-35.
Croisille, Jean-Michel 'L'art de la composition chez Suétone: d'après les vies de Claude et de Néron' *Annali dell'istituto Italiano per gli studi storici* 2 (1969/70) 73-88.
Dawson, H. 'Whatever happened to Lady Agrippina?' *Classical Journal* 64 (1968) 253-67.
Dupont, Florence 'La scène juridique' *Communications* 2.6 (1977) 62-77.
——— *L'acteur-roi* (Paris 1985).
Edwards, Catharine *The politics of immorality in ancient Rome* (Cambridge 1993).
——— 'Unspeakable professions: public performance and prostitution in ancient Rome' (forthcoming).
Frazer, R.M. Jr. 'Nero the artist-criminal' *Classical Journal* 62 (1966) 17-20.
Graf, Fritz 'Gestures and conventions: the gestures of Roman actors and orators' 36-58 in J. Bremmer and H. Roodenburg eds. *A cultural history of gesture from antiquity to the present day* (Oxford 1991).
Greenidge, A.J.H. *Infamia: its place in Roman public and private law* (Oxford 1894).
Griffin, M.T *Nero: the end of a dynasty* (London 1984).
Henderson, John 'Tacitus/the world in pieces' *Ramus* 18 (1989) 167-210.
Levick, B. '*The senatus consultum* from Larinum' *JRS* 73 (1983) 97-115.
Makin, E. 'The triumphal route with particular reference to the Flavian triumph' *JRS* 11 (1921) 25-36.
Manning, C.E. 'Acting and Nero's conception of the principate' *Greece and Rome* 22 (1975) 164-75.
Morford, M.P.O. 'Nero's patronage and participation in literature and the arts' *ANRW* 2.32.3 (1985) 2003-31.
Nicolet, Claude *The world of the citizen in republican Rome* (London 1980).
Plass, Paul *Wit and the writing of history* (Madison 1988).
Saller, R.P. 'Corporal punishment, authority and obedience in the Roman household' 144-65 in Beryl Rawson ed. *Marriage, divorce and children in ancient Rome* (Oxford 1991).
Wiedemann, T.E.J. *Emperors and gladiators* (London 1992).
Woodman, A.J. 'Amateur dramatics at the court of Nero: Tacitus *Annals* 15.48-74' 104-28 in T.J. Luce and A.J. Woodman eds. *Tacitus and the Tacitean tradition* (Princeton 1993).
Yavetz, A. *Plebs and princeps* (Oxford 1967).

6

Nero at play? The emperor's Grecian odyssey

Susan E. Alcock

'The Greeks alone are worthy of my genius; they really listen to music.'[1] Such – according to Suetonius' account – was Nero's motivation in launching his sixteen-month expedition to Greece in the years AD 66-67. Certain episodes of the sojourn are well-known; indeed they number among the most familiar of Nero's plunges into megalomania and hybris. Olympic gambols, unfinished canals, and short-lived liberations together present a crescendo of hilarity and of horror in most versions, both past and present, of Nero's Grecian odyssey. After such lunacy, his hurried return to Rome, and subsequent shabby death, seem but natural consequences.

In a volume devoted to a reconsideration of the emperor and his milieu, the time Nero spent in Greece (or, more properly, the Roman province of Achaia) stands out as an obvious target for a second look. This chapter reviews and proposes alternative interpretations for Nero's supposed madcap antics, while also suggesting the presence of more coherent policies at work. Such a reevaluation is aided by other recent scholarship: for example, a study of emperors 'on the road', and of the 'royal progress' as an instrument of imperial manipulation, provides a framework within which Nero's time abroad loses something of its frightening peculiarity.[2] A more critical stance towards the available Roman source material – chiefly Suetonius and Tacitus – and a recognition of the degree to which they are shot through with invective also affect our readings of the emperor's behaviour. The intention here is certainly not to whitewash Nero, to over-turn all past judgments and 'rehabilitate' him.[3] But the question can fairly be asked: just how bizarre *was* his behaviour in Greece?

Acts of madness?

Of the recorded events of Nero's journey, most startling and to some most repugnant was the emperor's personal participation and, predictably, his victories in various Greek competitive games. His antics at Olympia were recalled with derision by Suetonius:

> On several occasions he took part in the chariot racing, and at Olympia drove a ten-horse team, a novelty for which he had censured King Mithridates in one of his own poems. He lost his balance, fell from the chariot and had to be helped in

6. Nero at play? 99

again; but, though he failed to stay the course and retired before the finish, the judges nevertheless awarded him the prize.⁴

In order to accommodate the emperor, all of the major panhellenic festivals of the province were rescheduled, crammed within just over a year so that Nero could achieve his declared ambition of becoming *periodonikes* (i.e. winner of the 'Grand Tour', the panhellenic circuit). Dio Cassius reports that, on Nero's return to his capital, 1808 crowns from various festival victories were carried in triumph through Rome, where the emperor was hailed hysterically as Olympian Victor, Pythian Victor, Nero Hercules, Nero Apollo, 'the only victor of the Grand Tour, the only one from the beginning of time ... '⁵

Nero's fascination with sanctuaries extended apparently beyond agonistic competition. He stole, it was claimed, numerous statues from major Greek cult places, not least some '500 statues of gods and men' from Delphi; Olympia too suffered. Most of these were shipped back to Rome for the emperor's pleasure. Most notorious was his removal of the Eros of Thespiai in Boeotia, the beautiful image of Love carved by Praxiteles which served as that community's chief deity. This Eros had previously been removed to Rome by Caligula, though Claudius later returned it; Nero in turn, however, was unable to resist its temptations. In light of Nero's known sexual proclivities (or, at least, those alleged by our sources), the motive behind this particular crime seems all too obvious.⁶

Another Neronian undertaking which has attracted some scorn, both ancient and modern, was the proposed canal through the Isthmus of Corinth. Nero, that 'lover of the incredible' as Tacitus called him, himself took a mattock (made of gold, according to one version of the event), and 'at a trumpet blast broke the ground and carried off the first basket of earth on his back ... '⁷ While this particular imperial venture has been regarded in a variety of ways, at worst it was condemned as an act of outrageous hybris. Flamboyantly begun, the canal was never completed, being left abandoned with Nero's departure for Rome and subsequent death.

Last (but very far from least) to be mentioned is Nero's ultimate grandiose and irresponsible gesture: the liberation of the entire province of Achaia from Roman rule and Roman taxation. The emperor himself made the proclamation (he was, after all, a crowned herald) 'amidst the multitude' in the context of the panhellenic games at Isthmia. His grandiloquent speech on that occasion has been preserved in an inscription found at Akraiphia in Boeotia, where a local *euergetes* proposed a decree in honour of Nero Zeus Eleutherios:

> Unexpected is the gift, men of Greece, with which I present you – though perhaps nothing can be thought unexpected from munificence such as mine – and so vast that you could not hope to ask for it. Would that I could have made this grant when Hellas was in its prime, so that there might have been more men to enjoy my grace. Not through pity, however, but through goodwill I now make you this benefaction, and I thank your gods, whose watchful providence I have always experienced both on sea and land, that they have afforded me the opportunity of so great a benefaction. Other emperors have freed cities; Nero alone a whole province.⁸

A second look

Each of these episodes requires individual re-evaluation, not only by recognising the bias of the accounts usually quoted, but by placing them within a wider context. Again, the question can be put: just how bizarre *was* this behavior? Are there no precedents for it, no successors? Can any more general and positive policies be detected beneath the standard hostility of our sources?

There can be no question but that Nero's *personal* participation in the various Greek sacred games was unprecedented. Other members of the imperial family before him (Tiberius prior to becoming emperor; Germanicus) had participated vicariously by financing teams in the equestrian events, following patterns of behaviour set by aristocratic Greek families and by Hellenistic monarchs such as Attalus of Pergamon.[9] Attendance and involvement in other aspects of festival life were also common for influential Romans visiting Greece. The panhellenic sanctuaries especially had long served as a focus for the patronage of external benefactors: at Olympia, for example, both Agrippa and Herod provided major financial support after the Civil Wars, a period of special duress for the sanctuary as for the country at large. Also to be acknowledged is the long-lived imperial encouragement of games in the east, as a means of spreading largesse and fostering local support. Aelius Aristides points to this development in his mid-second-century AD panegyric, *Regarding Rome* (*Oration* 26):

> And the whole inhabited world, as it were attending a national festival, has laid aside its old dress, the carrying of weapons, and has turned, with full authority to do so, to adornments and all kinds of pleasures. And all the other sources of contention have died out in the cities, but this single rivalry holds all of them, how each will appear as fair and charming as possible .... Indeed the cities shine with radiance and grace, and the whole earth has been adorned like a pleasure garden. Gone beyond land and sea is the smoke rising from the fields and the signal fires of friend and foe, as if a breeze had fanned them away. There has been introduced instead every kind of charming spectacle and a boundless number of games. Therefore the celebration of national festivals, like a sacred and inextinguishable fire, never ceases, but passes at different times to different people, yet always is somewhere.[10]

Nero's activity could thus be viewed simply as an extension – admittedly a major extension – of Roman interest and participation in these festivities. At this point it is worth noting the all-embracing rhetoric with which he accepted his victories: 'Nero Caesar wins this contest and crowns the Roman people and the inhabited world, that is his own.'[11]

As for removing statues from religious contexts, rather than being perceived as merely a peculiar quirk on Nero's part, such behaviour must also be taken as continuation of a very long-lived trend. Nor was this simply a matter of the theft of art works. Appropriation by victors of the prized possessions of the defeated boasts a long history in the Mediterranean world. Many Romans before Nero (Marcellus, Sulla, Augustus himself) in their time carried off the images of gods, heroes and famous men from Greek cities and sanctuaries. Augustus, for exam-

6. Nero at play? 101

ple, removed the cult image, as well as the tusks of the Kalydonian boar, from the sanctuary of Athena Alea in Arcadian Tegea. Such statues, or other objects, were often taken back to Rome to be re-employed in a new and specifically Roman context; sometimes, however, they were instead transferred to different parts of the same province. In Greece, Augustus 'transplanted' cult images from the punished regions of Aetolia and Achaea to the new and favoured foundations of Nikopolis (Victory City) in Epirus and the Roman colony of Patras. Far from proving a matter of artistic connoisseurship, these acts must be taken as deliberate moves in a game of domination and symbolic control.[12] Transferral or removal of cult images, emblematic of the identity of a community or a people, serves to undercut local loyalties and to disrupt pre-existing networks of influence and authority. Similar tactics are observed in many imperial settings, as a means to punish the disobedient, to convince the recalcitrant and to honour the victors and their allies.

Such acts of cult displacement could be interpreted as purely punitive measures. With Nero, however, there is an alternative, or rather an additional, possibility – namely that the transfer of cult statues could also be viewed as a *sharing* of them. This reading suggests that in Nero's time the movement of these objects to Rome was less a power ploy and more a means to unite the peoples of Greece and Rome through their shared veneration of the same respected images. If that was indeed the intention, however, the Greeks certainly failed to appreciate it; their dismay at the loss of sacred possessions is evident. Divine vengeance was often claimed to strike those who removed beloved deities. Sulla, for instance, among his other depredations stole an image of Athena from Alalkomenai in Boeotia. Retribution followed: 'After these mad outrages against the Greek cities and the gods of the Greeks he was attacked by the most foul of diseases. He broke out into lice, and what was formerly accounted his good fortune came to such an end.' After recounting the history of the Eros of Thespiai, Pausanias remarked: 'Of the pair who sinned against the god, Gaius [Caligula] was killed by a private soldier ... The other, Nero, in addition to his violence against his mother, committed hateful crimes against his wedded wives ... ' Pausanias moreover spoke of the 'universal irreverence of Nero' – and of how it was eventually punished.[13]

As for the canal intended to pierce the Isthmus of Corinth, it is only fair to report that this particular project always received mixed reviews in the ancient sources, even being presented in the 'commendable' section of Suetonius' *Life of Nero*. Other commentators too thought the canal an impressive idea; Apollonius of Tyana supposedly acknowledged the magnificence of the project, while predicting it would never be completed. Certainly, other rulers were claimed to have entertained the scheme before, including the Archaic tyrant Periander, the Hellenistic king Demetrius Poliorcetes, and the Romans Julius Caesar and Caligula. In the century after Nero, Herodes Atticus mourned his inability to undertake such a superhuman and immortal feat, which 'he longed to do, but never had the courage to ask the emperor to grant him permission, lest he should be accused of grasping at an ambitious plan to which not even Nero had proved himself equal ... '[14] It is suggestive that the notion of a Corinthian canal has often won Nero disdain, whereas the similar ambitions of Julius Caesar or even of

Caligula are not mocked. Moreover, of these various attempts, Nero's project clearly emerges as the most committed and efficiently executed. Substantial progress, over a short period of time, was achieved through imported labour, including some six thousand captives sent by Vespasian after the Jewish revolt. A cross-Isthmus canal, actually following the line of Neronian cuttings, was only successfully completed in 1893. Evidence of Roman shafts and channels discovered at that time indicates that as much as an estimated one-fifth of the canal had actually been dug.[15]

Despite the claim that the Peloponnesus, newly made an island, would have been renamed Neronnesus, contemplation of a canal through the Greek isthmus cannot be dismissed as just a megalomaniac's fantasy. Pragmatic arguments for the work could be cited. Such a canal, as many have realised, would facilitate sea communications between the eastern and central Mediterranean, providing an alternative to the notoriously dangerous sailing route south of the Peloponnesus (under Cape Malea). According to Suetonius, Nero voiced the hope that the canal 'might benefit himself and the Roman people';[16] the benefits to the economy of Greece, particularly, should also not be underestimated. Other canals were apparently proposed and even begun by Nero, one from Ostia to Rome and another linking Lake Avernus to the Tiber. Sometimes considered as further examples of Nero's 'passion for the incredible' (indeed, it is in this context that Tacitus refers to Nero as *incredibilium cupitor*), these Italian canals are now being reassessed as showing a genuine interest in waterways, in reducing hazardous sea passages and in facilitating the grain supply of Rome.[17]

Apart from practical advantages, however, such canals would have acted as tangible symbols of imperial domination. In this sense, the Isthmus project fits well within one important dimension of the Roman treatment of Achaia (and indeed of other provinces), relating to a growing sense of central control over provincial territory. Systems of cadastral organisation, the redivision and redistribution of land, are one facet of this treatment, as are the building of roads and of aqueducts, long-distance linear features which cut across formerly impermeable civic boundaries. Canal-cutting, with its drastic alteration of the natural order, clearly relates to these phenomena. Provincial landscapes were seen as something to be moulded and altered according to Roman wishes; the imperial authority possessed the confidence to modify and divide the world in new ways. Yet a sense of danger and of transgression still hung about such symbolic acts, as emerges clearly in ancient discussions of Nero's canal. Pausanias spoke of it in relation to other failed attempts:

> He who tried to make the Peloponnesus an island gave up before digging through the Isthmus. Where they began to dig is still to be seen, but into the rock they did not advance at all. So it still is mainland as its nature is to be. Alexander the son of Philip wished to dig through Mimas, and his attempt to do this was his only unsuccessful project. The Cnidians began to dig through their isthmus, but the Pythian priestess stopped them. So difficult it is for man to alter by violence what Heaven has made.

Dio Cassius reported of Nero's project: 'Men shrank from it ... because, when the first workers touched the earth, blood spouted from it, groans and bellowings were heard, and many phantoms appeared ... ' According to pseudo-Lucian, the work was begun with hymns sung – by Nero, of course – to praise and to appease the local gods (Amphitrite, Poseidon, Melikertes, Leukothea).[18] Generally, Nero is portrayed as timorous, fearful of the whips of festival judges, and so on. Yet poor omens in this case were said merely to have spurred him into being the first to break the soil, a commitment echoed in the very size of the labour force he was said to have given over to the project.

Finally, there is Nero's liberation of the Greeks, a deed often regarded as a parody of Flamininus' respected proclamation of Greek freedom after the Second Macedonian War, some 250 years before. Flamininus' decree had also taken place within the context of the Isthmian games. Calling Nero's act a 'parody' sets the usual tone for its consideration, and the import of the gesture (admittedly short-lived) has tended to receive little probing scholarly attention. Quite a bit of the modern literature on the subject, for example, has revolved around the single issue of whether the liberation occurred in November 66 (and thus soon after Nero's arrival in the country) or in 67 (and thus as the resounding climax to a year of madness).[19] Currently, the latter year is generally accepted as correct.

The proclamation of freedom can, however, be assessed in a different way, as it probably would be if someone other than the obviously irresponsible Nero (Hadrian, for instance) had been responsible. Potency of the 'freedom of the Greeks' as a concept, manipulated by monarchs right back through Hellenistic times, is often underestimated by modern scholars too aware of the 'realpolitik' of the situation. Genuine political advantage could be wangled through such a gift, as can be glimpsed in the sources, especially in Nero's enduring popularity in the east. Admittedly, such a wholesale grant of freedom and tax immunity sounds wildly extravagant. On closer examination, however, the scale of the gesture diminishes. A not inconsiderable portion of the senatorial province of Achaia was already 'free and immune', including two of its largest civic units, Athens and Sparta. The province as a whole was quite small and relatively poor, factors which both lessen the financial loss to the Senate and enhance the value of the grant to the Greeks themselves. None the less, compensation for the imperial 'whim' was made to the Senate by the emperor's gift of Sardinia, a fertile, reasonably well-endowed secondary province; good evidence exists for a change in that island's status. Moreover, the periodic liberation of favoured cities or islands (Cyzicus, Rhodes) was hardly an unknown feature of Roman rule, as Nero himself observed in his liberty proclamation. As Sartre has recently remarked: 'What must have surprised contemporaries was more the number of beneficiaries, rather than the nature of the measure itself.' For this same period, Sartre has also observed a process of 'deprovincialisation' of the east to the benefit of client princes, suggesting the Achaian measure accorded with wider Neronian foreign policy.[20]

One of Vespasian's initial moves on becoming emperor was to revoke this grant, earning (according to Philostratus) cold words from Apollonius of Tyana: 'You have, they say, enslaved Hellas, and you imagine you have excelled Xerxes. You are mistaken. You have only fallen below Nero. For the latter held our liberties in his hand and respected them. Farewell.'[21] Vespasian's quick action has frequently been taken as proof of just how foolish the whole affair had been in the first place, as further evidence of Nero's folly. A closer reading of some of our sources for the period following the liberation suggests, however, a somewhat different explanation. Pausanias, for example, tells us:

> The Greeks ... were not to profit by the gift. For in the reign of Vespasian, the next emperor after Nero, they became embroiled in a civil war; Vespasian ordered that they should again pay tribute and be subject to a governor, saying that the Greek people had forgotten how to be free.

An inscription found at Epidauros, now dated to AD 67-68, refers to times 'most painful and most perilous'.[22] For all its small size, Achaia had been the scene of several rebellious outbreaks in the early first century AD, as well as periodically thereafter. Vespasian's revocation, then, may have been provoked by misbehaviour in Greece, and by that emperor's own well-attested sense of economy, rather than by the inherent unacceptability of such a grant of freedom.

Itineraries and motives

Working at this level of revisionist thinking, much more could be said about each individual aspect of Nero's time in Greece. Yet more is required than justifying particular episodes, finding parallels, or noting extenuating circumstances. Instead, can Nero's time in Greece be considered within a more general framework, can any overall patterns be discerned in his behaviour – some method, as it were, to his madness?

One useful start can be made by examining what we know of Nero's Greek itinerary. The only real 'stops' of which we can be relatively sure are his attendance at various festivals (panhellenic and civic), as well as some time in Corinth.[23] The only instance of a visit to a locale of a slightly different sort was that for an experimental sounding of the supposedly bottomless Lake Alcyon in the Peloponnesus. Here Nero seemingly demonstrates an interest in natural phenomena deliberately reminiscent of Alexander the Great, a ruler whose powerful image drew Nero, as other Roman leaders, to emulation.[24] On the whole, however, games and festivals dominate our accounts of Nero's imperial progress through Greece. Does this apparent concentration merely reflect Nero's obsession with self-glorification, his 'thirst for popularity'? Was Greece, to Nero, simply a theatre?

Any simple answer to that question evaporates as one contemplates the role of festivals in Achaian provincial life. It is clear that such celebrations – at the traditional panhellenic centres of Olympia, Delphi, Nemea, and Isthmia, as well as at other important cities such as Nikopolis or Argos – acted as increasingly necessary arenas for communication, competition and self-representation under the empire. The need for such arenas had been greatly accentuated with the loss of Greek political independence, and the subsequent denial of other avenues for individual and communal display. Plutarch (who may himself have been at Delphi at the time of Nero's visit) makes clear the centrality of agonistic festivals as venues for the interaction of provincial elite families.[25] Nor was attendance limited solely to Achaian residents: the presence of Romans in the audience, as well as luminaries from other Greek and non-Greek provinces, created a highly cosmopolitan gathering. Sanctuaries were thus attractive locations in every sense of the word, obvious places to present oneself in a variety of guises: in other words, to perform. A significant audience was present, therefore, to witness Nero's performance, not only as an 'artist' but as a ruler too. Competition and agonistic victory – as always – worked to establish authority in Greek society. Nero, however, extended his claim to glory and respect through his triumphs more widely: 'Nero Caesar wins this contest and crowns the Roman people and the inhabited world, that is his own.' Apart from sheer self-glorification, the emphasis here lies on bringing the Roman people, and the empire as a whole, within the Greek religious sphere, while – conversely – integrating his influential audience within the empire at large.[26]

Considering where Nero did *not* go likewise provokes some interesting observations. No visit was made (and this is stated explicitly in the sources) to Athens or to Sparta. Given the itinerary of practically every other Roman visitor to Greece, this neglect is peculiar in the extreme – all the more so, considering the length of Nero's stay. Moreover, the reasons adduced for avoiding these cities are unconvincing: Sparta because of its unsympathetic Lycurgan regimes (cold baths and laconic speech clearly not being to Nero's taste); Athens because of Nero's fear of matricidal guilt coming home to roost. Suetonius reported solemnly that at Eleusis Nero 'dared not participate when a herald ordered all criminals present to withdraw before the ceremonies began' – surprising behaviour indeed for a man accustomed to playing Orestes.[27]

But why else might an emperor choose to avoid these cities, the two major centres of Greece's antique glory? The fact that Nero chose to spend at least some time in Corinth may help to clarify matters. The Roman colony of Corinth, destroyed by Mummius in 146 BC and refounded by Julius Caesar in 44 BC, served as Achaia's capital. The colony acted as a unifying, pro-Roman force in provincial life, being tightly linked by its institutional character, location, colonists and monuments with the core city of Rome. It is worth noting that control of the Isthmian games (scene of Nero's proclamation of freedom) offered one channel by which Corinth promulgated its imperial message.[28] Now if Nero had wished to visit 'Old Greece', the cultural paradise of the Classical age, he undoubtedly would have gone to Athens and Sparta – as all other Romans did, before and after. By avoiding these, and instead basing himself in part at the colony of Corinth, the emperor encouraged a new conception of Greece: not as a land of the past, but as part of the imperial present. And an honoured part, as Veyne notes, with Nero's freedom: 'Greece was part of the empire, no longer as a province, but with the same claims as the cities of Italy.'[29] Nero's emphasis on festivals and sanctuaries can also be viewed in this light. Augustus previously had employed the Delphic Amphictyony as one means to promote provincial unity at the expense of individual and divisive Greek polities.[30] By staying in Corinth and by presenting himself at festivals, Nero likewise evinced an interest in Achaia as a whole, and as a functioning unit, rather than as a collection of separate cities. In other words, this emperor visited Roman Greece, rather than a museum of its Classical past.

Nero celebrates then, not the 'traditional' Greece, but an imperial Achaia. Judging by his known actions, some strands of a general policy can now be recognised: a desire to encourage Achaia, to link east and west, to promote and integrate Greek culture within the empire. Given the deep-rooted ambivalence of Romans toward the land Pliny once termed 'pure and genuine Greece', such an agenda contributed to the hostility shown towards Nero in the Latin sources.[31] Nero's policies may also in part have fallen victim to the time of their proposal. Dio Cassius explicitly contrasts this emperor's time in Greece with that of his 'good' Roman ancestors:

> But he crossed over into Greece, not at all as Flamininus or Mummius or as Agrippa and Augustus, his ancestors, had done, but for the purpose of driving chariots, playing the lyre, making proclamations, and acting in tragedies. Rome, it seems, was not enough for him ... [32]

Those ancestors, however, right down to Augustus and Agrippa, represent the early days of contact and incorporation, an era of force and punishment (even when cloaked by Augustus in the guise of 'preserving' Greek traditions and institutions). Nero, reigning in a time of assimilation rather than of active conquest of Greeks, attempted a new formula for their treatment; yet it was strongly rejected by certain influential groups at the imperial centre of Rome.[33] On the other hand, if we move forward to the figure of Hadrian, another emperor who spent a considerable period of time in Achaia and who also worked from a consciously philhellenic position, we see that his admiration of Hellenism then proved acceptable. Hadrian could safely patronise cities and sanctuaries, dedicate poems in the Valley of the Muses, and (compared to Nero) leave many traces of himself across the province in the form of monuments and financial benefactions. Yet the emperor as cultural hero was no longer a vulnerable figure. What had changed? By Hadrian's time, the Greeks had been safely 'distanced', their culture lionised but contained securely within a Roman framework, in which Greece was viewed as a museum of its own past achievements. Hadrian's deep devotion to Athens, notably his creation of the Panhellenion (which, in Oliver's words, made Athens 'morally and intellectually ... a second capital of the empire') is especially worth comparing to Nero's Greek strategy.[34] Hadrian's conception of Greece belongs to the world of the Panhellenion, and of the Second Sophistic: not the world, I would argue, that Nero had envisaged for Achaia.

The Greek response to Nero merits a final thought. Abject sycophants, passive onlookers, well-paid judges: the ambivalent attitudes and outright malice of our sources unfairly colour present-day perceptions. Instead, we must accept that with Nero, as with all emperors, the Greeks adapted to a new and powerful presence in their midst, employing language and ritual evolved since the days of the Hellenistic monarchs. If sycophancy is not an accusation hurled by modern scholars faced with Hadrian's gigantic Olympieion, forested with 136 statues of the emperor within the *temenos*, then it is illogical to revive an out-dated sense of disgust with the Greeks for yielding to Nero's supposed blandishments.[35] Moreover, Nero's gift of freedom was not forgotten by Greeks in the empire

6. Nero at play?

and signs of their appreciation endure. Among the elite, it is reflected in the judgments of Plutarch, who said that the gods themselves owed Nero, though a soul in torment, a kindness for his gift to the 'noblest and most beloved' nation; or in those of Pausanias, who likened Nero to a 'noble soul ruined by a perverted education'.[36] At lower levels of society, the popular support which greeted the 'false Neros' (*Nero redivivus*) was clearly not insignificant, even if aided and abetted by Parthian intervention.[37] Difficult as it is to discern through the *damnatio memoriae*, the Greek response to Nero must be appreciated as part of an active and positive agenda, as the new provincials adjusted to their still relatively recent annexation by Rome. When it is finally accepted that Greece was more than merely a hapless stage for imperial self-glorification, then we can turn to a newly intriguing question – namely, what impact Nero's interest and support may have had upon the difficult business of being a Greek within the Roman empire.[38]

Notes

1. Suetonius, *Nero* 22.3 (translations of Suetonius are by Robert Graves).
2. See Halfmann 1986 pp. 33-4, 156, though – disappointingly – for the most part he dismisses Nero's journey as being made for purely personal and selfish reasons.
3. Note the similar conclusions of Levi (1982), speaking as president of the Société Internationale d'Études Néroniennes; see also Veyne 1985-6 p. 705.
4. Suetonius, *Nero* 24.2. Cf. Dio Cassius 62.14.1.
5. Dio Cassius 62.20.5; 21.1. Bradley (1978a) has reconstructed the sequence of the major festivals in which Nero competed as follows: Actian, Pythian, Isthmian, Nemean, Olympian, Actian, Pythian, Isthmian. This list, of course, does not include the smaller civic games Nero undoubtedly attended.
6. Eros of Thespiai: Pausanias 9.27.1-4. Theft of statuary from Delphi, Pausanias 10.7.1; and from Olympia, Pausanias 5.25.8-9; 5.26.3.
7. Suetonius, *Nero* 19.2. For other accounts of the digging of the canal, see Dio Cassius 62.16.1-2; Philostratus, *VA* 4.24. On the golden mattock, pseudo-Lucian, *Nero or The Digging of the Isthmus* 3.
8. *SIG*[3] 814, translation M.P. Charlesworth, quoted in Grant 1970 p. 189; Holleaux 1888; Oliver 1971. In this inscription, Nero's name clearly suffered a later *damnatio memoriae*. For ancient references to the liberation, see Plutarch, *Flamininus* 12.8; Suetonius, *Nero* 24.2; Pausanias 7.17.3, Pliny, *Nat. Hist.* 4.6.22.
9. Moretti (1957): no. 538 (?Attalos); no. 738 (Tiberius); no. 750 (Germanicus); nos. 790-5 (Nero); see Veyne 1985-6 pp. 713-14. Cf. Finley and Pleket 1976 pp. 72, 107, where Nero's personal 'lunatic Games performance' is derided.
10. Aelius Aristides, *Oration* 26, *Regarding Rome* 97, 99; Behr 1981 pp. 94-5; Oliver 1953; Finley and Pleket 1976 p. 109; Harmon 1988. For the proliferation of games in Roman Greece, see Spawforth 1989.
11. Dio Cassius 62.14.4
12. Athena Alea: Pausanias 8.46.1-5. Nikopolis and Patras: Pausanias 7.18.8-9; 7.21.1. For other examples of Roman appropriations, see for example: Pausanias 7.22.5, 9; 9.33.6; 10.21.6; Strabo 8.6.23; Suetonius, *Caligula* 22. For the close identification of a god with its image, Lane Fox 1986 pp. 133-7. On the general phenomenon of 'displaced cult', see Alcock 1993 pp. 175-80; Gordon 1979.
13. Pausanias 9.27.4; 10.7.1. On Sulla, Pausanias 9.33.6. For a different Greek

perspective on the Roman appropriation of statues, compare Dio Chrysostom, *Oration* 31.151.

14. Philostratus, *VS* 551-2; *VA* 5.7; 4.24. For previous attempts, Pliny *Nat. Hist.* 4.4.10-11 who noted that the fate of individuals like Demetrius, Caesar, Caligula and Nero proved the undertaking 'to have been an act of sacrilege'.

15. On the archaeological evidence for Nero's canal, see Gerster 1884; Engels 1990 pp. 59-60. On the Jewish captive labour force, Josephus, *BJ* 3.10.10.

16. Suetonius, *Nero* 37.3. On the dangers of the sea passage, Pliny, *Nat. Hist.* 4.4.10, see also Philostratus, *VA* 4.24.

17. Suetonius, *Nero* 16.1; 31.3; Tacitus, *Ann.* 42. For a reassessment of these undertakings, see Bradley 1978b pp. 101, 115, 182; Griffin 1984 p. 109. Suetonius appears to approve the Isthmian plans of Caligula, *Caligula* 21.

18. Pausanias 2.1.5-6; Dio Cassius 62.16.1-2; pseudo-Lucian, *Nero or The Digging of the Isthmus* 3. The sacred implications of redirecting rivers are made clear in Tacitus' account (Ann. 1.79) of a debate about altering the course of Tiber tributaries; in that case nothing was done. One example of a mythical 'taming' of waters is given in Dio Cassius 4.35.3-4. For Alexander the Great's interest in canals, see Strabo 16.1.11. Broader discussions of provincial landscapes and of imperial symbolic geography are provided in Purcell 1990 and Nicolet 1991.

19. Plutarch, *Flamininus* 12.8; Gallivan 1973b; Bradley 1978a; Halfmann 1986 pp. 173-7; Veyne 1985-6 p. 709.

20. Sartre 1991 p. 44. On Sardinia's change in status: *CIL* 10.7852; Gallivan 1973b p. 233; Bradley 1978a pp. 68-70. On the landscape of Roman Sardinia: Rowland 1984; Rowland and Dyson 1991.

21. Philostratus, *VA* 5.41, where he also says: 'Nero freed the Hellenes in play, but you have enslaved them in all seriousness. Farewell.' For Vespasian's action: Suetonius, *Vespasian* 8.4.

22. Pausanias 7.17.4; *SIG*³ 796A with Momigliano 1944 p. 116. Philostratus (*VA* 5.41), on the other hand, claimed that with freedom 'the cities regained their Doric and Attic characteristics, and a general rejuvenescence accompanied the institution among them of a peace and harmony such as not even ancient Hellas ever enjoyed'.

23. For a recent review of the chronology and sequence of events in Nero's visit, see Bradley 1978a.

24. Lake Alcyon: Pausanias 2.37.5. Alexander's plan to cut a canal may have helped to inspire Nero's Isthmian attempt, just as his reported inability to complete it (Pausanias 2.1.5) may have consoled the emperor. As another example of such emulation, Nero apparently intended to launch an eastern expedition, no less ambitious than that of Alexander himself, to the Caspian Gates. For this purpose, he raised a new crack legion called 'The Phalanx of Alexander the Great': Suetonius, *Nero* 19.2; Pliny, *Nat. Hist.* 6.15.40. Kolendo (1982) argues that this project was designed largely as an ideological exercise, distracting attention from internal difficulties by planning a campaign of spectacular expansion, one rivalling or even surpassing those of Alexander. Men were also sent to investigate the source of the Nile, partly out of 'devotion to truth', partly in connection with another planned campaign, Seneca, *QN* 6.8.3; Pliny, *Nat. Hist.* 6.35.181; see Veyne 1985-6 pp. 711-12.

25. Jones 1971 pp. 16-17 on Plutarch's Pythian visit and pp. 39-47 on the society of Plutarch and his wealthy compatriots. Cf. Plutarch, *Quaestiones Convivales* 628A-B, 638B, 674F, 675D, 723A; Jones 1970; Spawforth 1989 pp. 196-7.

26. Veyne explores in a different fashion the meaning of these agonistic victories in a thoughtful account of a course presented in the *Annuaire du College de France*. The 'voyage' of Nero to Greece serves as the notional focus of discussion, but the bulk of his essay deals with the utopian political philosophy of that artist-king, in which the ruler

6. Nero at play? 109

becomes an all-powerful creator, personal excellence becomes the means of attaining legitimacy, and the governed obey out of love and admiration for the glorious genius who governs. Veyne finds Nero's enactment of his chosen role wanting, however, and his personal behavior at Olympia bizarre and misjudged, commenting: 'Nero passionately loved power, but he lacked a political sense': Veyne 1985-6 p. 723 and *passim*.

27. Suetonius, *Nero* 34.4. For Nero's refusal to visit Athens and Sparta, Dio Cassius 62.14.3-4. Momigliano, for one, thought such behavior a sure sign of Nero's 'psychological problems,' see Momigliano 1934 p. 737.

28. Alcock 1993 pp. 168-9; for a collection of evidence about Roman Corinth: Engels 1990. The Isthmian Games 'were wont to draw crowds of people ... ' Strabo 8.6.20.

29. Veyne 1985-6 p. 709.

30. Larsen 1958; Oliver 1983 pp. 101-2.

31. Pliny, *Epist.* 8.24.1; Petrochilos 197; Wardman 1976 pp. 1-24. On the 'temptation of philhellenism', see Griffin 1984 pp. 208-20. On the other hand, it is worth noting that Nero did not vastly increase the number of Greeks receiving Roman citizenship: Griffin 1984 pp. 211-13; Warmington 1969 pp. 52-3, 58.

32. Dio Cassius 62.8.2-3

33. Veyne (1985-6 pp. 723-37) analyses the subjectivity of response to Nero, and his utopian philosophy of rule, within various social groups of the empire.

34. Oliver 1983 p. 104. On the Panhellenion, see Spawforth and Walker 1985; 1986. For Hadrian's time 'on the road': Halfmann 1986 pp. 188-210.

35. For a more sophisticated analysis of the imperial cult in the east, see Price 1984. On the Olympieion, e.g. Abramson 1974.

36. Plutarch, *De sera numinis vindicta* (On the Delays of the Divine Vengeance) 567F-568; Pausanias 7.17.3. See also Philostratus, *VA* 5.41: 'Nero restored the liberties of Hellas with a wisdom and moderation quite alien to his character ... .' This does not prevent Greek authors, with hindsight, from ultimately passing a negative judgment on Nero: cf. Philostratus, *VA* 5.7 and the accusations of Dio Cassius (62.11.1) about Nero's 'devastation' of Greece, 'precisely as if he had been sent out out to wage war, notwithstanding that he had left the country free ... '

37. Suetonius, *Nero* 57.1-2; Bowersock 1987 pp. 308-10; Gallivan 1973a; Grant 1970 pp. 206-8; Momigliano 1934 pp. 741-2. Of Nero, Dio Chrysostom remarked in his *Oration* 21.10 : 'even now everybody wishes he were still alive. And the great majority do believe that he is ... '

38. On the quest for a Greek cultural identity under the empire, see Elsner 1992. I would like to thank John Cherry and Peter Garnsey for their helpful comments.

Bibliography

Abramson, H. (1974) 'The Olympieion in Athens and its connections with Rome', *California Studies in Classical Antiquity* 7 pp. 1-25.

Alcock, S.E. (1993) *Graecia Capta: the landscapes of Roman Greece*, Cambridge.

Behr, C.A., ed. (1981) *P. Aelius Aristides, The Complete Works. Volume 2: Orations*, pp. 17-53. Leiden.

Bowersock, G.W. (1987) 'The mechanics of subversion in the Roman provinces', in *Opposition et résistance à l'empire d'Auguste à Trajan*. Geneva.

Bradley, K.R. (1978a) 'The chronology of Nero's visit to Greece AD 66/67', *Latomus* 37 pp. 61-72.

—— (1978b) *Suetonius' Life of Nero: a historical commentary* (Collection Latomus 157), Brussels.

Elsner, J. (1992) 'Pausanias: a Greek pilgrim in the Roman world', *Past and Present* 135 pp. 3-29.
Engels, D. (1990) *Roman Corinth: an alternative model for the classical city*, Chicago.
Finley, M.I. and Pleket, H.W. (1976) *The Olympic Games: the first thousand years*, London.
Gallivan, P.A. (1973a) 'The false Neros: a re-examination', *Historia* 22 pp. 364-5.
—— (1973b) 'Nero's liberation of Greece', *Hermes* 101 pp. 230-4.
Gerster, B. (1884) 'L'Isthme de Corinthe: tentatives de percenant dans l'antiquité', *BCH* 8 pp. 224-32.
Gordon, R.L. (1979) 'The real and the imaginary: production and religion in the Graeco-Roman world', *Art History* 2 pp. 5-34.
Grant, M. (1970) *Nero*, New York.
Griffin, M.T. (1984) *Nero: the end of a dynasty*, London.
Halfmann, H. (1986) *Itinera principum: Geschichte und Typologie der Kaiserreisen im römischen Reich*, Stuttgart.
Harmon, D.P. (1988) 'The religious significance of games in the Roman age', in W.J. Raschke, ed., *The Archaeology of the Olympics: the Olympics and other festivals in antiquity*, pp. 236-55. Madison.
Holleaux, M. (1888) 'Discours de Néron prononcé à Corinthe pour rendre aux Grecs la liberté', *BCH* 12 pp. 510-28.
Jones, C.P. (1970) 'A leading family from Roman Thespiae', *HSCP* 74 pp. 223-55.
—— (1971) *Plutarch and Rome*, Oxford.
Kolendo, J. (1982) 'Le projet d'expedition de Néron dans le Caucase', in J.-M. Croisille and P.M. Fauchère, eds., *Neronia 1977 (Actes du 2e colloque de la Société Internationale d'Études Néroniennes, Clermont-Ferrand, 27-28 Mai 1977)*, pp. 23-30. Clermont-Ferrand.
Lane Fox, R. (1981) *Pagans and Christians*, Harmondsworth.
Levi, M. (1982) 'La S.I.E.N: sa raison d'être, ses buts', in J.-M. Croisille and P.M. Fauchère, eds., *Neronia 1977 (Actes du 2e colloque de la Société Internationale d'Études Néroniennes, Clermont-Ferrand, 27-28 Mai 1977)*, pp. 9-10. Clermont-Ferrand.
Momigliano, A. (1934) 'Nero' in *CAH X: The Augustan Empire*, pp. 702-42. Cambridge.
—— (1944) 'Review of *CAH Volume X: The Augustan Empire*', *JRS* 34 pp. 109-16.
Moretti, L. (1957) *Olympionikai. I vincitori negli antichi agoni olimpici* (Memorie della Classe di Scienze morali e storiche dell'Accademia dei Lincei, volume 8, ser. 8a). Rome.
Nicolet, C. (1991) *Space, Geography and Politics in the Early Roman Empire*, Ann Arbor.
Oliver, J.H. (1953) *The Ruling Power*, Philadelphia.
—— (1971) 'Epaminondas of Acraephia', *GRBS* 12 pp. 221-37.
—— (1983) *The Civic Tradition and Roman Athens*, Baltimore.
Petrochilos, N.K. (1974) *Roman Attitudes to the Greeks*, Athens.
Price, S.R.F. (1984) *Rituals and Power: the Roman imperial cult in Asia Minor*, Cambridge.
Purcell, N. (1990) 'The creation of provincial landscape: the Roman impact', in T. Blagg and M. Millett, eds., *The Early Roman Empire in the West*, pp. 7-29. Oxford.
Rowland, R.J., Jr. (1984) 'The Roman countryside of Sardinia', in M. Balmuth and R.J. Rowland, Jr., eds., *Studies in Sardinian Archaeology*, pp. 284-300. Ann Arbor.
Rowland, R.J., Jr. and Dyson, S. (1991) 'Survey archaeology in Sardinia', in G. Barker and J. Lloyd, eds., *Roman Landscapes: archaeological survey in the Mediterranean area*, pp. 54-61. London.
Sartre, M. (1991) *L'Orient romain*, Paris.
Spawforth, A.J.S. (1989) 'Agonistic festivals in Roman Greece', in S. Walker and A. Cameron, eds., *The Greek Renaissance in the Roman Empire* (*BICS* Supplement 55), pp. 193-7. London.
Spawforth, A.J.S. and Walker, S. (1985) 'The world of the Panhellenion: I. Athens and Eleusis', *JRS* 75 pp. 78-104.

——— (1986) 'The world of the Panhellenion: II. three Dorian cities', *JRS* 76 pp. 88-105.
Suetonius (1957) *The Twelve Caesars*, translated by Robert Graves. Harmondsworth.
Veyne, P. (1985-6) 'Histoire de Rome', *Annuaire du College de France* 1985-6 pp. 705-37.
Wardman, A. (1976) *Rome's Debt to Greece*, London.
Warmington, B.H. (1969) *Nero: reality and legend*, London.

7

Constructing decadence: the representation of Nero as imperial builder

Jaś Elsner

> There was nothing, however, in which he was more ruinously prodigal than in building.
>
> Suetonius, *Nero* 31.1[1]

On one thing the historical tradition hostile to Nero is agreed: his profligate excess surpassed even itself in his imperial buildings, and especially in the *Domus Aurea*, the imperial villa Nero built in the centre of Rome.[2] In this chapter, I compare posterity's representation of Nero's building activities with other imperial programmes of construction by other Julio-Claudian emperors. By placing the emperor's buildings within an ancient Roman debate on the nature of the principate, one can see architecture as a three-dimensional and visual dynamic of self-presentation, in which rulers used buildings both as a method of self-presentation to the populace and as a means of distinguishing themselves from their imperial predecessors within what had rapidly become a tradition of successive emperors. Yet building was always an ambiguous theme in the invective of Roman moral rhetoric. As Julio-Claudian buildings became increasingly lavish, in the attempt to surpass previous emperors, they became increasingly open to the charge of luxury and decadence. Nero's very need to surpass his ancestors in imperial architecture primed the guns of those historians whose project was to condemn him.

Introduction

The fierce and productive academic debate in recent times on the nature of the Roman principate has tended to obscure the fact that there was an equally fierce – and perhaps still more interesting – debate on this same issue in ancient times.[3] In epic poetry, Lucan's *Bellum Civile* (however one chooses to read it, or chose to do so in the reign of Nero) is on some level an explicitly political riposte to the imperial politics of the *Aeneid*. In history, the works of Tacitus are an extended meditation on the nature of imperial government from the standpoint of a neo-republican imagination. In drama, the *Octavia* – a rare non-Senecan tragedy to have survived from Roman literature – dramatises a debate on the principate between the characters of Nero and Seneca (vv. 440-592). Nero

7. Constructing decadence

argues that the sword, the destruction of enemies and fear itself are the principal bulwarks of an emperor's power (vv. 443, 457-8); while Seneca argues the case for fostering one's subjects' loyalty and love (vv. 444, 457-8). As with Lucan's indebtedness to Virgil, and Tacitus' opening in the *Annals*, inevitably the debate turns on a comparison of Nero's reign with that of Augustus (vv. 472-532).

However, it turns out that Seneca and Nero subscribe to different versions and views of the Augustan principate. For Seneca,

> the first Augustus, his country's father, gained the stars and is worshipped in temples as a god. (vv. 477-8)

But Nero replies,

> He who earned heaven by piety, the deified Augustus, how many nobles did he put to death, young men and old, scattered throughout the world, when they fled their own homes through fear of death ... all by the proscription lists delivered to grim destruction. (vv. 504-9)

The meaning of the principate in ancient times was ambivalent, contested and open to debate. The existence of this Roman debate – attested as early as the reign of Nero by the *Bellum Civile* and the *Octavia* – is crucial. For it reminds us that we cannot regard imperial activity in isolation. Julio-Claudian emperors acted and were viewed in the knowledge that their office was in the direct line of their descent from Augustus.

In his moral epistle on mercy, addressed to Nero, Seneca explicitly compares the emperor with his predecessors:

> It is a mighty burden that you have taken upon yourself; no one today talks of the deified Augustus or the early years of Tiberius Caesar, or seeks any model he would have you copy but yourself ... (*De Clementia* I.1.6)

Nero is burdened with the heritage of his office (despite, indeed because, 'no one today talks of' his ancestors), yet he must act not as them but as himself. Ultimately, an emperor – always merely the next candidate to slot into the line of imperial purple – could not just emulate previous models, but had to create and foster his own image: 'the standard for your principate is the foretaste you have given' (ibid.) Seneca's keen awareness of the imperial problematic of tradition and innovation also motivates the implicit contrast between Claudius and Augustus in his *Apocolocyntosis*. There, writing about Claudius in a satiric vein, Seneca puts his condemnation at the court of heaven into the mouth of Augustus – implying that Claudius failed to live up to the imperial tradition he inherited (*Apocoloc.* 10-11). Just as Julio-Claudian portraits reflected the portraiture of Augustus (whether by imitation or innovation),[4] so their every gesture represented a new act in imperial self-definition, which could be directly compared with what had gone before. The fulfilment of the imperial office was beset by a permanent anxiety of influence.

In this chapter, I concentrate on one specific but significant area in the public activity of the emperor – namely, the act of building in Rome. Nero himself was an outstanding builder, praised even by hostile sources such as Tacitus for the excellence of the rebuilding of those parts of Rome damaged by the great fire of AD 64 (*Annals* 15.43). In a remark recorded by a fourth-century historian, Nero

> was so effective for five years, especially in improving the city, that Trajan with justice declared that all other emperors fell far behind Nero's five years.[5]

Since such praise represents a rare match struck in the general darkness of history's subsequent abuse of Nero, his buildings certainly made a deep and at least in some respects positive impression – even on a hostile posterity. Before exploring them, and their textual representations, in more detail, let us briefly glance at the kind of activity which public building had become in the hands of the emperors, and how it was regarded.

Augustus' building programme had transformed the city of Rome.[6] In combination with Agrippa, he had reconstituted the visual environment of the city, not only in its ancient centre but also in the Campus Martius outside the pomerium, the traditional and augurally constituted boundary of Rome. By the time of Hadrian, this remarkable project of imperial construction had come to be a commonplace in descriptions of Augustus' reign. Hence Suetonius' well-known comment (*Aug.* 28):

> Since the city was not adorned as the dignity of the empire demanded ..., he so beautified it that he could justly boast that he had found it built of brick and left it in marble.

Not only did the first princeps build lavishly, but he also ensured that the edifices he constructed would forever be linked with their author's name. Apart from inscriptions on individual monuments, Augustus made his own record of the whole project of his buildings in Rome as chapters 19-21 of the *Res Gestae*, his autobiography. This was inscribed in two bronze columns engraved after his death in front of the mausoleum of the Julio-Claudian emperors, and copies were set up in temples elsewhere in the empire, notably in Asia Minor.[7] This two-fold Augustan programme in the realm of building – the actual construction of large numbers of prestige buildings and the careful public record of whom these buildings were inaugurated by – had a remarkable impact on the definition of the principate in Rome.[8] Buildings were the most direct, visual and experiential evidence of the emperor's activities. Thereafter no emperor could afford not to emulate the first princeps. The pattern of imperial building became – like that of imperial portraiture – one of emulation, imitation and improvement.

If Augustus' principate created the parameters of public and private activity by which the new role of emperor was to be defined, that of Tiberius established this group of imperial definitions through a basic continuity. The setting up of the *Res Gestae* in Rome, and its inscription in cities like Ancyra, Apollonia and Psidian Antioch in Asia Minor, were acts accomplished in Tiberius' reign. As Tiberian statements, they showed (no less than Tiberius' deification of Augustus)[9] the essential cohesion to be envisaged between the two reigns. As early as

7. Constructing decadence 115

AD 30, the Roman officer Velleius Paterculus was concluding his *History of Rome* with a grandiose (if evidentially thin) peroration in the penultimate chapter on Tiberius as imperial builder:

> What public buildings did he construct in his own name or that of his family! With what pious munificence, exceeding human belief, does he now rear the temple to his father! With what a magnificent control of personal feeling did he restore the works of Gnaeus Pompey when destroyed by fire. For a feeling of kinship leads him to protect every famous monument. (II.130.1)

To be seen as a worthy emperor, Tiberius had to be perceived as a worthy builder.[10] Thereafter, in the writings of the Roman empire, it became a cliché of imperial history, biography and panegyric to enumerate at least some of their subjects' buildings. The apogee of this tradition is Procopius' *De aedificiis*, an entire panegyric devoted solely to Justinian's buildings.

A further element in the public dissemination of buildings under the principate was their representation on coins, as well as in inscriptions and literary texts.[11] This practice had begun in the Republic, but became assimilated to imperial propaganda under Augustus. It meant that prestigious edifices in Rome, whether built by the Emperor or not, could be associated with him in the perceptions of a large social stratum in the empire, through being represented on his coinage. By combining images of important buildings with brief texts announcing what they were, and, on the coin's obverse, portraits of a particular ruler, such numismatic propaganda went a long way to establishing the image of emperors as builders. Augustus had a number of his most prestigious monuments marked in this way – his triumphal arches,[12] some of his temples,[13] his equestrian statues.[14] Later emperors chose to be represented not only on the obverse of coins with their own buildings (such as Claudius or Nero with their triumphal arches)[15] but also with earlier monuments, especially those set up by Augustus. For instance a copper coin of Nero issued in Lyons, the main mint in the west of the Empire, shows Augustus' *Ara Pacis* on the reverse (see Plate 6).[16] Here not only was an important Augustan monument being associated with Nero, but its particular thematic resonances (to do with peace) were significant.

Yet the incorporation of public and private building into the very definition of the principate was tinged with ambiguity, even paradox. While mighty buildings were the rightful acts of great men, they were also – in Roman moral discourse – a sign of luxury, decadence and vice.[17] The grandeur of an emperor's buildings could signal his greatness, as in Strabo's contemporary account of Augustan Rome (*Geography* 5.3.8), Pliny the Younger's panegyric of Trajan (51-2) or Suetonius' *Life of Augustus* (28-9). But that very grandeur could be a sign of wanton, profligate and outrageous excess. Despite the approving remarks of Trajan and Tacitus on some aspects of Nero's building programme, it would be upon Nero as builder that the full weight of Roman rhetoric's moral censure of extravagant building would descend.[18]

This chapter, then, traces a double theme. On the one hand, I shall explore Nero as builder. That is, the emperor in his necessary (indeed, defining) role as one who initiated new and outstanding buildings in the city of Rome. This was not an easy role, since every move in it, every building, could be matched against the previous history of imperial building, the previous history of imperial self-definition in its most visual form. If an emperor's buildings fell short of the high standards set by his predecessors, then implicitly he was unworthy of his office. If he surpassed them, he risked the accusation of morally reprehensible luxuriousness. On the other hand, I shall examine the *representation* of Nero as builder in the historiographic tradition – that is, Nero's image as builder *after* his fall, when posterity had already decided that he was wicked. I shall argue that the ambiguity implicit in the theme of building – coupled with Nero's deliberate construction policies – allowed his buildings to be rhetorically exploited against Nero as proof of his monstrosity, once the tradition had decided that his memory was to be damned.

Buildings and the rhetoric of imperial degeneracy

In Suetonius' *Life of Caligula*, the trope of imperial buildings plays an interesting role. Concluding his introductory account of Gaius' early life and reign (1-21), Suetonius lists his public works in Rome (chapter 21) – the temple of Augustus, the theatre of Pompey, the initiation of an aqueduct from Tibur and an amphitheatre. He mentions also Gaius' works at Syracuse (including the repair of the city walls and the temples of the gods), as well as his plans to rebuild the palace of Polycrates at Samos and the temple of Didymaean Apollo at Ephesus. The brief survey of buildings ends with Caligula's aim to construct a city in the Alps and to dig a canal through the Isthmus at Corinth. Essentially these projects fall into the classic categories for imperial building – centred primarily on sacred and secular constructions. The provision of buildings for leisure activities (such as the theatre and amphitheatre) is matched by public utilities (such as the aqueduct and walls of Syracuse). The construction of projects grandiose enough to be worthy of an emperor (the palace at Samos, the canal, the city in the Alps) is balanced by the temples in Rome, Syracuse and Ephesus. This is a carefully constructed and balanced list, on the lines of the rather longer one designed by Augustus for his *Res Gestae*.[19] None the less, it is a catalogue charged with potent and possible ambiguities pointing proleptically to the tyrant that Caligula would become. The palace at Samos explicitly recalls the tyrant Polycrates, the canal through the Isthmus evokes the canal at Athos dug by the Persian king Xerxes in his attempt to enslave Greece,[20] the city in the Alps suggests the Alpine feats of Hannibal who had attempted to conquer Rome.

Then, at the opening of chapter 22, Suetonius breaks off:

So much for Caligula as emperor; the rest of this account must deal with the monster.

The acts of the monster include a number of building projects, listed separately from the previous list:

He built out a part of the Palace as far as the Forum, and made the temple of Castor and Pollux its vestibule (22.2).

7. Constructing decadence 117

> He built a bridge over the temple of the deified Augustus, and thus joined his Palace to the Capitol. Presently, to be nearer yet, he laid the foundations of a new house in the court of the Capitol. (22.4)

This remarkable break from emperor to monster, and the ability of buildings to stand as evidence under either heading in Suetonius' rhetoric, is significant. The buildings of the monster are those which appear to transgress the precise and anciently established boundaries of function and situation, either by combining sacred and secular (including the temple of the Dioscuri into the vestibule of the palace, building a house in the temple of Capitoline Jove) or by uniting previously discrete and distinct parts of the city (the Palatine and Forum, the Palatine and Capitol).

Yet Suetonius' categories by which buildings are to be impugned for monstrosity are not stable. In his account of Augustus' public works (*Augustus* 29), Suetonius notes that the first emperor

> reared the temple of Apollo in that part of his house on the Palatine for which soothsayers declared that the god had shown his desire by striking it with lightning (29.3).

Gaius' linking of his own house with that of a god could not have had a better precedent, a precedent which the biographer appears to approve. Yet, if lightning had struck the house of Caligula, we can imagine what the portent would have been made to mean in Suetonius' rhetorical hands ... It was only the general success of Augustus, the fact that he was a 'good emperor', deified at his death, that allowed his house on the Palatine to stand posthumously for his good qualities. Likewise, had Caligula proved worthy to be a *divus* at his death, his building ambitions in the heart of Rome would not have been the acts of a monster.

It is this quality of 'judgment through hindsight' that must make us wary of the textual tradition. The historians were above all rhetoricians, and buildings had the potential to occupy any position, positive or negative, in their highly rhetorical accounts. Above all, we need to worry when we find the 'evil emperors' lumped together as if their actions were simply and inevitably variations on the same theme – a series of reversals of the norms of *natura*. Within ten years of Nero's fall, the Elder Pliny wrote:

> Twice we have seen the whole city encircled by imperial palaces, those of Gaius and Nero, the latter's palace, to crown all, being indeed a House of Gold. (*Natural History* 36.111)

This passage is frequently quoted as if it reported the truth.[21] But whether it was really the case that both emperors attempted to ring the city with palaces, and whether such actions represented deliberate policy (with Nero emulating Gaius), what matters to Pliny is something quite different from factual veracity. In the context of a lament about modern extravagance, his account is a polemical attempt to associate what he implies are extreme acts of degenerate modernity with emperors whose names were already a byword for unrestrained excess.

Pliny's whole argument is highly rhetorical. We learn that the 'lands of those who made this empire great occupied a smaller space than those emperor's sitting rooms' (36.111). Moreover, the *Domus Aurea* did not encircle Rome (except in Pliny's rhetorical flight of fancy); it linked the Palatine and Esquiline hills in the middle of the city.

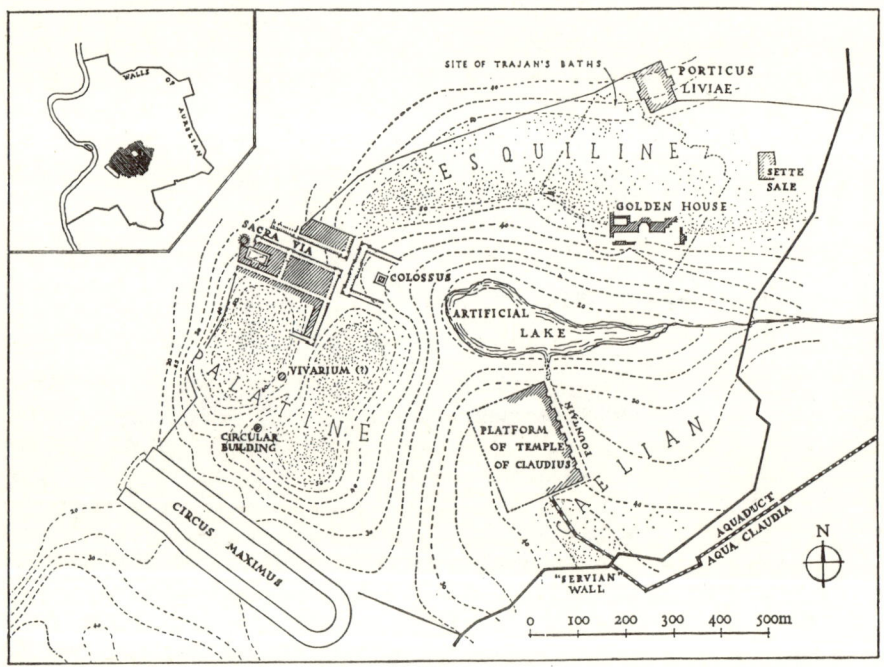

Nero's *Domus Aurea*, AD 64–8. Plan of the probable extent of the park.

In effect, almost as soon as Vespasian had taken over the empire, we can see in Pliny a highly mythologised and polemical version of Nero, in which his activities, his buildings and the nature of his principate become mapped – together with the principate of Caligula – onto a negative ideal of how not to be an emperor. Despite antedating Tacitus and Suetonius, Pliny (like the author of the *Octavia*) presents no more objective an account than they. Together, these writers provide a polemical rhetoric which hardly deserves to pass under the unproblematic guise of 'the evidence'. Nor can we rely on later sources (themselves reliant on Pliny and his Flavian contemporaries) such as Pausanias, writing in the second century AD of Gaius and Nero as a 'pair who sinned against the god' (*Description of Greece* 9.27.3–4).

Nero's building policy in the context of the Julio-Claudians

Most commentators, especially those who look at the material remains of Neronian building (architectural, visual and archaeological), rather than at the writings of the ancient historians, are agreed that it represented an outstanding and innovative phase in the history of Roman art and architecture.[22] Those who have explored the economic and managerial implications of imperial building are likewise agreed on the general competence and good timing of Nero's construction measures in Rome.[23] These conclusions are a long way from the impression of outrageous excess on which our ancient literary sources unite. In this section I shall briefly outline a sketch of Neronian building policy in relation to the activities of earlier emperors.

It is clear that Nero's principate opted for a series of innovatory and even controversial gestures in the realm of public art. The Elder Pliny (no friendly source, as we have seen, since he completed and revised his *Natural History* under the Flavians) remarks on Nero's colossi – not only the huge bronze statue which stood in the vestibule of the *Domus Aurea* facing the Sacra Via and the Forum (34.45-6), but also the enormous portrait painted on linen 120 feet high which he labels 'an insanity of our age' (35.51). Nero's triumphal arch on the Capitoline Hill (see Plate 7), voted in celebration of Corbulo's Armenian victories in AD 58, has been described as 'revolutionary' and 'remarkable'.[24] His baths were outstanding. As Martial wrote (also under the Flavians)

> What is worse than Nero? What is better than his baths? (7.34.4).

From Claudius, Nero had inherited an extensive and effective series of pragmatic structural improvements in the city of Rome. Claudius had undertaken a number of major projects including the completion of the aqueducts started under Gaius (the Aqua Claudia and the Aqua Anio Novus),[25] the building of the harbour at Ostia,[26] and the draining of the Fucine Lake, 53 miles east of Rome.[27] These projects, along with the construction of granaries in both Ostia and Rome,[28] ensured stability in both water and grain supplies to the city.

No laudatory list survives of Nero's own buildings – such even as Suetonius includes in his account of Caligula the pre-monster. But from isolated references and archaeological excavation, some picture can be painted of his public building in Rome. This fits well with the range of projects planned by previous emperors. Nero completed the harbour at Ostia,[29] and went so far as to issue a coin in AD 64 depicting the harbour on the reverse (see Plate 8).[30] In addition to the arch, Nero dedicated a provision market, the Macellum Magnum, in AD 59, his new baths north of the Pantheon in the Campus Martius, and a gymnasium closely linked to the baths. Other significant public buildings included the amphitheatre in the Campus Martius erected in AD 57 and the completion of a circus begun by Caligula.[31]

These constructions are hardly out of keeping with previous imperial activity. They continue the policy of endowing the city with public buildings whose functions were highly suited to the needs and entertainment of the populace.

Significantly, but not unexpectedly, we find the literary sources turning these monuments to rhetorical effect against Nero, despite the fact that they are little different from what we might have expected from any emperor – good or bad. For Suetonius, Nero's amphitheatre was the excuse to put 400 senators and 600 knights onto the stage (*Nero* 12.1). According to Tacitus, at the consecration of the gymnasium, 'oil was distributed to the equestrian and senatorial orders', which he acidly describes as 'a Greek form of liberality' (*Annals* 14.47). The gymnasium's main virtue, in Tacitus' account, was that it was struck by lightning and burned to the ground: 'A statue of Nero inside was melted into a shapeless mass of bronze' (*Annals* 15.22). All this is simply gratuitous – but it set the literary tone for what became (and still are) the standard rhetorical associations of Nero's buildings. By the third century, Philostratus could happily present 'the occasion of Nero's completion of the most magnificent gymnasium in Rome' as marked

> by the fact that Nero was in extra good voice when he sang on that day, and he sang in the tavern which adjoined the gymnasium, naked except for a girdle round his waist, like any low tapster. (*Life of Apollonius of Tyana* 4.42)

Thus a myth is born.

The principate's own presentation of these public buildings was sober by comparison. We have no Neronian texts to compare with the *Res Gestae*, but the coin record – an official and officially sanctioned document – is hardly outrageous. Just as Augustus had celebrated peace by closing the doors of the temple of Janus Geminus (*Res Gestae* 13), so Nero closed the gates of this temple in 66 and celebrated the event in a number of coin issues from both Rome and Lyons (see Plate 9).[32] His own buildings were represented on coins mainly issued after the fire of 64.[33] They included the arch (coin struck in 64-5, see Plate 7),[34] the Macellum Magnum (coin issued 64-6, see Plate 10),[35] and the temple of Vesta which Nero probably rebuilt after the fire (coin struck 64-5, see Plate 11).[36] Our literary sources do not record the reconstruction of this highly significant temple (despite attesting its destruction in the fire – Tacitus *Annals* 15.41), yet the coins suggest that Nero himself emphasised its importance.[37] These coins, in addition to those representing the Ara Pacis and the Ostia harbour, show a propaganda of typical Julio-Claudian balance, whereby honorific imperial monuments (such as the arch) are matched by public buildings of popular utility, such as the harbour and the market, and by the temples of Vesta, Janus and Pax Augusta. It is noteworthy that, while the texts never associate Nero with temple building or restoration, three out of the six coin types that have survived representing buildings associate the emperor with sacred edifices.

By contrast with (and indeed pointedly ignoring) all this, our literary sources focus on a radically different area of Neronian building. All Nero's gestures – whether innovatory or traditional – paled before what our ancient sources see as the outrage of the Golden House (for its extent, p. 118 above). In the words of Suetonius (*Nero* 31.1-2):

> He built a house stretching from the Palatine to the Esquiline, which he called the *Domus Transitoria*; and when it was burned soon afterwards, rebuilt it under the new name of the *Domus Aurea*. The following details will give some notion of its

1. Sample advertisement for Munsingwear rayon boxer shorts, from the campaign book for *Quo Vadis* (1951).

2. Sample poster advertising the reissue of *The Sign of the Cross*, from the campaign book of 1944.

3. Cecil B. DeMille directs the filming of *The Sign of the Cross* (1932).

4. Nero shows his court plans for rebuilding Rome, from *Quo Vadis* (1951).

5. Nero plays as Rome burns in *Quo Vadis* (1951).

6. Neronian coin showing the Ara Pacis, reverse.

7. Neronian coin showing Nero's arch, reverse.

8. Neronian coin showing the harbour at Ostia, reverse.

9. Neronian coin showing the closure of the gates of the Temple of Janus Geminus, reverse.

10. Neronian coin showing the Macellum Magnum: *left* obverse; *below* reverse.

11. Neronian coin showing the Temple of Vesta, reverse.

7. Constructing decadence 121

size and magnificence. A huge statue of himself, 120 feet high, stood in the entrance hall; and the pillared arcade ran for a whole mile. An enormous pool, more like a sea than a pool, was surrounded by buildings made to resemble cities, and by a landscape garden consisting of ploughed fields, vineyards, pastures and woodlands – where every variety of domestic and wild animal roamed about. Parts of the house were overlaid with gold and studded with precious stones and mother-of-pearl. All the dining rooms had ceilings of fretted ivory, the panels of which could slide back and let a rain of flowers, or of perfume from hidden sprinklers, fall on his guests. The main dining room was circular, and its roof revolved slowly, day and night, in time with the sky. Sea water, or sulphur water, was always on tap in the baths. When the palace had been decorated throughout in this lavish style, Nero dedicated it, and condescended to remark: 'Good, now I can at last begin to live like a human being!'

Before looking more closely at the *Domus Aurea*, we should note that it belongs to a more strictly *private* sphere of imperial building than the temples, markets and theatres of the official documents and coins. Emperors did not represent their palaces, gardens or villas on their coinage, nor did they advertise details of their domestic buildings in official documents such as the *Res Gestae*. At the same time, imperial palaces were not 'private' in any modern sense of the word. Emperors concluded much of their official business in these 'private' residences – for instance meeting delegations of clients as is memorably recorded in Philo's account of the embassy of Alexandrian Jews to Gaius (*De Legatione* 181, 351f.). Under the Julio-Claudians, such 'private' spaces had become increasingly lavish and luxurious. The jewel-bedecked windows ordered by Gaius for his residence at the Horti Lamiani, while Philo and his colleagues trembled before the emperor's wrath (*De Legatione* 358, 364), have been matched by archaeological discoveries on the site of these gardens.[38] The remarkable grotto which served Tiberius as a dining room at Sperlonga,[39] and the extraordinary nymphaeum of Claudius recently discovered at Baiae,[40] only serve to confirm the extent and lavishness of such 'private' imperial luxury.

The *Domus Aurea* was in one sense a natural and direct continuation of this Julio-Claudian tradition. Its huge atrium and vestibule (in which the Colossus stood and towards which the Via Sacra was partly realigned and redirected) was a grand Neronian version of the patron's meeting place with his clients.[41] The luxurious excesses of the Golden House, against which the sources rail, are again in line with the general luxury of early imperial dining-rooms and villas. For instance, the nymphaeum of the *Domus Aurea* with its revolutionary ceiling mosaics depicting Ulysses and Polyphemus,[42] is iconographically and thematically related (as well as in terms of its innovatory lavishness) to the decor of the Sperlonga cave and the Baiae nymphaeum.

But while in itself the *Domus Aurea* may have been just one further step in the developing visual and architectural language of imperial luxury, in one crucial aspect it represented a radical act of innovation. Nero had placed a spectacular example of a lavish rural villa (the kind of villa suited to Sperlonga, Capri or Baiae) in the heart of Rome.[43] This, in retrospect, was to prove unforgivable. As Tacitus puts it (*Annals* 15.42):

Nero turned to account the ruins of his fatherland by building a palace, the marvels of which were to consist not so much in gems and gold, materials long familiar and vulgarised by luxury, as in fields and lakes and the air of solitude given by wooded ground alternating with clear tracts and open landscapes.

The outrage of *rus in urbe* (bringing the countryside into the city) was, like the building of villas into the sea,[44] a transgression of the discrete boundaries of *natura* approved by Roman custom and upheld by moral rhetoric. It represented an attempt, in Tacitus' words (*Annals* 15.42),

> to try the force of art even against the veto of nature.

But the *Domus Aurea* added to this transgression a further confusion of boundaries hitherto experienced as distinct. Like the house of Caligula which impinged on the Forum and was ultimately linked by a bridge with the Capitol, one crime of Nero's palaces (committed by both the *Domus Transitoria* and the *Domus Aurea*) was to attempt to unite discrete and distinct spaces in the geography of Rome. Both Neronian palaces straddled the Palatine and Esquiline hills, with the *Domus Aurea* apparently incorporating most of the Caelian Hill too.[45] Not only was the Golden House represented as encroaching on the spatial integrity of the city, it was seen as having become the city. As Suetonius put it, purportedly reporting a contemporary epigram (*Nero* 39):

> Rome has become a house; citizens, emigrate to Veii;
> But watch out that the house does not extend that far too.

It was this usurpation of the city by the 'hated hall of a cruel king' which motivated Martial's jibe (*Liber de Spectaculis* 2.4):

> One house took up the whole of Rome.

And, to add insult to injury, the 'house' which had taken over the city was itself filled with 'buildings made to resemble cities' (Suetonius, *Nero* 31).

Conclusion

The relationship of the *Domus Aurea* to the 'monstrous' building of Caligula should make us wary. For Nero was, even in what posterity would later make out were the most scandalous excesses of his building, not as untraditional as the scholarly literature's emphasis on Neronian innovation may lead us to assume. On the contrary, everything about the *Domus Aurea* – lavish gardens, an attempt to link the Palatine with other hills in the city, luxurious decoration and fittings – all this was presaged by previous imperial building in Rome and in Italy. Nero simply went one step further than his predecessors, as he did in the design of his arch, and as he had to do in what I have suggested was an incremental visual discourse of building by successive emperors in the city. What is at stake is whether what Nero did was by definition outrageous by every standard of Roman taste and decorum (as the literary sources imply) or whether it *became*

7. Constructing decadence

the supreme symbol for outrageousness only when (and because) Nero was overthrown.

At the beginning of this chapter, I argued that imperial building was one of the emperor's most significant public activities, and that it encapsulated both the self-presentation of emperors by contrast with their predecessors and a public definition of their relationship with the populace. If we exclude the evidence of the literary polemics from Pliny and Martial to Tacitus, Suetonius and third-century writers like Dio Cassius and Philostratus (all biased against Nero and all probably embroidering on the same anti-Neronian sources), then there is little scandalous about his buildings. The range of kinds of monuments he constructed is traditional, the record of numismatic propaganda is sober and unexceptional, the innovations are all motivated by a tradition of imperial innovation in which Nero's moves were the next step. Moreover, no positive account of his works has been allowed to survive, although there must have been some.

My contention is that if Nero had not been overthrown in 68, if his reign had lasted as long as that of Augustus, or even that other philhellene builder Hadrian, there would have been nothing prodigal even about the Golden House. Certainly the history of imperial construction and the later topography of the city of Rome would have been very different. But the historians' rhetoric would have turned in the opposite direction – towards panegyric and not abuse. Instead, after the instabilities of 69, it fell to Vespasian to restore Rome.[46] His projects were traditional – for instance, the rebuilding of the temple of Capitoline Jove (sacked in the fighting of 69), a temple of Honos and Virtus, a temple of Peace. In part, his works specifically responded to Nero, contradicting with temples and public buildings the excesses of what Flavian writers were already portraying as a monstrously extravagant regime. The artificial lake of the *Domus Aurea* became the Colosseum, the temple of the Divine Claudius on the Caelian (which Nero had never got round to building) was completed, the colossus was rededicated to the sun. Vespasian's coins depicting buildings emphasised temples – both those he had built himself (like the Capitol) and previous sacred dedications, including the temple of Vesta restored by Nero.[47] Inevitably, given the image of Nero, Vespasian as builder and propagandist initiated a return to less daring and grandiloquent public gestures. Vespasian slotted into the tradition of the principate by not being another Nero, and by helping to construct a Nero like whom he could never be. As a result, Vespasian could be innovative by being conservative, and thus – as emperor – was perfectly placed to merit the approbation of the moral rhetoric of Roman historiography.

In effect, Nero only became an outrageous and prodigal builder when he fell from power. Then, the rhetoric of history turned against him and he was condemned in every respect – especially in the most visible and rhetorically potent elements in his reign, his private life and his public works. Essentially, the ancient historians made a brilliant and persuasive job of reversing causalities. Their combined argument was that the outrageous nature of Nero's actions, epitomised by murder and debauchery in private and by buildings and theatrical antics in public, caused his fall. My suggestion is that, at least in the context of his buildings, their outrageousness, and the polemic poured upon them, were not a cause but, in fact, the result of his fall.

By being toppled, Nero did more than end the Julio-Claudian dynasty. He ended also the radical nature of early imperial experimentation with the city of Rome. The *Domus Aurea* became the ultimate, notorious, stage in the Julio-Claudian pattern of luxurious encroachment onto the rest of the city, begun as early as the extensions of Augustus' house on the Palatine into a palace under Tiberius. As such, and as the supreme monument of an emperor instantly vilified, it was – along with Nero's building projects in general – damned by the rhetoric of history.

Notes

1. An editor (especially) needs editing: I am grateful to Peter Garnsey, Valerie Huet and Jeremy Tanner for their suggestions.

2. See e.g. Griffin 1984 ch. 8 'The Tyranny of Art' pp. 119-42.

3. On the modern debate see e.g Price 1980 pp. 28-43; Wallace-Hadrill 1982 pp. 32-48; Millar 1984 pp. 37-58; the essays in Raaflaub and Toher (eds.), 1990.

4. On Julio-Claudian portraiture, see Ziss 1975 and Jucker 1981 pp. 236-316.

5. Sextus Aurelius Victor, *Liber de caesaribus* 5.1-2 (cf. also the *Epitome de caesaribus* 5.2-5) with Anderson 1911 pp. 173-8. My apologies for a longish note on the so-called 'quinquennium Neronis', or Nero's period of five (good) years. Following Victor, who is himself purporting to quote Trajan, it has become traditional to assume that Nero had five good years before he went bad, and that these years were associated with his building programme. The only conceivable good years in Nero's reign (according to the Tacitean-Suetonian account) were the early ones, good by comparison with what came later and good because Nero's regents, Burrus and Seneca, were in control. Unfortunately, these were not the years when Nero did much building. Accordingly the debate has raged – was the quinquennium the first five years of Nero's reign, as argued by Lepper (1957) and Murray (1965), or the last, as argued by Thornton (1973), or indeed the middle ones, as argued by Hind (1971 and 1975)? All such argument assumes that the quinquennium must have existed and that we can believe a couple of fourth-century sources. One wonders. As Griffin points out (1984, p. 84), Nero had to be 'good' first in order to be bad later, and in order that the bad look worse. Here he conforms to the same pattern as Suetonius' Caligula and Domitian (*Gai.* 13-21, *Dom.* 4-10). Might one not suggest, as with so much else in the Neronian phantasmagoria, that the quinquennium Neronis is but another stitch in the tapestry of later myth-historical embroidery?

6. Gros 1976; Simon 1986; Zanker 1988; Favro 1992 pp. 61-84.

7. On the buildings section of the *Res Gestae*, see Sablayrolles 1981 pp. 59-77 and Elsner forthcoming.

8. cf. Millar 1984 pp. 57-8.

9. On this see Vell. Pat. II.124.3, 126.1; Suet., *Aug.* 97 and 100.

10. On the buildings of Tiberius, see Blake 1959 pp. 10-18.

11. For an account of some aspects of 'the persuasive language of imperial coinage', see Wallace-Hadrill 1986 pp. 66-87.

12. See Hill 1989 p. 53 (cf. Zanker 1988 pp. 55 and 188).

13. Hill 1989 p. 27.

14. ibid. pp. 66-7

15. ibid. pp. 50-1, 53-4. See also Kleiner 1985 pp. 99-138.

16. Mattingly 1923 no. 361, p. 271, pl. 47.2. It seems more natural to assume that this coin, with its inscription ARA PACIS, should refer to the Augustan altar in Rome (with e.g. Platner and Ashby 1929 p. 31) than to invent an altar of Pax at Lyons solely on the evidence of the coin – as does Mattingly 1923 p. clxxx.

7. Constructing decadence 125

17. A clutch of texts which denounce luxury through the image of luxurious building: Cato fr. 139 (in *Orationum Reliquiae* ed. M.T. Sblendorio Cugisi, Turin, 1982); Cic., *Pro Sest.* 43.49; Sall., *Cati.* 12.3-4, 13.1, 20.11; Vell. Pat. II.33.4; Hor., *Od.* II.15, 18, III.1, 24, *Epist.* I.1.83-7; Petron., *Sat.* 120.87-9; Sen., *Epist.* 90.8-10, 122.8. See especially the discussion of Catharine Edwards 1993, ch. 4: 'Structures of Immorality: Rhetoric, Building and Social Hierarchy'.

18. For an account of this, focussing on the *Domus Aurea*, see Morford 1968 pp. 158-79.

19. See Elsner forthcoming for a detailed account.

20. Herodot. 7.22-4; cf. the reference to Caligula outdoing Xerxes' 'famous feat of bridging the Hellespont' at Suet., *Gai.* 19.

21. See e.g. Wiseman 1987 p. 409 or Purcell 1987 pp. 198-9. On the exaggeration of this text as an account of both Nero and Gaius, see Van Essen 1954 pp. 371-98, esp. p. 373.

22. Ward Perkins 1956 pp. 209-19, esp. p. 219; MacDonald 1965 pp. 3-46; Boethius and Ward Perkins 1970 pp. 211-16, 248-50; Kleiner 1985 pp. 73, 89 and 92.

23. See Balland 1965 pp. 349-93, esp. 391-3; Thornton 1971 pp. 621-9; Phillips 1978 pp. 300-7; Thornton 1986 pp. 28-44, esp. p. 39; Thornton and Thornton 1989 pp. 96-101, 119-20.

24. Kleiner 1985 pp. 89 and 92.

25. Thornton and Thornton 1989 pp. 93-6; Blake 1959 pp. 26-8.

26. Thornton and Thornton 1989 pp. 77-91; Meiggs 1973 pp. 54-8.

27. Thornton and Thornton 1989 pp. 56-76.

28. Blake 1959 pp. 28-30.

29. Thornton and Thornton 1989 pp. 87-8, 96.

30. Mattingly 1923 nos 131-5, pp. 222-3, pl. 41.7.

31. On these projects see Blake 1959 pp. 33-6; on the gymnasium see Tamm 1970.

32. Mattingly 1923 no. 64, p. 209, pl. 39.17-18; nos 111-13, p. 215, pl. 41.1; nos 156-67, pp. 229-31, pl. 42.6-7; nos 198-204, pp. 238-9, pl. 43.8-9; nos 225-33, pp. 243-4, pl. 44.5-6; nos 319-22, p. 263, pl. 46.2; nos 374-5, p. 273, pl. 47.6; Hill 1989 pp. 10-11.

33. On the dates of the coin issues representing buildings, see Sydenham 1920 p. 63 (Ara Pacis: 60 or 64), pp. 91-2 (Janus Temple: 64-6), p. 97 (Arch: 64-5), p. 105 (Vesta Temple: 65), p. 106 (Macellum: 65-6), p. 108 (Ostia: 64-5); Mattingly 1923 p. clxviii (Macellum: 64-6), p. clxxiv (Janus Temple: 64-7), p. clxxv (Vesta Temple: 64-5), p. clxxviii (Arch: 64-5); and Sutherland 1987 p. 82 (Ostia: after 64).

34. See Mattingly 1923 nos 183-90, pp. 234-5, pl. 43.3; Kleiner 1985 pp. 99-138.

35. Mattingly 1923 nos 191-7, pp. 236-7, pl. 43.5-7; nos 335-7, p. 266, pl. 46.6; Hill 1989 p. 40.

36. Mattingly 1923 nos 101-6, p. 213, pl. 40.10-13; Hill 1989 pp. 23-4.

37. It appears from Tac., *Hist.* I.43 that the temple had been rebuilt in time for Galba's ally Piso to be murdered there in early 69.

38. See Cima 1986.

39. See Sauron 1991 pp. 19-42; Lavagne 1988 pp. 515-58; Andreae 1982 pp. 103-85; Stewart 1977 pp. 76-90; Conticello and Andreae 1974.

40. See Lavagne 1988 pp. 573-7; Andreae 1982 pp. 199-220; Zevi and Andreae 1982 pp. 114-56.

41. Tamm 1963 pp. 102-8.

42. See Lavagne 1970 pp. 673-721; Sear 1977 pp. 90-2; Lavagne 1988 pp. 579-88.

43. See Purcell 1987 pp. 198-203; Griffin 1984 pp. 133-42.

44. For this particular assault on *natura* see Hor., *Od.* II.18.17-22; Papirius Fabianus in the Elder Seneca, *Contr.* II.1.11-12; Petron., *Sat.* 120.87-9.

45. On the topography of the *Domus Aurea*, see Van Essen 1954 and generally, Boethius 1960 pp. 94-128.

46. On Vespasian's buildings see Homo 1949 pp. 365-81, Blake 1959 pp. 88-91 and Boethius and Ward Perkins 1970 pp. 217-24

47. Vespasian's coinage includes images of the restored temple of Jupiter Capitolinus (see e.g. Mattingly 1930 no. 614, p. 133, pl. 23.14; Hill 1989 p. 25), of the Augustan temple of Vesta on the Palatine (Mattingly 1930 no. 90, p. 17, pl. 2.17; Hill 1989 pp. 31-2) and the Ara Providentiae Augusti (Mattingly 1930 no. 611, p. 132, pl. 23.12; Hill 1989 p. 64), of the temple of Vesta in the Forum, restored by Nero (Mattingly 1930 no. 664, p. 151, pl. 26.9; Hill 1989 p. 23), and of the temple of Isis probably built by Gaius in the Campus Martius (Mattingly 1930 p. 123, pl. 22.7; Hill 1989 pp. 28-9). The famous coin showing the Colosseum was issued by Titus in 80-1 (Mattingly 1930 'Titus', no. 90, p. 262, pl. 50.2; Hill 1989 pp. 40-1).

Bibliography

Anderson, J.G.C. (1911) 'Trajan on the quinquennium Neronis' *JRS* 1 pp. 173-8.
Andreae, B. (1982) *Odysseus: Archaeologische des europäischen Menschenbildes*, Frankfurt.
Balland, A. (1965) 'Nova Urbs et "Neapolis", remarques sur les projets urbanistiques de Néron', *MEFR* 77 pp. 349-93.
Boethius, A. (1960) *The Golden House of Nero*, Ann Arbor.
Boethius, A. and Ward Perkins, J.B. (1970) *Etruscan and Roman architecture*, Harmondsworth.
Blake, M.E. (1959) *Roman construction in Italy from Tiberius through the Flavians*, Washington, D.C.
Cima, M. (1986) 'Il "prezioso arredo" degli Horti Lamiani', in M. Cima and E. La Rocca (eds.), *Le tranquille dimore degli dei: la residenza imperiale degli Horti Lamiani*, catalogue for an exhibition of the same name in Rome (1986), Venice, pp. 105-44.
Conticello, B. and Andreae, B. (1974) *Die Skulpturen von Sperlonga*, Antike Plastik 14, Berlin.
Edwards, C. (1993) *The politics of immorality in ancient Rome*, Cambridge.
Elsner, J. (forthcoming) 'Inventing imperium: texts and the propaganda of monuments in Augustan Rome', in J. Elsner (ed.), *Art and text in Roman culture*, Cambridge.
Van Essen, C.C. (1954) 'La topographie de la Domus Aurea Neronis', *Mededelingen der Koninklijke Nederlandse Akademie van Wetenschappen* 17 pp. 371-98.
Favro, D. (1992) 'Pater urbis: Augustus as city father of Rome', *Journal of the Society of Architectural Historians* 51 pp. 61-84.
Griffin, M.T. (1984) *Nero: the end of a dynasty*, London.
Hemsoll, D. (1990), 'The architecture of Nero's Golden House' in M. Henig (ed.) *Architecture and architectural sculpture in the Roman Empire*, Oxford, pp. 10-38.
Hill, P.V. (1989) *The monuments of ancient Rome as coin types*, London.
Hind, J.G.F. (1971) 'The middle years of Nero's reign', *Historia* 20 pp. 488-505.
——— (1975) 'Is Nero's quinquennium an enigma?', *Historia* 24 pp. 629-30.
Homo, L. (1949) *Vespasien: l'empereur du bon sens*, Paris.
Jucker, H. (1981), 'Iulisch-Claudisch Kaiser- und Prinzenporträts als "Palimpseste" ', *JDAI* 96 pp. 236-316
Kleiner, F.S. (1985) *The arch of Nero in Rome* (Archaeologica 52), Rome.
Lavagne, H. (1970) 'Le nymphée au Polyphème de la Domus Aurea', *MEFR* 82 pp. 673-721.
——— (1988) *Operosa antra*, Rome.

Lepper, F.A. (1957) 'Some reflections on the quinquennium Neronis', *JRS* 47 pp. 95-103.
MacDonald, W.L. (1965) *The architecture of the Roman empire*, vol. 1, New Haven.
Mattingly, H. (1923) *Coins of the Roman empire in the British Museum*, vol. 1, London.
――― (1930) *Coins of the Roman empire in the British Museum*, vol. 2, London.
Meiggs, R. (1973) *Roman Ostia*, Oxford.
Millar, F. (1984) 'State and subject: the impact of monarchy', in F. Millar and E. Segal (eds.), *Caesar Augustus: seven aspects*, Oxford.
Morford, M.P.O. (1968) 'The distortion of the Domus Aurea tradition', *Eranos* 66 pp. 158-79.
Murray, O. (1965) 'The "quinquennium Neronis" and the Stoics', *Historia* 14 pp. 41-61.
Phillips, E.J. (1978) 'Nero's new city', *Rivista di Filologia* 106 pp. 300-7.
Platner, S.B. and Ashby, T. (1929) *A topographical dictionary of Rome*, Oxford.
Price, S.R.F. (1980) 'Between man and god: sacrifice in the Roman imperial cult', *JRS* 70 pp. 28-43.
Purcell, N. (1987) 'Town in country and country in town', in E.B. MacDougall (ed.), *Ancient Roman villa gardens* (Dumbarton Oaks colloquium on the history of landscape architecture 10), Washington, D.C.
Raaflaub, K. and Toher, M. (eds.) (1990) *Between republic and empire: interpretations of Augustus and his principate*, Berkeley.
Sablayrolles, R. (1981) 'Espace urbain et propagande politique: L'organisation du centre de Rome par Auguste (Res Gestae 19 à 21)', *Pallas* 28 pp. 59-77.
Sauron, G. (1991) 'De Buthrote à Sperlonga: à propos d'une étude récente sur la thème de la grotte dans les décors romains', *RA* pp. 3-42.
Sear, F.B. (1977) *Roman wall and vault mosaics*, Heidelberg.
Simon, E. (1986) *Augustus: Kunst und Leben in Rom um die Zeitenwende*, Munich.
Stewart, A.F. (1977) 'To entertain an emperor: Sperlonga, Laokoon and Tiberius at the dinner-table', *JRS* 67 pp. 76-90.
Sutherland, C.H.V. (1987) *Roman history and coinage 44 BC – AD 69*, Oxford.
Sydenham, E.A. (1920) *The coinage of Nero*, London.
Tamm, B. (1963) *Auditorium and palatium* (Stockholm studies in classical archaeology 2), Stockholm.
――― (1970) *Neros Gymnasium in Rom* (Stockholm studies in classical archaeology 7), Stockholm.
Thornton, M.K. (1971) 'Nero's new deal', *TAPA* 102 pp. 621-9.
――― (1973) 'The enigma of Nero's quinquennium', *Historia* 22 pp. 570-82.
――― (1986) 'Julio-Claudian building programs: eat, drink and be merry', *Historia* 35 pp. 28-44.
Thornton, M.K. and R.L. (1989) *Julio-Claudian building programs: a quantitative study in political management*, Wauconda, Il.
Wallace-Hadrill, A. (1982), 'Civilis princeps: between citizen and king', *JRS* 72 pp. 32-84.
――― (1986) 'Image and authority in the coinage of Augustus', *JRS* 76 pp. 66-87.
Ward Perkins, J.B. (1956) 'Nero's Golden House', *Antiquity* 30 pp. 209-19.
Wiseman, T.P. (1987) 'Conspicui postes tectaque digna deo: the public image of aristocratic and imperial housing in the late republic and early empire', in *L'urbs: espace urbain et histoire* (Collection de l'École Française de Rome 98), Rome.
Zanker, P. (1988) *The power of images in the age of Augustus*, Ann Arbor.
Zevi, F. and Andreae, B.(1982) 'Gli scavi sottomarini di Baia', *La Parola del Passato* 203 pp. 114-56.
Ziss, K. (1975) *L'iconographie des princes Julio-Claudiens à temps d'Auguste et de Tibère*, Warsaw.

Part III

Tropes of Literature

8

Persius and the decoction of Nero

Emily Gowers

Stumbling towards his last stage role, a tragic death in rags, Suetonius' Nero scoops up some water from a puddle and scoffs to his depleted audience: *Haec est Neronis decocta* ('This is Nero's boiled-down water').[1] Nero's contemporary, Persius, seals his last will and testament, the posthumously published *Satires*, with a similar-sounding metaphor: *si aliquid decoctius audis* ('if you are willing to hear something more boiled-down').[2] In Nero's case, we have Pliny to explain the point of the joke: among Nero's more harmless experiments was the invention of concentrated water, heated to boiling point, then cooled with snow.[3] With Persius, we have to turn to the etymology of 'satire' ('full, or satisfied, dish') to see the irony: one tiny text will boil down the bloated stuffing of Lucilius and the bland concoctions of Horace into an intense and biting concentrate, a medicinal dose of vinegar or hellebore.

This paper will take the metaphor of 'decoction' that the two texts share, and suggest that the repetition is more than a coincidence, that these two Neronians' final solutions give us a taste of their place in history, as thwarted latecomers, burnt-out prodigies and pre-destined bankrupts. By Nero I do not mean the historical figure, but the myth of Nero, created not only by the man himself but also by the later historians who wrote his life: Suetonius, Tacitus and Dio. However, what is strange about Nero's Rome is that his contemporaries provided the material from which to build myths. I shall suggest that Persius, like other Neronian writers, played a vital part in shaping those later biographies.

With their galloping consumption of the genres of Augustan poetry – satire, epic, pastoral, panegyric – Neronian writers seem to have some premonition that they will die young, and that their era will only briefly survive them.[4] The anonymous eulogist of Piso ('not yet in his twentieth year'), Persius, writing his will and looking ahead to his grandsons, or Lucan measuring his full-grown epic against Virgil's juvenilia:[5] most Neronians write as though they are conscious that the heat is on, that they will be burnt out all too soon. In retrospect, even their style seems infected by the spirit of the age. Seneca, in Fronto's eyes, was propelled by hectic hurry into epigrams that were like 'febrile little plums'.[6] And the model for all this feverish haste was Nero himself. Or so it seems.

Neronian literature, more that that of any other period in Rome, demands to be read in the shadow, or rather, glare, of its ruler. The sun-king always penetrates the dark studies and rural retreats that confine Neronian writing.[7] Calpurnius' shade-seeking eclogues, for example, end up in the heat-haze of the urban amphitheatre; their hero is not *lentus in umbra*, at ease in the shade, but *lentus ab urbe* (7.1), glued to the city and its glittering emperor.[8] Petronius' Trimalchio, a tyrant at the provincial dinner-table, apes feasts in the metropolis.[9] The *Aetna* poet asks his Muse for the causes of fire, to name the force that rages against *imperium*, and wields its screaming heat (*quid fremat imperium, quid raucos torqueat aestus*), and one answer to these natural questions is: Nero himself.[10] In short, we cannot help reading Nero into Neronian literature.

That is why, in accounts given by the historians and biographers, Neronian literature is always born of an interaction, negative or positive, between Nero and his writers: joint texts emerge from royal soirées, Seneca prompts panegyrics, Petronius' deathbed 'confessions' are an alternative *res gestae Neronis*, Lucan steals the emperor's thunder and vents it into a latrine.[11] The most literary of emperors is the one who is most often ghosted or parodied by his own contemporaries. He provides the inspiration, the context, for their own prolific output, just as they write the script and pile up the baroque concentrate of Nero for later chronicles. According to another set of myths, though, Neronian literature exists in spite of Nero. Under so-called Neronian repression, a literary ferment seethes; writing thrives on opposition, on being stifled and kept in the dark. Tacitus, for example, records that Veiento's books were snapped up while suppressed, and forgotten as soon as they were published.[12] Calpurnius' hissing grape-press brings it home: 'the wine-presses are squeezing wet grapes, and seething juice froths with hoarse whispering.'[13]

Persius' satires are a special case, since satire is writing that, in theory, cannot exist without contemporary reference. And in this area comes the oddest Neronian 'fulfilment' of all: instead of Horace's neutral compromise, which, most unsatirically, propped up the Augustan regime, we have Persius' muzzled underground bark, the best advertisement for imperial indifference, and an indirect sign of the independence that satire needs if it is to be the vehicle of a society's free speech. Nero, we are told, was remarkably tolerant of lampoons; or is that too hard to believe?[14] Is the truth that he was really autistic? Was this king Midas really deaf to his barber's whispers, like Persius' Natta, buried in layer after layer of insensible fat?[15] The historians, after all, make Nero so unaware of the outside world that he thought he could live as a private citizen, acting unconscious of the long goodbye symphonies performed by his own audience (spectators feigned death at Nero's theatre so that they could be carried out).[16]

Even Persius, a satirist who manages so well to insulate himself from the outside world, cannot be read without letting Nero in. Prize open the seal, and we find a subversive cackler, muttering secrets into his hole in the ground. Dig around, as the scholiasts did, and we unearth Nero too, hinted at by unnaturally loud stage whispers, a tyrannical emperor ridiculed by a naughty boy behind his back. The legend according to which Persius' tutor Cornutus posthumously censored his explicit allusions to King Midas (at 1.121) is just the sort of invention we would expect: Nero is always in the back of our minds when we read Persius.[17]

In the case of satire, the myths are naturally those of perfect opposition: the emperor and the satirist, King Midas and the barber, obscene voluptuary and chaste Stoic novice. So much so that the similarities between the two have been obscured. Perhaps we should really see all Neronian poets as doubles for the emperor, pseudo-Nerones.[18] Nero and his writers, despite the gulf between them, shared the inherited burden of Augustan perfection, the responsibilities of early promise and the expected standards of another Golden Age. According to Suetonius, Nero promised to rule *ex Augusti praescripto*, according to the example laid down by Augustus.[19] For a writer, the words *ex praescripto* would have had a different meaning: the Augustans had already written everything in advance, timed the golden age of literature in one glorious *kairos*, or perfect hour. Everything to come was fated to be 'late'. The metaphor of 'decoction' explored here is one of many links between myth and literature that help to shape the Neronian legacy.

Let us look at the word in more detail. *Decoquere* literally means 'to boil down', usually of liquids. It is very frequent in Pliny, who writes for example of boiling down grape juice (*sapa, mustum*) and other substances into half, or, more usually, a third of their original volume.[20] 'Boiling down' was also seen as a distorted function in nature, an over-hastened version of the 'cooking' (Greek *pepsis*) of plants by the sun. Over-cooking by too intense a heat, according to Pliny, leads to a premature hardening of grapes: *acini decocuntur in callum* ('young grapes shrivel into a hard lump').[21] The word can also be used metaphorically: of stewing or shrivelling one's body, in a bath, for instance, or of reducing the excesses of early rhetorical exuberance.[22] It can also signify squandering one's worldly substance, or being insolvent.[23] Whatever the particular meaning of the word – becoming shrivelled, skimmed, concentrated, boiled away or broke – it always involves the idea of a final stage, a last burning out of substance.[24] Its mirror opposite in this context is precocity – *praecoquere, praecox* – ripening too early. Both these organic stages can be seen as significant metaphors for Nero's reign and Neronian literature. If Augustus timed his reign for the perfect *kairos* and seized the chance of mature government while the time was ripe,[25] then Nero's age was a conflation of infantile precocity and premature decline. Both Nero and the Neronians tried to speed towards a revival of Augustan maturity; outgrown adolescents took on themselves too great a task, and withered away too soon.

But this is not just the perspective of hindsight. What soon emerges is that it is not only the later historians reconstructing Nero's life – Tacitus, Suetonius, Dio and Pliny – who are drawn to organic metaphors of precocity and decline to describe the Neronian predicament, but Nero's contemporaries too. The conclusions we should draw from this are not entirely clear. There will always be the problems of chronology and truth: are the lives of the poets as mythical as those of their emperors; are we inevitably reading into Neronian writing the myths we have shaped with hindsight; or is there some sense of urgency in the contemporaries themselves that sets the temperature for all later representations of this age?

Nero

The more concrete events are as follows: Nero was a young man when he began his reign and still young when he died. There was a fire, some *spectacula*, many deaths. Out of this is shaped the grand opera of Neronian mythology. The source of the metaphor of decoction may lie in a simple matter of numbers. Compare the length of the two reigns: Augustus ruled from an indefinite date between 31 and 27 BC to AD 14 (44–41 years), Nero from 54 to 68 (a little under 14 years, more or less a third of that time).[26] Comparisons of this kind were common in antiquity. Vespasian dreamed that he saw a balance with himself and his sons on one side, Claudius and Nero on the other: each side would reign for the same space of time.[27] Vespasian's mother, Suetonius tells us, dreamed in organic metaphors about the future of her children: the first was thin and soon withered (*exilem et cito arefactum*), the second was strong and tall, and the third was the image of a tree, which meant that he would be a Caesar.[28] Nero was a Caesar, but he, too, turned out to be quick-withering. If *decoquere* in its literal sense of concentrating liquids means reducing to a third of the original volume, then Nero's reign was a decoction of his great-grandfather's, bringing with it its own pungent end, the end of the house.

In the historians' eyes, then, Nero was fated to be a man in a hurry. If he was to concentrate Augustus' lifetime into his own short span, he had plenty of catching up to do. His youth seemed no handicap: for a boy who spurted at eleven, Augustus' Trojan games were child's play. His puberty was public (he shaved his beard at his own Juvenalia); and of all the premature honours offered by the senate he refused only one, the title of Pater Patriae (Father of his Country) – on grounds of implausibility.[29] He soon towered over his genuine rival Britannicus,[30] and propagated his own image by surrounding himself with perfect physical specimens of outsize youth.[31] Later he outgrew adolescence without achieving genuine maturity, discarding his tutors for the guidance of his own ancestors.[32] His reign had a permanently childish colour, even after he had shaken off childhood.[33]

Nero's mental activities, whether artistic or sadistic, were propelled by the same sense of impatience. We are told that he could not wait for the five-yearly festivals in Greece to come round again, so he conflated them all into one year, speeded up their anniversaries. His own festival, the Neronia, was also revived before time (*cum tardum videretur*, 'because it seemed too slow').[34] At first he resisted the attempts of the Senate to bring the new year in early in his honour; later he jumped the gun by re-naming April, May and June *Neroneus, Claudius* and *Germanicus* after himself, leaping in ahead of Julius and Augustus.[35] He was so impatient for the death of his old aunt Domitia that he could not even wait for her to die naturally of old age. Leaning over her sickbed, he allowed her to stroke his downy beard ('for he was already well-grown'), and, when she said, 'As soon as I hear this is gone I shall die happy', he replied, 'I'll shave it off at once', and had her dispatched within days of her already imminent death. The two poles of maturity – puberty and death – were unnaturally induced in the same instant.[36]

In other Neronian scenarios, Augustan *maturitas* is replaced by Nero's unnatural contempt for the old, which leaves behind memorable images of youth and age jostling together: we are told that he made octogenarians dance at his Juvenalia; jeered at the prematurely grey hairs on one of his victim's heads; had Thrasea killed because he had a gloomy expression like that of a tutor; Pallas killed because he guarded his fortune by living too long (*longa senecta*); and even had grain that was corrupted by age thrown into the Tiber.[37] But in the end it was grey-haired Galba, kept on ice since boyhood, who had the last laugh.[38]

There are two classic models for understanding this emphasis on Nero's impatience and his artificially speeded, ultimately fruitless life. One is the Roman moralisation of luxury. The other is the model of good growth and its perversion in the vegetable world, set out most clearly in Detienne's analysis (1977) of the Greek myth of the Gardens of Adonis.[39] Impatience was always one of the motives ascribed to the production of luxurious goods. Seneca, for example, compares the topsy-turvy quality of contemporary Roman morals to a notorious dish of seafood in which all the most expensive fruits of the sea were scandalously commingled. Incomprehensibly to us, he attributes the concept to impatience: the dish is designed for people who do not have time to savour each ingredient individually, but want to engulf the lot in one mouthful. *Sapores coguntur in unum* ('all the flavours are forced into one taste'), as he puts it. The same words are used by Suetonius of Nero's treatment of the festivals: *cogi in unum annum* ('forced into one year').[40]

As for vegetable analogies, it may seem artificial, perhaps, to graft Greek mythology on to Rome. But the Gardens of Adonis alluded to by Plato and Aristophanes provide the best analogy for the fast-burgeoning, quick-withering growth of this suspiciously Hellenophile emperor. The Athenian festival of Adonis, with its little pots of ephemeral herbs, belongs, according to Detienne, at one end of a mythological spectrum modelled directly on types of organic development. Normally the processes of human life appear to follow those of nature: the sun cooks the earth, which in turn cooks the juices of plants: man reproduces this with the 'cooking' of agriculture, the 'cooking' of sperm in the male, the infant in the female, and, of course, cooking in the kitchen. At the other extreme, the world of extra-marital and sterile love mimics sterility in nature: perfumes, the empty spices that stimulate unproductive love-making, are at the opposite end of the plant scale from sexual suppressants like lettuce. The festival of Adonis took place in midsummer: stifling heat was the right temperature for burning spices and inciting unnatural lust, and for the rapid growth and sudden withering of the symbolic gardens.[41]

This contrast between normal growth and sterile precocity is what shapes the mythology of Nero's reign into the polar opposite of that of Augustus. The snippet of information in Suetonius, for example, that Nero's surviving admirers used to plant spring and summer flowers on his grave looks like an allusion to the myth of eternal ephebic youth.[42] Vegetable metaphors crop up, too, in the narration of post-Augustan dynastic struggles. As Pliny's strained analogies between the plant world and the human world show (in his hands, modern horticulture, like modern civilization, becomes a catalogue of abortions, adoptions and adulteries[43]), the language of the nursery-man can be fruitfully transplanted to historiography. Pliny tells us, for example, that all trees mature more quickly (*celerius adolescunt*) if the suckers are removed and nourishment concentrated into one stem (*unam stirpem*).[44] This was a recipe for dynastic continuity too. Nero was a grafted plant, ousting the genuine stock with the same 'peculiar impudence' shown, Pliny tells us, by plums grafted on to nut trees, which 'keep the appearance of their parent stock, but acquire the juice of the new plant'.[45]

Tacitus preserves the fruit-growing image at *Ann.* 13.14: Britannicus was the *veram dignamque stirpem* ('the true and genuine stock'); Nero was *insitus et adoptivus* ('grafted and inserted') into the Claudian house by the harmful actions of his mother.

Nero's fast burgeoning seemed at first to presage a new spring for Rome, after an alternating succession of imperfectly aged rulers: a late-comer, a hooligan and a dotard. The images of his early years are always of golden rebirth.[46] Tacitus presents Claudius' premature senility as the autumn to Nero's false spring: during one ripe October near the end, he makes Messalina cavort in vintage costume ('When Autumn was fully grown (*autumno adulto*), she celebrated a mock grape-harvest all over the house. Wine-presses were squeezed, vats flowed, her women dressed in skins and frolicked like sacrificing or raving Bacchantes. She herself had flowing hair and shook a thyrsus; at her side was Silius crowned with ivy, wearing buskins and tossing his head, while all around him a deranged chorus wailed'), before being carried off in a wheelbarrow like a pile of dead leaves.[47]

But precocity always had its nemesis in early withering. The word *praecox*, precocious, early-ripening, may look like the opposite of *decoctus*, but the two can sometimes be used interchangeably. Pliny, as we saw, uses *decoquere* of grapes blighted by untimely heat (*calore intempestivo*): 'Young grapes shrivel (*decocuntur*) into a hard lump.' But in another passage he describes exactly the same process, and uses *praecoquere* instead: 'Harm is done by the heat, and the young grapes are ripened before time (*praecocuntur*) into a hard lump.'[48] Aristotle in the *Physics* puts among things that grow and wither away 'the precocious flowering of the sensual adolescent and the accelerated growth of corn that has not been firmly embedded in the ground'. Or, as Simplicius puts it: 'just as a great heat hastens germination of corn, sensuality and the quest for pleasure provoke a more rapid growth; premature adolescence results in premature old age.'[49] The proverb 'You are more sterile than the gardens of Adonis' sums it up: too sudden growth is ephemeral and never reaches maturity. Plato's word for these immature gardens, *paidia*, is also the one Dio uses to describe the interests like water-organs that Nero never outgrew.[50]

Nero's choice between the women in his life is that of an Adonis, too. The faithful wife Octavia is unfairly declared sterile, while Nero sheds his seed on fruitless ground: first the marriage with the male Pythagoras; then Poppaea, the beauty who 'could not distinguish between husbands and adulterers', prayed that she would die in her prime, and who was embalmed, oriental-fashion, stuffed with Arabian spices, in clouds of incense.[51] Nero's only scion, the Infanta Claudia Augusta, is nipped in the bud: the fuss and pomp surrounding her birth (including a Temple of Fertility) are dismissed by Tacitus as *fluxa* (transient), because of her early death.[52] This sense of foreboding about precocity is also contained in the prophetic juxtapositions of youth and old age in accounts of Nero's reign. In Tacitus' dialogue between Seneca and Nero, Nero admits that, while Seneca's gifts to him are permanent, his own to Seneca (which include villas and gardens) are perishable.[53] Ephemeral sensationalism is also the basis of Nero's building programme. The theatre, for example, which once had a permanent site (Tac. *Ann.* 14.21: *perpetuas sedes*), is transformed into a short-lived bloom, continually raked up and planted from scratch (*immensum sumptu singulos per annos consurgeret et destrueretur*), forced into yearly bloom like those hardy quinquennials, the festivals, that the edifice contained.[54]

In the natural world, as well, Nero's reign is staged as an Adonia, midsummer madness under blazing Sirian heat. Neronian meteorology is always high-temperature, Neronian scenographics always cataclysmic: the earthquake in the theatre at Naples, comets (presaging heat and destruction), the fire he fiddled to destroy the city. Even in his 'Games for the Eternity of the Empire', Nero put on a strange rehearsal for the end of the Julio-Claudian house: a performance of Afranius' *Incendium*, in which the furniture carried out of the burning house was up for grabs by the public.[55] The universal conflagration prophesied by the Stoics came virtually to pass in Nero's reign: when someone said, 'When I am dead, may the earth be consumed by fire', the impatient emperor replied, 'No, rather while I live.'[56] Meanwhile, Tacitus' backdrop to Nero's performances, Corbulo's campaigns, spanned record extremes of temperature: bitter cold in Armenia (icy ground had to be dug up before the tents could be pitched; a soldier's hands froze until they dropped off from the stumps 13.35); until spring burgeoned, again strangely out of step with Nero's deceptive adolescence (*donec ver adolesceret* 13.36); finally, drought and extreme heat (14.24: *penuria aquae, fervida aestas*). Tacitus even sees a sinister new twist in Nero's modernisation programme, when the old winding streets of Rome were cleared to make way for shadeless boulevards: 'Without the protection of shade, they blazed with a more unbearable heat.'[57] Dio's 'Golden Days' of Nero degenerate all too soon into an unremitting glare.[58]

The vegetable world withers at Nero's hands, too. Tacitus' ironic chronicling of the miraculous rebirth of the Ruminal fig tree has to be seen in the context of many more appropriate natural metaphors for a destructive reign scattered through the anecdotes.[59] Livia, we are told, planted trees that died shortly before Nero's death, perfectly spanning the Julian dynasty. Pliny saw in his youth the trees kept 'evergreen and young' (*virides iuvenesque*) by Caecina Largus, until Nero unnaturally 'hastened' (*adcelerasset*) their end in the Great Fire. And a cypress tree in the precinct of Vulcan fell down and was left lying in Nero's last years.[60]

Like the backdrops to his reign, Nero's body is also the site of extreme clashes in temperature. Seethingly hot by nature, he needs to compensate with artificial cooling devices.[61] *Neronis decocta*, Nero's drink of water boiled, then cooled by snow, appears in another guise as a bathing fetish: warm baths in winter, icy plunges in summer.[62] Both habits are frowned on by the moralists. In Pliny's opinion, the craze for iced drinks involves an unnatural confusion of the seasons.[63] Seneca, too, chastises those whose heartburn makes them long for snow. At the other extreme, he also condemns stewing in hot baths (*decoquere corpus*). *Decoquere* this time suggests the final, shrivelled stage of the human body.[64]

Nero's need to cool down was sometimes metaphorical too: Lucan's biographer tells us that he left in anger during one of the poet's readings, and called a meeting *refrigerandi sui causa* (to pour cold water over the whole performance). Other odd details of his regimen seem to have had the same purpose: the lead plates he used to preserve his voice were also the ancient equivalent of cold showers; the chives he ate to ease his throat sound like a memory of those refrigerating anti-Adonian salads.[65]

Nero's regimen for his own body sets the style for his treatment of other people's bodies as well. In Tacitus' chronicle, death scenes are normalised into a monotonous-seeming routine.[66] Each one, however, is an imaginative variation on the twin themes of haste and over-boiling that characterise the reign as a whole; each death a different kind of concentration. For example, Nero's saunas and Poppaea's beauty treatment (she loved to soak (*macerare*) her body in a 'stew' of asses' milk[67]), find their perversion in Octavia's murder. The innocent girl dies in an over-heated bath, smothered by the steam.[68] Haste is the constant factor in all Neronian deaths, whether in their individual speed, their accumulative acceleration, or their effect on the life-span of the victims. The death of Vestinius, for example, involves speeding up a vigorous life unnaturally and bringing it to a premature, over-heated end: 'Everything was hurried through in a trice ... still vigorous, he was carried into the bath, and plunged into hot water.'[69] Seneca's own disquisitions on the uselessness of soaking (*decoquere corpus*) in the bath-tub[70] are prophetic of his own suffocation: 'He got into a pool of hot water ... he was lifted into a bath and was stifled by the steam.'[71] For Martial, the baths of Nero allow the heat and intemperance of their founder to linger on: 'The sixth hour is hot with the excessive heat of Nero['s baths].'[72]

Another method of death is poisoning, the paramount example here being the death of Britannicus. Tacitus tells us that Nero got past the tasters by cunningly producing a harmless hot drink, which he then cooled down with poisoned water.[73] Preparing the poison took several stages, each one producing a stronger concentrate.[74] Nero had first tried it out on a pig. When the animal took too long to die, he boiled the poison up again: *iterum ac saepius recoctum*. Or, as Tacitus puts it: *decoquitur virus cognitis antea venenis rapidum* ('the poison was boiled down, once previous tests of its ingredients had proved that it would work fast').[75] Surfacing once again, the word *decoquere* reminds us that Nero as poisoner uses the same techniques from his mindless experiments with iced water. And the word *rapidum* is the essence of this reign, where concentration of time and potency are simultaneous.[76]

One more typically 'Neronian' death-scene involves the simultaneous dispatching of a daughter, a father and a grandmother (Tac. *Ann*. 16.11). Fate, Tacitus says, at least observed the proper order of death and allowed the girl to die last. But this almost simultaneous destruction of three generations is reminiscent of a passage in Pliny which says that vines that display three stages at once — ripeness, swelling and blossoming (*alia maturescunt, alia turgescunt, alia florent*) — are called mad, *insanae*.[77] Nero was himself a plant forced on a hot-bed: to hurry through these conflated deaths and *then* pass retrospective sentence was, for Tacitus, another sign of his own disregard for proper seasons, his own insanity.[78]

Seen in retrospect, Nero's early growth marked him out for a premature end, a final show of fireworks before the end of the Julian house. An indefinite *nondum*, 'not yet', the word that casts the opening blight over Calpurnius' Indian summer, was also the tactful answer to Nero's impossible questions. When Nero asked Passienus Crispus if he had slept with his own sister, '*Nondum*' was his politic reply.[79] The word has a special resonance for Nero's reign: it suggests temporising in the face of imminent doom, staving off the end. Suetonius' Nero, faced with death, protests that the fated hour has not yet come: *nondum adesse fatalem horam.*[80]

Even so, Nero had already missed his chance. In a rhetorical context, Quintilian sees early exuberance as a positive starting-point from which a more temperate eloquence can be honed down: 'I like to see the raw material somewhat excessive and more extravagant than it need be. From that starting-point the years will skim off (*decoquent*) much of the froth.'[81] Here *decoquere* stands for a constructive process. But Quintilian is also wary of the dangers of precocity, how it may not always bear fruit: 'the kind of talent that ripens early is rarely fruitful.'[82] Seneca might have learned something from Alexander's philosopher-tutor Callisthenes, who announced sagely that he prayed for 'late immortality' (*sera immortalitas*) for the young king, because the same fruit could not be precocious and long-lasting (*nullum esse eundem et diuturnum et praecoquem fructum*).[83] Or again from Cicero, who accused another moral bankrupt, Antony, of precocious insolvency in his teens: *praetextatum te decoxisse.*[84] The extra anomaly lies in the fact that *decoxisse* should refer to the last stage of life, *praetextatum* ('wearing the teenage toga') to the first. Like Antony, Nero conflated the two stages.

That explains why the words *Neronis decocta* in Suetonius' death-scene (48) also contain an allusion to bankruptcy, burning out, the final mean end. Nero's ironic name for the stagnant puddle concentrates all the sybaritic drinks and scalding poisons into his moment of nemesis. On the way, his horse had been thrown by the smell of a corpse thrown into the road, an omen that marks out the final stage of a rapidly boiled life: putrefaction. And under Suetonius' autopsy, Nero's precocious body ends up like that of an etiolated, rotting plant, gone to seed: spotty and smelly (*corpore maculoso et fetido*), with a thick neck (*cervice obesa*), projecting stomach (*ventre proiecto*) and weedy legs (*gracillimis cruribus*). Though his robust physique supported him through the rampings of luxury, this victim of a rapid spurt shrivelled early.[85] Aulus Gellius, discussing the change in meaning of the word *mature* from 'at the right time' to 'too soon, hastily', defines ripe fruit as that which is neither 'raw and bitter' (*cruda et inmitia*), nor 'over-luscious and rotten' (*caduca et decocta*).[86] Nero's decocted life inverts the Augustan text *speude bradeos* ('hasten slowly') to create its own rushed fruitlessness. His death is not just *acerba*, prematurely raw and bitter, as Tacitus describes the funeral rites of Britannicus, but also prematurely corrupted.[87] That final meaning of *decoctus* is embedded in an *exemplum* from Epictetus, which lays down Nero's enduring legacy to history. Some men, he says, have a bad image attached inextricably to their names; when people are offered coins, for example, they are superstitious about taking any which have the heads of bad emperors on them. If it is Trajan, a man will say, 'Give it here.' If it has the Neronian imprint (*Neronianon charactera*), he will say, 'Take it away, it's unacceptable, it's rotten (*sapron*).'[88]

Persius

According to the historians, then, Nero's reign tried unnaturally to collapse a lifetime into its short span: it was both callow and raw, and prematurely rotten.

However we are to explain it, the poetry of Nero's contemporary Persius is also obsessed with conflating the normal stages of life. How does Persius so conveniently squeeze the essence of this reign into his six satires?

Once again, the arithmetic is surprisingly neat. If Nero's reign was a boiled-down third of Augustus', then the same is true of Persius: his six satires are exactly a third of his Augustan predecessor Horace's eighteen. Nero's decoction of his great-grandfather's reign is figured on the page in Persius' concentrated epitome of Horatian satire. What are we to make of this? Persius could hardly have known in advance that Nero's reign would be so short. Can we countenance the theory of the *Vita* that Cornutus shortened the book to make it seem 'more complete': did he lop off the end of the book to simulate a perfect Neronian decoction? Or must we once again believe in a spirit of the age, impelled by a sense of urgency, rushing ahead to its prematurely shrivelled end?

In one sense, Persius' concentrate and Nero's arrive at the same solution from different directions. Persius offers his reader *aliquid decoctius* (1.125), satire modestly diminished. According to Suetonius, Nero once promised a literary audience *aliquid sufferti* ('something full, puffed out'), which, paradoxically, would have been a more 'natural' form for the bloated form *satura*.[89] Did Suetonius choose *aliquid sufferti* as an ironic parody of Persius' *aliquid decoctius*, an empty promise that Nero would default on at his bankrupt death? Nero's most monstrous projects – the history of Rome in 400 books, the epic on Troy, the colossal statue, and the longed-for grand slam of Greek prizes – are at the opposite aesthetic extreme from Persius' precious elixir.[90] But most of them were unfinished. When Nero asked Cornutus for advice on his 400-book history, the philosopher replied that it was too long and no one would read it. Nero pointed out that Chrysippus had written more books. Cornutus replied: Yes, but his books show men how to live.[91] Persius' concentrate, a digest of Chrysippus' Stoic stockpile, is also opposed by its moral seriousness to anything Nero wrote. Behind *aliquid decoctius* is a pun on *aliquid sapientius*, 'something more flavoursome, more pungent', and also 'something wiser'.[92] Persius' saintly epitaph in the *Vita* (a pure and virtuous young man, devoted to his female relations, who knelt at the feet of the philosophers, who met Seneca too late to be taken in by him, who chastised even the emperor for his sins) is anti-Neronian in its construction.

Here, however, I shall consider what Persius has in common with Nero, and how his feverish last words, spoken in retreat from the hectic city (*turbida Roma* 1.5), take the temperature of Neronian Rome.

Persius Flaccus, like Nero, took the name of his ancestor, grafting himself on to the branches of Horatius Flaccus while also adopting himself into the hard philosophical school of Cornutus (cf. *cornea fibra* 1.47, 'horny fibre').[93] Even his name, Persius Flaccus, suggests both precocity and premature decay. *Persicum* is the Latin for a peach, a horticultural usurper and lightweight. Martial writes about precocious peaches grafted onto apricot trees: 'Early peaches. We were once cheap peaches on our mothers' branches. Now we are precious peaches on adopted branches.'[94] Calpurnius, too (whether or not he is Neronian), uses an image of peaches grafted on to plum-trees: 'my skill marries the pear to the apple, and forces grafted peaches to supplant precocious plums.'[95] Persius ripened early; still covered with peachy down, he provides us, next to Lucan, with the most convenient contemporary template or obverse for the precocious emperor. Lucan's reverence for Persius ('he so admired Persius's poems that ... he could not restrain himself from shouting that these were real poems and his own just child's play') anticipates Crashaw's gift to Cowley of two green apricots, which, he protests, have more in common with the giver than the precociously mature younger man.[96]

Flaccus, by contrast, should be a synonym for *decoctus*; *aliquid decoctius*, writing in its last, burnt-out, boiled-down phase, is what Persius offers us. Peaches, according to Pliny, were the most ephemeral of fruit (*non aliud fugacius*), lasting only two days at most after they were picked.[97] Persius' name, then, sums up what is distorted about his notion of time. A split adult on the brink of civic life, a novice who takes on the voice of his tutor, Persius leaps ahead of Nero, sums up his life for him. He looks ahead with foresight as clear as the historians' retrospective vision over his own tiny span, from uncooked childhood to life's rotten legacy. A sense of lateness hits him prematurely; his youth is pre-doomed. The chaste epitaph in the *Vita* is belied by Persius' text itself, a stew of secretions, obscene organs, the body stripped down to its offal: a hard recipe for adolescence. The concentrate Persius sets his sights on at the beginning is not a pure elixir but a dose of decay, a vision of the world as a rotten abattoir of stinking flesh: it boils down what Nero has to show for himself at the end.

There is no space here to stretch tiny Persius on the rack to his full extent. Just a few passages will show how he leaves behind the traces for later interpretations of Nero.

Satire 1, with its disembodied voices and ostentatious false starts, offers posterity a simulacrum of Nero's lost works, the focus of dispute among the historians. For Tacitus, Nero's 'literary circle' was a pretext for plagiarism, the joint conflation of disjointed ideas. Yet Suetonius claimed to have seen Nero's rough jottings with his own eyes, a muddle of crossings-out.[98] A pool of voices, or one split and undecided one, speaking to thin air? Who will read this, Persius asks (1.2). The answer boomerangs back: no one. Suetonius pierces Nero's bubble of pretence too. The emperor did not rule by consensus but by reading proposals in solitary confinement: 'Whenever he withdrew for consultation, he did not discuss anything with other people or openly, but made them each write down their opinions, and he would read them in secret, then pronounce on the matter according to his own whim, but as though it were the view of the majority.'[99] Whether they are collaborative efforts (Persius edited by Cornutus, Nero ghosted by Seneca) or the products of a split mind, both writers' works invite explanations of their disjointedness. With self-centred Nero, we have the beginnings of the myth of artistic loneliness. He was an autistic who needed an audience. He toyed with his water-organs in moments of crisis, but sent word to a star actor that he was taking advantage of the emperor's busy days.[100] He landscaped the Golden House in the form of a wilderness (*in modum solitudinum*), but still considered Rome itself, the theatre of Pompey and the Circus Maximus, not a big enough arena for his talent.[101]

Persius, like Nero, is a divided voice on his own private stage. Just as the solid singularity of Augustus split into a lucky dip of rulers, alternating old and young, so Persius banishes the middle men of Horace, all that easy *mediocritas*, and takes every part, tutor and pupil, reprobate and mature instructor, for himself. Not for him the carefree *mañana* of his uncles on their sunbeds, or the ease of the rent boy, transformed from blooming youth into the withered onions and boiled buttocks of sad old age.[102]

The beginnning of Satire 3 is the best example of Persius' conflation of times. The satirist lies in bed, with the noonday sun beating down on his ruminations. An invisible friend stirs him: *iamdudum coquit* ('it's been baking for ages'). The weather and time outside the darkened room set the temperature and the clock for Neronian writing: just before high noon, *kairos*, yet burdened with a sense of lateness.[103] It is the morning after the night before, and hungover Persius needs to be boiled down, skimmed like a jar of Falernian wine.[104] A specific time, a specific temperature, perhaps, but this is also the poem where Persius anatomises himself not just as a fermenting jar of must, but as an unbaked piece of clay (21-2: *maligne/ respondet viridi non cocta fidelia limo*: 'when struck the pot rings false – responds/ But grudgingly, with its green clay as yet unfired'). He is prematurely rotten and still uncooked at the same time.[105] Outside the window is stale pastoral: the herd under the flattened tree, the crops roasted by the insane dog-star (*siccas insana canicula messes/ iam dudum coquit* 5-6), the weather for withering Adonian gardens.[106] The satirist calls for an audience, but again no one is there.

Persius staggers to his writing desk, and a dialogue between philosopher and voluptuary begins. A controversy has raged for years over the number and identity of the speakers at this point in the poem. For Housman, the voices were internal, two halves of the split Persius, an argument that came from common sense, a sense of the 'split' decorum of hotch-potch satire. His opponents have argued, on grounds of logic, that the voices must come from two distinct sources; a companion is clearly alluded to in the first few lines of the poem, and he must play the role of stern mentor to Persius' crapulous student.[107]

A closer look at the text shows that the companion is little more than a figment of Persius' hallucinations. He no sooner speaks than he evaporates: nothing could be more explicit than 7-8: *ocius adsit/ huc aliquis. nemon?* ('Quick, someone,/ Come here! What, no one?'). The best support for Housman's theory that both the remaining voices come from inside Persius himself is also inside the poem. The simmering froth in Persius' head boils over in an explosion of satirical bile: *turgescit vitrea bilis:/ findor, ut Arcadiae pecuaria rudere credas* (8-9 'Vitreous bile begins to swell/ And I explode, braying like all Arcadia's mokes'). There in the word *findor* (literally, 'I am split in two') is the first intimation of the poet's split personality, the gossiping barber who grasses on Rome's ass's ears, and the man who brays like a raucous ass himself.

The biggest clue to the poem's meaning is the secretaire under Persius' nose. This has been overlooked by most scholars, except for one with an interest in ancient palaeography,[108] and it is not analysed in any of the standard close readings of the poem.[109] We need to be much more myopic. There on the writing desk are the raw materials for split satire: a jungle of reed-pens, a rough notebook of twin-tone, shaved parchment (*positis bicolor membrana capillis* 10), and the final blank sheets for the testament (*chartae* 11). The false starts, the rough workings are all on view; they are part of the finished product. Yellow on one side and

8. Persius and the decoction of Nero

white on the other,[110] the parchment is not only satirically multi-coloured. It also takes on the complexion of the ephebic predicament, shows us the two faces of the satirist in this poem: the pallid student, brimming with mental health; the sick voluptuary, who collapses in the bath with jaundiced skin.[111] Like Nero's, Persius' puberty is on show: *positis capillis* suggests not just that the parchment is shorn of its raw animal hair, but also that the book is personified as a Roman adolescent, shaving his first peachy fuzz and dedicating it.[112] The pens, too, are the tools of Persius' style (*harundo* 11; *calamo* 12; *fistula* 14). How many are there: three separate ones, or one, whose name is split three ways? A knotty pen (*nodosa harundo* 11), in any case, is among them: *nodosus* is the word for riddles of the sphinx or hieroglyphics, a good word for crabbed, inscrutable writing, secrets in code.[113] The ink is blackly satirical (*nigra sepia* 13),[114] but Persius is at the mercy of an unpredictable, uneven instrument. Either the pen clogs up, clotting at the nib, or else it runs too thin, leaving a watery line (12-13). Neronian satire, he is suggesting, cannot help deviating from the measured uniformity of Horace; it is born out of splenetic irritation with its raw materials (14: 'we complain ... '; 19: 'How work with such a pen?'). Worse still: when the pen does work, the nib splits and starts to draw two separate lines: *dilutas querimur geminet quod fistula guttas* (14). Persius is describing the splitting of the ways for Neronian youth: the primrose path that Nero took to the eternal bonfire, and the straight and narrow route to Stoic salvation. The bifurcated pen traces the outline of the Pythagorean letter Y that figures later in the poem (56-7), standing for the divided paths of life.

One voice in Persius' head preaches salvation; the other is irredeemable but can see his inevitable end. The uncooked youth bubbling and spitting in bed is always looking ahead to the final stage of putrefaction. The unbaked pot (*non cocta fidelia* 22) of the beginning soon decomposes into tainted gifts, stinking storage-pots in the larder (*multa fidelia putet* 73). Nero's *nondum* is attached to a jar of sprats on the point of going off (*maenaque quod prima nondum defecerit orca* 76). Wine in Persius is flat (*vapida* 5.148, 6.17) or vinegary ('the tattered dregs of dying vinegar' 4.32); onions droop (*marcentis bulbos* 4.36); porridge is tainted with grease (6.40). Persius' *aliquid decoctius* is not the pure distillation the word suggests, but a storeroom of rotten matter, best before yesterday.[115]

The word 'yesterday' comes into its own in Satire 5, which broadens out into a panorama of Rome: no longer the darkened closet with its *bicolor membrana*, but *mille hominum species et rerum discolor usus* ('Men's types are legion, polychrome their use of things' 5.52). The satirist stands at the crossroads in central Rome, seeing the split path branching ahead of him (*iter ambiguum ... ramosa compita* 34, 35).[116] With his tutor Cornutus he has achieved the only balance in the universe, with Libra and the Twins poised in equilibium, matching their unequal ages (*tempora* 47). Everyone else under the sun, in a world where even the merchandise has taken on the polar complexions of human skin ('wrinkled peppercorns and grains of pallid cumin' 55), has the wrong texture: gone swollen and turgid in sleep (*hic satur inriguo mavult turgescere somno* 56), boiled away into bankruptcy with gambling (*hunc alea decoquit* 57), or into putrefaction with lust (*ille/ in venerem putris* 57-8). Persius' *aliquid decoctius* is a vision of the world burnt out before time, like Pliny's insane vines or simultaneously ripening and rotting figs. Cawing *iam cras hesternum consumpsimus* ('we've used up yesterday's tomorrow' 68), the unbaked youth looks ahead to his own sun-shrivelled old age and back at the future he has already consumed.

In the last poem (6), where Persius foretells his early death and the squabbles among his heirs, his legacy turns out to be that of a bankrupt, the squandered, boiled-away substance of adolescence. His *nepos* ('grandson' or 'spendthrift'), angry that his ancestor has run through his capital (*rem curtaveris* 6.34), and left what elsewhere Persius allows to be rated at a dented 100-as (ass?) piece,[117] reinflates himself on goose-guts (*satur anseris extis* 6.71). Persius ends by taunting his reader with the notion of infinite quantity, Chrysippus' heap without limits (80). But the final impression is of shortcoming, of ambiguous promise, a diminished legacy ('The total's less'. It's less for me – for you, all there,/ However small': *'dest aliquid summae.' minui mihi, sed tibi totum est* 64-5).[118] Persius' satire, his *aliquid decoctius*, is all that remains.

The barber Persius mutters his secrets into a bed of reed-pens, conflates yesterday and tomorrow, unripeness and rot, youth and age. Did he set the scene for Suetonius' death of Nero? King Midas, who turned Rome to gold, cuts a swathe through another bed of reeds (*per harundineti semitam* 48.3), and tells himself the truth as he sees the hot drinks and vaporous baths of his past drained away into a rotten puddle.

Two hundred years after Nero's death, Florus, with the benefit of hindsight, divided the history of Rome into 'Four Ages'. The age of kings was Rome's infancy, the early republic her adolescence, the 150 years down to Augustus her robust youth (*iuventus imperii et quasi robusta maturitas*), and beyond that came decline into old age. Or, as Florus puts it, after Augustus Rome *consenuit atque decoxit*: Rome grew old and rotted away.[119] That word *decoquere* again, the distillation of Persius and Nero's bitter endings. Oddly enough, Florus probably inherited his scheme of Four Ages from the Neronian Seneca, who allegedly brought the last stage forward to the time of Augustus and the loss of *libertas*, when Rome reverted to a combination of child-like dependence and helpless decrepitude.[120] Did Seneca include Nero's reign in this final stage, or did he represent it as a new beginning? His original words do not survive, so we do not know whether he too used the word *decoquere*.

If Seneca had lived, what would he have made of his pupil's legacy? In another context, he wrote: 'It is less shameful to default on (lit. "boil away for") a creditor than on the promise of your own talents': *minus autem turpe est creditori quam spei bonae decoquere*.[121] But perhaps Alexander's tutor was wrong, after all, when he said: 'The same fruit cannot be precocious and long-lasting.'[122] The myths have arrested the Neronians permanently in a state of unfulfilled promise, and that is why their boiled-down lives remain so potent.[123]

*

A postscript on Calpurnius, another poet who conflates time, but whose own time has now been thrown into doubt. Once again, an established, mature genre has to be rewritten: pastoral is peopled with callow youths with skin as soft as quinces (2.87; cf. *praecoquibus prunis* 2.43) and tired old men. The poet's pipe is made from a seasoned reed (*matura harundine* 1.17) handed on from an old man, but writing for Nero is still green on the tree, not yet dried out: *arenti nondum se laxet hiatu* 1.22; *viridas etiam nunc ... rimas* 22). Summer, too, is staving off its end (*nondum solis equos declinis mitigat aestas*), while the shade is long-lived (*annosa umbra* 2.21). Fruitfulness comes at all seasons, from glistening figs in scorching summer (*praetorrida aestas* 2.80) to the ripe nuts (*maturis nucibus* 2.82-3) splitting their green husks in the December sun. Does Calpurnius' oozing wine-press (1.2-3) provide the imagery for Tacitus' Messalina in autumnal rig (11.31)? Or is it that, with Tacitus' 'autumnal' representation of Claudius' reign and the false, spring-like resurgence of Nero at the back of our minds, we read something more significant and doomed into what is essentially a copying from Virgil? Is the heat of the sun (*iam fremit aestas* 4.168) really more intense in Calpurnius? And does the voice of the late-comer Lycidas (*serus ades, Lycida* 6.1), 'spurting a dribbling tune from a dry throat, squirting out words in gulps' (6.3-4), sound like a peculiarly Neronian voice, harsh, uneven and failing in its pretensions? It may be clutching at straws, but it will always be tempting to claim Calpurnius for a Neronian.

Notes

1. Suet. *Nero* 48.3. All references to Suetonius from now on are from *Nero* unless otherwise stated.
2. Pers. 1.125. All translations of Persius from now on are from Lee 1987.
3. Plin. *Nat. Hist.* 31.40.
4. See Henderson (1993).
5. *Laus Pisonis* 260. *Vita Lucani*; cf. Stat. *Silv.* 2.7.73f.
6. Fronto 2 p.102 (155N): *febriculosis prunulis*.
7. The long list of solar images that Griffin 1984 pp. 216-18 rejects could be read perversely as impressive evidence for a sun-cult of Nero.
8. Why is it so important that Calpurnius should be Neronian? See Champlin 1978, 1986, for arguments that he is not, resisted strongly by e.g. Townend 1980, Mayer 1980. The fact remains that it is more interesting for us to read Calpurnius in the light of Nero. See the postscript at the end of this chapter.
9. See Veyne 1961.
10. *Aetna* 3.
11. Tac. *Ann.* 14.16; *Ann.* 13.3; *Ann.* 16.19; Suet. *Vita Lucani*: Lucan once relieved himself loudly in a public latrine while declaiming half a line of the emperor's verse (*sub terris tonuisse putes*: 'You'd think it thundered underneath the earth').
12. Tac. *Ann.* 14.50; cf. Cremutius Cordus: *Ann.* 4.35.
13. Calp. Sic. 1.2-3.
14. Suet. 39.
15. Suet. 6.3: Nero raised by a dancer and a barber as his tutor. Hor. *Sat.* 1.7.1 on *sermo* as barbers' gossip (a poem where one of the protagonists is called Persius). Natta: Pers. 3.31-4.
16. Dio 63.27.2; Suet. 23.2.
17. *Vita Persi*. In Persius' parody of contemporary poetics in *Sat.* 1, the scholiasts saw lines 93, 99-102 and 121-3 as allusions to Nero's own poems. The transsexual Attis (93), for example, was seen to refer to Nero's poem on the same subject (cf. Dio 62.20); a subconscious theory, perhaps, as the name *Nereus* appears in the next line. However, the theory that Nero wrote a poem on a one-eyed man (Suet. *Dom.* 1) seems to be a false

assumption from line 128, which is more probably a criticism of Horace's laughter at the provincial Aufidius Luscus in *Sat.* 1.5.34-6. Sullivan 1978, 1985, argues the scholiasts' case, though he thinks the Midas story a red herring.

18. On this phenomenon see Suet. 57.2.
19. Suet. 10.1.
20. e.g. Plin. *Nat. Hist.* 14.86: *decocto ad tertias partes*; 32.39: *decoctanum ad tertias partes*; 21.119: *decocta ad tertias*; 23.62: *vino ... decocto, donec tertia pars supersit.*
21. *Nat. Hist.* 17.226.
22. Sen. *Ep.* 108.16; Quint. *Inst.* 2.4.7.
23. See Crook 1967 p. 375: the word is used of ' "boiling away" one's property, i.e. losing it and so becoming insolvent, or of reducing one's assets by fraudulently disposing of part of them, or even of "boiling away" other people's property'; 'The most we can assert is that in classical times calling someone a *decoctor* meant usually that he was an insolvent and often that he was a dishonourable insolvent' (p. 376).
24. *OLD* s.v.
25. The ordering of time was central to Augustus' programme: the calendar, the horologium, the motto *speude bradeos* ('hasten slowly'). See Wallace-Hadrill 1987, Beard 1987.
26. 27 was the year he took the name Augustus and 'restored' the Republic: see Vell. Pat. 2.89; 31 the year of the vicotry of Actium and the defeat of Antony.
27. Suet. *Vesp.* 25.
28. Suet. *Vesp.* 5.2.
29. Suet. 7.1; Suet. 12.4 (Neronia), Dio 62.19.1 (Juvenalia); Suet. 8.
30. Suet. *Claud.* 43: C. wanted to give Britannicus the toga since his stature justified it, though he was still *impubi teneroque*, 'young and immature'.
31. Suet 19.2: Nero's legion of six-foot Italian tirones; 12.1: pyrrhic dances by Greek ephebes.
32. Tac. *Ann.* 14.52: 'Nero's childhood was undoubtedly over, and he had reached the full strength of youth: let him slough off his tutor; he had good enough teachers in his own ancestors.'
33. See Henderson (1989: 181-90) on Nero as ephebe. Tacitus's chosen image (*Ann.* 13.15) of Nero as the Saturnalian boy king (December 15th was his birthday: Suet. 6) lingers over the reign as a whole. Cf. Dio 61.4.2: Seneca had a taste for overgrown boys, *exoroi*, past their first bloom.
34. Suet. 23; 21.1.2.
35. Tac. *Ann.* 13.10; 16.12.
36. Suet. 34.5 (cf. Dio 61.17.1): the word used of Nero's beard, *lanugo*, is also commonly used of the downy skin of a fruit (*OLD* s.v.).
37. Dio 62.19.2, Suet. 11.1; Tac. *Ann.* 14.57; Suet. 37; Tac. *Ann.* 14.65; *Ann.* 15.18.
38. Suet. *Galba* 8: an incense-bearer's hair turned white, predicting that a young man would be succeeded by an old one. Cf. 4.1: Augustus had pinched his cheek as a boy and said in Greek 'You will take a nibble of my power'; 4.3: when Galba assumed the *toga virilis*, he dreamed that Fortune appeared to him and said unless he let her in at once she would fall prey to whoever she met first.
39. The two models are united in Pliny's account of the extravagant size of hothouse vegetables: *Nat. Hist.* 19.139.
40. Sen. *Ep.* 95.27; Suet. 23.1.
41. Detienne 1977 esp. pp. 10-14, 59-71, 118-31.
42. Suet. 57.1.
43. e.g. *Nat. Hist.* 17.8; 18.150; 16.1, 17.129, 15.41.
44. *Nat. Hist.* 17.95.
45. *Nat. Hist.* 15.41.

46. e.g. Sen. *Apocol.* 4: *aurea saecula*; Calp. Sic. 1.42: *aurea renascitur aetas.*

47. *Ann.* 11.31; 11.32: *vehiculo, quo purgamenta hortorum eripiuntur.* Cf. Sen. *Apocol.* 2 on Claudius' last autumn: 'ugly winter plucks the honours from rich autumn, Bacchus is told to grow old (*senescere*), and the late (*serus*) vintner picks the last few grapes.'

48. *Nat. Hist.* 17.226; 18.288.

49. Arist. *Phys.* 230b; Simplicius *In Arist. Phys.* 255a20f: both quoted by Detienne 1977 pp. 105, 119.

50. Plat. *Phaedr.* 276B; Dio 63.26.5: *epaizen.*

51. Tac. *Ann.* 13.45; Dio 62.28.1; Tac. *Ann.* 16.6, Plin. *Nat. Hist.* 12.83; cf. 13.22: Otho taught Nero to put perfume on the soles of his feet.

52. *Ann.* 15.23. Cf. *Ann.* 14.27: childless veterans; 15.19: childless candidates adopting children.

53. Tac. *Ann.* 14.55.

54. cf. *Ann.* 15.39: Nero built makeshift huts (*subitaria aedificia*) for the homeless after the Fire. A case could be made for reading Tacitus' murder of Agrippina (*Ann.* 14.8-9) as Nero's sudden rebirth, this time as a fully-grown prodigy. There are many hints of quasi-Caesarian section in her death-scene: the mother's slit stomach, the echo in her *tu quoque me deseris*, and the site of her burial, near the villa of the dictator Caesar. Even the instantaneous hatching of the Pisonian conspiracy (*coepta simul et aucta* 15.48) is no match for Nero.

55. Suet. 11.2.

56. Suet. 38.1.

57. *Ann.* 15.4: *nulla umbra defensam graviore aestu ardescere.*

58. 62.6.1.

59. *Ann.* 13.58. See Segal 1973; McCulloch 1980.

60. Dio. 63.29.3; Plin. *Nat. Hist.* 17.5; 16.236.

61. Plin. *Nat. Hist.* 7.45 calls Nero and Gaius the torches (*faces*) of the human race. Was Nero also personified as one of the five comets that flew over his reign? See Suet. 51 on his long hair (*comam*).

62. Plin. *Nat. Hist.* 31.40; Suet. 27.2.

63. *Nat. Hist.* 19.55.

64. *Nat. Qu.* 4b.13.11 *cor ipsum excoquit*; *Ep.* 106.16.

65. Plin. *Nat. Hist.* 34.166; 19.108. Cf. Plin. *Nat. Hist.* 19.64 on Tiberius and his hanging hothouses of cucumbers.

66. Tac. *Ann.* 16.16: 'All this slave-like impassivity and the huge loss of blood at home must weary the mind and stifle it with sorrow.' See also the brilliant essay by Barthes (1982), who describes Tacitean deaths in the language of vegetable proliferation: 'spread out in time, subject to a movement, like that of sprouts on a stalk' (166).

67. Plin. *Nat. Hist.* 11.238.

68. Tac. *Ann.* 14.5.4: *praefervidi balnei vapore enecaretur.*

69. 15.69: *omnia simul properantur ... vigens adhuc balneo infertur, calida aqua mersatur.*

70. *Ep.* 108.16.

71. Tac. *Ann.* 15.64: *stagnum calidae aquae introiit ... balneo inlatus et vapore eius exanimatus.*

72. 10.48.3: *inmodico sexta Nerone calet.*

73. *Ann.* 13.15.

74. Suet. 33: *quam posset velocissimum ac praesentaneum.*

75. *Ann.* 13.15.

76. cf. *Ann.* 16.14: Nero's impatience is infectious: Anteius swallows poison, but, disgusted by its slowness, he slits his veins instead (*tarditatem eius perosus intercisis venis mortem properavit*). Petronius' insouciance is played out in his defiantly prolonged death

(16.19). Plin. *Nat. Hist.* 22.92 sees Nero as the poison Agrippina brewed up for the world: *venenum alterum* (in the context of the mushroom that killed Claudius).
77. *Nat. Hist.* 16.115.
78. See Plass 1988 on the importance of the ridiculous (*ludibrium*) in Tacitus' portrayal of Nero.
79. Suet. *Vita Passieni Crispi.*
80. Suet. 49.2.
81. *Inst.* 2.4.7: *materiam esse primum volo vel abundantiorem atque ultra quam oporteat fusam. multum inde decoquent anni.*
82. *Inst.* 1 3.3: *illud ingeniorum velut praecox genus non temere umquam pervenit ad frugem.* Cf. *Inst.* 1.3.5: precocious boys are like seeds sown on the surface of the soil: they spring up too fast and bear no grain.
83. Curtius 8.5.15. Cf Sen. *Brev. Vit.* 6.2 on the precocious nerve of Livius Drusus: *tam praecocem audaciam*; *Inc. pall.* 95: *odi puerulos praecoqui sapientia* ('I hate precocious little boys').
84. *Phil.* 2.44.
85. Suet. 51.
86. 10.11.
87. *Ann.* 13.16 (he also speaks of *praematura mors*). Cf. one of Nero's posthumous victims, Fannius, who dreamed that Nero appeared to him and started reading from Fannius' history of those who had suffered at his hands. When Nero reached the third book, he vanished – a portent that the history would remain unfinished and Fannius himself would die a premature death (*acerba et immatura mors*: Plin. *Ep.* 5.5.4-6).
88. Epict. *Diss.* 4.5.16-17.
89. Suet. 20.2.
90. Persius (1.121.3) says he will not sell his secret for an Iliad; Sullivan 1985 sees this as a snipe at Nero's *Troica.*
91. Dio 62.29.2.
92. As I have suggested elsewhere, since *sapa*, grape-juice, was the substance most commonly 'decocted': see Gowers (1993:180-8) on Persius.
93. See Braund 1978 on *Aulus Persius Flaccus* as a too-good-to-be-true *farrago* of Horatius Flaccus' names or characters.
94. 13.46: *Persica Praecocia: vilia maternis fueramus Persica ramis:/ nunc in adoptivis Persica cara sumus.*
95. 2.42-3: *ars mea nunc malo pira temperat et modo cogit/ insita praecoquibus subrepere persica prunis.*
96. *Vita Persi.* I am grateful to Jeremy Maule for drawing my attention to Richard Crashaw's poem 'Upon two green apricocks sent to Cowley by Sir Crashaw'.
97. Plin. *Nat. Hist.* 15.40.
98. Tac. *Ann.* 14.16: *non impetu et instinctu nec ore uno fluens* ('not flowing from one impulse, inspiration or voice'). Suet. 52: *multa et deleta et inducta et superscripta inerant* ('there were many examples of words crossed out or inserted or written between the lines').
99. Suet. 15.1.
100. Dio 62.26.5, Suet. 41.2; Suet. 42. Cf. Dio 62.14.4: 'he possessed the whole world, but still he went on playing the lyre, making proclamations and acting tragedies.'
101. Tac. *Ann.* 14.52; Dio 62.8.3; cf. Tac. *Ann.* 15.33: he despised the theatre as 'too narrow for such a full voice'.
102. 5.179: *aprici senes*; 4.36: *marcentis bulbos*; 4.40: *elixas nates.* On age-differences in Persius see Henderson 1993.
103. Nero himself was soon on the turn: Tac. *Ann.* 14.52: 'Nero inclined to worse advisers' (*Nero ad deteriores inclinabat*).

8. Persius and the decoction of Nero   149

104. 3.3-4: *indomitum quod despumare Falernum/ sufficiat.*

105. The cooking imagery that unites crops, wine, clay-firing and the human body in this poem recalls the Greek analogies discussed by Vidal-Naquet 1981 in the context of the rituals that prepared the Athenian ephebe for adult life. His article in the original French was called 'Les jeunes, le cru, l'enfant grec et le cuit'. See further Gowers (1993: 180-8) on Persius.

106. Is the dog-star an image for the satirist himself, who growled the *canina littera* ('dog's letter') in Satire 1 (109-10), and ends up condeming his own insanity in this poem (*non sanus* 3.118)? As a child he threw the *damnosa canicula*, the unlucky dog, in dice (3.49).

107. Housman 1913; accepted by Nisbet 1963 p. 53; rejected by Hendrickson 1928 p. 335. Reckford 1962 p. 495 detects three voices: the satirist, and the two voices of the student and the philosopher. Rudd 1970 p. 286 gives two voices to Persius (the narrator and the student), with the companion as the philosopher.

108. Johnson 1973.

109. Hendrickson 1928, Reckford 1962, Nisbet 1963, Dessen 1968, Jenkinson 1973.

110. See Johnson 1973: parchment was dyed on one side to help the ink to take (cf. Isid. *Orig.* 6.11.4).

111. 85: 'Is this your pallor?'; 94: 'You're pale, dear boy.' 'It's nothing.' 'Well, whatever it is,/ Best get it seen to. Your skin's yellow – quietly swelling.' The pot in line 24 is made of *lutum*, mud, uncooked, but destined to turn into the muddy yellow skin of the roué (*lutea pellis* 95), who ends up bedaubed (*lutatus* 104) with funeral perfumes.

112. cf. Suet. 12.4 on Nero: *barbam primam posuit*: 'he shaved off his first beard.'

113. The word is re-used in Apul. *Met.* 11.22 of Egyptian writing. Not enough has been written on the debt of Apuleius' prologue (*Met.* 1.1) to the *semipaganus* (half-initi-ate) Persius: not a stinging vinegary assault like Persius', but one so gentle and seductive that readers only notice on a second glance that the author is teasing their own asses' ears (*aures remulceo*). Did Apuleius take his *Aegyptia argutia* ('Egyptian sharpness') from Persius' *nodosa harundo*?

114. Trailing a path from Horace's venomous cuttle-fish ink at *Sat.* 1.4.100: *nigrae sucus lolliginis.*

115. Yesterday: cf. *oscitat hesternum* (3.59); *hesterni Quirites* (3.106).

116. Later he is 'torn apart by a double hook' (*duplici in diversum scinderis hamo* 5.154).

117. *Curto centusse* 3.191; cf. *curta supellex* 4.52 ('clipped equipment').

118. The *Vita* tells us that Persius advanced only so far (*aliquatenus*) in philosophy, and that Cornutus had to clip off the end of his unfinished work to make it seem complete.

119. Florus *praef.* 4-8.

120. Seneca the Elder fr. 4 (ed. L. Hakanson 1989 = Lact. *Inst. Div.* 7 15.14). See Griffin 1972 p. 10, arguing that Seneca's *Histories* were written by the Younger not the Elder Seneca: the quotation about the Four Ages 'suits the philosophical son better than the unspeculative father'.

121. *Ep.* 36.5.

122. See above p. 139.

123. My greatest debt in this chapter is to John Henderson, who taught me about ephebes, precocity and the gardens of Adonis, and who makes me think I have already come too late to Neronian literature.

Bibliography

Barthes R. (1982) 'Tacitus and the funerary baroque' in *A Barthes Reader* ed. S. Sontag, London, pp. 162-6.
Beard M. (1987) 'A complex of times: no more sheep on Romulus' birthday' *PCPhS* 213 pp. 1-15.
Braund D. (1978) 'Persius and Horace' *Farrago* (magazine of Cambridge Classics Faculty) October pp. 18-21.
Champlin E. (1978) 'The life and times of Calpurnius Siculus: technique and date' *JRS* 68 pp. 95-110.
—— (1986) 'History and the date of Calpurnius Siculus' *Philologus* 130 pp. 104-12.
Crook J.A. (1967) 'A study in decoction', *Latomus* 26 pp. 361-76.
Dessen C.S. (1968) *Iunctura callidus acri: a study of Persius' satires*, Urbana/Chicago/London.
Detienne M. (1977) *The Gardens of Adonis: spices in Greek mythology*, Sussex.
Gowers E. (1993) *The Loaded Table: representations of food in Roman literature*, Oxford.
Griffin M.T. (1972) 'The Elder Seneca and Spain' *JRS* 62 pp. 1-19.
—— (1984) *Nero: the end of a dynasty*, London.
Harvey R.A. (1981) *A Commentary on Persius*, Leiden.
Henderson J. (1989) 'Tacitus: the world in pieces' *Ramus* 18 pp. 167-210.
—— (1993) 'The pupil as teacher: Persius' didactic satire' *Ramus* 20.
Hendrickson G.L. (1928) 'The Third Satire of Persius' *CPhil* 23 pp. 332-42.
Housman A.E. (1913) 'Notes on Persius' *CQ* 7 pp. 12-32.
Jenkinson J.R. (1980) *Persius*, Warminster.
Jenkinson R. (1973) 'Interpretations of Persius' Satires 3 and 4' *Latomus* 32 pp. 521-49.
Johnson R.R. (1973) 'Bicolor membrana' *CQ* n.s. 23 pp. 339-42.
Lee G. and Barr W. (1987) *The Satires of Persius* tr. G. Lee, introd. and comm. by W. Barr, Liverpool.
Mayer R. (1980) 'Calpurnius Siculus: technique and date' *JRS* 70 pp. 175-6.
McCulloch H., Jr (1980) 'Literary augury at the end of *Annals* 13' *Phoenix* 34 pp. 237-42.
Nisbet R.G.M. (1963) 'Persius' in J.P. Sullivan (ed.) *Critical Essays in Roman Literature: satire*, London pp. 39-71.
Plass P. (1988) *Wit and the Writing of History: the rhetoric of Roman historiography*, Madison, Wisconsin.
Reckford K.J. (1962) 'Studies in Persius' *Hermes* 90 pp. 476-504.
Segal C. (1973) 'Tacitus and poetic history: the end of *Annals* 13' *Ramus* 2 pp. 107-26.
Sullivan J.P. (1978) 'Asses' ears and Attises: Persius and Nero' *AJP* 99 pp. 159-70.
—— (1985) 'Callimachean critiques: Nero and Persius' in *Literature and Politics in the Age of Nero*, Ithaca, NY, pp. 74-114.
Townend G.B. (1980) 'Calpurnius Siculus and the *Munus Neronis*' *JRS* 70 pp. 166-75.
Wallace-Hadrill A.F. (1987) 'Time for Augustus: Ovid, Augustus and the *Fasti*' in *Homo Viator* ed. M. Whitby, P. Hardie and M. Whitby, Bristol, pp. 221-30.
Veyne P. (1961) 'Vie de Trimalcion' *Annales* no. 2 pp. 213-47.
Vidal-Naquet P. (1981) 'Recipes for Greek adolescence' in R. Gordon (ed.) *Myth, Religion and Society*, Cambridge, pp. 163-85.

9

Deceiving the reader: the political mission of Lucan *Bellum Civile* 7[1]

Jamie Masters

1. Historical distortion

We are by now quite used to the idea that Lucan distorts history for his own ends. Not always, of course; on the contrary, during this century we have come to know that *for the most part* he is accurate in matters of fact. This discovery has been a necessary corrective to the sort of scholarship (well exemplified by Heitland) which wrote Lucan off as a hopeless incompetent who could never get anything right;[2] and it was Pichon – in other respects no friend to the poet – who struck one of the first blows in defence of the new position: 'In a word, when he is dealing with topography, chronology, strategy or tactics, Lucan almost always displays the conscientiousness and the seriousness of a well-informed expert'.[3] Subsequent work on the poem, generally more sophisticated in its methods, has none the less come to the same conclusions; so, for instance, Grimal: 'If one can generalise ... one would conclude that, without doubt, Lucan's documentation concerning the material facts he reports or assumes knowledge of is very precise, and that chronology in particular is scrupulously respected.'[4] Of course, as Grimal is careful to point out, given the fragmentary nature of our sources, it is not always possible to be sure; but when we *can* check Lucan's account against the information given us in the sources, it is surprising how often the more obscure details can indeed be vindicated. The implication is, of course, that Lucan had a fairly detailed knowledge of the events of the civil wars; or rather, knowledge of the traditional accounts of those events. He may not always have used that knowledge; but even where he did not, we can at least acquit him of ignorance. In short, Lucan shows that he is *capable* of getting his facts right; so when he does distort history, we have good reason to suppose that he is doing so deliberately; that he is lying.

In fact, it has long been known that the out-and-out lie is just one of the techniques Lucan employs for his historical distortions. As often as not the game consists precisely in 'getting the facts right', in telling a new history that is none the less woven, somehow, from the givens of the old.[5] If there are details that cannot be assimilated into the new design, they are simply omitted;[6] and it is always possible to tamper with those parts of history that are a matter of speculation rather than fact – the interpretation of motive, in particular.[7] Similarly, there are always gaps in recorded history (because there is a hierarchy of events, because the historian cannot tell everything), spaces that can be filled with invented material which does not contradict the 'facts' but can cast a new light on them; and who can absolutely *deny* (for instance) that Caesar cut down the first tree in the Massilian grove,[8] or that he visited the ruins of Troy en route to Egypt?[9]

These techniques, including the lies, have proved easy to fit into a political reading of the poem: Lucan, so the story goes, is anti-principate, pro-republican, and he distorts history 'largely in order to sustain his portrait of Caesar as a devil incarnate, of superhuman energy but addicted to cruelty'.[10] Immediately we need to qualify. Hostility towards Caesar is clear, for time and time again it is trumpeted from the rooftops, loudly, furiously, passionately; there may be exceptions, and one can question whether explicit rage must necessarily be an index of the poet's political beliefs; but for all its ironies the poem will, at least, stoutly resist being read as *favourable* to Caesar. Beyond that basic donnée, however, we are treading on more treacherous ground. The scholarship is all but unanimous in asserting that part and parcel of Lucan's condemnation of Caesar is his exoneration and glorification of Pompey, and those who fought with him to preserve senatorial *libertas*. Lounsbury, writing of Lucan's account of Pharsalus, is a typical example:

> The battle is described, and its catastrophic consequences examined in detail by Lucan. The responsibility for the defeat, therefore, will entail great blame for the man or men on whom it falls. It is Lucan's intention ... to place that blame elsewhere than on the Senate and its leader Pompey – which required the omission and distortion of much evidence.[11]

Such a reading, however, does seem to go against much of the spirit of the poem. Granted, explicit authorial approval of Pompey is not hard to find (particularly in books 7 and 8), but this is so often qualified, undercut by irony, or simply contradicted, that it is hard to come away from the poem without having felt its deep ambivalence about Caesar's great rival. Whatever else the poem may be, it is hardly a hagiography; and the unease about Pompey extends to the senatorial party as a whole.[12] The most we can say – and it certainly should be said – is that there is a persistent thread of pro-Pompeian rhetoric throughout the poem; not indeed *consistent*, not enough to justify a simple pro-Pompeian reading of the poem as a whole; but enough to cast a shadow.

The poem is, then, explicitly hostile to Caesar, and rather less certainly favourable to the republicans. It is an obvious next step to equate Caesar with Caesarianism, and find in the poem evidence of Lucan's implacable hatred of Nero; and for those who have ignored or suppressed the negative aspects of Lucan's portrayal of Pompey and the senators, it is easy to represent Lucan as a republican propagandist, using the victims of the civil war as symbols of the righteous struggle that he is now urging, against the tyranny of Nero, in the name of Roman liberty. Even those who have tried to respond to the ambiguities of Lucan's allegiance to Pompey have not, in fact, been able to offer much more. They have urged us to accept Pompey's sins as a mark of his humanity – as if he

9. Deceiving the reader

was a frail, complex, flawed man, who none the less did what he could for his *patria*, and so, fundamentally, a sympathetic character; they have argued that senatorial *libertas* as an ideal can be abstracted from its particular, imperfect, instances; they have run to the shelter of Cato as the one perfect embodiment of *libertas*, the one candidate for unqualified sainthood, and the one guarantor of the poem's propagandistic purpose; or or they have explained the lack of authorial consistency by presuming that Lucan changed his mind as the poem progressed, and failed to smooth over the contradictions before he died. The bottom line has always been the same: the poem is anti-Neronian propaganda.

So be it – for now. But to return: it has usually been recognised that while historical distortion is one of Lucan's most useful propagandistic devices, these 'political' distortions are not the whole story, and that there are other examples in which a simple political bias is not so easy to discern. These were well dealt with by Syndikus: the omission of military details (strength of armies, tactics, etc.),[13] the compression of whole trains of events into a superficial line or two,[14] the excision of any element which would tend to clarify the workings of cause and effect, the replacement of rational motivation with the irrational and the arbitrary,[15] the inclusion of the superfluous and the privileging of the insignificant.[16] In Lucan, we discover, the plot tends to fall by the wayside: it is not clear what happens, why it happens, or why it is important to know that it happens:

> In Lucan's account, on the other hand, an enormous number of vague details are compressed together. Nothing is prepared for, nothing explained, nothing linked. Lucan simply juxtaposes events as he finds them in his sources, often without any concern for whether his account still makes overall sense.[17]

These effects are obviously deliberate, as Syndikus noted,[18] and it is by no means clear that they are all made to serve the end of glorifying the republic or vilifying Caesar (or of endorsing whatever political position Lucan is supposed to have entertained). Where the scholarship has bothered to account for these other deformations of the historical tradition (and often it has not, preferring only to gesture in their direction before moving on to more overtly political material), it has had to find an aesthetic, a literary, purpose. Such an account, at its most contemptuous extreme, is offered by Robert Graves in the introduction to his Penguin translation:

> Lucan may also be called the father of the costume film. If lopped of all digressive rhodomontade, the *Civil Wars* is a script which could be put almost straight onto the floor. It consists of carefully chosen, cunningly varied, brutally sensational scenes, linked by a tenuous thread of historical probability; and alternated with soft interludes in which deathless courage, supreme self-sacrifice, memorable piety, Stoic virtue, and wifely devotion are expected to win favour from the great sentimental box-office public ... Lucan must, I think, have been so single minded a rhetorician that all his values were melodramatic ones. Unless a situation yielded a surprising paradox – the cruelty of Caesar's clemency, the loyal comradeship that the Oderzo Gauls showed by brutal murder, or the unkindness of the Roman refugee who gave Pompey's body decent burial – it did not interest him.[19]

Fortunately Graves betrayed himself by the very extremity of his position, and his hostility towards the poet has since become infamous. But even so, if we strip away the obvious scorn, his comments have much in common with the other, more objective, attempts to explain the aesthetics of the *Bellum Civile*. So, according to Syndikus, for example, what Lucan sacrifices in the way of clarity is compensated for by an increased *vividness*; clearing away the clutter of events allows him to bring to the fore what is emotionally powerful, or rhetorically striking.[20] More than that, when dealing with material so multifarious and of such scope as the recent civil war, some reshuffling – in the name of economy and efficiency – is a *sine qua non* for the epic poet.[21]

Neither of these explanations is, however, entirely satisfactory. As even Syndikus pointed out,[22] Lucan's distortion of history, and in particular his devastation of its narrative continuity, goes far beyond the requirements of epic recasting. It should be possible to write emotionally and powerfully, and to concentrate the attention on vivid set scenes of an exemplary character, without sacrificing *so much*. For Graves it had obviously been *too* much; for Lintott too, who was as flatly objective as Graves was furiously partial, Lucan's methods were unconventional enough to require some kind of apology:

> Even in the period before Pharsalia it is difficult to comprehend the course of the civil war from Lucan's account alone. On the other hand Lucan's work was never meant to be a primary source or indeed a history in our sense of the word. His method is to present epic scenes or episodes, speeches in character, and his own personal statements linked together by compressed pieces of narrative – a sort of oratorio technique. Moreover he is often allusive rather than explicit when describing the action. He seems to have expected the reader either to be content with a vague impression or to recognise the allusions through familiarity with the history. This technique is clearly not that of a historian, but nevertheless shows respect for the facts of history.[23]

But Lintott has made a important step forward: the poem, he says, is not history; but it does *allude* to history. Since it is not possible to understand Lucan's account without reference to the standard prose accounts, we need not suppose that it was ever meant to stand on its own. Put simply, Lucan's poem cannot *replace* his sources; it is *parasitic* on them. In some ways the suggestion is useful because it offers a way of putting Lucan's poem, and his readers, back where they belong into the world of *doctrina*, of learned allusion – which was just the sort of literary environment Graves was trying to deny. But it also provides a very neat solution for the elliptical nature of Lucan's narrative: Lucan doesn't tell his story straight because he doesn't have to; there is no need to spell out the details if everyone knows the story already.[24]

This account can explain a lot, but it is still not enough. In Lintott's gentle vision, the plot shrinks because Lucan's epic technique is (like an oratorio) simply unsuited to the ordered unfolding of a complicated narrative. Details fall out – at the risk of mystifying some readers who have to be 'content with a vague impression' – but he knows that most readers are capable of filling in the gaps from their own knowledge. But no: what is missing from this account is any recognition of the violence, the heresy, the will-to-travesty of Lucan's relation-

9. Deceiving the reader 155

ship with his source material. It is not that he regretfully lets details fall out in some worthy epic cause; often he marks off for slaughter just those details which would allow his story to make sense. For what Lucan confronts us with is a narratological policy which eschews the straightforward and puts a premium on disorder, discontinuity, and, of course, deception. Johnson was the first (and recently, at that) to take this particular bull by the horns, and is worth quoting at length:

> Had he wished, for instance, Lucan could probably have written a 'normal' epic about Caesar's Civil War which, placing the proper emphasis and blame on the reactionary senators who abused Pompey's gifts and used his failings, would have linked events vividly and clearly, would have dramatised the influence of human volition and human choice on these events and their connections ... Instead ... this epic consistently saps the comforting logic of chronology by obscuring transitions from one event to another, by expanding various kinds of digressions and by vividly dramatising the irrelevant and the unreal. Even after allowing for the complexity of the historical materials in question and admitting that their wide distribution over space and time rendered unity of action more than difficult for Lucan, we may argue that Lucan deliberately complicates and further distorts the complex untidiness of the story he has chosen to tell.[25]

A fine analysis of the symptoms; now for the diagnosis.

> Since he sees what happens in history not as the effort by human beings to impose rational patterns by rational actions on an intelligible world but, rather, as the blind reflexes of unknowable and irrational mechanisms, the very concept of unity of action is useless to him except insofar as it represents a false and dangerous myth (disorder masquerading as order) that satire may demolish in order to let its poet approach the truth of chaos.[26]

We started with the statement that Lucan distorts history for his own ends. The position is uncontroversial; the difficulty arises only when we try to determine what 'his own ends' were. In the standard formulation, some are propagandistic, and some are literary; but what is required, and what I think Johnson actually provides (as we shall see shortly), is a reading which unites both phenomena.

One popular suggestion runs as follows: Lucan, who has made it his job to discredit Caesar and the dynasty that followed him, finds a natural opponent in Vergil, the poet who went a long way toward creating the very myths that Lucan is so anxious to destroy. Flatly contradicting Vergil's melancholic optimism, and at every turn giving the lie to Vergil's implication that an Augustan golden age was worth even the price of civil war, Lucan opposes Vergil as much on the stylistic as on the political plane: when he annihilates epic narrative, the target is really Vergil; and when he attacks Vergil, the target is really Caesarianism.

Now, the opposition of Lucan to Vergil on a *poetic* level (his imitation and subversion of specific Vergilian episodes and general Vergilian rhetoric) is well known, and it does seem to offer another very powerful explanation of Lucan's tortured epic technique. But the extension of this familiar argument into *politics* rests on two interrelated premises: first, that Lucan was – as a card-carrying member of the 'Stoic opposition' – radically opposed to the principate; and second, that (in Lucan's eyes) Vergil represented support for the imperial regime, or at the very least, consent to it.[27] In response to the second premise, it should be obvious that Vergil might have represented any number of things to Lucan, since political sycophancy is only one of any number of Vergilian characteristics. Most of the others are 'literary'; any one of them might furnish fuel for opposition; and indeed, nearly all of them do. If it seems plausible that Lucan saw Vergil principally as an imperial spokesman, that is only so because we are sure (for other reasons) that Lucan hated the emperors. Take away *that* certainty, and it would become possible (though I have never seen it done) to take the argument in a totally different direction. Rather than making Lucan's political beliefs logically prior to his poetic credo, we might go so far as to suppose that it was Lucan's inevitable clash with Vergil – inevitable because of an 'anxiety of influence'[28] – that led him to proclaim so noisily a political ideal that was so outrageously anti-Vergilian; that Lucan's poetics are prior to his politics. An extreme position, since it appears to deny Lucan any sincere political opinions; how seriously I would entertain it will emerge as this chapter progresses.

Opposition to Vergil is not the only candidate for an interpretation that will unite 'political' and 'literary' distortion. An alternative is offered by Rambaud, and it is grounded in his hypothesis that Lucan's poem is intended as a deliberate counterpoise to Julius Caesar's own *De Bello Civili*. What applied to Vergil now applies to Caesar: Caesar is, of course, a natural representative of Caesarianism, and it is not so easy to imagine Lucan choosing to rival Caesar for purely 'literary' reasons; opposing Caesar politically, then, and seeking to reverse the oh-so-subtle bias in Caesar's account of the civil war, Lucan also opposes Caesar's historiographical method, by choosing to write in the style of the Sallustian monograph (which tends to be organised around themes), rather than Caesar's own annalistic style (which claims to be objective, day-to-day reportage).[29] Now comes the cunning part. To write a historical epic requires, as we have noted, some degree of 'literary' recasting; so too the translation of an annalistic source into a kind of Sallustian monograph will involve inevitable distortion, compression, omission. That is par for the course; but, says Rambaud, this strictly literary policy can be made to work in a propagandistic cause. Precisely because one expects the poet to rearrange his material for aesthetic reasons, those distortions which are most damaging to Caesar seem to be more innocent (less politically motivated) than they actually are:

> Lucan is quite open in his policy of omission, and one cannot, at first sight, blame him for cuts which appear only to serve artistic purposes ... But it is not without a certain partiality, which one can detect in the choice of the parts sacrificed.[30]

But here we face the same problem again: such a position assumes that we know Lucan's political motives. So long as we believe that, as Rambaud puts it, 'Lucan's constant concern was to defend the memory of Pompey' (p. 155), the idea that Lucan used literary distortion as a way of smuggling in political partiality seems fairly plausible. If we do *not* accept that Lucan was a republican apologist, we are, more or less, back to square one.

9. Deceiving the reader

When we return to Johnson we find most of the themes I have reviewed above developed to a new level of sophistication. In his account, the 'literary' phenomenon (the incoherence and obscurity that he argues lies at the heart of Lucan's tortuous aesthetics) is a product of an implied philosophical position (the 'broken machine') which informs, or is informed by, Lucan's political beliefs. It is not only opposition to Vergil that stimulates the atrocities of his narrative technique; it is opposition to all narrative – history, epic, opposition to anything that *makes sense* in a world that makes nothing but nonsense. Politically, Lucan is an idealist whose idealism has gone sour. Once the champion of lost Roman freedom, he soon finds himself prey to a pessimism which drives him to lay bare his own (and others') self-deception. Caesar, Pompey, Cato, everyone and everything is victim of his acerbic wit and ruthless malevolence;[31] there is no hope, only Nero and a world gone mad:

> Whatever pure hymn to freedom, virtue, and history he initially intended to write, at some early point he found himself writing about the past he loved, in which all that he valued had been possible but in whose reality he no longer believed, and he found his poem screaming dreadful things about the present, whose monstrous reality he could neither deny nor alter. From the strain of this ambivalence and the trauma of this disenchantment burst the rich flood of sarcasm which came increasingly to shape his poem as he endeavoured to complete it.[32]

Johnson's vision of Lucan's politics is undoubtedly a great improvement, recognising as it does Lucan's ambivalence towards Pompey, Cato and the republican senators. And yet even here we have not managed to discard entirely the notion that the poem is some kind of political credo. For all its contempt for the men who, historically, represented the struggle against tyranny, the poem is still clearly anti-Neronian – 'screaming dreadful things about the present' – and, if not an apology for Pompey, it is at least a sincere and passionate lament for the loss of, or the loss of belief in, Roman liberty. Thus: 'Lucan loves the idea of freedom, despairs of it, and he hates, with a violence beyond any control that art might bestow, the monsters who have been complicit in the destruction of the reality and the idea of Roman freedom.'[33] Johnson may argue (and with this I would agree) that the poem is often hilariously funny; but this, he argues, is 'gallows wit', 'the comic-ugly', 'the laughter of outrage' – bitter, satirical, and always in the end 'deadly serious'.[34] In short, Lucan is always sincere, and the poem, with all its contradictions, is an accurate mirror of his tortured political beliefs; Lucan is an anguished, but ultimately *committed* writer.

It is political commitment that I want to deal with in this chapter. We have looked at a number of the accounts the scholarship has offered to explain the historiographical method of the *Bellum Civile*, and in their different ways each has seen politics at the bottom of it all. Each has claimed that Lucan was earnest in support of a political position – whatever political position the poem is seen as advocating. The passion that we find in the poem: that is surely the authentic voice of the poet. In the pages that follow, I wish to question radically the possibility of such a reading; not, indeed, by abandoning intentionality altogether – for in spite of its flaws, the construction of the poet's 'intention' is, at the least, rhetorically compelling. Instead, I shall be working towards a intentionalist reading of my own. My hostility towards the most straightforward of the 'propagandist' readings will be clear; and since Johnson's more sophisticated approach, provocative as it is, and so devoid of close scrutiny of the text, is bound to be at best controversial, I will devote much of my attention to demonstrating why we cannot read the poem as a simple pro-republican political tract – why, in fact, Johnson's contribution was so much needed. In the end, naturally, I will have to differ from Johnson too. But for now, the immediate need is to escape from the generalisations we have been dealing with up till now, and turn to the poem itself to see how, in detail, it stands up as propaganda.

2. The representation of political bias

Book 7 has always been a favourite locus for Lucan's 'propagandist' readers, since it is here that he comes out explicitly and without equivocation in support of Pompey; here, too, that he makes – again explicitly – the connection between the struggle for freedom at Pharsalus and the continuing struggle against tyranny under Nero.[35] It offers some of the most famous (and extreme) examples of historical distortion, most of which are found to have an overtly pro-republican bent; and Lucan's interpretative asides are a rich hunting-ground for anti-Caesarian proselytising. Literally central, if we accept (as I do not) the hypothesis of a planned twelve-book format,[36] and certainly climactic, book 7 is seen as central to the poem's meaning; and as the central expression of Lucan's political beliefs.

Explicit support for the Pompeian cause – what, indeed, could be more explicit than the following?

> o summos hominum, quorum fortuna per orbem
> signa dedit, quorum fatis caelum omne vacavit!
> haec et apud seras gentes populosque nepotum,
> sive sua tantum venient in saecula fama
> sive aliquid magnis nostri quoque cura laboris
> nominibus prodesse potest, cum bella legentur,
> spesque metusque simul peritura<mark>que</mark> vota movebunt,
> attonitique omnes veluti venientia fata,
> non transmissa, legent et *adhuc tibi, Magne, favebunt.*

[O highest of men! Fortune sent portents of their greatness throughout the world,
and every sky made room for their destinies!
Even among later races and the peoples of our descendants, these events
– whether they become immortal by their own fame alone,
or whether the pains I take over my work can also
be of benefit to great names, when the wars are read about –
these events will excite hope and at the same time fear and unfulfilled prayers,
and everyone will be thunderstruck reading of those fates as if they were still to come
and not in the past, *and they will still be on your side, Pompey.*]

(*B.C.* 7.205-13)[37]

9. Deceiving the reader

There is no gainsaying it: Lucan tells you that when you read his *Bellum Civile* (and even if you don't) you will be on Pompey's side. It is an extraordinary claim, clear and unambiguous, and it is, so far as I can tell, unique in epic. Epic poets simply don't tell you whose side you are supposed to be supporting; nor, indeed, do historians. As it happens, either genre may be the vehicle for the most blatant propaganda, and may use the most transparent of techniques to ensure that there can be no mistaking where the reader's sympathies ought to lie; but nowhere, I think, does the author actually *predict* the response of the reader in this way.

A little more detail is required before we can continue. Taking lines 205-10 on their own for a moment, it is clear that what we have is the beginning of a fairly conventional statement about poetic *fama* ('fame').[38] The poet marvels at the greatness of the heroes whose history he is telling, and promises them eternal renown in his poem, since it will be read for generations to come. But there is a new element in Lucan's version of this standard topos: the conceit that his heroes are not entirely dependent on the poet for their fame. Presumably it is a compliment: they are so great that their own fame may well last independently ('whether they become immortal by their own fame alone', 208); the poet himself is, at best, merely helping them on their way to eternity ('or whether ... my work can also be of benefit to great names', 209-10[39]). Strangely, these 'highest of men' are as yet unspecified: there may be a hint of Pompey's name in *magnis ... nominibus* (209-10),[40] but the reference is vague, and would apply just as easily to other 'great names' – even, indeed, to Caesar.[41]

The passage is, so far at any rate, a generalised celebration of the greatness of *all* its heroes. We may suspect, and in fact we almost certainly *do* suspect, that such impartiality, improbable as it is, is a sham; but there is nothing yet in the text to allow us to be sure. Lines 211-12, however, introduce a startling new element to the *fama* topos: that the poem (or whatever) will create the impression that the war is happening all over again, so that the readers will experience the same hopes, fears and disappointments as the original combatants. Here Lucan's objectivity has been eroded: there must have been hopes and fears on both sides, but 'unfulfilled prayers' belong to those who wish things hadn't turned out the way they actually did – that is, the supporters of the losing side. For an epic poet this is daring enough, but even this is hardly sufficient preparation for the way in which Lucan's bias reasserts itself, brazenly, in a punchline which is carefully postponed to the last words of the passage: *and they will still be on your side, Pompey*.

We could not expect this punchline because such a thing is unheard of in epic. The relative impartiality of the introduction combines with our generic expectations to make the final four words doubly startling. Some might say, therefore doubly persuasive. I think not. Rather, this carefully contrived shock has the effect of highlighting the fact that Lucan is seriously tampering with the laws of epic objectivity; and this is something that can easily backfire. We might be impressed because the breaking of rules is one of the signs of 'passion', and 'passion', like 'commitment' and 'sincerity', commands respect; but there is a difference between recognising passionate commitment to a political ideal, and being persuaded oneself of that ideal. More to the point, Lucan runs a very real risk of alienating his reader, either by apparently being swept off in a frenzy of fanaticism to which the reader may not necessarily assent, or by alerting the reader to the fact that she or he is being so obviously manipulated – so explicitly appealed to as if by an author who has an axe to grind and a case to plead.[42]

But there is more to say before we can start drawing conclusions. In the first place, let us look again at the innovation of *sua tantum fama* ('by their own fame alone'). Not only is it unusually humble (in a topos which often asserted the *poet's* claim to immortality as something at least as important as the claims of the subject matter), but the idea that the poet is some kind of optional extra, only incidental to the processes by which one earns eternal renown, actually contradicts the fundamental premise on which the topos is based. Poetry (or literature in general) *is* the process by which one earns eternal renown, and great deeds die without a poet to celebrate them; *fama* and poetry are often virtually synonymous. One of the effects of this innovation we have noticed already: it is a compliment to the characters in Lucan's poem to imply that they do not require his services. Of course, if we insist on Lucan's bias, then it is not clear that he would want to compliment *all* of his characters in this way; perhaps, then, more generally, it is an assertion of the overriding importance of this battle (more than other battles), above and beyond anything that Lucan could write about it. This would certainly serve his 'propagandistic' purposes, for after all it hardly goes without saying that Pharsalus was the great turning point of history, that this *was* the memorable event *par excellence*; though it is central to Lucan's position that it was.[43] But even more than this, we can see that Lucan's humble pose functions as a guarantee of his credibility: you will come to the same conclusion (that Pompey is the good guy) whether you read Lucan or don't read Lucan. Lucan's poem and *sua tantum fama* do not conflict; they are simply different ways of expressing the same thing (in fact, by the end of the sentence, they are the same thing).[44] In other words, Lucan could not be convicted of contaminating or distorting the truth we all know. No propaganda here!

At this point we may well laugh. This appeal to a non-literary *fama*, to *fama* itself that exists and spreads unaided, independent of the immortality conferred by the poet, is an appeal to an idea of fame as somehow 'in the air', so widespread that it is not to be pinned down precisely to any one source, but is simply one of the things 'everyone knows'. Call it 'rumour', call it 'popular mythology', call it what you will, this is the kind of *fama* with a hundred mouths and a hundred tongues, which mixes truth with lies and swells as it travels.[45] To be sure, it is sometimes truthful, but there is no way of telling; and if Lucan expects us to believe the account offered in his poem because it does not contradict *fama*, then that is not, really, much surety. For both *fama* and poetry are traditions, and both are subject to error and distortion; one cannot guarantee the credibility of the other any more than the blind can lead the blind.

To the hostile reader, then, Lucan would appear to be begging the question of his reliability. Worse than that, though, it is not even clear that Lucan *does* have *fama* to support him. For it is hardly indisputable that (in particular) the lost cause of Pompey and the republican senators was still, at the time Lucan was writing, high in popular regard. Of course, there may be evidence for a tendency among certain imperial historians to write favourably about the defeated opposition of the civil war period; but we cannot deduce, from what might be exceptional cases, that this was the conventional story – the 'accepted truth' –

9. Deceiving the reader

of the civil war, even among the Roman aristocracy. Most likely, there was no *universally* 'accepted truth'; and among conflicting truths, a radically different 'official version' will have been a force to reckon with. Lucan, here at least, does not reckon with it at all. Similarly, we should note that in allowing for one alternative route to eternal fame, Lucan excludes any other. As far as he is concerned, there are only two ways of learning about the great men of the civil war: either through his poem, or through their own *fama* (which is able somehow to disseminate itself unaided). What has been left out, of course, is any mention of *other* literary accounts of the civil war (of whatever political colouring). In this passage, it is as though they did not exist; and because they do not exist, there can be no opposition to the account offered in the poem.

Such a position is, of course, a blatant falsity. But it is the least of our problems. So far, we have been working on the premise that Lucan is at least trying to appear sensible; that there is a surface plausibility to his position, even if it falls apart under closer scrutiny. After all, it makes sense for propagandists to imply that the cards are already stacked in their favour; that what they say is entirely natural, everyone knows it is true, and there never has been anyone who could deny it – even if ultimately it is not clear that these implications are justified. What does not make sense is for the propagandist to imply something that is manifestly impossible; and yet this is exactly what Lucan does.

For it is quite obvious that Lucan is posing as an eyewitness of the events he is relating.[46] We are, we Neronians are, the 'later races and the peoples of our descendants' – from the point of view of the 40s BC; we are the ones who will be moved, who will read, and who will favour (*legentur, movebunt, legent, favebunt*, all future tenses); some day, says Lucan, as if surveying the future from Pharsalus, these events will be immortal (*venient in saecula*, again future tense) simply by virtue of their own *fama* – and perhaps he can help them on their way with his poem – but in any case, with a contrived naïvety, he imagines that future years will interpret the war exactly as he does. It is on this basis alone, presumably, that he is at all *qualified* to replay in his poem the events of the war 'as if they were still to come and not yet in the past':[47] it is his status as eyewitness that gives him the authority to magic the reader back into an eyewitness's shoes. And it is on this basis, too, that he is able (as we have seen above) to ignore the existence of accounts other than his own – accounts which, in reality, he must have used as his sources: at this stage in history, with the blood (let us suppose) still warm upon the battlefield, these accounts simply don't exist yet. Lucan's *is* the only one.

His pose as an eyewitness is reinforced by a number of other passages in the poem where, often jarringly, he drops his epic narrator's persona and speaks as a contemporary of the events he is relating; a device which has been well recognised.[48] It goes without saying that Lucan has other poses too, and as often as not he is happy to reveal himself as the sarcastic Neronian of the 60s AD (a gesture that can, in its place, be equally jarring);[49] but we must at least recognise that the 'civil war contemporary' is a coherent role available for the poet to adopt at a moment's notice. Obviously it is all a rhetorical matter of 'subjectivity' invading and dispelling epic 'objectivity' in the name of passion and commitment; but it is more than that, too. For it highlights one of the major problems

Lucan must face as a 'Pompeian apologist', as against a proliferation of other histories more or less favourable to Caesar: Lucan, writing more than a hundred years after the event, just doesn't have the same authority as his sources – so on what grounds can he repudiate them? His answer is as simple as it is outrageous: he appropriates for himself the ultimate authority, the authority of one who was there and saw it all, a *carte blanche* to contradict anything and everything, anybody and everybody, he wants to.

Of course it is all nonsense; and no one could possibly take it literally. But we should, at least, take it *seriously*. For however easy we feel about dismissing this pose as 'mere rhetoric', however disinclined we are to press the poet on the basis of what is only a pretence, a question has been raised about the credibility of Lucan's account – and he doesn't have an answer. Not only has he no answer, but he makes things worse by continuing to defy the historical tradition, capriciously, extravagantly, and with an often bizarre disregard for plausibility. At every stage, faced with an ever more outrageous reworking of history, we will forced to confront anew the worthlessness of his testimony.

Is Lucan, then, 'pleading a case'?[50] Certainly he is, transparently so, with fanatic zeal and rhetorical vigour. To persuade you of his sincerity, he shatters epic objectivity, he makes the poem into a political forum in which only one voice is heard and you, the reader, must vote his way, he batters you down with the conviction of a man who has seen it all and now lives to tell the tale. We cannot fail to recognise here the white heat of pro-Pompeian ardour; but in recognising, precisely in recognising, we cannot fail to disbelieve. It is all too much; it is all too blatant; and it all too obviously runs itself aground. And so what we are left with is a choice: either Lucan, as a propagandist, is extraordinarily inept, and has a monumentally unrealistic conception of just how much a reader's intelligence can be insulted; or he never intended that his 'case' should convince anyone. Naturally, I take the latter view: the view that we are dealing not with propaganda, but with the semblance of propaganda; not with political bias, but with the representation of political bias.

The larger consequences of this argument I will reserve for my concluding section; but in the meantime, let me sketch out some of the more immediate implications. What I am claiming is that Lucan – the 'real' Lucan – is not *necessarily* a committed Pompeian. The passage we have been examining is the most overtly pro-Pompeian statement in the poem; and yet it is at best questionable, and at worst preposterous. We are forced – Lucan forces us – to conclude that this 'passionate outburst' is a pose, a rhetoric, a voice which is *adopted* but not definitely *endorsed* by the author of the poem. Since the political alignment of the poem is already subject to so many variations – since, for instance, the treatment of Pompey elsewhere wavers so bewilderingly between eulogy and satire – none of this should, in fact, come as much surprise. Simply in order to reconcile the embarrassing number of mutually conflicting authorial statements and reconstruct a single, consistent meaning for the poem, we have *always* been compelled to read some of those statements as insincere, ironic, ambiguous (or, dishonestly, as 'mistakes'). Of course, it would be entirely wrong to argue on the basis of 'ironies' of the *fama* topos in book 7 that Lucan's message is really *anti*-Pompeian. The passage certainly encourages us to question Lucan's Pompeianism, but far more than that it encourages us to question the whole business of political persuasion, the whole business of the epic poet being involved in politics. Because Lucan 'cheats', we cannot trust him – we are invited to deconstruct his propaganda *qua* propaganda – but our opinion of Pompey, and our construction of Lucan's opinion of Pompey, might ultimately survive even this. The most one could say is: if we are to support Pompey, it won't be for the reasons Lucan has given us; and if we are supposed to believe that Lucan is a Pompeian, he is playing his cards very close to his chest. *Very* close.

3. The death of Domitius and other damned lies

And so back to historical distortion. Book 7 offers us a rich field, too rich, obviously, for a chapter of this size; and so I will restrict the scope of my discussion more or less to a single exemplary episode. My choice of the passage describing the heroic death of Domitius at Pharsalus is not (entirely) fortuitous: although its precise 'moral' is still a matter of controversy,[51] it is none the less universally agreed that Lucan has here distorted history for *some* political end, and the episode features prominently in most accounts of the political outlook behind the poem. It is thus an ideal test-case for Lucan's 'propagandistic' techniques, and will also provide us with a specific arena in which to confront the contemporary scholarship. Here, then, is the passage in question:[52]

> hic patriae perit omne decus: iacet aggere magno
> patricium campis non mixta plebe cadaver.
> mors tamen eminuit clarorum in strage virorum
> pugnacis Domiti, quem clades fata per omnis
> ducebant: nusquam Magni fortuna sine illo
> succubuit. victus totiens a Caesare salva
> libertate perit: tunc mille in volnera laetus
> labitur ac venia gaudet caruisse secunda.
> viderat in crasso versantem sanguine membra
> Caesar, et increpitans 'iam Magni deseris arma,
> successor Domiti; sine te iam bella geruntur'
> dixerat. ast illi suffecit pectora pulsans
> spiritus in vocem morientiaque ora resolvit.
> 'non te funesta scelerum mercede potitum
> sed dubium fati, Caesar, generoque minorem
> aspiciens Stygias Magno duce liber ad umbras
> et securus eo: te, saevo Marte subactum,
> Pompeioque gravis poenas nobisque daturum
> cum moriar, sperare licet.' non plura locutum
> vita fugit, densaeque oculos vertere tenebrae.

> [Here perished the whole glory of our country: in a huge heap there lay
> on the fields patrician corpses with no plebeians among them.
> However one death stood out amongst the carnage of famous men,
>   that of the pugnacious Domitius, whom fate had brought through every
>   calamity;
> never had he been absent whenever Pompey's fortune
> collapsed. Defeated so many times by Caesar, he nevertheless

> perished with his freedom intact. Now he fell gladly under a thousand wounds,
> and rejoiced not to receive Caesar's pardon a second time.
> Caesar saw him rolling his limbs in thick blood,
> and taunting him, said 'Now you are deserting the army of Magnus,
> Domitius, my successor; now the war is being fought without you.'
> But the breath beating Domitius' breast was enough
> to let him speak, and unlocked his dying mouth.
> 'Seeing that you have not yet achieved the dire reward for your crimes,
> but are uncertain of your destiny, and are still a lesser man than your son-in-law,
> I go to the Stygian shades, with Pompey as my leader, free
> and untroubled; that you will be crushed in savage war,
> and will pay a heavy penalty to Pompey and to me,
> is something I can hope for, since (*or* although) I am dying.' He said no more;
> his life fled him, and a dense darkness covered his eyes.]
>
> (B.C. 7.597-616)

Reading the passage, situated in the midst of Lucan's battle-narrative, without reference to any of the other historical accounts, we could summarise: Domitius dies of the 'thousand wounds' he has received in the fighting; Caesar confronts him gloatingly, but his enemy rebuffs him with arch-republican defiance, and with his dying breath predicts his eventual defeat. All in all, a 'glorious' death which sets the tone for Lucan's ethic of 'victory in defeat', and which cannot but reflect well on the cause that Domitius served. So far so good. But what of our other sources for the event? Caesar himself, in his own list of casualties, tells us that Domitius had fled from the Pompeian camp to the mountains, where he was killed by some cavalry.[53] In his deadpan way, of course, Caesar is implying that Domitius behaved like a coward and a weakling whose death was fittingly marginal; and so we have a right to be sceptical. A passage in Cicero has been adduced in support of Caesar's version, but in my opinion is inconclusive.[54] For the rest, Appian, Tacitus, and Suetonius offer only the bald fact that Domitius died at Pharsalus – where or how goes unremarked.[55] Caesar's account is, then, hardly canonical, but even if we were to suppose that it was not the only version available to Lucan,[56] then the 'no frills' version (the simple fact that Domitius fell at Pharsalus) is the only attested alternative. Clearly Lucan offers a version that is diametrically opposed to Caesar's; but it is highly unlikely that he is standing in any tradition of glorious death-scenes for this ambiguous republican hero.

The scene, then, is an invention of Lucan's (as all would agree). It is further obvious that what Lucan has done is to 'heroicise' Domitius' death, in the sense that he has contrived it to reflect a particular Homeric pattern: the death of Patroclus at the hands of Hector in *Iliad* 16.818-61. Lucanian scholarship tends to concentrate exclusively on the (very similar) death of Hector in *Iliad* 22.247-366,[57] but it is as well to be precise; and though *prima facie* the death of Hector seems more likely to have provided the model, in the end it is the death of Patroclus that seems to predominate.[58] Domitius, after all, is the companion and follower of Pompey (so especially 'nusquam Magni fortuna sine illo / succubuit', 601),[59] as Patroclus is of Achilles.

The parallels should, I think, be obvious; but it is the differences I am interested in. In the first place, Domitius' death-speech is not followed by any response from Caesar (Lucan simply stops, and returns to his pointedly vague depiction of the innumerable battle-casualties), although in both of the Homeric passages the victor has the final word. We can take this in one of two ways: either the poet *prevents* Caesar from having the last word, as if having the last word were some kind of moral victory which Lucan wants to reserve exclusively for Domitius;[60] or we are to imagine that no reply was necessary: Caesar did not have to waste his breath responding to the empty taunts of a dying man. Naturally our choice of reading will depend partly on whether we believe that the scene functions as a pro-republican exemplum; but we may incline more to the second interpretation when we look at Lucan's other major departure from his Iliadic models. For while Lucan certainly *alludes* to the Homeric topos whereby a hero is able to prophesy in the last moments before his death, Domitius' prophecy is not, in fact, a prophecy at all: it is only a hope ('sperare licet' – another hanging *para prosdokian*).[61] It is also, strictly, a false hope: what Domitius is saying is 'you have not won yet, and soon you will be defeated in battle in the same way as I have been defeated today' – and indeed, as Patroclus to Pompey's Achilles, he seems to be implying that Pompey will be the one to avenge his death and defeat Caesar. This will never happen; Caesar will never be 'saevo Marte subactum'; and his eventual downfall, long after he has won every battle and actually 'gained the reward for his crimes', will take place in a way that Domitius cannot envisage. The 'prophecy' is, in other words, marked by its very imprecision as an empty threat; and indeed Domitius himself (with a typically Lucanian twist) seems to be ironically aware of this. *Cum moriar, sperare licet*: not, surely, 'although I die, it is possible to hope' (as it is always translated);[62] but '*because* I die, it is possible to hope'. In other words: were Domitius to live, he would be forced to see Pompey defeated and Caesar victorious; it is his death which *deprives* him of knowledge of the future, and thus makes it possible for him still to hope.[63] If Domitius knows anything, it is the certainty of Caesar's victory; but death alone, gives him the opportunity to 'hope' for a revenge that will not come.[64]

Revenge: of course, as we read this scene, we are thinking of the Ides of March – and it is no accident that the death of Domitius is immediately preceded by a passage in which we see Brutus on the verge of assassinating Caesar some five years ahead of time (*B.C.* 7.586-96). This is itself, of course, another case of historical distortion, and a particularly blatant one at that. The technique is that of 'filling in the gaps': none of our sources, and presumably none of Lucan's, testify to Brutus' early assassination-attempt on the battlefield of Pharsalus, and this is hardly likely to be an accident of transmission. And yet Brutus was at the battlefield, bearing arms against Caesar; and since we know nothing about his movements from minute to minute, we are in no position to deny categorically that Brutus ever disguised himself in plebeian armour,[65] ever went near Caesar, ever entertained the thought that he could put a quick end to the battle by killing the enemy commander. On the other hand, we are not likely to believe it either – it is the sort of fact that is bound to be fictional, precisely *because* it is filling a gap in the sources (because we know that Lucan has no way of knowing that this really happened).[66] What is interesting about this particular fill-in is that it threatens to change the course of history (if Brutus were to succeed, there would be no civil war); historical distortion looks to be getting out of hand, and the poet is obliged to 'prompt' his character, forbidding him to ruin the play by anticipating his big scene. It is not, let it be said, unusual for Lucan to offer advice to, plea with, or castigate the characters in his poem (as part of his pose of being a civil-war contemporary); this, however, is the one place where it actually seems to work! But of course it has to; the effect of this brief tableau is precisely to show the poem striving to break the bonds of history, but ultimately bowing to the necessity of 'truth'.

False the anecdote may be; but the assassination of Caesar in 44 BC is true, and Lucan's explicit allusion to that assassination must have an effect on our reading of Domitius' dying words (some 20 lines later). Briefly, Domitius proposes a heroic pattern of killing and revenge which (as we have seen) is inaccurate. In fact, what revenge there is will come from a different source, for a different crime. By the time we come to Domitius' death, Caesar's punishment has already been (as it were) taken care of; and thus Domitius' expectation of an Achilles-like avenger of his own death appears as an irrelevant side-issue.[67] Caesar will not merit punishment for killing Domitius; he will not deserve death until he has reached the height of power. Only then will he be worthy of assassination by Brutus:

> nondum attigit arcem,
> iuris et humani columen, quo cuncta premuntur,
> egressus meruit fatis tam nobile letum.
> vivat et, ut Bruti procumbat victima, regnet
>
> [He has not yet achieved the height
> nor has he reached the pinnacle of human justice, which stands above everything,
> and earned from fate so noble a doom.
> Let him live, and – so that he may fall the victim of Brutus' knife – let him be king.]

(B.C. 7.593-6)

So Lucan's allusion to a classic epic topos is – and not for the first time – heavily ironic: he plays on our generic expectations only to question them, allows us to be impressed by so 'heroic' a death only to point up the delusion behind it. But again, this is not the kind of irony that simply states one thing and means the opposite: though we have come some way from regarding the scene as straightforwardly encomiastic, it has not been shown (and I will not attempt to show) that Lucan's Domitius is in fact a villain or a fool. He may be a deluded hero, but he is still, arguably, a hero – perhaps, even, all the more sympathetic a hero *because* he is deluded. Let us then assume (as I am inclined to do) that under close scrutiny the passage still stands up as *sophisticated* encomium. It should be easy going now. Domitius is glorified; Lucan intended to glorify Domitius; Lucan intended that his readers should be convinced by this glorification; to glorify

9. Deceiving the reader

Domitius is to endorse the politics he represents (whatever they may be); Lucan intended to persuade his readers to support those politics; Lucan is a propagandist.

This argument simply will not do. We have established that Domitius is (in some sense) glorified; but what the reader is supposed ('intended') to make of it is a different matter altogether. This is hardly sophistry: it is an urgent and real problem, because no modern reader has *ever* been convinced that Domitius' death occurred in the way Lucan says it did. It is obvious to *us* that the whole thing is an absurd lie; but were Lucan's Roman readers in fact any less aware of the absurdity? There are many reasons for supposing that they were not so gullible; many reasons, further, for supposing that Lucan expected from his readers *anything but* open-mouthed, dimwitted assent.

The crucial question is this: were Lucan's (implied) readers able to recognise that Lucan's account of Domitius' death was a historical distortion (or, more to the point, that it differed radically from any other version)? In other words, did Lucan anticipate a readership that would in fact know of Domitius' death from other sources – and in particular the version presented in Caesar's commentary? The answer is surely yes. As we saw in the first section of this chapter, Lucan's poem in general 'was never meant to be a primary source or indeed history in our sense of the word' – with its omissions and obscurities, it can only be deciphered by a reader already very familiar with 'the facts'. We must therefore assume that the implied reader is someone who is quite capable of weighing up Lucan's account against knowledge derived from other sources. We could quibble about which sources – for instance, we could (implausibly) exclude 'Caesarian' sources and confine the reader only to, say, Livian sources – but since even the favourable sources can offer no more than the plain fact that Domitius died at Pharsalus, such a reader would be well aware that Lucan's episode, with its uniquely obtrusive Homeric patterning (there is, after all, no other such battle-scene in Lucan),[68] is at best a mountain made out of a molehill. That is to be cautious; as it is, nowadays few scholars would deny that Lucan wrote his poem as an 'answer' to Caesar's own *De Bello Civili* – which is to admit that the poem's readers might well have had access to Caesar's version of the story.

More than that, Lucan's version of the death of Domitius is, I would argue, *dependent* on Caesar's anecdote. It is paradoxical but none the less true that, for all the appearance of contradiction, Lucan has been very careful not to alter any detail we find in Caesar's account. Caesar says that Domitius died fleeing to the mountains; and although Lucan tells us that a huge pile of patrician corpses lay on the battlefield (597-8), he does not say that Domitius actually died among them – merely that his death was the most significant of the whole carnage.[69] The 'thousand wounds' from which Domitius dies are quite compatible with his slaughter by the cavalry who had (according to Caesar) hunted him down; and Caesar's appearance on the scene, with the ensuing exchange of words, is another case of 'filling in the gaps' – unlikely, but at least possible. Most striking is Caesar's address to Domitius: 'iam Magni deseris arma ... sine te iam bella geruntur' (606-7). Thus the character Caesar flings at Domitius the very reproach that the real Caesar had actualised in his own account of the scene – you have run away from Pompey's army; the battle is now being fought without you.

So it is that Lucan abides by the letter of the facts, by not by their spirit. After all, it is as clear as day that Lucan is *implying* that Domitius died on the battlefield (like Patroclus) among all the other corpses, and *implying* that he received his thousand wounds heroically in battle. Even the blatant reference to Domitius' desertion from the field can, at a pinch, be read more innocuously as a (singularly pointless) taunt: you are *de facto* leaving Pompey's army, because you are dying – henceforth you will have no part in the war. And indeed, that is how it has always been read.

But why, in fact, does Lucan go to so much trouble? Why bother to coincide with Caesar on so many points of detail? One possible answer might lie in Ahl's suggestion that the poem's historical accuracy is a kind of confidence-trick: Lucan's project is to 'maintain the illusion of historicity' so as to 'give the semblance of reality to what he describes, a factual underpinning for his vision which makes the vision itself very hard to refute'.[70] But that hardly applies in this case: by recalling Caesar's version so accurately, Lucan is begging too many questions. He is reminding the audience that there exists an account in which Domitius was nothing but a coward and a weakling;[71] and the only effect of his reworking is to demonstrate how a different bias can, with a little imagination, twist the same 'facts' into an entirely different kind of story. We are invited, that is, to watch the propagandist at work; to be entranced or shocked by his cavalier attitude to truth; to admire or condemn the flamboyance with which he plies the wicked little tools of his trade. So far from finding Lucan's vision 'very hard to refute', we will, in concert with the whole of Lucanian scholarship, feel no qualms about dismissing it out of hand for the outrageous lie it is. Whether or not Domitius died heroically on the battlefield of Pharsalus is not the issue. What matters – what fascinates and entertains – is seeing how closely Lucan keeps within his chosen parameters; how wittily he adapts his own bizarre and unashamedly antagonistic fiction to the 'facts' presented by the opposition. It cannot convince; but it can make us laugh.

4. Predictable responses to the *Bellum Civile*

The telos of my argument, then, is simple: Lucan's poem is a *reductio ad absurdum* of politically committed writing (as it is, indeed, of every other feature of Vergilian epic). Since it can instantly be *perceived* as loud and clumsy agitational propaganda, it cannot *work* as propaganda. Rather than assuming that Lucan tried and failed to persuade his readership to accept his passionate and often perverse political position, we should suppose that his *intention* was to 'fail', and in the process to parody the propagandistic devices of factual distortion and misinterpretation which inform his own work as much as his historical sources. The response of the 'intelligent reader' to Lucan's political tub-thumping is to be amused by it.

This may be as far as it goes. For the ideal reader living more or less in a vacuum, the *Bellum Civile* can work remarkably well as 'pure literature', with no larger purpose than to astound and exhilarate with its uncanny and perverse brilliance. Its message, if it has one at all, may be irresponsible and opportunistic (everything is fair game for the satirist) or nihilistic (all existing systems are ripe for deconstruction in this senseless world).[72] Ultimately what we will 'learn' from Lucan's propagandistic excesses is that truth is a matter of interpretation; history means what you want it to mean. Of course, there are politics involved in such a position; but it is the ease with which these politics can be abstracted and translated to any number of different political situations (including our own) which makes for the attractiveness of such a reading, and ensures Lucan's 'lasting appeal' – as one who could see beyond the pettiness of contemporary power struggles to the deeper lessons of history, rhetoric, and ideology.

Real readers, however, are not necessarily 'ideal': real readers cannot always be relied upon to see the ironies in overt political preaching. Although so far I have argued that no reader could possibly be convinced by Lucan's propagandistic excesses, it is clear that some readers *have* been convinced, if not necessarily of the validity of his 'republican vision', then at least of his intent to persuade. They may be guilty of misreading, but such misreadings are quite understandable and quite predictable, and it would have been naive of the poet to ignore them. So if we want to assess the potential impact of the *Bellum Civile* on a Neronian audience (as if it had ever been published in full),[73] we should be aware of a gradation of responses that have to be taken into account; but there need not be any great difference between the responses Lucan (would have) provoked and the responses he expected to provoke. He may well have anticipated that some readers would 'miss the joke'; and indeed, I will argue that misreadings form part of the plan.

On one level, the *Bellum Civile* is an appalling, dangerous and subversive poem. Its subject matter is basically taboo: we know of no other epic poem dealing with the civil war between Caesar and Pompey, and in historiography too there seems to have been some risk involved in treating any part of the civil war period. The actual degree of risk may have been exaggerated; but under the Julio-Claudians enough histories were suppressed for it to have been taken seriously. Showing any degree of sympathy for the forces opposed to Caesar was dangerous enough: Cremutius Cordus was tried and convicted merely for having called Brutus and Cassius 'the last of the Romans', so they said (see n. 76). Against such a background, the sustained violence of Lucan's bitter denunciation of Caesar, no matter how playful, no matter how ironic, seems to argue an almost suicidal disregard for political exigencies. If Lucan's poetic and political mission had simply been a matter of exposing propaganda techniques to mockery, he need not have chosen to dice with death by treating so controversial a subject in so provocative a way. That he *did* choose to do so, shows that there is more to the poem than an abstract lesson in ideological manipulation. The *Bellum Civile* is, on the contrary, the one poem that could *not* represent itself as an innocent *exempli gratia*; the one poem that was *bound* to call down upon itself the full force of imperial repression; the one poem that should not, under any circumstances, be written. ·

But if that is so, why did Lucan attempt to write it at all? Even if we grant that it was likely to be perceived as 'subversive' by some of its readers, the traditional answer, that the poem represents an idealistic but foolhardy attempt to rally senatorial opposition (or at the very least to register personal opposition to Nero), has little in its favour. Such an explanation may just be plausible if we consider the *Bellum Civile* as the product of Lucan's final year or two – the years after the ban, the years leading up to his involvement in the Pisonian conspiracy, when, writing more or less in isolation, he might feel free to express his anger with impunity. But it fails to take account of the fact that the poem was a troublesome and seditious project *from its very inception*; from a time, that is, when Lucan's relations with Nero were not strained (at least not demonstrably), when he was at the start of a promising and precocious political career, and when he would have had nothing to gain and everything to lose by stirring up opposition to his most powerful benefactor. And further, the traditional view cannot explain why Lucan was prepared to risk destroying his career (and even losing his life) by *revealing* his bitterness towards the Neronian regime in public recitations of the poem. As it is, we are asked to believe that the poem was at odds with his public career; which is tantamount to believing that Lucan was a fool. What we need to do instead is to ask how Lucan might perceive the poem, dangerous and subversive though it may appear, as (at worst) an innocuous adjunct to, or (at best) an intrinsic part of, his career strategy.

We need, therefore, to revise our simplistic view of the political milieu. Nero's regime was not the kind of dictatorship unable to tolerate any hint of subversion in its literary figures; and it is not clear that artists of conscience were compelled to choose between compromise and death. We can indeed point to instances of literary repression in the history of the principate; but as important as these are examples of ostentatious *permissiveness*. Not surprisingly, the behaviour of the reigning emperor towards his 'troublesome' writers became, in our sources, an index of the nature of his rule: tyrannical or benevolent. Augustus, the archetypal 'good' emperor, was renowned in later periods for his tolerance of dissent;[74] and Gaius, at the beginning of his reign, made a big show of reviving some works which had been suppressed for political reasons by his predecessor.[75] At stake was the principle of *libertas* – a slogan, perhaps, but in retrospect an important part of what the old Roman republic was supposed to have been about; and if it was desirable for the 'enlightened' emperor to suggest that the values of the Roman republic still lived on in his own reign, dissent in some form must be seen, if not to thrive, then at least to survive unpersecuted. Where it did not, we have the case of a Cremutius Cordus, whose prosecution under Tiberius is recorded in great detail by Tacitus, not because Cordus was a political figure of any great moment, but precisely because his fate illustrates a principle; namely (and this is quite explicit), how much things have changed since the enlightened days of Julius and Augustus, when a man could not be prosecuted simply because of something he wrote.[76]

On these grounds let us propose an alternative scenario for the context of the *Bellum Civile*; let us not fall into the trap of assuming that the Neronian regime was anything so simple as a tyranny, or that Lucan's story is anything so simple as the crushing of an hot-headed revolutionary. If we assume instead that Nero genuinely intended that his own principate should be looked on as an improvement on his predecessors', if he did want to be perceived as a new and better Augustus whose accession heralded a true golden age of culture, freedom, and prosperity, then he would have had every reason to eschew acts of literary censorship which would instantly be interpreted as a regression to the bad old

9. Deceiving the reader 171

imperial days – of corruption, coercion and despotism. Indeed, he would have had every reason to *encourage* his literary figures to express themselves freely; to discover that no writer need fear repercussions for treading on dangerous ground; to guarantee *de facto* that the spirit of Republican wit and ardour could be safely revived. Against a background such as this (indeed, *only* against a background such as this) Lucan's insanely provocative project would make perfect sense. It was be precisely *because* the civil war was a dangerous subject that he chose it for his *magnum opus* – and chose to treat it in so outrageous a way. If so much as a hint of pro-Republican sentiment could, before Nero's time, earn one the death-sentence, Lucan would show that in the new atmosphere of literary freedom even full-blooded anti-Caesarian hysteria could be tolerated, and enjoyed too (if we are privileged to understand the joke). Such a demonstration would be all the more powerful, coming as it did from a well-known court figure closely associated with Nero, one at the beginning of a political career and with so much to lose if imperial favour was withdrawn.[77]

In the end, imperial favour *was* withdrawn. We cannot be sure why; the story that got around (recorded by Tacitus and Dio) was that the musical emperor was jealous of Lucan's talent, but this seems a trivial motive for Nero's complete suppression of Lucan's public activities (and, in effect, the annihilation of his political career). Certainly, too, it is possible that Lucan miscalculated the depth of the emperor's tolerance, and that the published books of the *Bellum Civile* were what caused Lucan's downfall; but if so, it is extremely surprising that we hear nothing of it from our sources, who would surely have seized upon a blatant act of literary censorship as one more instance of Nero's tyrannical rule. Suetonius' account, that friction had been building up for some time for largely personal reasons, and that Lucan had been tormenting the emperor with more or less open insults (among them a 'libellous poem' which is almost certainly *not* the *Bellum Civile*),[78] suggests that he had been riding for a fall; and it may well be that Nero felt he had to put a stop to his impertinence, which was harmful not only to himself but to his network of friends. It is not a glamorous solution; but it is plausible. In any case, the ruination of Lucan's political career seems an entirely sufficient reason for his involvement in the conspiracy, and we have no need (nor any evidence) to suppose that there was any deep-seated anti-Caesarian idealism behind it.

I would like to draw these threads together by making a final proposition: that the essential plan of the *Bellum Civile* need not have changed at any point during the process of composition; that the same poem can be seen to fit into the context of early imperial favour or, later, imperial displeasure. As I have argued at length, the poem itself is too radically irresponsible for it to have been intended as any kind of manifesto for rebellion, or any serious attempt to persuade anyone of the justice of any cause. It can, however, be *misunderstood* as propaganda; or, more accurately, since it is not a very persuasive text, some readers may *decide* that it is propaganda which, in spite of its obvious faults, may still have a subversive effect on other readers. In the early stages of its composition this misunderstanding was an asset, since the princeps wanted it to be known that persecution of literary figures was a thing of the past. After the ban, the same qualities of the text took on a different meaning. The poem became, simply by virtue of the changed circumstances of its author (and later by virtue of his involvement in a conspiracy) a shrill protest against tyranny. Not a word of the existing books need have been changed;[79] and, similarly, there is no need to look for any major changes of mood in the books that were written later. The poem was, by coincidence or design, a litmus test for the character of the Neronian principate. If Lucan had survived, it would be a testimony to Nero's liberality; since Lucan was, for whatever reason, persecuted, it is now a scathing indictment of his tyranny. Both readings may, in fact, be wrong, because Lucan was interested in other things than the mere dissemination of a political message; but they are predictable. Lucan knew that he was not writing in a vacuum: poets have to write for readerships, and readerships always misread. What is fascinating about the *Bellum Civile*, quite apart from its abstract entertainment-value, is its success in being creatively misunderstood against a complicated political backdrop.

Notes

1. My thanks to Denis Feeney, Stephen Hinds and Jaś Elsner for their comments on this chapter; other debts are acknowledged along the way.
2. See e.g. Heitland 1887 pp. li-liii; Plessis 1909 p. 566; Postgate & Dilke 1978 p. 33.
3. Pichon 1912 p. 159 (my translation).
4. Grimal 1970 p. 105 (my translation); see also Lintott 1971 passim.
5. cf. Rambaud 1955 pp. 260ff.; Grimal 1970 p. 86; Ahl 1976 pp. 69-72; Esposito 1978 pp. 129-30.
6. Rambaud 1960 p. 158; Grimal 1970 p. 56; Lintott 1971 p. 489. Polybius criticised the historian Phylarchus for a similar distorting technique: 'Apart from this, Phylarchus simply narrates most of such catastrophes and does not even suggest their causes, without which it is impossible in any case to feel either legitimate pity or proper anger. Who, for instance does not think it an outrage for a free man to be beaten? But if this happen to one who was the first to resort to violence, we consider that he got only his desert, while where it was done for the purpose of correction or discipline, those who strike free men are not only excused but deemed worthy of thanks and praise ... ' (Polybius 2.56.13-14, the Loeb translation).
7. See Lintott 1971 p. 489; Ahl 1976 p. 70.
8. *B.C.* 3.399-452; Rambaud (1960 pp. 159-60), for one, appears to believe it.
9. *B.C.* 9.961-99; listed as 'pure fiction' by Lintott 1971 p. 489 and n. 3; though Zwierlein (1986 pp. 465-6) is willing to concede that it is at least possible.
10. Lintott 1971 p. 489.
11. Lounsbury 1976 p. 211.
12. See Johnson 1987 chapters 2 & 3 passim; and Masters 1992 pp. 74-90, 99-106.
13. Syndikus 1958 p. 17.
14. ibid. p. 12.
15. ibid. p. 17 and ff.; also Rambaud 1960 p. 158.
16. Syndikus 1958 pp. 8, 23-4, 30.
17. ibid. p. 13 (my translation); see also p. 31.
18. Syndikus 1958 p. 29.
19. Graves 1956 pp. xi-xii.
20. Syndikus 1958 p. 16; see also Rambaud 1960 pp. 158-9, Esposito 1978 p. 130, Bramble 1982 pp. 539-40, Fantham 1985 pp. 126-7 on the Caesarian mutiny.
21. Syndikus 1958 pp. 12-13; Rambaud 1960 p. 157; Ahl 1976 p. 71.
22. Syndikus 1958 pp. 24ff.

23. Lintott 1971 p. 493.
24. cf. Bramble 1982 p. 540: '[Lucan] begins to write his poem at a point where narrative has ceased to matter; his audience, with its knowledge of Livy, and of the paradigmatic history conveyed by the rhetoricians, is expected to supply the background, and the links.'
25. Johnson 1987 pp. 109-10.
26. ibid. p. 110. This is Johnson's vision of the universe as a 'broken machine', endlessly and predictably churning out destruction without meaning or reason; on which see also ibid. pp. 5-18.
27. Stressed by Ahl 1976 pp. 64-7, and Esposito 1978 p. 132.
28. On which see Masters 1992 ch. 1.
29. Rambaud 1960 p. 156-7.
30. Rambaud 1960 p. 159 (my translation).
31. On Cato, see Johnson 1987, ch. 2, esp. pp. 44-6; on Pompey, see chapter 3, esp. pp. 68-9.
32. Johnson 1987 p. 95. The quotation is typical: see also pp. 64-6, 85, 93ff., 122-3.
33. Johnson 1987 p. 72.
34. Johnson 1987 pp. 46, 45, 56 and 45 respectively; quotations chosen *exempli gratia*.
35. For instance 7.440ff. and 7.638-46.
36. On this issue, see Masters 1992, ch. 7.
37. My thoughts about this passage were clarified by an enjoyable discussion with Lucan enthusiast Neil Wright. These moments are rare and precious: thanks.
38. Verg. *Aen.* 9.446-9 (the apostrophe to Nisus and Euryalus) is probably the immediate model.
39. 'Sive aliquid magnis nostri quoque cura laboris nominibus prodesse potest', alluding to, and reshaping, Vergil's 'si quid mea carmina possunt' (*Aen.* 9.446).
40. For plays on Pompey's name 'Magnus', and particularly on the slogan 'magni nominis umbra', see e.g. Feeney 1986.
41. Taken this way by Postgate & Dilke ad loc.
42. Heitland, in his pejorative way, has hit the nail on the head when he remarks of Lucan's apostrophes that 'The poet's business is surely to develop his moral by the simple interaction of characters and circumstances. The reader should be left to judge: half the pleasure and most of the profit of poetry lies in the discovery of the moral significance of the characters and the meaning of the story, not by direct statement, but from the story and characters themselves. Now Lucan is always thrusting himself forward to tell us what it all means: and, whatever Roman audiences may have thought of the practice, on us *the effect is simply to destroy the illusions of poetry and bring us face to face with the orator*' (1887 p. lxxi, my italics). My argument is that 'Roman audiences' will have thought much the same as 'us'.
43. cf. Ahl 1984 pp. 44-6, distinguishing between 'two perspectives on what happened in the civil wars: the 'Actium School' of Octavian, and the 'Pharsalia-Philippi School' of his foes'. Let it be added that to insist on the *civil* wars at all as the crucial event of Roman history is already to make a political statement.
44. The syntax is awkward: although it is arguable that the phrase 'cum bella legentur' (210) must be taken as qualifying only the second *sive* clause (209-10), rather than the sentence as a whole (thus: 'or whether the care I have taken over my work can be of any benefit to great names, i.e. when my poem about the wars is read'), none the less the later 'legent' (213) does not appear to allow for any alternatives: everyone ('omnes' 212) is now a 'reader'. As an index of this confusion, witness the scholiast's attempt to explicate the sentence: 'ordo: haec apud seras gentes cum bella leguntur, spes et peritura vota movebunt' (*Adnotationes*, quoted by Housman ad loc.), which tidies things up at the

expense of suppressing the alternatives altogether, and making 'cum bella legentur' qualify the whole sentence (cf. Duff's translation).

45. Of course I am alluding to the famous personifications of *Fama* in Vergil *Aen.* 4.173ff. and Ov. *Met.* 12.39ff. (which are imitated and de-personified by Lucan in *B.C.* 1.466ff.).

46. This was something that Vergil too, Lucan's immediate model, had hinted at (quoted above): when he writes that the fame of Euryalus and Nisus will last 'so long as the house of Aeneas shall dwell by the fixed stone of the Capitol and the Roman Father shall have power', naturally we are aware (as Roman readers living during Augustus' principate) that we live at the end of a period lasting centuries during which those conditions have held true; and it is as if Vergil has stepped back in time so as to grant fame (retrospectively) to these two characters for all those 'future' centuries of Roman greatness leading up to our own age – as well as for our own future. In Vergil it is a hint, a hint of subjective involvement in his story; in Lucan it is the premise.

47. Thus Brisset 1964 p. 69.

48. See e.g. Syndikus 1958 pp. 39–43; Albrecht 1970 p. 273; Ahl 1976 p. 151; Williams 1978 p. 234; Esposito 1978 p. 131; Mayer 1981 ad 8.827; Johnson 1987 p. 7; and my own book (Masters 1992), pp. 5–6 and 78–9. Lucan is, in fact, only intensifying an existing epic tendency: so Lausberg 1985 p. 1571.

49. e.g. *B.C.* 7.640-6, 8.673.

50. So Lounsbury 1976 p. 210.

51. The problem is this: does Domitius represent the dying glories of republican idealism, or are we to recall that he is Nero's ancestor, and see in this episode one of the few traces we have left of Lucan's original intent to praise Nero? Those eager to read the poem as republican propaganda have tried to play down the importance of Domitius' connection with Nero (see Pfligersdorffer 1959 p. 356, Lounsbury 1976 pp. 224-7, Ahl 1976 pp. 49–54; argued against by Brisset 1964 p. 188, Mayer 1978) But it seems to me that the episode encourages us to confront it. Caesar addresses Domitius as 'my successor' (607), and while in dramatic context we know that Domitius had in fact been appointed as Caesar's successor in Gaul, the Neronian readership is surely being invited to savour the irony that Domitius' descendant would one day be Caesar's *imperial* successor – savour the moment in which the two halves of Nero's origins meet on the battlefield on opposite sides, making Nero a true product of civil war, where ancestor fights ancestor like brother fights brother and father fights son. A specific propaganda message is still possible (Nero might have the qualities of either the vicious Caesar or the virtuous Domitius); but I shall argue against any such interpretation.

52. A shortened version of this section of my paper presented at the APA annual general meeting in Chicago in December 1991; and a lengthier version at a seminar in Corpus Christi Oxford hosted by Robin Osborne nearly two months later. My thanks to all those involved; their often penetrating observations have been an important influence as I prepared my final version.

53. Caes. *BCiv.* 3.99.5: 'L. Domitius ex castris in montem refugiens, cum vires eum lassitudine defecissent, ab equitibus est interfectus.' Ahl (1976 p. 50 n. 60) interprets this as meaning that Domitius made a courageous last stand; surely he is wrong.

54. Cic. *Phil.* 2.71, cited by Lounsbury 1976 p. 223; cf. Ahl 1976 p. 50 n. 60. Cicero is accusing Antony: 'fueras in acie Pharsalica antesignanus; L. Domitium, clarissimum et nobilissimum virum, occideras multosque praeterea, qui e proelio effugerant, quos Caesar, ut non nullos, fortasse servavisset, crudelissime persecutus trucidaras' ['you had been a commander in the battle at Pharsalus; you had killed that most notable and noble man, Domitius, and you had followed up and cruelly butchered many besides, who had escaped from the battle, and whom Caesar might have pardoned, as he did several others']. There is no *necessary* implication here that Domitius was actually among those

who 'had escaped'. It remains possible, though, that Cicero was embroidering on information he found the Caesarian account; and indeed there is no *necessary* implication that Domitius was *not* among those who had escaped.

55. Appian *BCiv.* 2.82, Tac. *Ann.* 4.44.5, Suet. *Nero* 2.3.
56. As does Lebek (1976 p. 261 n. 23).
57. e.g. Lebek 1976 pp. 164-5 and n. 30 (citing Rutz and Nehrkorn).
58. In Lucan, Domitius is already dying of a thousand wounds when confronted by Caesar (603); similarly in *Iliad* 16, Patroclus has already been wounded by Euphorbus (with the help of Apollo) when confronted by Hector (806ff., cf. 849-50) – though Caesar does not strike the final blow as Hector does. Domitius' words of defiance, with his prophecy that Caesar will himself be defeated, closely parallel Patroclus' response to Hector (*Iliad* 16.843-54) – itself a defiant prophecy of Hector's death. Similarly Hector prophesies Achilles' death (*Iliad* 22.355-60), but this comes later on in the episode; and there is nothing in Lucan's scene to parallel the *first* exchange of words in which Hector begs for a decent burial, and Achilles harshly refuses (*Iliad* 22.337-54).
59. As usual, Lucan perverts his model with a classic *para prosdokian* hanging over the end of a line: Domitius had always had a part in Pompey's greatest – collapses. A joke at the expense of the Pompeian cause as a whole, rather than Domitius in particular (for presumably we are not meant to think of Domitius as a 'jinx').
60. So Lebek 1976 p. 265.
61. Noticed by Lebek 1976 p. 265.
62. I have consulted Duff, Bourgery & Ponchont, Ehlers, Griffa, and most recently Braund; Graves avoids the phrase.
63. Thus he is in the enviable position wished for at the beginning of book 2:

sit subitum quodcumque paras [sc. Iuppiter]; sit caeca futuri
mens hominum fati; *liceat sperare* timenti.

[Whatever you intend, Jupiter, let it come suddenly; let the minds of men be blind to future destiny; let him who fears be allowed to hope.]

(*B.C.* 2.14-15)

64. It has been suggested to me (see n. 52) that Domitius' 'prophecy', if read like an ambiguous oracle, does in fact come true when Caesar is assassinated. Plutarch records (*Caes.* 66.12-14) that Caesar fell beside the statue of Pompey 'so that one might have thought that Pompey himself was presiding over this act of vengeance' (thus 'paying a heavy penalty to Pompey' according to the prophecy); and 'saevo Marte' ('in savage war / by savage Mars') might allude to the Ides of March (the month of Mars). Presumably, Domitius knows none of this when he speaks, and so this oracular interpretation does not compromise the point I am making; and all in all I find the suggestion very attractive.
65. Why in plebeian armour? Presumably to avoid being killed, since Caesar has given instructions to his troops to kill only senators (578).
66. cf. Lounsbury 1976 p. 228, adding that '[Brutus'] conduct after the battle little accords with Lucan's ferocious zealot'.
67. This line of argument grew from a suggestion made by Ray Clare at a very early stage in the gestation of this chapter.
68. Thus there is little force in the argument that Domitius' heroic death is plausible because 'epic poems are like that'. Lucan's epic is not like that at all.
69. Noticed by Pichon 1912 p. 156 and Brisset 1964 p. 135.
70. Ahl 1976 pp. 71-2.
71. cf. O'Donnell & Jowett 1986 p. 16: 'Propaganda seeks to contain information in a specific area, and responses to propaganda are manipulated in an attempt to keep them

in the contained area. The recipient of the propaganda message is discouraged from asking about anything outside the contained area.'

72. So, approximately, Johnson 1987.

73. Probably in AD 64, Nero imposed a ban on Lucan's appearance in law-courts and on recitation or publication of his works. Before the ban, a good portion of the poem had been made public (possibly three books), but the remainder was suppressed until after Lucan's death – and, presumably, after Nero's (see Griffin 1984 pp. 158-9, and Masters 1992 pp. 216-34). Private circulation among friends would have been the only form of 'publication' open to him.

74. See e.g. Sen. *De ira* 3.23, Sen. *Ben.* 3.27, Sen. *Contr.* 2.4.13. Ovid is a difficult case to judge: he may not have been exiled, and if he was, it may not have been directly for his poetry. There is, let it be said, a darker side to Augustus' 'tolerance': but in comparison with his descendants he was regarded as having been remarkably benign.

75. Suet. *Gaius* 16.1.

76. Tac. *Ann.* 4.34-5; cf. Suet. *Tib.* 61.3; Dio 57.24.2-4.

77. Though I disagree with Ahl on the propagandistic purpose of the poem, I find myself in sympathy with his assessment of the Neronian regime: '... No work bears clearer testimony [than the *Bellum Civile*] to Nero's tolerance of criticism and senatorial values. I doubt it could have been produced and published under any Roman emperor but Nero ... It is the epic too dangerous for Octavian's contemporaries' (Ahl 1984 p. 70); and later, 'Perhaps the saddest irony of the Neronian age is that, in terms of literary freedom, it was more republican than the late republic – and with the same disastrous results ... Nero's artistic activities and his tolerance of differing opinions were seen as a weakness, not as anxiety to encourage poetry and art ... Nero's reign offered the chance of a restored republic under the transitional rule of an emperor who had no heir apparent, and who seems genuinely to have desired both popularity and acceptance by a restored aristocracy' (ibid. p. 77).

78. Suetonius *Life of Lucan*. The *Bellum Civile* may, of course, have been a contributory factor.

79. The biographer Vacca's statement, that Lucan published 'three books [of the *Bellum Civile*] which were as we see them now', implies precisely this.

Bibliography

Ahl, F.M. (1976), *Lucan: an introduction*, Cornell Studies in Classical Philology, Ithaca.
─── (1984), 'The rider and the horse: politics and power in Roman poetry from Horace to Statius', *ANRW* II 32.1: 40-110.
Albrecht, M. von (1970), 'Der Dichter Lucan und die epische Tradition', *Entretiens Hardt* 15 (Lucain), Geneva: 267-308.
Bramble, J.C. (1982), 'Lucan', in *The Cambridge history of classical literature*, vol. 2: 533-57.
Brisset, J. (1964) *Les idées politiques de Lucain*, Paris.
Duff, J.D. (trans.) (1928), *Lucan: the civil war*, Loeb Classical Library, Harvard.
Esposito, P. (1978) 'Il VII libro della Pharsalia e l' ideologia di Lucano (un ipotesi interpretativa)', *Vichiana* 7: 117-41.
Fantham, E. (1985), 'Caesar and the mutiny: Lucan's reshaping of the historical tradition in *De Bello Civili* 5.237-373', *CPh* 80: 119-31
Feeney, D.C. (1986) '"Stat magni nominis umbra": Lucan on the greatness of Pompeius Magnus', *CQ* 36: 239-43.
Griffin, M.T. (1984) *Nero: the end of a dynasty*, London.
Grimal, P. (1970), 'Le poète et l'histoire', *Entretiens Hardt* 15 (Lucain), Geneva, 51-117.
Graves, R. (trans.) (1956) *Pharsalia: dramatic episodes from the civil wars*, London.

9. Deceiving the reader 177

Haskins, C.E. (1887) *M. Annaei Lucani Pharsalia* (with an introduction by W.E. Heitland), London.

Heitland, see Haskins.

Housman, A.E. (ed.) (1970), *M. Annaei Lucani de bello civili libri decem*, reprint of 2nd edn. (1927), Oxford.

Johnson, W.R. (1987), *Momentary monsters: Lucan and his heroes*, Cornell Studies in Classical Philology, Ithaca.

Lausberg, M. (1985), 'Lucan und Homer', *ANRW* II 32.3:1565-622.

Lebek, W.D. (1976), *Lucans Pharsalia: Dichtungsstruktur und Zeitbezug*, Göttingen.

Lintott, A.W. (1971), 'Lucan and the history of the civil war', *CQ* 21: 480-505.

Lounsbury, R.C. (1976), 'History and motive in book seven of Lucan's Pharsalia', *Hermes* 104: 210-39.

Masters, J. (1992), *Poetry and civil war in Lucan's 'Bellum Civile'*, Cambridge.

Mayer, R. (1978) 'On Lucan and Nero', *BICS* 25: 85-8.

O'Donnell, V. and Jowett, G.S. (1986) *Propaganda and persuasion*, London.

Pfligersdorffer, G. (1959) 'Lucan als Dichter des geistigen Widerstandes', *Hermes* 87: 344-77.

Pichon, R. (1912), *Les sources de Lucain*, Paris.

Plessis, F. (1909), *La poesie latine*, Paris.

Postgate, J.P., revised by O.A.W. Dilke (1978), *Lucan De Bello Civili VII*, Bristol.

Rambaud, M. (1955) 'L'apologie de Pompée par Lucain au livre VII de la Pharsale', *REL* 33: 258-96.

——— (1960) 'L'opposition de Lucain au Bellum Civile de César', *Inf. Lit.* 12: 155-62.

Syndikus, H.P. (1958), *Lucans Gedicht vom Bürgerkrieg*, Diss. Munich.

Williams, G. (1978), *Change and decline: Roman literature in the early empire*, Berkeley.

Zwierlein, O. (1986), 'Lucans Caesar in Troja', *Hermes* 114: 460-78.

10

Nero, Seneca and Stoicism in the *Octavia**

Gareth Williams

According to Tacitus (*Ann.* 14.5), the night was quiet and the sea calm when Nero sent off Agrippina on the collapsible boat and made his first attempt on her life. A similar calm prevails in the *Octavia* as the ship's oars plough the sea in steady rhythm (315); but those conditions seem suddenly to change when the ship disintegrates (317-18). The effects of the shipwreck are typical of the literary tradition of storms at sea: desperate cries go up (319; cf. Virgil, *Aen.* 1.93, Ovid, *M.* 11.540), death is an ever-present vision (321; cf. *Aen.* 1.91, *M.* 11.738), struggling survivors cling to broken planks (323-4; cf. *M.* 11.559-60), while others swim for their lives (325; cf. *Aen.* 1.118). In *Tr.* 1.2 Ovid is caught in a raging storm on his voyage into exile:

> scilicet occidimus, nec spes est ulla salutis,
> dumque loquor, vultus obruit unda meos.
>
> [We are surely lost, there is no hope of safety,
> and as I speak the waters overwhelm my face.] (33-4)

Agrippina, like Ovid, has no hope of salvation (cf. *spes est nulla salutis*, 330), and as she speaks the waters similarly strike her face and drown her words (*feriunt fluctus ora loquentis*, 345). On the strength of these echoes Agrippina would appear to be a storm-victim; but the appearance is deceptive, and not just because she, like Ovid in *Tr.* 1.2, will survive the waves.

These staple characteristics of the literary storm tradition doubtless heighten the dramatic effect of Agrippina's sufferings at the hands of a son whose own savagery is compared earlier to the wild waves (cf. *saevior pelagi fretis*, '[he is] more cruel than the waters of the sea', 129). But the familar storm-apparatus is hardly what might be expected on as calm a night as that which Tacitus reports. Literary shipwrecks are invariably brought about by the raging of the elements, sometimes with divine complicity.[1] In the *Octavia* there is no storm, no natural disintegration of the boat through the buffeting of winds and sea, and Agrippina comes close to a death which is humanly contrived, not the work of nature. The poet's appeal to the literary storm tradition thus rings false; without the storm, the staple features of literary shipwreck as evoked in lines 319ff. lack their natural catalyst, and through this literary distortion the contrived circumstances of Agrippina's shipwreck are thrown into sharper relief.

10. Nero, Seneca and Stoicism in the Octavia

Nero clearly acts against nature in motive as well as means when he sends Agrippina to sea on the matricidal death-boat. The extended description of Agrippina's loyal attendants coming to her rescue in the sea at great risk to themselves (350-5) thus serves only to contrast with his own disloyalty and deceit (cf. 312), while the perverted sense of values which incites Nero to matricide is given verbal expression in his reaction to the news of her rescue through those loyal servants:

> Furit ereptam pelagoque dolet
> vivere matrem
>
> [He rages and grieves that his mother, snatched
> from the sea, is alive.] (361-2)

Nero would prefer to see her *ereptam*, 'snatched away', in the deathly sense of the word;[2] and the regular term for plaintive mourning, *dolet*, is paradoxically applied to the grief he feels at his mother's survival. Analogies from tragedy place the sheer scale of Nero's second, and successful, attempt on his mother's life in its proper perspective in lines 359-60, where the claim that posterity will never believe such horror echoes both Atreus' preface to his own heinous crime (Sen., *Thy.* 192-3) and Oedipus' acknowledgement of the future notoriety which his actions have earned him (Sen., *Phoen.* 264-7).[3] By redoubling his original crime in making good his mother's death, Nero merely piles one massive extreme (cf. 363) on another, and he does so with the impatient hurry (cf. *patitur ... moram sceleris nullam*, 'he allows no delay in the crime', 365) which marks out such slaves to dangerous passion as Seneca's Clytemnestra (cf. *maiora cruciant quam ut moras possim pati*, 'my torture is too great to allow delay', *Ag.* 131).[4] Indeed, Nero is no more able to control his criminal abandonment (cf. *ruit in miserae fata parentis*, 'he rushes to secure his wretched mother's death', 364) than Agrippina is able to control her own destiny amid the overwhelming waves (cf. *ruit in pelagus*, 'she rushes into the waters', 346); Octavia was right to compare his savagery to that of the wild seas (129). Agrippina herself acknowledges his monstrous nature when, true to the parallel accounts of Tacitus and Dio, she invites her final assailant to strike at her womb:

> 'hic est, hic est fodiendus' ait
> 'ferro, monstrum qui tale tulit.'
>
> ['It is this, this that must be pierced with the sword,'
> she said, 'the womb which bore such a monster.'] (371-2)[5]

In these lines a Senecan echo complicates the historical allusion. At the point of death by her own hand in the *Oedipus*, Jocasta similarly makes her womb the target:

> hunc, dextra, hunc pete
> uterum capacem, qui virum et gnatos tulit.

[Make this your target, my hand, this ample womb which bore my husband and children.] (1038-9)

By echoing Jocasta's cry, the poet has Agrippina condemn Nero as an inhuman monster like Oedipus, though with the ironic modification that Nero replaces Oedipus' parricide with matricide. Stabbed in the womb, both mothers victimise the original source of their own ruin – and Nero fares worse in comparison with Oedipus because, unlike Oedipus, he cannot claim to have sinned in ignorance.

These initial observations offer a convenient illustration of Nero's character as drawn more broadly in the *Octavia*. Nero is cast as a tyrant whose cruel excesses make him an ideal subject for a work illustrating the disastrous consequences of autocratic power which lacks moral direction. True, the Stoic code of moral conduct as presented in the play by the character Seneca is a lofty ideal which, as we shall see, Nero attacks with no little justification because of its failure to address the simple pragmatics of autocratic rule in the conspiratorial atmosphere of imperial Rome. For this reason it would be simplistic to insist on a straightforward contrast in the drama between good and bad, between Seneca's Stoicism and Nero's tyrannical evil, or to assume that Stoicism is presented as an ideological panacea, the only alternative to tyrannical misrule. The date and authorship of the play are crucial in this respect, for if Seneca is the author, his own character's failure within the play to bring Nero to Stoic reason could be viewed either as an admission of ideological defeat or as a despairing last effort at correcting a delinquent pupil.[6] But my conviction that the play is not Senecan[7] allows for the Stoic position of Seneca's dramatic *persona* to be treated with critical detachment by an author who depicts not just Nero's autocratic excesses, but also the weaknesses in Seneca's own doctrine. In what follows my first objective is to demonstrate how the author uses Stoicism to provide a moral criterion against which to judge the Neronian regime; my second objective is to demonstrate how Nero's victory over all opposition by the play's end despatches the ideal Stoic ruler to the philosophical wilderness.

1. Seneca and the Golden Age

Seneca's resignation to the vagaries of fortune (377-80) is very much in the character of the real Seneca; raised to the precarious pinnacle of high office (379), he is now vulnerable to the same dangers of fortune which he so often voices in his tragedies.[8] The idea is, of course, commonplace in Greek tragedy and bound to no one philosophical school, but here it is tailored to Stoic theory in Seneca's reflections on life in Corsica before being recalled to office at Rome (381ff.). There is no contradiction in the Epicurean overtones of *latebam* ('I was lying low', 381),[9] for Seneca's quiet life in exile enables him to cultivate a distinctively Stoic peace of mind. He is the *sapiens* who, through necessary philosophical contemplation (384), has attained the freedom of mind which comes with being one's own rational master (cf. *liber animus et sui iuris mihi*, 'my spirit was free and its own lord', 383) rather than a hostage to fortune or a slave to passion.[10] His, too, is the virtuous happiness (cf. *o quam iuvabat* ..., 'O what joy it was ...', 385) of the *sapiens* who lives in accord with nature (*Natura*, 386) and whose ordered soul is at one with the macrocosmic soul of the universe;[11] hence his contemplation of the sun, moon and stars in their fixed courses (386-90) amounts to no more than the confirmation of peace within his own self.[12] But on his recall to Rome this vision of cosmic order is shattered. That the world passes through fixed cycles towards eventual destruction and renewal was orthodox Stoic doctrine which Seneca mouths with guarded generality in line 391-5,[13] and with only an implied slur on the Neronian age (cf. *genus impium*, 'the impious race', 393); but his account of the dissolution of the Golden Age into progressively worse ages down to his own time (cf. *saeculo premimur gravi*, 'a grievous age afflicts us', 430) carries an unmistakable message: Nero's reign marks the nadir which precedes Stoic catastrophe.

In Seneca's *Apocolocyntosis* Nero's accession is prophetically cast as the beginning of a new Golden Age,[14] but in the *Octavia* the proven nature of his rule betrays that prior forecast. Now the fusion of literary and philosophical influences ensures that the Neronian age is cast as the extreme antithesis of the Golden Age and the embodiment of all the vices which are said from Hesiod onwards to characterise the Iron Age. The residual theme throughout the description of successive ages in lines 397-434 is man's gradual alienation from life in harmony with nature and his fellow man. In the Golden Age (397-406) literary precedents supply the standard characteristics.[15] Cosmic harmony prevails, with Justice and Faith making the easy transition from heaven to benign rule on earth (398-9) and with man living at one with nature in a relationship which expands the language of the microcosmic family to macrocosmic proportions (404-6). But the ages which succeed the Golden Age (406-15) mark man's steady alienation from nature until 'the restless race' (*[genus] inquietum*, 409) begins to exploit her in earnest. The earth is abused (414) and her once spontaneous munificence (cf. 405) violated; the language of daring (*auderet*, 410), guile (*decipere*, 412) and coercion (*extrahere*, 411, *premere*, 412) now characterises man's deteriorating relationship with the natural world.

The Iron Age dawns (416ff.), the earth is plundered through mining (416), arms are carried (418), land is divided (419), walled cities spring up (420), Justice departs (424): these regular characteristics of the literary Iron Age are invoked to negate every aspect of the Golden Age of lines 397-406.[16] But the poet nevertheless combines subservience to a familar topos with a creative contribution of his own. No longer safe in the hands of her once dutiful offspring (cf. 405-6), mother earth is plundered by acquistive man in search of iron and gold. *In parentis viscera intravit suae/ deterior aetas* ('the worse age intruded into its mother's innards', 416-17): man turns on his own nurturer in an act of cosmic matricide which immediately bears comparison with Nero's own matricidal crime.[17] Through his minister he uses the very symbol of the corrupt Iron Age, the sword (*ferrum*), to penetrate his mother's flesh (cf. 372) as Iron Age man once penetrated mother earth; he it is who, through his crimes, banishes Justice in his own time and soils her with the pollution of bloody murder (cf. 423); he is heir to a legacy of sin in the imperial house (cf. *series facinorum*, 'a series of crimes', 143) which is inspired by the same subservience to appetite (*regni cupido, sanguinis diri sitis*, 'lust for power, thirst for terrible bloodshed', 144) which is a vice in the Iron Age (cf. *cupido belli ... atque auri fames*, 'desire for war ... and hunger for gold', 425); and 'the grievous error' (*error gravis*, 428) which fuels the bane of easy living (*luxuria, pestis blanda*, 'luxury, a luring bane', 427) is evident in Nero's abandonment to the blandishments of love, a god who is later cast by Seneca as preying on 'human folly' (*mortalis error*, 558) and 'nurtured by slothful indulgence' (*luxu otio/ nutritur*, 562-3). When Seneca eventually heaps the vices of successively degenerate ages on his own age (429-30), the general corruption merely confirms the insinuation made against Nero in the preceding Iron Age (417-28). The nature of Nero's impious rule is reflected in the symbolic rule of criminality (*scelera regnant*, 'crimes hold sway', 431) and in the raging of impiety (431). Lust prevails (432) under a leader who is a slave to his own libido; and the plundering of the world's resources (433-3) takes place under a ruler who, through Agrippina, 'plundered' the world to become its master (cf. 155-6). Nero's first appearance in the play (437) is timed to perfection: he personifies the very vices which Seneca has just described.

2. Seneca and Nero

When Nero first appears, his agitated steps and fierce demeanour (435-6) betray his state of mind; hence Seneca's foreboding (*quid ferat mente horreo*, 'I tremble at the thought of what he brings', 436), for Seneca the character recognises the symptoms which Seneca the writer makes the outward mark of irrationality in the *De Ira*, where hurried steps and a harsh demeanour are but two characteristics of the angry man's loss of self-control and Stoic reason (1.1.3).[18] Seneca's foreboding is borne out in his ensuing exchanges with Nero (440-592). That Nero departs in this section of the play from many of the principles which the real Seneca had addressed to him in the *De Clementia* has long been observed,[19] but the author of the *Octavia* does not simply create a Nero who has demonstrably learnt nothing from his early mentor's guiding text. Nero proves to be deficient in each of the four primary virtues which equip the Stoic *sapiens*, practical wisdom, justice, self-control and bravery,[20] and in portraying this deficiency the poet casts Nero as the antithesis of the ideal Stoic ruler and the embodiment of all that is worst in that pejorative term in the *De Clementia*, the *tyrannus*. Octavia terms Nero a tyrant in line 33, 88, 110 and 250; in lines 440-592 Nero himself reveals why he deserves the insult.

At *Cl.* 1.7.1 Seneca lays down one precept which should inform the conduct of the ideal ruler:

optime hoc exemplum principi constituam, ad quod formetur, ut se talem esse civibus, quales sibi deos velit.

[I shall best establish this as the standard after which the ruler should model himself – that he should wish to be to his subjects as he would wish the gods to be to himself.]

The relationship drawn here between the gods, the ideal ruler and his subjects is not fulfilled in the *Octavia*. In response to the character Seneca's appeal that he make divine approval the determinant of his actions (448), Nero bluntly denies his own subordination to the gods (449); and far from treating his people as he would wish to be treated by the merciful gods, Nero replaces Stoic *virtus* with a despotic alternative (cf. *extinguere hostem maxima est virtus ducis*, 'a leader's greatest virtue is to destroy his enemies', 443) which enables him to sentence Sulla and Plautus to death on the merest suspicion of an impending coup (437-8).[21] Instead of protecting his citizens as he should in his role of *pater patriae* (cf. 444),[22] Nero victimises his subjects, in this instance Sulla and Plautus, to make his own safety his misplaced priority. His is a form of tyranny, then, which is a perversion of model Stoic rule because under his sway the ordered, hierarchical structure of citizenry, king and gods is thrown into disorder.[23] And Nero's understanding of his own power is shown in lines 451-4 to be anything but the Stoic ideal:

N: Fortuna nostra cuncta permittit mihi.
S: Crede obsequenti parcius: levis est dea.
N: Inertis est nescire quid liceat sibi.
S: Id facere laus est quod decet, non quod licet.

[N: My position makes everything possible for me.
S: Trust compliant fortune more cautiously: she is a fickle deity.
N: It is the fool's part not to know the extent of his power.
S: It is praiseworthy to do what is right, not what one may.]

In his interpretation of the nature of fortune, Nero proves to be devoid of the cardinal virtue of Stoic wisdom.[24] In using the term to describe his status as emperor and the limitless entitlements which come with that status,[25] he falls victim to false opinion according to the Stoic code: Stoic Fortune is not the immutable ally which he takes her to be when he claims her as his own (cf. *nostra*, 451), but a mercurial quantity which the *sapiens* treats with cautious moderation (452).[26] Misguided on this point, Nero is no closer to Stoic wisdom when he defines knowledge in line 453 in the tyrannical sense of understanding the extent of one's power (*quid liceat sibi*). Again, Seneca strives in vain to counter what he interprets as Nero's folly by making morally correct action (*quod decet*, 454) more laudable than actions based on the dangerous licence of being able to do as one pleases (*quod licet*, 454) – a licence which dispenses with the Stoic imperative of wise discrimination between right and wrong.

Nero's lack of Stoic wisdom inevitably strips him of self-control, the Stoic virtue which would impose moderation (cf. 452) on his limitless self-indulgence (451) and commit him to observing propriety (*quod decet*).[27] The sentence he passes on Sulla and Plautus reflects his lack of self-control in the face of his own suspicions, and it equally demonstrates his lack of Stoic justice, that primary virtue of knowing how, on the strength of proper judgment, to give every man his proper due.[28] Nero's is, by contrast, a code of justice based on his own self-interested interpretation of right and wrong, not the impartial code which Seneca urges him to invoke with *iusta impera* ('give just orders', 459). Nero's response – *statuam ipse* ('I shall myself decide', 460) – relegates the Stoic ideal of justice to his own whim and defies Seneca's appeal for consensus (460). Instead of consensus, the sword ratifies Nero's own personalised judicial code (461); an emperor who rules by fear has no alternative, as Nero makes plain in line 441:

iusto esse facile est cui vacat pectus metu.

[To be just is easy when the heart is free from fear.]

Now even if, with one commentator,[29] we concede the practical reasoning which lies behind Nero's case for defending his own position by the sword, the poet still damns him in a Stoic context by connecting him with the cruel tyrant exemplified in the *De Clementia*. At 1.12.4 Seneca contrasts the kindly rule of the ideal king with that of the tyrant who rules by fear:

> nam cum invisus sit, quia timetur, timeri vult, quia invisus est.

[For since he is hated because he is feared, he wishes to be feared because he is hated.]

Such a ruler is himself the slave to his own fears:

> tantum enim necesse est timeat, quantum timeri voluit, et manus omnium observet et eo quoque tempore, quo non captatur, peti se iudicet nullumque momentum immune a metu habeat.

[For he must fear as much as he wishes to be feared, he must watch the hands of every person, he must regard himself as a target even when no one is after him, and no moment must he have that is free from fear.] (1.19.5)[30]

Again, then, Nero's insistence that a ruler ought to be feared (457) betrays his failure to heed the lessons of the *De Clementia*. But as a victim of his own fears (cf. 441), Nero also falls short of the fourth cardinal Stoic virtue, bravery.[31] Instead of fearless commitment to Stoic reason and to the ideals of Stoic kingship, Nero's own brand of tyranny unites him and his people in a mutual bond of fear.

The schism which opens in lines 440-71 between Seneca's Stoic ideology and Nero's autocratic pragmatism widens in lines 472-592, when each judges the career and achievements of Augustus according to his preferred criteria. Now in the *De Clementia* Seneca cites Augustus as a model of clement rule – but not the youthful Octavian:

> Divus Augustus fuit mitis princeps, si quis illum a principatu suo aestimare incipiat; in communi quidem rei publicae gladium movit.

[The deified Augustus was a mild ruler, if one should undertake to judge him from the time of his principate; but when he shared the state with others [i.e. in the triumvirate], he wielded the sword.] (1.9.1)

Seneca reiterates the point at 1.11.1-2 in a contrived compliment to Nero: whereas Augustus' late clemency was born of weariness with cruelty, the new emperor's clemency is born of his immaculate character. In the *Octavia* Seneca's *dramatis persona* echoes that compliment in the form of an implied contrast in lines 479 and 482 between *fortuna* [*cruenta*] ('[bloody] fortune') and *incruenta* [*fortuna*] ('bloodless [fortune]'): heir to the Augustan legacy of secure *imperium*

(483), Nero is supposedly unsullied by the bloodletting which created it (479-81). On this occasion, however, the character Seneca plays down the pejorative aspects of Augustus' youthful character and concentrates on the Augustan principate as a model of sound and harmonious government which Nero would do well to emulate. In the Senecan gaze the mature Augustus proves to be an ideal Stoic ruler, a model of temperance whose own self-control is reflected more broadly in the controlled peace which pervades his age; hence Seneca uses the programmatic language of Stoic kingship to describe the Augustan legacy in lines 472-6 – the language of altruistic devotion to the national cause (*consulere patriae*, 'to have care for the fatherland', 473), the language of moderation (cf. *parcere afflictis*, 'to spare the afflicted', 473, *caede abstinere*, 'to abstain from bloodshed', 474, *tempus ... irae dare*, 'to be slow to anger', 474), and the language of imperialist and macrocosmic peace ([*dare*] *orbi quietem, saeculo pacem suo*, '[to give] calm to the world, peace to one's time', 475). In order to impress upon Nero the case for living at one with the people, not at variance with them, Seneca portrays the rule by consensus which Nero has eschewed (460-1) as basic to the Augustan heritage (485); hence Augustus bequeaths to Nero a state in which the senate, the equestrian order and the people are said to be united behind the new emperor (486-7) in a political concord which is universally reflected in the Augustan creation of global peace (488-90). In lines 472-91 a perfect vision emerges of the Augustan achievement because Seneca imposes his own chosen emphasis on his interpretation of the Augustan principate. Can Nero be brought to Stoic reason by such a display?

Unimpressed, Nero meets Seneca's philosophical loftiness with political pragmatism in lines 492-532, replacing the idealised vision of Augustus as a philosopher-king with what he presents as the harsh reality of the late Republic and Octavian's push for power. Caesar's assassination (500-2), the proscriptions under the second triumvirate (504-9), Philippi (515-16) and the civil war between Antony and Octavian (519-24): for Nero, Republican history holds a more pertinent lesson on how to treat opponents than the strictures of the *De Clementia*. In what amounts to a direct critique of that work, he turns on his former tutor by siding with the young Octavian, not the mature Augustus, as he sets out his own pragmatic view of government. For Nero it is madness (*dementia*, 496) not to act on the suspicion of possible subversion by ordering immediate death (496-8); for Seneca, by contrast, to condemn Sulla and Plautus on suspicion alone is an act of rashness (cf. 440) which signals Stoic *dementia*. *Dementia* has one meaning for Nero, another for Seneca, and the difference in interpretation lies in the difference between the political pragmatism of the one and the Stoic idealism of the other. For an autocrat such as Nero, the Stoic code of rule is but an idealistic vision which fails to address political reality.

3. Nero in love

Just as he urges that Nero indulge Fortune with Stoic moderation (cf. 452), so Seneca advocates equivalent restraint in love:

recedat a te (temere ne credas) amor.

[Let love depart from you; do not place rash trust in it.] (553)

Nero is beyond persuasion, ruled as he is by his passions; he is ready to declare his servitude to love's indomitable influence on the strength of his own convenient analogy of Jupiter's submission to Amor (554-6). That Nero submits to Cupid is in fact hardly surprising, for the two are cognate characters of similar fickleness and whimsical instability – as Seneca himself seems to recognise. Casting the notoriously winged and fleeting god as a force that appears irrepressible only to the deluded (*volucrem esse Amorem fingit immitem deum/ mortalis error*, 'human folly imagines the winged god to be an implacable deity', 557-8),[32] he reappraises Amor in language which, coincidentally or otherwise, partly reflects the emperor's own character:

> vis magna mentis blandus atque animi calor
> Amor est; iuventa gignitur, luxu otio
> nutritur inter laeta Fortunae bona.
> quem si fovere atque alere desistas, cadit
> breviaque vires perdit extinctus suas.

[Love is a mighty force of the mind and a luring heat of the soul; it is born of youth, it is nurtured by luxury and ease amid the bright gifts of Fortune; and if you cease to foster and feed it, it falls away and, once allayed, it quickly loses its power.] (561-5)

Amor has chosen a suitable victim. The easy living (*luxuria*) which Seneca detects as a vice in his own age (cf. 433) has nurtured Nero just as it nurtures Cupid (562-3); Nero, like Cupid (563), thrives under what he interprets as Fortune's benign gaze (cf. 451); and while Cupid flourishes when nourished and wilts when unsupplied (564-5), Nero jeopardises his people's loyalty according to the Stoic code by falling for Poppaea: the consequence of his passion is that in ceding to love of one kind, he is in danger of losing once and for all what Seneca portrays in the *De Clementia* as the Stoic king's greatest strength, his people's love for him (*amor civium*, 1.19.6). The character Seneca warns of the popular backlash which Nero risks by marrying Poppaea (572-3), but Nero, Cupid-like and resigned to Cupid's hold over him, is unstoppable in his erotic waywardness.

On the strength of his implied kinship with Cupid, Nero predictably counters Seneca's Stoic dismissal of Amor as a transitory illusion (557-65) by siding with Epicurus in lines 566-9. Lucretius is the intermediary who furnishes the essentials of Nero's dogma: Love is the cause of all creation (566; cf. *DRN* 1.4-5), the source of generative pleasure (*voluptas*, 567; cf. *DRN* 1.1), the gentle captivator of every wild animal (569; cf. *DRN* 1.14-16). But Nero's stated commitment to the Epicuran cause rings false in the light of his transparent failure elsewhere in the play to live the Epicurean life. Agitated (cf. 437-8), suspicious of unproven enemies such as Sulla and Plautus (cf. 469), ruling by fear in order to allay his own fear of overthrow (cf. 441), and given over to anger (cf. 255), Nero betrays at every turn his complete lack of *ataraxia*, the ultimate Epicurean goal. And though Epicurus himself makes bodily pleasures the source of maximum pleasure,[33] he does not endorse any and every hedonistic indulgence, for the hedonistic calculus balances pleasure against pain and determines action accordingly.[34] Now even if the allegation of Octavia's infertility was true,[35] Poppaea's attraction for Nero does not lie solely in her potential for child-bearing (cf. 591): he is clearly captivated by her surpassing beauty (544-6). But his passion is so overwhelming that the hedonistic calculus is beyond him, and because he fails to weigh the pleasure to be derived from Poppaea against the painful consequences of such a union (cf. 572-3), Nero is not quite the fully fledged Epicurean that he claims to be in lines 566-9. The suspicion remains that he merely disguises his reckless designs on Poppaea in the convenient language of philosophical conviction, perhaps sarcastically so in an open attack on Seneca's Stoic convictions; and though he swears allegiance to Amor in Epicurean cliché, Amor is anything but a source of *ataraxia* for one who is so ready to inflame his public to satisfy his own private passion.

Nero's response to this popular unrest amounts to an ironic admission of his own inner turbulence:

> libet experiri, viribus fractus meis
> an cedat animis temere conceptus furor.
>
> [I want to make trial whether, broken by my power,
> this rashly conceived madness will leave their minds.] (576-7)

Compare Seneca's appeal in line 553:

> recedat a te (temere ne credas) amor.
>
> [Let love depart from you; do not place rash trust in it.]

Nero refuses to recognise the possibility that the outbreak of what he interprets as civic *furor* is precipitated by the *furor* within himself (cf. *amor*, 553); that the rashness which he condemns in his people (cf. *temere*, 577) is characteristic of himself (cf. *temere ne credas*, 553); and that his determined effort to snuff out his people's *furor* (*libet experiri ... an cedat animis – furor*, 577) can hardly be reconciled with his determined disregard for Seneca's advice that he rid hemself of his own erotic *furor* (*recedat a te ... amor*, 553). Nero cannot accept Seneca's insinuation that the chaos which reigns in his own psyche is the catalyst for social chaos, and his harsh response in lines 576-7 to his people's stirrings merely evades the real issue as implied by Seneca – that self-correction is the only way to correct what Nero allegedly misinterprets as civic delinquency. Seneca once again tries to supply the Stoic corrective by advising calm compliance with the popular will (578), just as he earlier advised the emperor to indulge fickle fortune with cautious moderation (cf. 452). Seneca fails (cf. *liceat facere quod Seneca improbat*, 'permit me to do what Seneca disapproves', 589), and at the end of his encounter with his early mentor Nero is cast as an obdurate enemy of Stoic *ratio*. The Stoic code is redundant.

4. Choral factions and Neronian fire

The chorus of lines 273-376, 669-89, 887-98, 924-57 and 972-82 sympathises with Octavia, that of lines 762-79 and 806-19 with Poppaea.[36] The arrangement represents the divisiveness which Nero's lack of self-government has on his public. More specifically, the divided chorus takes into the public domain the private conflict of different ideologies between Seneca and Nero (440-592).

Like Seneca (553-5), the chorus of lines 273-376 envisages Octavia as the guarantor of stable continuity within the Claudian *gens* (278-81), only for that vision of ordered *imperium* based on hereditary succession to be shattered when Nero divorces Octavia. Like Seneca, who contrasts the enduring virtues which Octavia has at her command with Poppaea's transient beauty (547-50), this Chorus interprets Nero's divorce as a descent into moral decadence:

> sancta quid illi prodest pietas
>   divusque pater?
> quid virginitas castusque pudor?

[Of what avail to her is her sacred devotion and deified father? Of what avail her maidenly purity and unblemished decency?] (286-7)

Sancta pietas has already fled before Agrippina's atrocities (160), and under Nero Octavia's *sancta pietas* is similarly abused; it is left to the pro-Octavia faction to prove Seneca right when he warns Nero that *sancta pietas* will vindicate her in the form of popular opposition to the new marriage (572-3).[37] Octavia's supporters rise to the occasion by resurrecting the Republican spirit of 'true virtue' (*vera ... virtus*, 291) which avenged Virginia (295-9) and Lucretia (301-3), other victims of tyrannical excess, and which punished Tullia for her crime of Neronian dimensions agaist her father (304-8);[38] through these *exempla* traditional Roman *virtus* is invoked to combat the threat which Nero's own dissolute example poses to the traditional moral order. That Nero makes the wrong choice between the alternatives presented by Seneca in lines 547-50 – between Poppaea's fleeting beauty and Octavia's enduring virtue – is shown by the actions of the pro-Octavia faction in lines 682-9. When the rumour of the divorce is confirmed (669-75) and the Chorus rallies to the battle-standard of Republican *virtus* (678-81), the assault on Poppaea's statues (682-9) comes as proof of Seneca's claim that superficial beauty is all too transitory (550).

When the Messenger reports to the pro-Poppaea faction of the Chorus the smashing of Poppaea's images (794-9), its harsh response reflects its different values. Its opposition to the rioters means that in terms of the Republican *exempla* which the pro-Octavia faction adduces in lines 291ff., the pro-Poppaea faction sides not with the victims of tyrannical abuse, Virginia and Lucretia, but with the right of their abusers to violate with Neronian impunity. As the enemy of Republican *virtus*, this chorus predictably joins Nero in the moral abandonment which sees him favour Poppaea's beauty over Octavia's enduring virtues; indeed, the chorus surpasses Nero's own hyperbole: whereas Nero casts Poppaea as Helen's equal in his reconstruction of the Judgment of Paris (545-6), the Chorus makes Poppaea Helen's conquerer (*vincet vultus haec Tyndaridos*, 'she will outshine the face of Helen', 775). Like Nero, the Chorus falls victim to what Seneca portrays as the human folly of accepting Cupid as a remorseless god who brooks no opposition (cf. 557ff.). Its warning that the rioters will pay a heavy penalty for resisting Cupid (806-19) is an endorsement of tyrannical omnipotence – and an endorsement of Nero's own style of tyranny. In these lines, as elsewhere in the drama, Cupid's character proves to be uncomfortably close to Nero's.

So powerful is the fire which Cupid wields that even Jupiter's bolts are defeated by it (809), and Jupiter himself is taken captive (810). Nero has already conceded defeat to Cupid on the analogy of Jupiter's submission (cf. 554-6), and in lines 806-19 the parallel between Nero and Jupiter is resurrected. How, then, can Nero be likened to Cupid if he is already cast as Jupiter? Nero may be Jupiter-like in yielding to Cupid, but in seeing off the public opposition to Poppaea he acts with Cupid's remorselessness. In setting fire to Rome (cf. 831) to bring his subjects to what he would call their senses, Nero wields an incendiary weapon which vies with Cupid's own. When the Chorus states that Cupid will exact bloody reprisals for the slights against his authority (811-12), the price is that set by Nero in his own murderous response to the popular uprising (cf. 822-4, 830). When Cupid is said to be 'hot-headed, not slow to anger nor easy to be ruled' (*non est patiens fervidus irae facilisque regi*, 812-13), the description might equally apply to Nero's own hot-headed intemperance (cf. *regenda ... est fervida adolescentia*, 'fiery youth needs to be controlled', 446). With Nero's reappearance on the scene imminent (820), we might well wonder who is meant when the Chorus closes with shuddering uncertainty over what 'the unchecked power of the relentless god will do' (*quid ferat ... vis immitis violenta dei*, 818-19). Since Seneca had similarly shuddered on Nero's first appearance in the drama (436), the chorus' foreboding suggests that Nero's entrance will begin the terrible retribution of Cupid.

When the mob launches a torch-attack on the imperial palace (cf. 801, 851-2) and Nero responds by ordering Rome to be burnt to the ground, his order signifies Cupid's avenging fire:

> mox tecta flammis concidant urbis meis,
> ignes ruinae noxium populum premant
> turpisque egestas, saeva cum luctu fames.
>
> [Let Rome's roofs quickly fall before my flames,
> let fires, let ruins crush the guilty populace,
> and loathsome want and grief and dire hunger.] (831-3)

The holocaust turns Rome into a hellish apparition, a recreation of the Virgilian underworld which houses 'ill-counselling hunger and loathsome want' (*malesuada Fames ac turpis Egestas, Aen.* 6.276).[39] But the poet achieves a yet more brilliant effect by turning Nero's burning of Rome into an event of climactic significance: Stoic catastrophe beckons.

Seneca's Stoic vision of the world passing through fixed cycles to eventual destruction and renewal (391-5) now assumes crucial importance. Destruction comes when impiety reigns:

> tunc adest mundo dies
> supremus ille, qui premat genus impium
> caeli ruina.
>
> [Then for the world that last day
> is at hand to crush the sinful race of men
> with heaven's ruin.] (392-4)

That point is reached in the Iron Age of the corrupt Neronian present (cf. *saevit impietas furens*, 'raging impiety runs wild', 431). Now when in his prose works Seneca makes fire and inundation the two agencies of cosmic catastrophe, he reflects orthodox Stoic thinking.[40] These agencies rage with such force and frequency in his tragedies as to bear out Rosenmeyer's claim that 'the catastrophe of cosmic conflagration and inundation is deeply embedded in the structure and mood of Senecan drama'.[41] Could the same be true of the *Octavia*? Agrippina's ominous wedding-torch (cf. 24, 723), Nero's burning hatred of Octavia (cf. 132), his ardent passion for Poppaea (cf. 189), Agrippina's scorching anger at her son (cf. 331), the inflamed passions of Octavia's supporters (cf. 792) and their torch-attack on the palace (cf. 801), Nero's fiery response to the flames kindled against him by his people (cf. 822): through constant allusions to fire the poet sets up a series of repercussive incendiary devices which finally erupt in the great conflagration initiated by Nero himself (831-2). In fact, the fire broke out in AD 64;[42] by transposing it to the aftermath of the pro-Octavia rebellion of 62, the poet recasts history to meet the demands of his imagery. But in a play of such Stoic emphasis the fire carries a further implication. Blind to his own impiety (cf. *impius*, 363), Nero fires Rome to punish his disaffected subjects for what he interprets as their impiety (*impium plebis scelus*, 'the people's impious crime', 826). Seneca's Stoic conviction that catastrophe will purge the world of the 'impious race' (*genus impium*, 393) is borne out in an eruption of fire which is in fact a localised manifestation of Stoic conflagration.

This interpretation of the fire as the dramatic realisation of Stoic catastrophe finds support elsewhere in the portrayal of Nero as the catalyst of cosmic disorder. The comet which appeared in AD 60 was believed to portend a change of emperor, prompting Nero to remove his likeliest rival, Rubellius Plautus, to Asia.[43] But Seneca is careful to detect in the comet's appearance a cosmic endorsement of Nero's principate when, at *N.Q.* 7.21.3-4, he compares it with one which was seen during Claudius' reign: the comet of AD 54 is described as briefer, dimmer and smokier than the brilliant Neronian comet. But Seneca's tact is lost on Octavia when she predictably chooses to interpret the comet as a sign of cosmic irregularity (231-4) which portends the disastrous consequences of Nero's rule (236-7); unlike Seneca, she is not afraid to interpret the Neronian comet ominously.[44] Nero is further cast as a source of pollution to the cosmic *pneuma* (cf. *aether*, 236) through his own pernicious breath (*diro spiritu*, 235).[45] And like the Giants who disturbed the cosmic order by making their assault upon heaven, Nero, a worse scourge even than Typhon (238), threatens the cosmic scheme as the new enemy of the gods (*hostis deum*, 240). Through her crimes Agrippina 'broke the laws of nature' (*iura naturae ... rupit*, 163-4); Nero's own trail of cosmic disruption equally alienates him from the Stoic ideal of life in conformity with nature and the universal structures.[46]

The great conflagration rages, then, in a symbolically catastrophic climax to the earthly disturbance caused by Nero. But an obvious objection to interpreting the fire as a creative re-enactment of Stoic *ekpyrosis* is that the world which dawns after the conflagration is hardly cleansed of imperfection. At the end of the drama Nero lives on, the pro-Octavia rebellion is suppressed, Octavia herself embarks on a partial replica of Agrippina's death-boat (cf. 907-10) to go to certain death at Pandataria, and Poppaea is installed as the new imperial consort: the tide of corruption is hardly reversed by the poet's vision of *ekpyrosis*. How, then, can that vision be sustained? Nero's final departure from the Stoic code of Seneca lies in his perversion of the normal role and function of Stoic *ekpyrosis*. By purging the elements which resist him, Nero's *ekpyrosis* clears the way for him to take yet further the stages of his own depravity as emperor. Whereas Stoic *ekpyrosis* leads to the rebirth of a virtuous Golden Age, the Rome which survives Nero's fire remains in the Iron Age. By the end of the *Octavia* Seneca's Stoic theory of the cyclical ages (391ff.) is no longer sustainable and, like Atreus in Seneca's *Thyestes*, Nero's excesses within the drama go unpunished.

Conclusion

Our sole surviving *fabula praetexta* in complete form, the *Octavia* is not necessarily a typical example of the genre.[47] It is conceivable, for example, that the poet innovates by modelling his play on recent Senecan tragedies. But whether or not Seneca's influence ushers in a new or modified form of *praetexta*, the fact remains that Nero's character as drawn by the historians lends itself ideally to the Senecan mode of dramatic treatment. A villainous tyrant whose Stoic *dementia* is reflected in the cosmic, social and moral chaos which breaks out under his misrule, the Nero of the *Octavia* can scarcely be taken as a reliable guide to the nature of the 'real' Nero because his dramatic personality is shaped on the pattern of tyrannical behaviour set by the likes of Atreus in Seneca's *Thyestes*. Although the play is based on historical events amply corroborated by Tacitus, Suetonius and Dio, the poet is no slave to historical constraint, but a free agent who interprets recent history according to his own creative demands. Allowance must therefore be made for artistic licence before an conclusion is drawn about the impact of the *Octavia* on its contemporary Roman audience. Like Claudius in Seneca's *Apocolocyntosis*, Nero may be made to suffer posthumously at the hands of a dramatist who exaggerates all that was worst about the Neronian regime. If the play were Senecan, personal bitterness might have provided a motive for vitriolic excess late in life. But the prevalent view that the *Octavia* is post-Neronian allows the play to be taken as evidence of a Neronian 'myth' growing rapidly after his death. Given that autocratic villainy is a recurring phenomenon in Senecan tragedy, an author writing in the Senecan mode in the *Octavia* could not but treat the Neronian 'myth' with a pejorative emphasis – whatever the Neronian 'reality' may have been.

Notes

* The text used is that of Zwierlein (1986). I owe a debt of gratitude to Neil Hopkinson for helpful criticism and comments.

1. So e.g. Homer, *Od.* 5.291ff., Aesch., *Ag.* 646ff., Virgil, *Aen.* 1.65ff., Lucan, *B.C.* 5.620ff., Sen., *Ag.* 528ff., etc.

2. See *OLD* s.v. *eripio* 3a for examples.

3. Noted by Whitman (1978), 77 on 359.

4. For further examples of irrational impatience in Senecan tragedy see Whitman (1978), 77 on 365.

5. cf. Tac., *Ann.* 14.8, Dio 62.13.5.

6. But it is by no means clear that the real Seneca, Nero's teacher in oratory, ever fulfilled the role of philosophical adviser/instructor to the latter; see Rawson (1989), 247-8. Seneca's role as a restraining philosophical influence in the *Octavia* may be no more than dramatic invention.

7. The weight of scholarly opinion is against Senecan authorship on the grounds of a problematic textual transmission, style and language, content (Seneca's appearance in his own drama unlikely), and supposed allusions to historical events later than Seneca (e.g. Nero's death 'predicted' by Agrippina, 619ff.). So Herrmann (1924), Helm (1934), Herington (1961), Garson (1975), Carbone (1977), Barnes (1982), Kragelund (1982 and 1988), Rosenmeyer (1989) *et al.*; *contra*, Pease (1920 and 1924), Thomas (1945), Marti (1952), Whitman (1978) *et al.*

8. cf. (e.g.) *Ag.* 57ff., 101, *Tro.* 259ff., *Oed.* 11. For further examples see Whitman (1978), 79 on 377-80 with Tarrant (1976), 183 on 'Fortuna's malicious pleasure'.

9. cf. the Epicurean watchword *lathe biôsas* ('live low', fr. 551 Usener).

10. His is Stoic *apatheia*, on which see Sandbach (1975), 63 and Rist (1969), 26.

11. For discussion of the Stoic ideal of living in accord with nature, see Sandbach (1975), 52-9 with Rosenmeyer (1989), 136-7 for Senecan testimony and additional bibliography.

12. cf. *Dial.* 12.8.4, a passage which (as Whitman [1978], 79-80 and Ballaira [1974], 69 note) shares striking parallels in thought and expression with *Oct.* 386ff., and aptly so: when Seneca reflects on his Corsican life in the latter passage, he echoes a passage written in Corsica.

13. For discussion of the doctrine see Sambursky (1959), 106-8 and Sandbach (1975), 78-9 with Rosenmeyer (1989), 149: 'In Seneca's writings, both prose and dramatic, catastrophe is a pervasive memory and fear, a thought that colours all thinking about the constitution of the cosmos.'

14. *Aurea formoso descendunt saecula filo* ('a Golden Age descends on the beautiful thread [spun by the Fates]', 4.1.v.9). For additional examples of the same see Eden (1984), 76-7.

15. On the poet's choice of sources, especially Ovid, in constructing his Golden Age see Gatz (1967), 77-8.

16. See Gatz (1967), 78-9 for the poet's sources.

17. So Giancotti (1981), 88-9.

18. See Cacciaglia (1974), 84-5 for the manifestation in Senecan tragedy of the symptoms of anger as described in the *De Ira*.

19. See most recently Poe (1989), 450-1 and n. 59 for additional bibliography.

20. So Chrysippus (*SVF* 3.264, 265). For definition and discussion of the four virtues see Sandbach (1975), 42-3 (on Zeno) and 124-6 (on Panaetius; see also Rist [1969], 192-5). For present purposes I take the four virtues to be an orthodox Stoic position,

but for shifts of emphasis and refinements from the Early Stoa onwards (e.g. subdivisions of the four virtues) see Zeller (1962), 258 n. 2.

21. For background detail on the charges see Whitman (1978), 84.

22. *Servare cives maior [virtus] est patriae patri* ('it is a greater virtue for the father of the state to protect his citizens'): on *servare* as a key programmatic term in the *De Clementia* see Bellincioni (1984), 20-2. Nero refused the title *pater patriae* on his accession because of his youth (so Suet., *Nero* 8), and the historians do not mention him taking the title; but see Thomas (1945), 65 for numismatic evidence that Nero assumed the title in 57.

23. cf. Bellincioni (1984), 57-8 where *Cl.* 1.7.1 is cited to illustrate the relationship between the 'grandeur' (*maiestas*) of the ruler and that of the gods; at *Oct.* 578 Nero is cast as hybristic in his claim to divine *maiestas*.

24. On practical wisdom (*phronêsis*), defined as 'knowledge of the good and bad and indifferent' or 'what is and is not to be done and the indifferent' (*SVF* 3.262, 266), see Zeller (1962), 259 n. 2, Sandbach (1975), 42, 126 and Rist (1969), 192-3. *Phronêsis* is in fact one branch of wisdom, the other *sophia*, or 'knowledge of all things human and divine' (so Cic., *Off.* 1.153, Sen., *Ep.* 85.5 etc.); on the distinction see Zeller (1962), 258 n. 1.

25. For *fortuna* in this sense see *OLD* s.v. 11b with Whitman (1978), 86 on 451.

26. cf. n. 8 above.

27. On self-control (*sôphrosunê*), defined as 'knowledge of what should be chosen and what avoided and the indifferent' (*SVF* 3.262, 266) and linked by Panaetius with the notion of decorum (*to prepon*), see Sandbach (1975), 125-6 and Rist (1969), 195-6.

28. Justice (*dikaiosunê*), defined as 'knowledge which assigns to each man his due' (*SVF* 3.262, 266), is 'the virtue that arises from the social instincts' (Sandbach [1975], 124). By abusing Stoic justice Nero proves to be a tyrant bereft of social instinct and responsibility.

29. Whitman (1978), 93: 'Nero's reasoning [throughout his exchanges with Seneca] has been that of a tyrant, but his case is not weak. The philosopher king is an impossible ideal ... Nero's replies have a ring of truth about them.'

30. For further Senecan examples (prose and verse) of the tyrant ruling by fear to quell his own fear see Cacciaglia (1974), 89-90.

31. Bravery (*andreia*) is variously defined (see *SVF* 3.262 and 266 with Zeller [1962], 259 n. 3 for variants), but the quality amounts to fearless obedience to the law of reason. Cf. Sandbach (1975), 125: 'Bravery for Panaetius is freedom ... from fear.'

32. cf. Sen., *Phaed.* 195ff., where the Nurse similarly casts Amor as an illusory god who preys on human folly. She tries to dissuade Phaedra from pursuing her lustful designs on Hippolytus, only later to give way and support the attempt (cf. 267ff.). When Seneca echoes the Nurse's failed counsel, does he inadvertently foreshadow the failure of his own counsel? Nero, like Phaedra, is beyond reprieve.

33. D.L. 10.6 (fr. 67 Usener).

34. See further Rist (1972), 116-22 on 'the selection of pleasures'.

35. So Tac., *Ann.* 14.60 and Suet., *Nero* 35.2. But cf. *Ann.* 14.63, where Tacitus reports that 'forgetting his recent charge of sterility' (*incusatae paulo ante sterilitatis oblitus*), Nero accused Octavia of adultery and of procuring an abortion to hide in infidelity.

36. Most scholarship accept that, as in the *Agamemnon* and *Hercules Oetaeus*, the *Octavia* has two choral factions; but see Sutton (1982), 14-16 and 22 n. 21. Against Sutton, I fail to see how the chorus which condemns the pro-Octavia protest (781ff.) can be reconciled with the chorus which incites that protest (669ff.).

37. For *sancta pietas* as the people's devotion to Octavia and the Claudian house see Whitman (1978), 96 on 572 with *OLD* s.v. *pietas* 4a. But cf. Ballaira (1972), 105 on 572ff., interpreting 572 as appealing to Nero's moral duty to *sancta pietas*, not the people's. I favour the former interpretation without ruling out the latter.

38. See Whitman (1978), 73 on 296-300 and 301, and 74 on 304 for background to the three *exempla*. Zwierlein (1986) accepts Baehrens' transposition of 300 and 296-9 to follow 303, thereby allowing Virginia to succeed Lucretia in proper chronological sequence. My interpretation remains unaffected by the transposition.
39. Whitman (1978), 83 notes the parallel but makes nothing of it.
40. See *N.Q.* 3.27-30, *Dial.* 6.26.6-7, *Ben.* 6.22 with Rosenmeyer (1989), 148-51 on the traditions of conflagration and inundation in Stoic thought.
41. (1989), 156, citing various manifestations in the *Thyestes, Troades, Hercules Furens* and *Agamemnon* (pp. 152-8).
42. So Tac., *Ann.* 15.37, Suet., *Nero* 38, Dio 62.16.
43. So Tac., *Ann.* 14.22.
44. cf. Rogers (1953), 242, arguing that since the play is based on events in AD 62, the comet to which Octavia refers is not in fact that of 60, but 61. My interpretation remains unaffected. On the pejorative significance usually (though not always) read into comets in antiquity see *RE* 11.1143ff. s.v. Kometen.
45. On the universal *pneuma* as the source of coherence between all parts of the Stoic cosmos see Sambursky (1959), 1-7 with Rosenmeyer (1989), 93-4 and nn. 2 and 3 for further bibliography.
46. cf. n. 11 above.
47. On the *praetexta* tradition see Pedroli (1954), 9-63; Whitman (1978), 5 offers a succinct survey.

Bibliography

G. Ballaira, ed., '*Seneca*': *Ottavia* (Turin, 1974).
T.D. Barnes, 'The date of the *Octavia*', *MH* 39 (1982), 91-3.
M. Bellincioni, *Potere ed Etica in Seneca. Antichità Classica e Cristiana* 25 (Brescia, 1984).
M. Cacciaglia, 'L'etica stoica nei drammi di Seneca', *RIL* 108 (1974), 78-104.
M.E. Carbone, 'The *Octavia*: structure, date, and authenticity', *Phoenix* 31 (1977), 48-67.
P.T. Eden, ed., *Seneca: Apocolocyntosis* (Cambridge, 1984).
R.W. Garson, 'The pseudo-Senecan *Octavia*: a plea for Nero?', *Latomus* 34 (1975), 754-6.
B. Gatz, *Weltalter, goldene Zeit und sinnverwandte Vorstellungen. Spudasmata* 17 (Hildesheim, 1967).
F. Giancotti, 'Seneca personaggio dell' "*Octavia*" ', *Dioniso* 52 (1981), 67-107.
R. Helm, 'Die Praetexta "*Octavia*" ', *SB Berlin* 16 (1934), 283-347.
C.J. Herington, '*Octavia praetexta*: a survey', *CQ* n.s. 11 (1961), 18-30.
L. Herrmann, *Octavie: tragédie prétexte* (Paris, 1924).
P. Kragelund, *Prophecy, Populism, and Propaganda in the 'Octavia'. Museum Tusculanum* suppl. vol. 25 (Copenhagen, 1982).
—— 'The prefect's dilemma and the date of the *Octavia*', *CQ* n.s. 38 (1988), 492-508.
B. Marti, 'Seneca's *Apocolocyntosis* and *Octavia*: a diptych', *AJPh* 73 (1952), 24-36.
A.S. Pease, 'Is the *Octavia* a play of Seneca?', *CJ* 15 (1920), 388-403.
—— 'The *Octavia* once more', *CP* 19 (1924), 80-3.
L. Pedroli, *Fabularum praetextarum quae extant. Pubblicazioni dell'Istituto di Filologia Classica, Lydia* (Genoa, 1954).
J.P. Poe, '*Octavia praetexta* and its Senecan model', *AJPh* 110 (1989), 434-59.
E. Rawson, 'Roman rulers and the philosophic adviser', in M. Griffin and J. Barnes, eds., *Philosophia Togata: essays on philosophy and Roman society* (Oxford, 1989), pp. 233-57.
J.M. Rist, *Stoic Philosophy* (Cambridge, 1969).

—— *Epicurus: an introduction* (Cambridge, 1972).
R.S. Rogers, 'The Neronian comets', *TAPhA* 84 (1953), 237-49.
T.G. Rosenmeyer, *Senecan Drama and Stoic Cosmology* (Berkeley and Los Angeles, 1989).
S. Sambursky, *Physics of the Stoics* (London, 1959).
F.H. Sandbach, *The Stoics* (London, 1975).
D.F. Sutton, *The Dramaturgy of the Octavia. Beitrage zur klassischen Philologie* 149 (Frankfurt, 1983).
R.J. Tarrant, ed., *Seneca: Agamemnon* (Cambridge, 1976).
S.P. Thomas, 'De *Octavia praetexta*', *SO* 24 (1945), 48-87.
L.Y. Whitman, *The Octavia, Introduction, Text, and Commentary. Noctes Romanae* 16 (Bern, Stuttgart, 1978).
E. Zeller, *The Stoics, Epicureans and Sceptics* 2nd edn (New York, 1962), trans. by O.J. Reichel of *Philosophie der Griechen:* Vol. 3.1 (Leipzig, 1880).
D. Zwierlein, ed., *L. Annaei Senecae Tragoediae. Incertorum Auctorum Hercules* [*Oetaeus*], *Octavia.* OCT (Oxford, 1986).

11

Seneca's *Thyestes* and the morality of tragic *furor*

Alessandro Schiesaro

Thyestes is perhaps the work most often cited as a true representative of the tendencies and style of Neronian literature.[1] The temptation to read Atreus as a larger-than-life Nero is strong. In this way, the tragedy could easily become a document of sorts for the decadence of Neronian Rome, and at the same time a statement of moral resistance to that decadence. All this would be predicated, obviously, even if not explicitly, on a series of crucial assumptions. Some are quite general, such as that (the) tragedy reflects the social situation in which it was produced, or that Nero was in fact the cruel and rather quirky tyrant who sang while Rome burned.[2] I will not directly engage these assumptions, the former being too general, the latter being the overall concern of this volume as a whole. I offer here an analysis of the prologue of *Thyestes* which I hope will raise doubts about the possibility of such a reading, concentrating on a few items at the core of the play. In short, I will argue that certain modes of representation and signification that the prologue establishes – mainly but far from exclusively through interaction with previous poetic texts – cast the tragedy in a peculiar light from the beginning, a light which will not easily allow a moralising and centripetal reading such as the one alluded to above. In particular, I would like to claim that the modes of signification established by the prologue make the balance of moral responsibilities in the play difficult to determine, and at every stage force on the audience[3] the burden of discerning good and evil, illusion and reality, hypocrisy and sincerity, within the complicated framework established by the prologue.

At the same time I believe that this analysis can contribute to our understanding of the nature of Senecan tragedy and more specifically of Seneca's evaluation of the poetic word. While I will not focus in this paper on one of the most remarkable aspects of the play, the connotation of Atreus as a playwright, my reading of the prologue and its further ramifications will suggest that the poetic word, *qua* poetic word, is a vehicle of expression for realities which would otherwise tend to be repressed, and that the act of creation embodied in that word will necessarily be complicit with the nefarious contents it voices.

1. The poetics of *furor*

> Quis inferorum sede ab infausta extrahit
> avido fugaces ore captantem cibos,
> quis male deorum Tantalo visas domos
> ostendit iterum? Peius inventum est siti
> arente in undis aliquid et peius fame
> hiante semper?[4]

[Who is dragging me up from the home of the damned as I snatch at elusive victuals with greedy lips? What god, damn it, would again show Tantalus the houses of the living? Have they found something worse than parching thirst in the midst of water, than hunger always openmouthed?] (1-6)[5]

Thyestes begins by staging the process of its own construction. Tantalus not only wonders at the unexpected turn his punishment is taking, but also problematises the very existence – the theatrical essence – of the drama which is bringing him on the scene. His questions, while ostensibly bearing on his fate as a mythic character, also look in anguish at the unfolding of the tragic action. As if from the outside, he watches his becoming a character of a dramatic text. Who dragged him from the depths of the underworld and forced him to this stage? What is this novel situation worse than hell, one where, paradoxically, he is punished by being forced to punish others? Similarly, the subsequent fight between the Fury and Tantalus' shadow embodies a creative conflict that immediately traces a radical contrast between passive forces which try to resist the drama's violence and active forces which create and complicate the drama. Perhaps this initial metadramatic[6] reflection staged by *Thyestes* is disruptive enough to eliminate from the outset any pretence of reducing to a simple, effective formula the contorted and conflicting signifying strategies that the drama enacts. The reading exercise I propose moves towards a different goal: to trace and chart the polysemic density of *Thyestes*, its signifying conflicts, intertwining motifs and moral evaluations. I would like to read *Thyestes* as a real *tragedy*, and not simply as a touchstone where unambiguous moral principles are vented and advocated. Tragedy, that is, as an experience which Greek and Roman culture cannot help exploring, and to which any response is ultimately ambiguous, insufficient, always lacerating.

The harsh violence which dominates this prologue warrants foregrounding. Violence, at a minimal level, is encoded already in the prologue's dialogic form,[7] which opposes two parties with different levels of power and different opportunities to reinforce their words with deeds. Division, fracture and conflict impose themselves as dominating forces from the very first lines, when Tantalus' evoked shadow addresses his yet unknown counterpart. Tantalus, it should be immediately said, has a dramatic consistency which is not altered by the Fury's final, inevitable victory. He is a guilty man, as he readily admits: *me pati poenas decet/ non esse poenam* (87-8) ('I should suffer punishment, not be one'). His moral opposition to the Fury's demand is heightened by this admission. The Fury wants Tantalus to arouse on Earth new, terrible *scelera*. Tantalus resists in vain. Those *scelera* ('crimes') are the tragedy in and of itself, since *Thyestes* is precisely the tale of a compelling and memorable *scelus*.

Textual signals are uniformly pointed: this prefatory debate is a symbolic enactment of the birth of the play and an open (although far from 'objective') window on the creative forces that presided over its creation. Indeed, if Tantalus' firm advocacy of moderation won, there would be no *Thyestes* at all. Tantalus is utterly shocked at the request to come back on earth; his anguish is clear in the repeated questions in lines 1-5 (quoted above). *Iterum* ('again') is the key word here. Tantalus questions the senseless drama of re-enactment, and the novel 'invention' (cf. *inventum*, line 4); but what is personally and morally unacceptable is precisely what this tragedy and its poetics are made of: re-enactment, repetition, obsessive return of, and return to, what could (should) best be left unsaid.[8] The tragedy thus defies the (moral) option of a repressive silence. The Fury reminds Tantalus that his *scelus* would not be new: *epulae instruantur – non novi sceleris/ tibi conviva venies* (62) ('let the banquet table be laid, you will be a guest in a feast not unfamiliar to you'). The question that Tantalus utters here for the first time is also the key question of the play as a whole: *why* should this drama be repeated?[9] The Fury inspires *scelera*, the very *scelera* that make up the whole of *Thyestes*. Thus the Fury effectively inspires this poetry: from the very beginning of the play, there is no escaping the daunting connection between poetry and *scelera*. To stage *scelera* is indeed to make them happen: the poetry of *nefas* becomes a *nefas* itself.

Tantalus does try to resist. After much complaining he finally assumes a firm and fierce stance; he simply won't obey:

> Magne divorum parens
> nosterque, quamvis pudeat, ingenti licet
> taxata poena lingua crucietur loquax,
> nec hoc tacebo: moneo, ne sacra manus
> violate caede neve furiali malo
> aspergite aras. Stabo et arcebo scelus.

[Ah, great father of the gods, and mine too, however embarrassing, though my impertinent tongue be requited with great torment I will not keep silent. I warn you: Do not violate your hands with accursed murder, do not spatter the altars with insane wickedness. I shall stand fast and fend off the crime.] (90-5)

Tantalus' didactic attempts to impart moral guidance and avoid errors would befit a sage. His resistance, however, does not last long, as the Fury tortures him on stage:

> Quid ora terres verbere et tortos ferox
> minaris angues? Quid famem infixam intimis
> agitas medullis? Flagrat incensum siti
> cor et perustis flamma visceribus micat.[10]
> Sequor.

[Why are you brandishing your lash at my face, why do you menace me with writhing snakes? Why are you stirring the hunger in my inmost marrow? My heart is on fire with blazing thirst and the flame is licking through my scorched vitals. I yield.] (96-100)

Tantalus' words confess to the impossibility of his moral stance and his didactic purpose. The vehement words which describe his intentions (*moneo, stabo, arcebo*)[11] are suddenly and irrevocably reversed in the bitterly ironic repetition of a Stoic-sounding *sententia: sequor* is what the sage should say when facing destiny, since it is better to follow willingly than be dragged. The Fury's power is the power of unavoidable destiny. The Fury is the Muse of *scelus*, and her victory is the victory of poetry (of this particular brand of *poiesis*) against the repressive silence Tantalus advocates in vain.

Lines 96-9 make the language of erotic desire and creative impulses intersect, and cruelly deprive both of their comforting metaphorical value. The usual association of fire and eros connotes the Fury's order as an irresistible, sinful desire redolent of erotic passion. At the same time, these images are connected with the vocabulary of poetic enthusiasm, the burning power which moves poets to create.[12] In this respect the passage anticipates a central moment later in the play, where a revengeful Atreus strives to find inspiration for his new creation – the plot of his revenge and of the rest of the tragedy:

> dira Furiarum cohors
> discorsque Erinys veniat et geminas faces
> Megaera quatiens. non satis magno meum
> ardet furore pectus, impleri iuvat
> maiore monstro.

[Let the dread band of the Furies come, the fiend Discord, and Megaera, brandishing her twin torches! My heart does not burn with a great enough rage; I must be filled with ampler fiendishness.] (250-4)

Atreus, far from being tortured by the Furies, appeals to them to obtain the creative impulse to act, that is to produce a dramatic text which he will act out and force on Thyestes. Both passages substantiate the connotation of the Fury's impulse as a sinful *desire* which finds in poetry its final realisation. This *furor* cannot be resisted, and the play comes to light endowed with the sinister force of a victory against morality, reason, and *fas*.

In this same prologue Seneca also offers meaningful intimations about the literary background in which we should place those declarations of poetics. Three texts dominate the background to the prologue, but I will concentrate especially on the last and arguably most important one.

Friedrich Leo was the first to suggest a connection with the dialogue between Iris and Lyssa in Euripides' *Heracles* (822-74).[13] The actual verbal coincidences are faint, but the overall structure of the dialogue is close to Seneca's scene in important details. In particular, like Tantalus' shade, Lyssa does in fact try to resist, albeit unsuccessfully, Iris' commands. The Fury herself offers at least one other strong signal of intertextual self-awareness in her first, most effective speech:

> Ornetur altum columen et lauro fores
> laetae virescant, dignus adventu tuo
> splendescat ignis – Thracium fiat nefas
> maiore numero.

[Deck the tall column, make the doors green with festive laurel, light up a blaze worthy of your advent, repeat the Thracian crime with larger numbers.] (54-7)

Through allusive amplification (*maiore numero* 'with larger numbers') the Fury introduces here a field of intertextual connections which will prove important for the whole play: the Thracian *nefas* par excellence is the bloody story of Tereus, Itys and Procne, especially as told in Ovid's *Metamorphoses*. The Fury underlines her truly intertextual metadramatic dimension[14] by showing her knowledge of mythical and literary history, and by explicitly alerting us to the allusive resonances of the play. The agonistic stance expressed in the phrase *maiore numero* ('with larger numbers') acknowledges the new dimension that this dramatic repetition of *nefas* will assume. As we will see shortly, any repetition of *nefas* is necessarily worse than its model – more obsessive, more painful, more 'guilty'. At the level of poetics, the repetition will encourage the exploration of a more intensely expressive and emotionally loaded language.

The prologue shows a marked connection with the opening scenes of *Aeneid* 7.[15] The sequence of events in Vergil's poem is more complicated, but the basic pattern is the same. Enraged by the apparent triumph of the Trojans (286-322), Juno summons Allecto and commands her to bring *discordia* ('discord') and destruction into the Latin field (323-40):

> tu potes unanimos armare in proelia fratres
> atque odiis versare domos, tu verbera tectis
> funereasque inferre faces, tibi nomina mille,
> mille nocendi artes. fecundum *concute pectus*,
> dissice compositam pacem, sere crimina belli;
> arma velit poscatque simul rapiatque iuventus.

[For you can arm for battle brothers, though
they feel at one, and ruin homes with hatred;
and you can carry firebrands and lashes
beneath their roof; you have a thousand names,
a thousand ways of injuring; awake
your fertile breast and break this settled peace;
sow war and crime; let sudden quarrel spur
young men to want, demand, and seize the sword.] (335-40)[16]

The Fury's orders to Tantalus echo Juno's words:

> Ante perturba domum
> inferque tecum proelia et ferri malum
> regibus amorem, *concute* insano ferum
> *pectus* tumultu.

11. Seneca's Thyestes

[First confound your house, bring with you battle and lust for steel, the king's bane, rouse savage breasts to beserk rage.] (83-6)

The vivid expression *concute pectus* links the two texts as well as the insistence on *domus* as the target (*Aen.* 7.336 and *Th.* 83) and the use of *inferre* (337 and 84).

Furthermore the results of Juno's and the Fury's destructive orders are alike; the Fury points out to a bewildered and reluctant Tantalus the effects his presence has provoked in the house of the Pelopides:

> Sentit introitus tuos
> domus et nefando tota contactu horruit.
> Actum est[17] *abunde*. Gradere ad infernos specus
> amnemque notum; iam tuum maestae pedem
> terrae gravantur.

[The house senses your advent and shudders throughout at your tainted touch. You have played your part to the full. Off with you now to the infernal caves and your familiar river; now the earth is irked and chafed by your tread.] (103-7)

The Fury's words resonate with Juno's final admonition to Allecto:

> terrorum et fraudis *abunde est*:
> stant belli causae, pugnatur comminus armis,
> quae fors prima dedit sanguis novus imbuit arma.

> [There is enough
> of fear and fraud; the causes of the war
> are firm; they now fight hand to hand; the weapons
> that chance first brought are now stained with new
> blood.] (552-4)

When Allecto returns to Acheron at Juno's request, she relieves earth and sky of their painful burden:

> hic specus horrendum et saevi spiracula Ditis
> monstrantur, ruptoque ingens Acheronte vorago
> pestiferas aperit fauces, quis condita Erynis,
> invisum numen, *terras caelumque levabat*.

> [Here
> a horrid cave – the breathing vents of Dis,
> the savage one – appears; a huge abyss
> where Acheron erupts here opens its
> infectious jaws. In these the Fury hid
> her hated power, freeing earth and sky.] (568-71)

In *Th.* 107 Vergil's *terras caelumque levabat* becomes *terrae gravantur*, as the forces of evil once again oppress the Earth. The importance of the intertextual connection lies precisely in this indication of continuity; by pointing directly at *Aeneid* 7 and acknowledging Vergil's archetypal model as a poet of *furor* ('fury'),

Seneca reconstructs a meaningful *lignée* of literary history and invokes a powerful protector for his own nefarious endeavours.

Seneca deliberately points here to the second half of the *Aeneid*. The thematic connection, as we have seen, is clear. Juno's very words to Allecto (335 *tu potes unanimos armare in proelia fratres*, 'For you can arm for battle brothers') leave no doubt that the new battles in store for the Trojans will be of a different kind from those told retrospectively in the first six books. Actions performed in the present tense of narration correspond symbolically to their potential implications as prefigurations of a devastating internal conflict. Yet it is precisely this tale of horrors which is Vergil's *maius opus* (7.45, 'greater labour'), his *maior rerum...ordo* (7.44, 'greater theme'). These Vergilian echoes also show how Thyestes condenses the horrors of civil strife in the polarised contrast between two brothers. The theme had obvious, obsessive resonances in first-century Latin culture. By remembering Vergil, Seneca implicitly reflects, too, on a crucial issue of poetics, the very one that Tantalus had raised in his opening speech: why again? By alluding to Vergil, Seneca characterises his own writing as repetition, as a painful, irresistible return to horrors which had already been sung. Seneca thus places his tragedy in a tradition of *furor*-inspired poems (and actions) whose authoritative model he traces back to Vergil.[18]

The second half of the *Aeneid* forces on the reader a set of ethical dilemmas which the first, for all the suffering it described, did not present so poignantly. At the beginning of book 7 a happy ending is within reach; the decision to *re*-start the poem all over again, as it were, with a second proem, and to expand it considerably by a detailed account of a quasi-fratricidal strife is entirely Vergil's own: this time, no displacing or attenuation is possible. Poetic innovation and moral responsibility run parallel; the latter six books are morally more troubling because they represent new and 'unnecessary' amplifications of the plot, because they reproduce the physical horrors of war which the Trojan exiles hoped to have left behind, and above all because they give voice to the unsurpassed evil of civil war.

All the moral implications of these poetic strategies are active in Seneca's text, which – as a whole – stands as a challenge to the repressive decorum of silence. From a moral point of view, Seneca is as guilty as Vergil, since he chooses to re-tell a story whose devastating contents he knows well: once again, to sing of *nefas* is, in a sense, to perpetrate it. Seneca raises the stakes of his moral conflict by giving voice at the beginning of the play to an alternative which the *Aeneid* had only left implied: Tantalus does proclaim his intention to steer away from the Fury and her orders, but his ultimate defeat only amplifies the horror of *nefas*. Yet, after all, this is precisely what Vergil had done, and Seneca attempts in turn to displace moral responsibility by invoking such a mighty predecessor. The spiral of violence and poetry about violence, it seems, offers no escape.[19]

2. Tantalus' tongue

Even before we try to widen the theoretical implications of the metadramatic dialogue between the Fury and Tantalus, it will be useful to reflect briefly on the exegetical consequences that dialogue entails. The single most important interpretive gain afforded by recognising a layer of metadramatic reflection in the prologue is the difficulty it creates for simplifying the 'meaning' of the play as a whole. The sheer existence of a perceptible metadramatic layer in the play determines a complexity of voices, motives, contrasting forces and cross-references that make it virtually impossible to flatten the signifying force of the dramas. The metadramatic reflection acts as a bent mirror which multiplies and distorts, complicates and blurs our perception. The central action of the play – Atreus' revenge – will have to be perceived by the audience within the alienating frame provided by the prologue. A full understanding of the actions performed on the stage will have to be negotiated by keeping in mind what the prologue imposes on the rest of the play: an intrinsic complicity between the very existence of the tragic *nefas* and its representation. The audience is made to realise that the aesthetic pleasure afforded by the play is coextensive with that *nefas*. The play's very existence is in fact guaranteed by the unrelenting evil of characters necessary to it, such as the Fury and Atreus.

One problem with many interpretations of *Thyestes* is precisely that they neglect the structural importance of the prologue. By overlooking the prologue it is possible to see the core of the play in the contrast between two ethical types, Atreus and Thyestes, whose actions may bear comparison with, for instance, a character described in *de ira* or some sort of Stoic *proficiens*.[20] Constrained by the choice between a Stoic *proficiens* with doubtful credentials and a blood-thirsty tyrant, the audience might have reasons to be uncertain about the real interest of the play and to be surprised at the tragedy's strong emotional impact. The real dramatic and emotional crisis of the tragedy lies not so much in the choice between Thyestes and Atreus – both of whom are, for different reasons, unacceptable ethical prototypes – as in the ethically troubling connotations of the very act of representation which the prologue foregrounds. This breeds a complex activity of aesthetic approval or disapproval within the audience, as it is forced to negotiate the conflicting aspects of that representation.

The prologue offers a visual representation of the power of poetry, the source of its inspiration and ethical status. At the same time, the prologue also creates a pattern of representation which is essential to the structural organisation of the whole tragedy. The Fury and Tantalus cease to act, but they are not meant to disappear. The whole tragic action will unfold before their eyes, and Tantalus will be forced to watch the monstrous banquet he has unavoidably, if unwillingly, inspired: *mixtus in Bacchum cruor/ spectante te potetur* (65-6) ('wine mixed with gore will be drunk before your eyes'). Tantalus, once he has performed his starting task, becomes a spectator himself, an impotent, horrified prisoner. The conflict between the Fury and Tantalus draws a line between active and passive forces, performers and spectators, power and powerlessness. It is a meditation on the implications of poetry and its effects on both author and audience.

If the debate between the Fury and Tantalus actually illuminates the genesis of the play, then conflict and violence define it. This conflict is, we have seen, between silence and speech, between avoiding a *scelus* ('crime') or enacting it (95 *stabo et arcebo scelus*, 'I shall stand fast and fend off the crime.'). This contrast foregrounds in turn a set of qualities that are part of Tantalus' mythical record and that Seneca elliptically but surely introduces into his text. Immediately before his refusal to enact the *scelus*, Tantalus refers in lines 90-3 (quoted above) to the excessive past loquacity that warranted his punishment. *Loquax...lingua* ('my impertinent tongue') is an explicit reference to a lesser known side of the myth of Tantalus, in which the gods punish him for revealing their secrets to human beings.[21] The prologue of Euripides' *Orestes* refers to Tantalus' *akolasia* ('intemperance'), and it has been persuasively shown that largely through Euripides' example Tantalus is later consistently identified as the paramount example of 'supremely audacious verbal hubris'.[22] In *Thyestes* Tantalus vows to overcome his hard-learnt lesson of restraint and to say what he feels in spite of his past punishments (93 *nec hoc tacebo*, 'I will not keep silent'). This restraint ultimately amounts to the suppression of the *scelus* ('crime') and its incarnation in the poetic word which the Fury tries to elicit instead. In the reversal of roles brought about by the prologue, Tantalus is tortured by the Fury for his reluctance to speak, and once again sins by forcibly overcoming this reluctance.

The prologue's reference to Tantalus' past raises an interesting interpretive point. Tantalus' own past error characterises the essential nature of the confrontation between him and the Fury as the contrast between a repressive (and ultimately defeated) silence and an avoidance of *scelus* which is, too, realised in linguistic terms. At the same time, this reference strengthens the equation of silence and inaction on the one hand, and word and action on the other. The Fury's victory is presented as a lifting of the morally conscientious veil of repression that Tantalus advocates. The prologue's dialectic between repression and its removal structures the creative struggle represented in the play.[23] Recognising the connotations this opposition introduces bears fruit in the analysis of the play as a whole. In a very important sense *Thyestes* can be read as an experiment in the nature and limits of poetic (tragic) language and an answer to the problem of the relationship between poetry and reality. If the conflict that pitches Tantalus against the Fury is also a conflict between the words of tragedy and the silence which the avoidance of tragedy would preserve, then the prologue itself represents poetry as the medium through which objectionable *scelera* can be expressed, and against which the moral restraint personified by Tantalus' shadow remains fatally impotent. Not only are words deeds, as the double aspect of *scelus* itself powerfully suggests, but the words of poetry represent a decisive victory against the repressive morality of silence and *fas*. In giving voice to *nefas*, poetry reverses the repressive instance that *nefas* encodes.

At a more radical level, the presentation of Atreus' deeds as an intrinsic victory over repression, as well as the collusion established between poetic word and *scelus*, gives *scelus* an emotional appeal which defies the feeble attempts at moral correctness which other parts of the play appear to advocate. The audience's attempt to identify their emotions with any given character is upset beyond repair by the play's intricate metadramatic structure. For any action represented in the play must not only be interpreted and judged *per se*, but, as we have seen, the very act of its representation carries upsetting ethical connotations.

The most important case is Atreus himself. The text constantly challenges its audience about the ethical status of Atreus and his actions, but also questions the ethics of the author's choice to represent them. Thus the possibilities of emotional identification offered to the audience are multiplied and result in a potentially endless set of conflicts. The audience has to 'decide' every time not only whether it sides with Atreus or not, but also whether it can enjoy the aesthetic emotions offered by Seneca's poetry without colluding *ipso facto* with their powerful overcoming of *fas*. Conversely, the audience might sometimes sympathise with Tantalus' advocacy of silence and simply wish that the whole tragedy, with all its content, did not exist at all. Nevertheless, not only do the *scelera* perpetrated by Atreus confront the audience at every single word, but also the *scelus* of the play's very existence.

From this perspective it may be useful to reflect for a moment on what would happen if the tragedy did not have its metadramatic prologue. Then the conflict between the unimplemented – but righteous – silence ethically advocated by Tantalus and the triumphing *furor* of poetry would not lend to the conflict staged by the play the character of a battle between repression and the removal of repression. Deprived of this polymorphic prologue, the actions later staged in the play would create a simple opposition between the oppressing force of Atreus' violence and the moral values defended, however faintly, by Thyestes, the *satelles* ('minister') and the Chorus. As it is, the prologue introduces a dynamic force which compels those otherwise simple values to undergo multiple transformations and interactions.

The metadramatic prologue, of course, complicates rather than simplifies, since it forces the audience to a stereoscopic vision in which the actions and utterances of the play should be constantly seen at both a metadramatic and dramatic level, and as such deals a blow to any attempt to reduce *Thyestes* to sweeping, reassuring generalisations. It also casts in a different light a problem which has long been at the very heart of Senecan criticism, namely whether we should read the tragedies as a reversal, that is mere negative illustration of values and ideas advocated in Seneca's own prose-works.[24] The very structure of the play works towards a multiplication and diffraction of meanings that makes any attempt at summary comparison with other texts extremely difficult. What the prologue impresses upon us is first and foremost the lacerating power of the poetic word, which imposes on its creator and its public a dramatic set of moral implications which cannot necessarily be composed into a reassuring unity.

The contrast between the conflicting drives personified by the Fury and Tantalus carries over from the prologue and pervades a much larger portion of the play. This contrast generates in the text a series of oppositions subordinate to and dependent on that basic opposition between silence and tragedy so powerfully won by the words of tragedy in the prologue. Like that basic opposition, this series of oppositions within the play as a whole can be construed as a conflict between repression and its removal.

The extension of this pattern of oppositions highlights the functional correspondences which link several characters in the tragedy. Just as the contrast between Tantalus and the Fury pitches one of the principal moving forces of the tragedy against the potentially most effective obstacle to it, other dramatic confrontations at other levels of the play reflect the same antithesis. The *satelles'* initial reaction to Atreus' plans in the second act is precisely one of resistance. Functionally, then, the *satelles* and Tantalus are paired together in their vain attempt to stop Atreus and the Fury respectively. Atreus complains about his inactivity (176-8: *ignave, iners, enervis.../ inulte*; 'spiritless, nerveless, spineless...vengeanceless), and braces for new, spectacular actions, indeed for a new *scelus* (203). The *satelles*, on the contrary, advocates the restrained morality which Tantalus had unsuccessfully embraced, and tries to counter Atreus' machinations with a series of invitations to desist from the proposed *scelus*.[25] As in the prologue, if Atreus yielded to the *satelles*' invitation, there simply would be no tragedy at all. Once again, the intimate connection between the unfolding of the plot and Atreus' moral responsibility is foregrounded. The equivalence between *nefas* as an action and a poetic representation of that action is notably strengthened in Atreus' self-presentation at lines 176ff. Atreus plans to perpetrate a *nefas* (193) of unsurpassed atrocity, one which can therefore aspire to immortal fame: *age, anime, fac quod nulla posteritas probet,/ sed nulla taceat* (192-3; 'up, my soul, wreak a deed no posterity can approve but none ignore'). The remarks that follow after a brief altercation with the *satelles* show that Atreus, as we have seen before, is prey to the same *furor* of poetic creation that the prologue had symbolically represented in Tantalus' forced subjugation to the Fury's irresistible force of inspiration at lines 250-4.

The same pattern recurs in the dialogue between Tantalus and his father Thyestes in lines 404ff. Here, too, the contrast between father and son focuses on Thyestes' reluctance to further the dramatic plot (436 *placet ire, pigris membra sed genibus labant*; 'I decide to go on, but my knees falter') and Tantalus' insistence that he follow the prescribed series of events (440 *evince quidquid obstat et mentem impedit*; 'overcome whatever it is that obstructs and impedes your purpose'). Thyestes' final words (488-9 *Eatur. Unum genitor hoc testor tamen:/ ego vos sequor, non duco*; 'but on we go. In this one point I assert my fatherhood: I will follow, not lead you'), in fact, follow very closely Tantalus' shadow's ultimate confession of defeat: *sequor* (100; 'I follow').[26]

Finally, in the first meeting between the two brothers, Thyestes incarnates a role which by now the audience of the tragedy has learnt to recognise as inevitably devoid of practical effectiveness, and whose moral consistency is at least doubtful: Thyestes does indeed try to resist Atreus' enticements, much as Tantalus had done in the prologue, and as the *satelles* had perfunctorily attempted to do in the first act, but Thyestes' sudden and rhetorically startling surrender to Atreus' argument stirs neither the possible compassion for Tantalus' suffering while he is tortured, nor the extenuating acknowledgment of the *satelles* undeniably weaker position: Thyestes, whose superficially vocal determination had started to vacillate while talking to his son, acquires in this central scene of the play the role, so far new for him, of a moving force, and in this way he signals his final change of status from victim to accomplice.

The whole tragedy hinges on the antithesis of two series of characters who are functionally similar: on the one hand the Fury, Atreus and Tantalus, on the other Tantalus' shadow, the *satelles*, Thyestes. The two groups possess different degrees of textual knowledge, and stand in different positions with respect to the metadramatic aspect of the play: the first group includes all the forces who work for the tragedy and its full accomplishment, those whose *furor* in carrying out the proposed *nefas* is coextensive with the removal of the repression that lifts the play from silence into existence. The second group is made up of potential, would-be

11. Seneca's Thyestes

upholders of that repression, of the characters who try, with different degrees of determination and textual credibility, to stop the ruinous series of events which their antagonists are carrying out. This contrast is further reinforced by the fact that the two groups represent authors and victims of deception.[27] The moving forces of the tragedy, *furor*, *nefas* and *furor*-inspired poetry, are the consummate deceivers, against which Tantalus', Thyestes' and the *satelles'* moralising attempts are completely ineffectual.

The systematic correspondences among the characters of the play embody the dialectical contrast between repression and removal of repression which we have identified in the prologue, and represent a reiteration and expansion of the basic conflict between the poetic word and morally justified silence. This contrast is in turn the foundation of another series of contrasts that are posited and invited by this primary one, and to all of which we should apply the same intimation of a Freudian dialectic: *nefas* and *fas*, *ratio* and *furor*, honesty and deception, to name just a few, present themselves not only as modular replicas of the pattern established at the beginning of the play, but also as causally dependent on this pattern and subject to the same reversal of roles that the underlying pattern of repression and its removal powerfully invites.

After showing that the symmetrical opposition of functionally similar characters extends the contrast between victory and defeat which was ostensibly exposed in the prologue through the whole tragedy, it would be necessary to follow the alternating vicissitudes of the characters in various stages of the play, to reflect on how and why they are winners or losers, and to identify the implications of their victory and defeat. Even if this is not possible in this paper, the observations which I have developed so far, on the multilayered structure of the tragedy and on the system which seems to organise its characters' functions, illustrate that the theme of victory and defeat will not be applied only to the most obvious case, Atreus' victory over Thyestes, but also to the other sets of characters involved in the same structural arrangement, such as, again, Tantalus, the *satelles*, and, to a certain extent, the Chorus.

The contrast between Atreus and Tantalus on the one hand, and the *satelles* and Thyestes on the other, reflects the similar contrast between the Fury and Tantalus' shadow represented in the metadramatic prologue, since it carries over into the action the constitutive hesitation between furthering the dramatic plot and preventing it from developing. Just as the metadramatic contrast, moreover, this hesitation too is qualified by the opposition between repression and removal of repression that I traced in the prologue. We must therefore apply to the bulk of the play and to the utterances and actions of its characters, the suspension of judgment which the fundamental tension inscribed in the prologue requires, and which seems the only appropriate response to the set of contrasting connotations which the prologue and its ramifications assign in a most disconcerting fashion to different sides of the play. Among other things, we must also be prepared to recognise that Atreus, the playwright with hands drenched in blood, stands out in the play as the embodiment of a victory against the constraints of moral repression that is inextricably connected with the force and pleasure of poetry.

Notes

1. This chapter was originally written for this volume and the conference organised by its editors in Cambridge in December 1991. The scope of the essay has become much enlarged since then, and I can offer this section only as a rather general indication of a more exhaustive reading of *Thyestes* which I hope to accomplish elsewhere. I am most grateful to the participants in the Cambridge seminar and several friends for criticism and encouragement. I also wish to thank the Magie Publications Fund of the Classics Department at Princeton and the University Committee on Research in the Humanities and Social Sciences for financial support.

2. The question of the dating of the tragedy inevitably arises in this connection, and here I must offer a declaration of disengagement and scepticism at the same time. The disengagement is prompted by the fact that conclusive demonstrations are hardly to be expected given the nature of our evidence, even if Fitch's recent study (1981, esp. 303-7) has been greeted (perhaps justifiably) with much interest. Fitch's metrical analysis points to a late date for *Thyestes*. On the other hand, I remain sceptical that even a more precise dating could much assist the process of interpretation: even if we knew precisely the year in which a given play was written, we would still lack information on elements of great importance, such as the audience envisaged by the author and the forms of theatrical production. Under these circumstances a precise date would do little more than encourage the direct superimposition of external data and historical facts on the text.

3. This is not the place to discuss the issue of recitation vs representation of Seneca's tragedies, but I will refer throughout to the 'audience' because the dramatic form normatively presupposes its existence.

4. The text is quoted from R.J. Tarrant 1985.

5. Translations from *Thyestes* are from Hadas 1965, with occasional revisions.

6. Calderwood 1971 pp. 4ff. has useful remarks on this notion of metadrama, which is not limited to 'forays across or...around the borders between fiction and reality', but is based on the assumption that plays are 'also about' plays.

7. The idiosyncratic qualities of this particular prologue become apparent in a comparison with the similar prologue of *Hercules Furens*. The enraged Juno who delivers the entire prologue of *HF* is in many respects parallel to the Fury: both superhuman characters provide the impetus which sets in motion the dramatic action, and correspond in function to the creative stance which underlies each tragedy as a whole. Moreover, Juno's words and attitude also establish a close connection with the role of Juno in *Aeneid* 7. However, the two prologues differ significantly in several respects. Juno's speech is not a dialogue and does not stage a conflict between a sinful creative impulse and a moral resistance to the creation of *nefas* represented in *Thyestes* by the Fury and Tantalus' shadow respectively. This structural difference deprives the prologue to *HF* of the dialectical contrast between silence and speech, which, I argue, is central to *Thyestes*.

8. The prologue of *Agamemnon* is centered as well on the topic of return and reiteration. While the relative chronology of *Ag.* and *Th.* in Seneca's literary production cannot be certain, in mythical time the actions of *Ag.* come after those narrated in *Th.*, and are in fact a direct consequence of them. The ghost of Thyestes in the prologue recalls very effectively Tantalus' shadow, especially since they both insist on their preference for the underworld to the devastation awaiting them on Earth. Thyestes' exclamation at line 11 – *libet reverti* – means precisely that he would rather return to the underworld than assist in the terrible revenge which is about to happen. It should be noted, however, that according to Fitch's metrical study (above n. 2), *Ag.* would have

been written before *Th*. For a more sceptical position on the dating of *Ag.*, prior to Fitch 1981, see Tarrant 1976 pp. 5-6.

9. It is tempting to charge *transcribor* (13) with metadramatic resonances.

10. cf. *Aen.* 7.457 (Allecto and Turnus): *effata facem iuveni coniecit et atro / lumine fumantis fixit sub pectore taedas*.

11. cf. the behaviour of *virtus* in *v.b.* 15.5: *illa fortiter stabit et quidquid evenerit feret*; the imperturbability of the *sapiens* in front of natural disasters: *stabit super illam voraginem intrepidus* (n.q. 6.32.4); *ben*. 5.2.4: (*vir bonus*) *ad ultimum usque vitae diem stabit paratus et in hac statione morietur*; Iocasta's attempt to stop the massacre at Thebes: *ibo, ibo et armis obvium opponam caput, / stabo inter arma: petere qui fratrem volet, / petat ante matrem* (Ph. 407-9). The original suggestion, however, is again Virgilian: cf. *Aen.* 7.373ff. (Allecto and Latinus): *His ubi nequiquam dictis experta, Latinum / contra s t a r e videt penitusque in viscera lapsum / serpentis furiale malum totamque pererrat*.

12. The most explicit Latin statement for this notion of poetic enthusiasm, ultimately Democritean and Platonic, is perhaps Cic. *de or*. 2.194: *Saepe enim audivi poetam bonum neminem...sine inflammatione animorum existere posse et sine quodam adflatu quasi furoris*; cf. also Tusc. 1.64, and Pease's commentary ad locos for further indications. A relevant poetic passage is Ov. *fast*. 6.5-6: *est deus in nobis, agitante calescimus illo: / impetus hic sacrae semina mentis habet*.

13. Leo 1912.

14. The Fury's intertextual competence becomes in the context of this prologue one of the ways in which she acquires a metadramatic status, in so far as her references to other poetic texts work as a reflection on the genesis of the play and its modes of signification which goes beyond the dramatic level acted on the stage.

15. Tarrant 1985 has useful notes (listed at p. 85 n. 2) on several of these passages. The model had been pointed out by Monteleone (1980, pp. 77ff.), who does not make any suggestion on its possible significance.

16. Translation from Mandelbaum 1961.

17. This use of *ago* (which is absent in the Virgilian model) can be considered a technical theatrical term: cf. *OLD* s.v. 25 and 43. But the very form *actum est* is often used to describe a situation deteriorated beyond repair, and in the Fury's mouth it is appropriate to preserve as well this sense of ultimate destruction.

18. *Thyestes* differs from the *Aeneid* in another relevant detail. Whereas in *Aen*. 7 Allecto is instructed by Juno, in the tragedy the Fury (who structurally parallels Allecto) acts of her own accord, and the absence of a divine figure prevents a further displacement of moral responsibility on the gods. The Fury has learnt her lesson, and now acts of her own initiative.

19. I offer further indications on this topic in Schiesaro 1992.

20. Information on previous treatments of the play along these lines, and a new proposal, in Lefèvre 1985. A related issue which I will not consider here is how much the Chorus is left unscathed by the cognitive turmoil that the prologue forces on the audience and can thus be seen as a reliable embodiment of a superior moral stance.

21. Willink 1983; cf. Willink 1986 pp. 4-10.

22. Willink 1983 p. 32.

23. The conceptual framework underlying these remarks is ultimately indebted to Francesco Orlando's books now grouped as a series under the general title of 'Letteratura, ragione e represso', and partially translated into English in Orlando 1978.

24. An articulate discussion of various points of view and their implications can be found in Biondi 1989 pp. 35-62. Dingel 1974 stresses the incompatibility between the tragedies and Seneca's prose works.

25. The overall behavior of the *satelles* is more complicated, as he ultimately changes

his initial attitude, accepts Atreus' point of view, and tries to expose the weak points of his plot rather than insist on the need for restraint.

26. Note also that Tantalus' exhortation in the two following lines (489-90: *respiciet deus bene cogitata. Perge non dubio gradu*) echoes a similar command on the Fury's part: *perge, detestabilis umbra* (24-5).

27. Tantalus' position warrants a more detailed analysis which I cannot offer here. For instance, it is necessary to consider to what extent Tantalus might be voicing Thyestes' own ambivalent thoughts and emotions.

Bibliography

Biondi, G.G. (1989), ed., *Seneca, Medea Fedra*, Milan.
Calderwood, J.L. (1971), *Shakespearean Metadrama*, Minneapolis.
Dingel, J. (1974), *Seneca und die Dichtung*, Heidelberg.
Fitch, J.G. (1981), 'Sense-pauses and relative dating in Seneca, Sophocles and Shakespeare', *American Journal of Philology* 102, pp. 289-307.
Hadas, M. (1965), *Roman Drama*, Indianapolis-New York 1965.
Lefèvre E. (1985), 'Die philosophische Bedeutung der Seneca-Tragödie am Beispiel des "Thyestes" ', *Aufstieg und Niedergang der römischen Welt* 32.2, pp. 1263-83.
Leo, F. (1912), *Plautinische Forschungen*², Berlin.
Monteleone, C. (1980), 'I modelli di Seneca nel prologo del "Thyestes" ', *Giornale Italiano di Filologia* n.s. 11, pp. 77-82.
Orlando, F. (1978), *Toward a Freudian Theory of Literature with an Analysis of Racine's Phèdre*, Baltimore and London.
Schiesaro, A. (1992), 'Forms of Senecan intertextuality', *Vergilius* 38, pp. 1-8.
Tarrant, R.J. (1976), ed., *Seneca, Agamemnon*, Cambridge.
Tarrant, R.J. (1985), ed., *Seneca, Thyestes*, Atlanta.
Willink, C.W. (1983), 'Prodikos, "Meteorosophists" and the "Tantalos" paradigm', *Classical Quarterly* 33 pp. 25-33.
Willink, C.W. (1986), ed., *Euripides, Orestes*, Oxford.

12

Educating Nero: a reading of Seneca's *Moral Epistles*

Yun Lee Too

I

Ancient and modern scholars depict Nero's Rome as one in which the philosopher is a figure alienated from society: imprisonment, exile and death are his lot, as the fates of the Musonii, Rubillinus Plautus and Apollonius of Tyana attest.[1] Imperial philosophy gains its authority in this manner from a separation between state and wisdom, from a stark contrast between the former's corruption and the latter's virtues.

The problem with this model is that it is of course an exaggerated caricature. It is a terrible travesty which has ruthlessly suppressed the evidence that spoils the picture or else employs the exception to insist on the rule.[2] Seneca, despite committing suicide on the orders of Nero (Suet. *Nero* 35.5; Dio 62.25.3; Tac. *Ann.* 15.63), is the obvious odd-man-out, excluded to uphold the pattern of the uncompromised and persecuted intellectual. For Seneca's biographers, his wealthy patrician background, his role as the emperor's tutor, and his career as court adviser call his identity as philosopher into question. Nevertheless, in this chapter I shall attempt to argue that it is exactly Seneca's collusion with state and emperor which ultimately enables the philosopher to empower philosophy and which allows philosophy to have any impact upon the state. To make my point I shall concentrate on two aspects of Seneca's pedagogical identity, of his role as teacher to the elite of Rome. I shall first examine briefly how the Roman biographical and historical traditions portray the philosopher as Nero's tutor; secondly, I shall recover the generally overlooked didactic *persona* that Seneca constructs for himself as instructor of Lucilius in one of his late works, the *Moral Epistles*.

II

Suetonius, Tacitus and Dio provide us with the authorised version of Seneca's career as teacher. For these writers and for the majority of modern scholars,[3] this is the story of disappointed opportunity, of how Seneca taught Nero to be a wicked tyrant, of how the philosopher became responsible for the corruption and excesses of the emperor-to-be. The narrative begins with Suetonius, who informs us that, when Nero lived in the house of his aunt Domitia Lepida, he was tutored by a dancer and a barber, figures who personify corruption and debauchery (*Nero* 6.3). According to the Suetonian account, Seneca enters the picture once Nero has been adopted by the emperor Claudius: the philosopher is hired to be the boy's tutor (*Nero* 7.1). Nevertheless, he is to be not so much a teacher of philosophy and morality, as an instructor in the workings of empire. Suetonius observes that Agrippina prohibited Nero from learning philosophy, which she regarded as a hindrance to political authority. Nero was rather to learn what the historian ironically, in the light of his subsequent actions as tyrant-king, terms 'liberal arts' (*liberales disciplinas*) (*Nero* 52). Other Roman writers also point to Seneca's complicity in the construction of Nero's power. Tacitus relates that Agrippina recalled Seneca from exile to fulfil her aspirations for her son to dominate (*ad spem dominationis*, *Ann.* 12.8); Dio says that Agrippina had her son trained for power precisely by handing him over to Seneca (60.32.3). Power and domination are the programme of Senecan pedagogy.

Following the authorised version, Seneca's teaching marks less a departure from the training of Nero's dancer and barber, as some have assumed, than a more efficient, more successful version of it. This is because Seneca is the teacher-producer (*didaskalos*) of the imperial drama of authority. Continuing to influence his pupil during his youth and in the early years of his reign (cf. Tac. *Ann.* 14.52), the philosopher scripts the opening acts of Nero's reign. He composes the speech that the emperor delivers at the funeral of Claudius (*Ann.* 13.3; Quint. 8.5.18). (Seneca also produces the *Apocolocyntosis*, the speech which, in ridiculing the dead emperor and his fate in the afterworld, perhaps raises queries about the construction of the new emperor's authority through the official funeral oration.) Following this, the philosopher scripts the orations that the emperor presents to assert his imperial identity in the Praetorian Camp and in the Senate (Dio 61.3.1). It is in light of these events that Tacitus goes so far as to characterise Seneca as the person who constructs the voice of the emperor, and even as the very 'voice of the emperor' (*vox principis*, *Ann.* 13.11). For Dio, Seneca emerges most clearly as teacher-producer when the imperial drama explicitly turns into drama. When the historian describes how Seneca, together with Burrus, standing behind the scenes, urges and supplies the cues to Nero's performance as a lyre-player, he describes them appropriately as the teacher-producers (again *didaskaloi*): 'and Burrus and Seneca, as teacher-producers, stood by him [Nero], offering prompts ...' (62.20.3).

The success of Senecan pedagogy for Nero – the horrifying accounts of the emperor's tyranny in the historians are the evidence – is, none the less, the compromise and so the failure of Senecan philosophy. Dio, in particular, draws attention to contrasts between the teacher's discourse of philosophy and morality and his enactment of corruption and power:

> And in other things he did everything entirely opposite to what he taught as philosophy. For although accusing tyranny, he became the teacher of a tyrant; despite running down powerful acquaintances, he did not distance himself from the palace; and while himself finding fault with flatterer, he cultivated Messalina and the freedmen of Claudius ... (61.10.2).

Seneca emerges from this paragraph as the hypocrite, as the political machinator who has donned as his disguise a mask of morality, a discourse of respectability. It is by this rift between word and deed that the teacher has empowered the student, even to the extent of giving the student authority over the teacher. Nero learns well the lesson enacted by his hypocrite pedagogue. When the emperor commands the philosopher to put an end to his life, Suetonius tells us that he invokes the language of morality to cover his exercise of power. Nero swears that he himself would have preferred to die than to harm his old *praeceptor* (*Nero* 35.5).

III

The end of Nero's youth marks the end of Seneca's career as his tutor. Tacitus ominously observes, 'indeed the end of Nero's childhood and the strength of adolescence were at hand: taught enough by sufficiently learned elders he threw off his teacher' (*Ann.* 14.52). Soon afterwards Seneca formally ends his relationship with Nero on the pretext of ill-health and a desire to study following the death of Burrus (*Ann.* 14.56; Dio 62.25.3). He retires from the state – or so it would appear – in AD 62. Between 62 and his death in 65, the author writes, among other works, the *Moral Epistles*. Modern scholars tend to regard this text as the quintessential expression of Seneca's withdrawal from empire and return to philosophy. Yet the extent to which the *Moral Epistles* can be read as the conclusion to the author's political existence is open to question. Andrews expresses his doubt that Seneca could ever stand back from the state after returning from exile precisely to be the tutor of Nero, and perceives this return to 'philosophy' as a death-delaying tactic.[4] Later Foucault throws into question the marginality of the philosopher when he raises the possibility that this text might be one in which its writer redefines in retrospect his position *within* Rome.[5]

To develop the suggestions of Andrews and Foucault and above all, to interrogate the stereotype of the alienated intellectual of Rome in the late first century, I shall draw attention to the fact that even here Seneca recalls his former politically active role within the state. Overlooked by the majority of readers, the *Moral Epistles* provides the unauthorised version of Seneca's pedagogical identity, one which significantly qualifies how we perceive the authorised account of the philosopher's education of Nero in the historians and biographers. Through vocabulary which characterises the author as teacher and the addressee of the letters as student – 'you must be educated' (22.1); 'I exhort you' (23.1; 34.2); 'learn' (23.2); 'I shall teach' (37.11) and so on – he recreates in the *Moral Epistles* his identity as a teacher. Now Seneca rehearses and revises his prior relationship with the boy-emperor with a member of the senatorial class named Lucilius, under the ironic guise of urging his addressee to stand back from participation in the state.[6]

IV

In the *Moral Epistles* Seneca rehearses the dichotomous relationship between word and deed by which Dio would later characterise his career. But whereas Dio saw this as the strategy by which the evil Rome of Nero was created and legitimated, Seneca employs this as the means by which he now undermines the authority of the *respublica*. As we shall see, the author deauthorises hypocrisy as a political tool precisely by making apparent his own hypocrisy. The philosopher presents his own doctrine as one which seeks to close exactly the gap between word and deed, between appearance and reality. At *Epistle* 108.35 Seneca prescribes the following ideal of language to Lucilius, 'I advise that ... profitable teachings and magnificent and spirited sentiments are immediately transferred into actions (*in rem transferantur*)'. Seneca demands that words be 'transferred' into things. It would appear that the aim of his imperative is to cancel out the traditional rhetorical opposition between word and deed, although it is also the case that the imperative itself acknowledges and affirms the opposition it attempts to void. Accordingly, this imperative raises questions about whether the moral project of enacting one's own language can be fulfilled by the philosopher himself. Elsewhere in this letter Seneca insists on the importance of rejecting the word–deed dichotomy. At the beginning of the epistle he expresses his disapproval of students who attend philosophical schools merely to pick up delightful words (*verba*) and not to acquire things (*non ut res excipiant*, 6). At the end he reiterates his message, exhorting his reader as follows: 'Let us learn so that what were words become deeds' (108.36) and 'let them do what they say' (108.38).

In the context of Stoic metaphysics, a 'thing' is something material; and because materiality is what constitutes being, a thing *is*. Furthermore, only material 'things' act upon other 'things' and can be acted upon. Because 'things' act (cf. *facit*, *Ep.* 65.4), they are what the Stoics termed 'causes'.[7] It is important to realise that for the Stoic, language was not always a 'thing'. When words express *relationships between things*, they are 'sayables' (*lekta*) and, like time, space and void, have no material existence and being.[8] Words can, however, be things when they are vocalised because as voice (*phonē*) they are constituted by vibrating air (Diogenes Laertius 7.55). Voiced words in turn act: as Seneca observes in *Ep.* 56, they might wake up a sleeping person or ruin his concentration when he is trying to study. In the *Moral Epistles*, however, Seneca's overriding concern is with the ethics rather than the metaphysics of 'word' and 'thing': the writer's aim is to provide a prescription for a way of life. Elsewhere in the work, the author continually rejects any discrepancy between saying or writing one thing and doing something else. In the collection's first epistle, the philosopher tells Lucilius to do what he portrays himself as doing in his own writing, 'therefore, do (*fac*), my Lucilius, what you write you do to fill the time' (1.2). Subsequent letters emphasise the importance of having a correspondence between word and deed in variety of different ways.[9] The numerous articulations of the ethical principle suggest that the mere words are themselves less significant than actions. Indeed, to drive home just this point that *opera* should always take precedence over *verba*, Seneca brings *Epistle* 98 to a close by querying 'what need is there for words (*verbis*)? Let us go to the present matter (*in rem praesentem*)' (98.18). The author's instinct is to squeeze out words altogether. The 'present matter' in this letter is remaining steadfast in the face of death and pain; in several other epistles in the collection the important *res* is having a proper attitude towards death (cf. 70.6; 17.11; 98.17).

Seneca's rejection of hypocrisy in these passages is precisely what draws to our attention the inconsistencies between his philosophical discourse and his own behaviour, even within the limited context of writing a work like the *Moral Epistles*. The ideal so fundamental to the moral doctrine of the work, namely that one should do what one says or writes, is disturbed by the signs that the letters are after all only fictional. For previous readers, the most compelling argument for viewing the letters as a literary project undertaken by the author himself is that the passage of time indicated in the epistles is too compressed to allow for an actual correspondence between Seneca and Lucilius, and to permit the intellectual and moral development of their addressee.[10] Letters seem to be exchanged within days regardless of the fact that one of the correspondents is often said to be far away from Rome. Furthermore, M. Griffin proposes that Seneca discourages his audience from assuming that his epistles are historical by deliberately confusing the temporal references that are present in the work.[11] That Seneca is allying himself with Epicurus and Cicero by writing fictional letters, as Bourgery and Sykutris were among the first to suggest, does not excuse the author's departure from his imperative to enact language.[12] If the epistles are fictional, then there is a deliberate gap between the philosopher's instruction to Lucilius to turn his language into something and the unreal or fictional frame in which the imperative is cast.

The fictional character of the letters is only the most obvious violation of Seneca's moral principle that one must enact one's language. The epistolary genre conventionally assumes that two different individuals participate in an exchange of language. Fictional epistles announce their literary form by upholding the pretence of communication between an author and an addressee. Thus the philosopher frequently characterises his letters as a conversation between himself and Lucilius. At 67.2, for example, he writes of the exchange of letters between himself and his addressee as a *sermo*, cf. 'as if I were speaking with you', 67.2. At 89.23 Seneca speaks of the importance of rehearsing one's epistle with interlocutors, 'say these things to others, write so that you yourself may hear while you speak, so that you may read while you write'. Nevertheless, Seneca's construction of his addressee, Lucilius, in the *Moral Epistles* suggests that he is prepared to violate and destabilise even the indications that the work is an epistolary fiction. The philosopher undermines the epistolary convention that one writes, or rather in this case, appears to write to another person. Griffin draws our attention to the unstable, shifting relationship between author and addressee: sometimes Seneca is patronisingly superior to Lucilius; at other times, he resembles his 'student'; in still other letters, he suggests that he will be taught by Lucilius.[13] This is an instability which proceeds from the author's deliberate and well signalled subversion of the epistle as one half of a dialogue, as part of an exchange with another person. At 3.2 the philosopher declares that even when communicating with one's friend, i.e. Lucilius, the priority lies in deliberation about oneself, 'indeed consider all things with a friend but begin first with yourself'. Discourse about oneself precedes and threatens to displace epistolary discourse. It is worth noting that when Seneca gives Lucilius an injunction to convey learning and knowledge to others at 89.23, he describes this above all as an act of communicating with oneself, 'Say these things to others, so that you yourself hear while you speak; write, so that you read while you write ...'. Elsewhere, e.g. at *Epp.* 28.10 and 58.5ff., as G. Misch observes, Seneca conducts a conversation with himself, a monologue.[14]

Bourgery and Grimal propose that the *Epistles* constitute an interior or self-dialogue – the author writes or talks only to himself.[15] Indeed, in numerous letters Seneca conspicuously raises a question about whether his epistolary project requires an addressee.[16] But it is particularly near the beginning of the collection that Seneca explicitly challenges the fiction that the *Moral Epistles* (appear to) participate in an exchange of letters between two friends by emphasising his composition as a dialogue with himself. At 6.7 Seneca cites from Hecato, an author he has been reading, 'I began to be my friend (*amicus esse mihi coepi*)'. Seneca signals that he is beginning to be his own friend, the individual to whom a letter writer conventionally directs his discourse – in this case, Lucilius. In the very next letter the philosopher displaces Lucilius. He declares that to teach oneself is to expend effort in the least wasteful manner, 'there is no reason for you to fear that you have wasted labour (*operam*) if you have taught yourself'[17] (7.9). In fact teaching himself is precisely what Seneca reveals himself to have been doing up to this point in the epistle. An intrusive and jarring reference to a second person in the following section of the letter serves to demonstrate that the author has up to now turned in upon himself, 'but I shall communicate with you (*tecum*) lest I teach only myself today' (7.10). The word *tecum* reveals to us that until 7.10 the letter has been a self-dialogue rather than the representation of a communication between the two designated as author and addressee. Despite the introduction of a second-person presence through the word *tecum* Seneca refuses to sustain this characterisation of the discourse of a letter as dialogue, for he immediately proceeds to cite Epicurus as his authority that one person can be at once both his own performance and his own audience (7.11). It is this assimilation of first and second persons to one another which enables the author to claim that Lucilius is continually with him: 'I ask about you and inquire from all who come from that region what you are doing, where and with whom you pass the time. You cannot respond. I am with you' (32.1) and 'you are always with me' (64.1). Because Seneca constructs Lucilius in terms of himself, so present is the addressee that the need for even the pretence of exchanging letters is ultimately called into question.

V

The author's internalisation of dialogue can be constructed as an important moment in the development of subjectivity. Misch and Festugière do not see the subversion of address in the *Epistles*; rather they regard the precedence given to the 'I' as an important contribution to the development of individuality in Western literature which descends from the Socratic emphasis on self-knowledge.¹⁸ This, however, is to oversimplify Seneca's construction of self in the text and to misread the work as a straightforward depiction of self, i.e. as 'autobiography'. Seneca resists exactly this naïve interpretation of both the first and second persons as *himself*. The author rather asks us to ascribe the collapse of epistolary dialogue to his creation of an extraordinary literary identity or *persona* for himself. As a result of this *persona* 'he' cannot be assimilated to any figure constructed by the literature of the Greek and Roman philosophical traditions; through it 'he' himself becomes a text.

I suggest that in the context of the *Epistles* the philosophical identity which Seneca writes for himself and 'Lucilius' is that of a literary text. The author begins *Ep.* 6 with a startling admission of self-knowledge: he has been 'transfigured': 'Lucilius, I understand that I am not only emended (*emendari*) but that I am transfigured (*transfigurari*) … And this is itself the plot (*argumentum*) of a soul translated (*translati animi*) into something better because it sees the faults which it did not previously know' (6.1). In *Ep.* 94 Seneca declares that the Stoic cannot be a wise man until his soul has been 'transfigured (*transfiguratus*)', supporting his statement with the authority of Marcus Agrippa (94.48). Scarpat Bellincioni regards the *transfiguratio* of the Stoic as his transformation into a godlike being.¹⁹ But this gloss on *transfiguratio* fails to take into account that the language of Stoic self-perfection consists in vocabulary that one might also use in referring to a literary composition: the soul is characterised as a narrative – note *argumentum* – to be corrected (*emendari*, 6.1).²⁰

There is further support for viewing the moral project that Seneca undertakes in the *Epistles* as a literary enterprise. The philosopher encourages himself in the form of his alter ego, his 'addressee', to begin composing his soul as soon as possible in order to have longer to enjoy it: 'continue as you began and hurry as much as possible so that you can have a longer time to enjoy an emended and composed mind (*emendato animo et composito*). Certainly you should enjoy even while you emend (*emendas*) it, even while you compose (*componis*) it' (4.1). It becomes apparent that psychological 'emendation' and 'composition' are metaphorical, for in *Ep.* 16 the philosopher urges 'Lucilius' to 'write' the soul as if he were composing a rhetorical oration: ' … it [philosophy] forms and fashions the soul, disposes (*disponit*) life; rules actions and shows what must be done or omitted' (16.3). Accordingly, when Seneca says to 'Lucilius' 'you are my work (*meum opus es*, 34.2)', we are to understand *opus* as connoting a literary work, specifically the literary text which the author presents as the *Moral Epistles*. To invoke a play of words which Seneca invites us to see, this textualised addressee, this *opus*, is the friend upon whom the philosopher, as Stoic, is obliged to expend his effort and labour, also *opus*, according to the doctrine of *Ep.* 9 (9.7; 95.5; 48.7).

The preceding passages imply that the philosopher is an artist (*artifex*) – specifically a literary artist – who writes himself and the world around him (cf. 85.41; *De Beata Vita* 8.3), perhaps, just as the emperor composes and enacts his drama of state.²¹ In turn the text of the soul assimilates to itself other modes of textuality, most immediately that of the written and spoken word. Language must conform to a person so that any hypocritical discrepancies between word and deed/thing/reality disappear. In a further elaboration and refinement of this ideal, Seneca prescribes a symmetry between speech and the person who produces it in the *Epistles*: 'philosophy teaches to do, not to say, and demands this ... that one's life is not dissonant with one's speech or with itself' (20.2); 'let one's speech agree with one's life' (75.4); and 'one's pronunciation, like one's life, should be composed' (40.2). On the basis of the assumption that speech parallels an individual's character and *vice versa* it is reasonable to assume that the historian Tanusius is tedious because his *Annals* are long-winded (93.11). *Epistle* 114, in particular, emphasises the relationship between the text and reality as Seneca argues that language betrays a person's life, 'the speech of individuals is like their life' (114.2). The idea that language is determined by one's nature is the central theme of *Epistle* 114 and provides the explanation for why different 'styles' enjoy a vogue at particular moments: the individual, as a member of society, reflects in the way (s)he speaks or writes the character of that society (esp. 1-3). *Epistle* 114 is important because it implicitly asks us to consider that the language of the text is a mirror for Neronian society; Seneca's failure to fulfil his own language is a reflection of the hypocritical politics on which the Roman ruler lays the foundations of imperial power.

Despite stressing the importance of composing one's own speech so that it agrees with one's self, Seneca is adamant that psychological composition should always take precedence over literary composition — and that the 'text' of the soul should ultimately displace the literal, spoken or written text.[22] At *Ep.* 115 Seneca warns, 'let not properly woven words (*verba contexta*) and pleasantly fluid speech seduce you; let them go as they will provided the soul stands composed (*animo composito*)' (115.18). The warnings to give precedence to the 'writing' of the soul are numerous in the *Epistles* because Lucilius is the reader who pays too much attention to words (*verba*), to literary texts and their language, and not enough to the *res* that they signify. For instance, at *Ep.* 71.6 Seneca must tell him to set aside 'that game of literary philosophy which reduces the most magnificent thing (*rem*) to syllables'. Even late in the collection Lucilius has to be criticised for taking issue with the literal *compositio* of the books on civic law and politics of Seneca's teacher, Fabianus Papirius: the addressee has neglected their philosophical content ('finally having to to be concerned with philosophy, you find fault with his composition ... he composed morals (*mores*) not words and wrote them for the soul not the ears', 100.1-2). Seneca must remind his addressee that Papirius is more intent on composing himself — as Lucilius should also be — than his words and thus with writing for the soul rather than for the ears: indeed Papirius is engaged in writing a composed and tranquil soul (100.8). In other late letters Lucilius is warned not to allow himself to be carried away by verbal composition and neglect the more important issue of the soul's composition (115.1; 100.1; 115.18). Even at this stage in their correspondence Lucilius fails to make the necessary connection between words and things; he is unable to compose them into their proper relationship.[23]

Yet there is a further textual authority to which the text of the soul is subordinate. Seneca declares in one of his letters that it is the easiest 'thing' to live according to nature (*Ep.* 41.8). At *Ep.* 45.9 the philosopher speaks of the blessed man who employs nature as his teacher and composes himself according to its laws. Seneca does not, however, remove the possibility that there may be a discrepancy between word and thing by transforming the one into the other when he envisages things as words. At *Ep.* 107.9 the author reveals that by living according to nature, an individual's soul is reconciled with only another 'text':

> ad hanc legem [naturae] animus noster aptandus est; hanc sequatur, huic pareat, et quaecumque fiunt debuisse fieri putet nec velit obiugare naturam. Optimum est pati quod emendare non possis, et deum quo auctore cuncta proveniunt sine murmuratione comitare
>
> [Our soul is fitted to this law [of nature]; let the soul follow it, obey it, and think what happens should happen and not wish to rebuke nature. It is best to endure what you cannot change and without grumbling to accompany god by whose authorship everything happens.][24]

The law of nature is a text author(is)ed by god (*quo auctore*; cf. *Ben.* 4.7.1 for god as *auctor*).[25] It is a text which resists emendation (*quod emendare non possis*), presumably because god is to be conceived of as a perfect author.

VI

From the preceding discussion, it becomes clear that even if Seneca provides a prescription for a symmetry between words and deeds or persons, what he prescribes must prove antithetical to the ideal of reification. Seneca does not himself manage to turn all his own words into deeds as he demands in *Ep.* 108. In fact, I have argued, he removes the disparity between world and word by assimilating the first to the second: he disables the conventional opposition between things and words by asking us to view all things and persons as metaphorical texts. But what does it mean for Seneca to make use of this textual metaphor in the *Moral Epistles*? To phrase this question more poignantly, how does the figure of metaphor stand with regard to the moral doctrine of the work?

Critics such as Steyns, Coleman, and Armisen-Marchetti regard metaphors as an important element of Seneca's communicative strategy. Metaphors convey philosophical ideas, or else enhance doctrine.[26] Seneca himself lists metaphor, conventionally termed 'transferences of words' (*translationes verborum*) amongst the various figures which assist speaker and hearer in coming to terms with his philosophical teaching.[27] Yet scholars fail to perceive that in the *Moral Epistles* metaphor is invariably introduced in a negative context. At *Epistle* 114.1 the author associates the use of metaphor (*translationis iure*) with a breakdown of moral values in society. In *Epistle* 108, the letter which I have emphasised as being significant for Seneca's ideal of how words should relate to things, we see that the author also declares a prohibition against employing neologisms, fictive words, 'unworthy metaphors' (*translationes inprobas*) and '[unworthy] figures of speech' (35). Armisen-Marchetti suggests that 'unworthy metaphors' are those which lack clarity.[28]

Seneca, however, does not reject just 'unworthy metaphors'; he rejects the figure of metaphor as a whole, as is suggested by his redefinition of *translatio* ideally as a transfer from words to things (108.35). To see why the philosopher is obliged to do so, it is important to recognise that he articulates the ideal of Stoic morality, in particular where it concerns psychological self-composition, in terms of space and motion. Wisdom is viewed as being expansive and requiring as much latitude as possible in the soul (*Epp.* 88.33-5; 74.25).[29] Seneca privileges psychological space at the expense of literal, physical space. So, in contrast, the Stoic must learn to circumscribe and compress his body so that it takes up as little space as possible ('limit the body', 15.3; 'for this reason compress yourself as much as possible; look into yourself', 28.10). 'Lucilius', furthermore, is told to imagine his lifetime as a mere point that is not to be and cannot be extended into any direction (*in hoc punctum coniectus es*, 77.12). But more prominent than the use of space in the construction of Senecan ethics is the use of motion. Throughout the work Seneca defines true peace of mind as being able to resist the urge to move from one place to another, since literally shifting from place to place stands in contradiction to the doctrine of psychological composition presented by the author. In *Epistle* 28 Seneca observes of Lucilius, who has undertaken a long journey, 'now you do not travel but you wander, are driven, and shift from place to place (*locum ex loco mutas*), although that which you seek, [namely] to live well, is located everywhere (*omni loco*)' (28.5). Lucilius has yet to grasp that the ideal life is not tied to any one location but is ubiquitously available. Elsewhere in the collection of letters Seneca explicitly forbids such migration because it is the mark of an unstable soul, 'I do not wish you to change place (*mutare te loca*) and leap from one place to another first and foremost since such constant movement is the mark of an unstable soul (*instabilis animi*)' (69.1).

Significantly, the image, perhaps the metaphor, of changing 'places' is also extended to Seneca's critique of individuals who dart from text to text and from author to author rather than concentrating on reading one text at a time (cf. *locorum mutationibus*, 2.1). Moving from text to text provides us with an image which stands in contrast to the 'plot of the composed mind' (*argumentum compositae mentis*, 2.1; 45.1). If the ethics of space and motion apply to language, then there is a problem with metaphor, at least as it is conventionally presented in the Latin rhetorical treatises. According to writers prior to and contemporary with Seneca metaphor or *translatio* is depicted as involving a 'transference' of a word from one thing or place to another thing or place. The writer of the *For Herennius*, an anonymous rhetorical treatise composed in the early first century AD, speaks of *translatio* as follows, 'a word is transferred from one thing to another thing because it will seem right that it can be transferred on account of their similarity (*propter similitudinem*)' (4.34.45). This author regards metaphor as a verbal transference justified or motivated by an apparent similarity between the objects. In Cicero's *Concerning the Orator* 3.38.155 Crassus views metaphor as a transference of word (*verbum transferendum*) from one object to another either for stylistic embellishment or else to make up for the absence of a word to denote an object.[30] Similarly Quintilian adheres to this definition in his *Institutes of Oratory* (post AD 96) when he suggests that metaphor lies in the transference of a noun or verb from its 'proper' or natural place to another place which lacks a 'proper' word or to where it would be better (8.6.6).

By expressing the concept of metaphor in terms of space and motion, Roman rhetorical writers produce a metaphor for metaphor. To be consistent with his own ethical construction, Seneca must reject the metaphorical commonplace of metaphor just as, *qua* Stoic, he rejects everyday language and its commonplaces (*communes locos*, 52.8) – this is the language of the *turba*, who are ignorant of morality (44.6). Nevertheless, as Steyns observes, the *Moral Epistles* contain numerous metaphors. In fact, they contain by far the majority – nine out of ten – of the metaphors which occur in Seneca's prose works.[31] Metaphor is the means by which the author expresses his ethical ideals: space and movement articulate lack of virtue and a disturbed condition of the soul; the images consciously evoke the conventional metaphor of metaphor. But it is the crux of the difficulty that Seneca has also used metaphor to express, of all things, the wise man's composed soul: as we have seen, the Stoic sage has a soul which resembles a composed text. In an age emblematised above all by a poet-actor emperor, becoming the Stoic 'wise man' means becoming a metaphor, a rhetorical figure which is conceived of in terms which make it antithetical to the ideal stability of mind possessed by the perfect Stoic. The means by which Seneca expresses the wise man calls into question the possibility of the wise man.

VII

Seneca presents us with a philosopher's dilemma: language and its various structures are the means by which we try to communicate; however, they are also the obstacles to communication – here of philosophical ideals. My reading of the *Moral Epistles* does not stop with the recognition that Seneca's pedagogy fails due to the limitations of language and following this, with a blanket statement that pedagogy of every kind is always doomed to failure and frustration.[32] I would like to suggest that the failure of the didactic project he undertakes with 'Lucilius' in the early 60s has a purpose beyond the demonstration that pedagogy is a suspect activity, as indeed it is in the *Epistles*. The problems of language and of the enactment of language raised by the teaching of Lucilius, I venture, have significant implications for Nero's political authority and, particularly, for Seneca's complicity in empire.

Just what these repercussions might be for the state and its leader, Seneca subtly signals in *Ep.* 108, the letter which I regard as holding a particularly important place in the *Epistles*. In this letter the author criticises a particular type of reader: this is the reader concerned only with style and language to the extent that he takes no notice of a work's content. Such an individual will become so absorbed with problems of syntax and etymology – the example he gives is of someone who comments that certain compound words, i.e. *reapse* and *sepse*, should be two words instead of one (108.32; cf. 48.6ff.; 71.6; 88.3; 113.26). Seneca takes this reader to task for turning philosophy into mere philology (108.23). He names this transformation of one study into the other an 'unworthy translation', using the very word which he elsewhere uses to denote the figure of metaphor. But the critique of the philological reader in *Epistle* 108 is especially significant because it is now given a context which clearly exposes the implications of Seneca's own pedagogy in the *Moral Epistles*. It is important to notice that the word-splitting philologist of *Ep.* 108 is specifically a reader of Cicero's *Republic*; he is thus a reader who fails to get beyond the words of this text to its larger ideas and so to the very 'thing', the 'public thing' or *res publica*, which is signified by the work and after which the work is named.

Seneca's philologist is Seneca's own *Doppelgänger*. When the philosopher engages in a pedagogy which prescribes things and deeds rather than words but deliberately continues to privilege words and texts over things, he represents himself as being able to disempower the state, figured as the public thing, the *res publica*. Moral philosophy is cast in the *Moral Epistles* as a sophisticated art of political (de)composition. It is the means by which Seneca declares that when he withdraws from the state he takes the state with him and more importantly, by which he pre-empts the attempt of subsequent biographers and historians to credit him with the writing and directing of the state in his capacity as Nero's teacher.[33]

Notes

1. See Philostratus *VA* 4.35; and 4.46, for the exile of the Stoics Rubellinus Plautus and Musonius Rufus; Tacitus *Annals* 15.71, for the imprisonment of the Babylonian Musonius and Apollonius of Tyana; Philostratus *VA* 7.16, for the death of Seneca. See also Ramsay MacMullen 1966 pp. 46-94.

2. See Rutherford 1989 pp. 66-77.

3. Murray (1965 pp. 41-61), however, argues that the initial period of Nero's rule, the golden *quinquennium*, is due in large part to the prominent position of Seneca at court.

4. Andrews 1930 p. 624.

5. Foucault 1986 p. 86.

6. Griffin 1976 p. 350.

7. Frede 1980 esp. pp. 219-30.

8. Sextus Empiricus *M* 8.11-12; cf. Diogenes Laertius 7.57; see Imbert 1980 p. 193.

9. e.g. 20.1; 20.2; 24.15; 52.14; 71.1; 98.17.

10. Those who believe the letters are or may be fictional include: Albrecht 1989 p. 114, n. 25; Bourgery 1911 pp. 49-55; Griffin 1976 p. 349, n. 4 and 416-19; Leeman 1951 pp. 175-81; Maurach 1970 p. 21, n. 37. Albertini (1923) maintains their historicity.

11. Griffin 1976 pp. 348-50.

12. Seneca is at pains to point out this by his reference to the Roman epistolarist par *excellence* at *Epp.* 118.1 and 21.4. Bourgery 1911 pp. 48-51 and Sykutris 1931 col. 204.

13. Griffin 1976 p. 417. Coleman (1974 pp. 287-8, n. 4), observes that even after 124 letters we get only a vague impression of author and addressee.

14. Misch 1950 pp. 421-2.

15. Bourgery 1911 p. 54; Grimal 1979 p. 229.

16. e.g. 10.1; 26.7; 27.1; 57.6; 68.6; 89.23.

17. Ms. δ omits 'if' (*si*).

18. Misch 1950 pp. 417-35 and Festugière 1954 pp. 59-61 but 62-5.

19. 1986 p. 2.

20. For *argumentum* in the sense of a 'plot' of a play or narrative, see, for example, Plautus *Amphitryo* 51, 96; Terence *Andria* 6; Cicero *Letters to Atticus* 1.19.1; 9.10.1; 10.13.2; 15.4.3. For *emendare/emendatio* meaning the correction of a literary text, see Cicero *Letters to Atticus* 2,16.4; *Orator* 46.155; Quintilian 1.5.34; 2.4.10 (of a child learning rhetoric); 2.4.13; 2.2.7; 8.2.4 and *passim*.

21. Thus the Stoic also is depicted as composing the world around him: e.g. deeds or things (e.g. *res*, 24.6), friends (9.5), poverty (27.9), peace and quiet (e.g. 9.8; 56.6).

22. For the use of *compositio* to refer to the style or disposition of a literary text, see

Seneca *Ep.* 100.7; 114.15; *For Herennius* 4.12.18; Cicero *Concerning the Orator* 3.52.200; *Brutus* 88.303; *Orator* 54.182; *Quintilian* bk 9 *passim*.

23. Lucilius' deficiency in reading has perhaps been prescribed by an earlier namesake, the satirist whom Horace criticised for failing to compose his words properly (*Sat.* 1.4.8; 1.10.1-2). In contrast the addressee of *De Tranquillitate Animi* and *De Otio* learns to live up to his name 'Serenus' with the aid of the calming, tranquillising discourse of Seneca's texts.

24. cf. 17.90 and 44.5.

25. In *De Beneficiis* 4.7.1-2 Seneca declares that 'nature' and 'god' are interchangeable terms.

26. Steyns 1907 p. 112.

27. McCall 1969 pp. 61 and 166-77.

28. So Armisen-Marchetti 1991 pp. 126-9.

29. cf. Armisen-Marchetti 1991 pp. 118ff. Appropriately, Seneca uses the image of displacement to describe greed, a vice which is implicitly opposed to the ideal of self-sufficiency or *autarcheia*; cf. 36.6.

30. Also *De Oratore* 3.39.157; *Orator* 27.92; and Quintilian *Inst. Orat.* 8.6.6.

31. Steyns 1907 p. 112.

32. For this view of pedagogy, see, for instance, the essays in Johnson, ed., 1982.

33. Versions of this chapter were delivered at the Nero-colloquium and at the Ancient Philosophy Seminar in Cambridge. My thanks to the participants of both seminars for their comments, discussion and criticisms.

Bibliography

Albertini, E. (1923), *La composition dans les ouvrages philosophiques de Sénèque*, Rome.

von Albrecht, Michael (1989), *Masters of Roman prose from Cato to Apuleius. Interpretative studies*, tr. Neil Adkin, Leeds.

Andrews, Alfred C. (1930) 'Did Seneca practise the ethics of his *Epistles*?' *CJ* 25 pp. 611-25.

Armisen-Marchetti, M. (1991) 'La métaphore et l'abstraction dans la prose de Sénèque' in Grimal (1991) pp. 99-131.

Bourgery, A. (1911) 'Les lettres à Lucilius sont-elles de vraies lettres?' *Révue de Philologie* 35 pp. 40-55.

Coleman, R. (1974) 'The artful moralist: a study of Seneca's epistolary style' *CQ* 24 pp. 276-89.

Festugière, André (1954), *Personal religion among the Greeks*, Berkeley.

Foucault, Michel (1986), *The care of the self. The history of sexuality*, vol. 3, tr. Robert Hurley, New York.

Griffin, Miriam (1976) *Seneca: a philosopher in politics*, Oxford.

——— and Barnes, Jonathan (1989) *Philosophia togata: essays on philosophy and Roman society*, Oxford.

Grimal, Pierre (1979), *Sénèque ou la conscience de l'empire*, Paris.

——— (1991), *Sénèque et la prose latine*, Geneva.

Imbert, Claude (1980) 'Stoic logic and Alexandrian poetics' in Schofield, Burnyeat, Barnes (1980), *Doubt and dogmatism: studies in Hellenistic epistemology*, Oxford, pp. 182-216.

Johnson, Barbara (ed.) (1982) *The pedagogical imperative: teaching as a literary genre*, Yale French studies 63, New Haven.

Kaster, Robert (1988), *Guardians of language: the grammarian and society in late antiquity*, Berkeley and London.

Leeman, A.D. (1951) 'The epistolary form of Seneca (ep. 102)' *Mnemosyne* 4, ser. 4 pp. 175-81.
McCall, Marsh H. (1969), *Ancient rhetorical theories of simile and comparison*, Cambridge, Mass.
MacMullen, Ramsay (1966), *Enemies of the Roman order: treason, unrest, and alienation in the empire*, Cambridge, Mass.
Maurach, G. (1970), *Der Bau um Senecas Epistulae Morales*, Heidelberg.
Misch, Georg with E.W. Dickes (1950), *A history of autobiography in antiquity*, vol. 2, London.
Murray, Oswyn (1965) 'The quinquennium Neronis and the Stoics' *Historia* 14 pp. 41-61.
Parker, Patricia (1987), *Literary fat ladies: rhetoric, gender, property*, London.
Rawson, Elizabeth (1989) 'Roman rulers and the philosophical adviser' in Griffin and Barnes (1989) pp. 233-57.
Rutherford, R.B. (1989), *The meditations of Marcus Aurelius: a study*, Oxford.
Scarpat Bellincioni, Maria (1986), *Studi Seneca e altri scritti*, Brescia.
Steyns, D. (1907), *Étude sur les métaphores et les comparaisons dans les oeuvres en prose de Sénèque le philosophe*, Ghent.
Sykutris, J. (1931) 'Epistolographie', *R-E* Supplement Band 5, Stuttgart, cols. 185-220.

13

Famous last words: authorship and death in the *Satyricon* and Neronian Rome

Catherine Connors

The *Satyricon*, with its carnivalesque mixture of elements of high and low cultures, its obsessions with food, sex and death, and its incessant manipulations of reality through artifice, seems a perfect mirror of Neronian tastes. But in bringing a Neronian context to bear on readings of the Satyricon, we must first recognise that we cannot be absolutely certain either that the Satyricon is Neronian in date or that it should be attributed to the Petronius described by Tacitus as Nero's *elegantiae arbiter* (arbiter of elegance).[1] In the first section of this chapter, I use literary analysis to expand the argument made by Rose (1971) that part of the *Satyricon* was composed after the death of Lucan in April of 65. In the second section, I situate this literary analysis within a discernible pattern associating death and the production of texts in Roman, and especially Neronian, culture.

Many attempts to consider the *Satyricon* in the context of Neronian culture investigate the possibility of a relationship between Lucan's *Bellum Civile* and the poem on the same theme produced by the *Satyricon*'s disreputable poet Eumolpus (*Sat.* 119-24). Some have viewed Eumolpus' poem as an exercise in epic composition not related in any significant way to Lucan's poem.[2] But the subject matter (the civil war between Caesar and Pompey) does not seem to have been popular in poetry generally and so invites comparison with Lucan's handling of the subject. Eumolpus' prefatory remarks on the appropriate representation of the gods in an epic on civil war (*Sat.* 118) also seem to indicate that the poem responds to the revolutionary elimination of speaking roles for the gods in Lucan's *Bellum Civile*.[3] I have discussed some of the literary complexities of Eumolpus' poem at length elsewhere;[4] here I limit my remarks to the passage which is arguably the most densely allusive in the whole poem: its ending.

After an account of the human and divine causes of the civil war, and of Caesar's movements toward Rome and Pompey's flight from the city, Eumolpus' poem breaks off abruptly with a totalising impulse, an attempt to embrace the entire civil war within its language. Discordia addresses Caesar and Pompey and bids them set the events of war in motion. The final line (295) narrates all the other events of the war and beyond: 'whatever Discordia commanded took place.' I would like to argue that lines 292-4 attempt to embrace not only the events of the war but also the specific representation of them in Lucan's text:

> '... nescis tu, Magne, tueri
> Romanas arces? Epidamni moenia quaere
> Thessalicosque sinus humano sanguine tingue.'
> factum est in terris, quicquid Discordia iussit.

['... Magnus, don't you know how to protect the Roman citadel? Seek the walls of Epidamnus and stain the Thessalian bays with human blood.' Whatever Discordia commanded took place on earth.] (292-5)

Discordia commands Pompey to flee Rome, to seek the walls of Epidamnus, and to stain the *sinus* (literally curved or enfolding places, often bays) of Thessaly with blood. I will return to Epidamnus in a moment, but first I wish to investigate line 294. The form of the line is drawn from Lucan's description of the first moment of armed conflict at Pharsalus, in which the earth of Thessaly is tainted with blood: *primaque Thessaliam Romano sanguine tinxit* ('[Crastinus' lance] first stained Thessaly with Roman blood', Luc. *B.C.* 7.473).[5] The conceit of Thessalian *bays* (*sinus*) stained with blood seems to expand the reference further to include Lucan's account of Pompey's arrival at the sea in his flight from Pharsalus after the battle: *litora contigerat per quae Peneius amnis / Emathia iam clade rubens exibat in aequor* ('he [Pompey] had reached the shore where the Peneus river, now reddening with Emathian slaughter, ran out into the sea', Luc. *B.C.* 8.33-4.) It is worth noting that Lucan, by emphasising the river's reddening with the word *rubens*, in effect gives Pompey a 'Rubicon' of his own.[6] Thus, using a technique exploited frequently in epic poetry and recently studied by P. Hardie, the poet combines allusions to different parts of an earlier poem in order to analyse or embrace the structure of the earlier poem:[7] the line *Thessalicosque sinus humano sanguine tingue* combines a verbal reminiscence of the beginning of bloodshed at Pharsalus with a conceptual evocation of Lucan's description of the aftermath of bloodshed at Pharsalus.

The range of references to Lucan's poem in Discordia's command at the close of Eumolpus' poem expands even further. By referring to Pompey's presence at the walls of Epidamnus, that is Dyrrachium, Discordia alludes to the very last lines of Lucan's *Bellum Civile*, which ends abruptly when Lucan's Caesar remembers Scaeva holding back Pompey at the walls of Epidamnus; in both Eumolpus' poem and in Lucan's the name Epidamnus operates on the level of history to bring up the fact that Pompey failed to press his advantage against Caesar there,[8] and it operates through a well-known etymology from *damnum* to suggest that this failure was Pompey's ruination:[9]

> captus sorte loci pendet; dubiusque timeret
> optaretne mori respexit in agmine denso
> Scaevam perpetuae meritum iam nomina famae
> ad campos, Epidamne, tuos, ubi solus apertis
> obsedit muris calcantem moenia Magnum.

13. Famous last words

[Caught by the destiny of the place he hangs in the balance; uncertain whether to fear or hope to die he looked back in the close-packed line of battle to Scaeva who already had earned a name of perpetual fame, at your battlefields, Epidamnus, where alone when the walls were breached he besieged Magnus trampling down the ramparts.] (10.542-end.)

Just as the final line of the *Satyricon*'s poem ('Whatever Discordia commanded took place on earth') encompasses all the events of the war and its aftermath, so too the immediately preceding lines (292-4) encompass all of Lucan's poem, allusively extending from Pompey's escape from Italy, on to the campaign at Pharsalus, Pompey's flight from Caesar after the battle, and finally Caesar's memory, at the noticeably abrupt end of Lucan's *Bellum Civile*, of Pompey's failure to win decisively at Epidamnus.

Rose, in order to date the composition of this part of the *Satyricon* to the period following the death of Lucan, argues that Petronius knows where Lucan's poem ends and is here 'using a neat variation of the last lines of the tenth Book to end his own poem'.[10] But the author of the *Satyricon* does not engage in this type of complex allusion simply in order to allow scholars to date his work. Sullivan has argued that throughout Eumolpus' poem Petronius is mocking Lucan in order to win favour with Nero, and this may indeed have been one way in which the text of the *Satyricon* was received during Nero's lifetime.[11] The poet Eumolpus is in some ways clearly represented as a figure of mockery; an earlier poetic recitation on the Fall of Troy is met with a shower of stones from bystanders (*Sat.* 89-90). But the reconstruction of stable, clearly defined philosophical or literary factions at the court of Nero is problematic.[12] Therefore, I would like to suggest a different framework, one not based primarily on identifying Petronius and Lucan as members of opposing factions, for interpreting an intertextual relationship between the ends of Lucan's and the *Satyricon*'s civil war poems. That is, I shall try to situate the *Satyricon*'s response to Lucan's apparently unfinished civil war poem in what I would like to term a Roman discourse of authorship and death. By observing how the deaths of certain authors are described and interpreted in Roman culture, we may be able to understand more about various ways in which the *Satyricon*'s allusion to the end of Lucan's *Bellum Civile* might be read in Neronian Rome.

For Romans, death was connected to texts in two very obvious ways. The text of an epitaph reminded the living of the dead; and Romans with property could exert control over that property even after death through the text of their wills. Death could also be connected with or mediated through authorship in subtler ways as well. In a passage introducing the group of Nero's victims which included Petronius, Tacitus compares his death notices to grave monuments of famous men: *detur hoc inlustrium virorum posteritati, ut quo modo exequiis a promisca sepultura separantur, ita in traditione supremorum accipiant habeantque propriam memoriam* ('Let this be granted to the future fame of illustrious men, that just as in their funeral procession they are distinguished from common burial, so too may they receive and possess their own memorial in an account of their last moments' Tac. *Ann.* 16.16). One particularly self-conscious instance of what we might call the textualisation of death is found in Seneca's *Moral Epistles* (77.20). In offering advice to Lucilius about the appropriateness of suicide in certain situations, Seneca explicitly figures suicide as the construction of a text or performance by an author: *quomodo fabula, sic vita: non quam diu, sed quam bene acta sit, refert. nihil ad rem pertinet quo loco desinas. quocumque voles desine: tantum bonam clausulam impone* ('As in a play, so in life: it doesn't matter how long it is but how well it is acted. It matters not at what point you stop. Stop wherever you like: just put a good clausula at the end.').[13] The word *clausula* can denote two types of textual closure. It can refer to the end of an extended text such as a letter or play, often with a witty or memorable twist.[14] Or it can refer specifically to the final group of syllables in an artfully constructed sentence. In a neat coincidence of form and content which reinforces the textual figure, this is the end of the letter, and *clausulam impone* form a cretic + trochee, one of the clausulae recommended and favoured by Cicero.[15]

In one type of 'utterance' in this discourse of authorship and death, a text is produced or re-enacted in the final moments of life.[16] The paradigm here is the *Phaedo*, Plato's account of Socrates' final discussion of the nature of the soul before his execution by hemlock poisoning. We can perceive Seneca's re-enactment of Socrates' death in Tacitus' narrative (*Ann.* 15.60-4): Seneca dictates a text of his own (probably philosophical), and then drinks a poison 'by which those condemned by a public judgment of the Athenians were put to death'. Thrasea Paetus seems to construct his last moments as an intertextual re-enactment of Seneca's death scene, and while waiting for the decision of the Senate he participates in a discussion of the nature of the soul (Tac. *Ann.* 16.34-5). He is also known to have written a biography of Cato which may have been Plutarch's source for the scene in which Cato reads the *Phaedo* twice in the hours before his suicide (Plut. *Cat. min.* 68.2, 70.2; cf. Seneca *Epist.* 24.6-8).[17] What we might call a serious 'utterance' in this discourse uses the textual devices of re-enactment of Socrates' death, philosophical reflections on immortality of the soul, and in Seneca's case, the production of his own text.

The discourse of authorship and death also embraces parodic or playful 'utterances' (texts produced or re-enacted in the final moments of life). Indeed, the Socratic paradigm already contains some lighter moments. Socrates says he has been busy in prison composing a versification of some fables of Aesop's (*Phaedo* 61b). When Socrates versifies Aesop, the boundaries between serious and playful moral teaching all but disappear because Aesop was viewed as a playful teacher of serious lessons. For example, to introduce a fable attributed to Aesop, Aulus Gellius says that he ' ... was rightly considered a wise man since he taught and recommended what it was beneficial to instruct and to advise not in a cheerless and domineering way, as is the custom of philosophers, but instead having invented witty and delightful stories he instilled in the minds and hearts of men things that had been wholesomely and providently considered, with a certain pleasant attraction of their attention' (*Attic Nights* 2.29.1). Later in the dialogue, Socrates' glance at the executioner when he asks whether there is enough hemlock for him to pour a libation before drinking it is glossed as 'mischievous' by Burnet.[18]

Among Roman 'utterances' in the discourse of authorship and death one could classify as playful or parodic Lucan's and Petronius' death scenes as told by

13. Famous last words 229

Tacitus. Lucan, instead of looking outward for a philosophical paradigm to re-enact in his death, turns inward and uses his own poetry as the script for his death: 'remembering a poem he had written in which he had said that a wounded soldier died a death of the same type, he repeated those very verses and this was his final utterance.'[19] So too, as many have observed, Tacitus' Petronius participates in the discourse of authorship and death by pointedly not being Seneca, by not participating in philosophical reflections, and by going in to dinner and allowing himself a nap so that, according to Tacitus, he might efface the appearance of suicide from the moment of his death. Petronius is said to have used his last moments in listening to frivolous verses and in composing, signing, and sending a list of Nero's *flagitia* (disgraceful actions) to Nero himself, and finally breaking his signet ring.[20] It is important to note that despite the obvious differences between Seneca's and Petronius' death scenes, both are composed and interpreted within the same discourse: so Tacitus describes what Petronius did not hear about from his companions as well as what he did hear: *nihil de immortalitate animae et sapientium placitis, sed levia carmina et facilis versus* ('[they said] nothing about the immortality of the soul or of the beliefs of wise men, but rather spoke trivial poems and offhand verses').[21]

The fictional narrative of the *Satyricon* too represents parodic or bizarre 'utterances' in the discourse of authorship and death; these involve false deaths. Trimalchio views a mere mishap as a near-death and commemorates it with the construction of a text: when the acrobat falls on him he calls for writing materials and composes and recites a banal verse on the unpredictability of life (*Sat.* 55.2-3).

I am mainly interested here in the *Satyricon*'s representation of the poet Eumolpus and his 'utterances' in the discourse of authorship and death. Although Eumolpus is clearly represented as a bad poet in the *Satyricon*, he is also the focus of some of the novel's most self-conscious literary effects. As the stormy seas wash over Lichas' ship, Eumolpus spends what might well be his final moments writing a poem on a huge piece of parchment (*Sat.* 115). While the ship founders, Eumolpus remains within the captain's cabin writing poetry. After the ship begins to break up in the storm, Encolpius and Giton hear loud cries emanating from the captain's cabin. It sounds like a beast trying to escape, but when they open the door they find Eumolpus crying out in a fever of composition. Eumolpus, imprisoned in his own creation, though he does not cry out to be saved from shipwreck still cries out in pain at the difficulty of writing, of struggling with his poem at its end: he says '*laborat carmen in fine*' ('the poem is in difficulties at its end,' *Sat.* 115.4). In truth, Eumolpus' literary efforts are not really interrupted by the shipwreck, or by the arrival of his rescuers, but by the intractability of the poem itself. His struggle to compose in the midst of a deadly storm puts his life even more at risk: he tells his rescuers to leave him alone with his poetic work, but they insist upon intervening and carry him to safety. Because the ship of poetry was in antiquity a common metaphor for literary creation,[22] when the novelist sets the scene of Eumolpus' struggle with poetry on a storm-tossed ship, the explicit and literal wreck of Lichas' ship is matched by the implicit and metaphorical shipwreck of Eumolpus' poem.[23] And when Eumolpus announces shortly afterward that his Civil War poem has not yet received the final touches (*ultimam manum*, *Sat.* 118.6), the shipwreck becomes an elaborately detailed account of the same unfinished and endless ending of Eumolpus' poem that we have investigated above.[24]

The pseudo death-throes of Eumolpus in the final surviving chapters of the *Satyricon* could be read as a parodic exercise in the discourse of authors-soon-to-be-dead; where Seneca offers the example of his life as an inheritance to his friends (Tac. *Ann.* 15.62), Eumolpus offers his body, and he debases the paradigmatic philosophical discourse on the soul's ability to survive the death of the body when he offers a history of cannibalism (*Sat.* 141), in which we might say that the body 'survives' the absence of the soul by becoming part of the flesh of those who eat it. Thus, whenever he is (or pretends to be) near death, Eumolpus produces bizarre utterances in the discourse of authorship and death.

Suetonius' account of Nero's final moments (Suet. *Nero* 49.1) also offers an example of an utterance in the discourse of authorship and death. When Nero perceives that the end is near, he bids his followers to make preparations for proper burial. These preparations include digging a grave, procuring fire and water for the disposal of the body, and even collecting any available pieces of marble to assemble in a makeshift monument. Nero says over and over as his companions carry out his orders, '*qualis artifex pereo!*' ('What an artist dies with me!'). Nero's repeated phrase participates in the discourse of authorship and death in several ways. On one level he ironically deprecates the impromptu memorial whose construction he directs, but he also celebrates, perhaps less ironically, his own role as artist and poet. More speculatively it might be added that the poet Nero will have been well aware that Horace closed his third book of Odes with the announcement *exegi monumentum aere perennius* ('I have built a monument more lasting than bronze') and that Ovid, alluding to Horace, proclaims at the end of his *Metamorphoses, iamque opus exegi* ('Now I have completed my work', *Met.* 15.871). When Nero marks the close of the artfully manipulated narrative that is his life with a remark that calls attention to his status as a monument builder, perhaps he ironically recapitulates a gesture of closure that is familiar from poetry in which poets call their work a monument that will triumph over their mortality. But where Horace and Ovid use this gesture of closure, the comparison with monument building, to announce their literary and artistic immortality, Nero may reverse it to confront his mortality. At the same time, the Suetonian emphasis on Nero's hesitation and fumbling in his attempts to control his destiny by commiting suicide (*Nero* 47-9) undercuts Nero's pose as an artist who artistically contrives the script of his final moments.

The capacious discourse of authorship and death thus allows utterances ranging from the seriously philosophical to the self-consciously literary to the determinedly frivolous: Seneca tries to die a re-enactment of Socrates' death, Lucan dies the death of one of his poetic soldiers, and Tacitus' Petronius dies a death scripted like the Menippean satire of the *Satyricon* (verse is heard in Petronius' last moments with exactly the kind of easy spontaneity which we see in the *Satyricon*). For Seneca, Lucan and Petronius, and perhaps for even Nero himself, the moment of death is artfully contrived to be the final utterance of a writing life. It is not possible to know precisely who does the contriving: both the ones dying and the biographers and historians who record their deaths are complicit in framing a suicide as a scene of the production of a text.

A second manifestation of the discourse of authorship and death originates not in a biographical or historical account of the author's final moments, but in the final moments of the text left behind. Thus, to take the most obvious example first, the composition of the *Aeneid* was known to have been interrupted by the death of its author, who ordered that it should be burned because he had not yet given it the final touches (*summam manum*). The half-lines which remained in the text were clear signals of the ultimately unfinished state of the poem, and it has been argued that when Ovid claims at *Tristia* 1.7.11-40 to have burned his *Metamorphoses* because it was unfinished when he went into exile, he is modelling his account of his poetic career on Vergil's deathbed scene.[25] The literary work dictated by Seneca in his last moments, which Tacitus explicitly says was published (*Ann.* 15.63), will have been received as a composition whose end coincided with the death of its author. So too, Lucan's *Bellum Civile* has been received as a text whose composition was interrupted by the death of its author; stories circulated that Lucan gave instructions for some revisions at his death (Suetonian Life), or that the first seven lines were added by a literary executor (Voss codex). But by far the most interesting aspect of the reception of Lucan's text as unfinished is the end of the narrative in Book 10. Lucan's *Bellum Civile* ends as Caesar is surrounded by unrest in Alexandria; the poet also looks unmistakably ahead to Caesar's assassination (e.g. Luc. *B.C.* 10.528-9: *dum patrii veniant in viscera Caesaris enses / Magnus inultus erit*, 'until the swords of the Roman fatherland plunge into Caesar's belly, Magnus will be unavenged'). Caesar's own account of his war, his *De Bello Civili*, ends at almost the same moment with unrest at Alexandria.[26] Working within the conventions of a culture which could view death as an act of closure exerted upon a text, Lucan has a discourse of authorship and death available to suggest that Caesar's Civil War text was brought to an end by the death of its author. At the end, after the uncovering of the Pisonian conspiracy, Lucan will have known that his own *Bellum Civile* could be read as a text brought to its end by the death of its author, and can use this knowledge to imply that Caesar's death imposed closure on Caesar's account of the civil war.[27]

I suggest, then, that the 'interrupted' narrative of the *Satyricon*'s Civil War poem, by alluding as we have seen to the 'interrupted' end of Lucan's *Bellum Civile*, participates in this same discourse of authorship and death. The author of the *Satyricon* reads Lucan's ended text / life in just the same way as Lucan reads Caesar's ended text / life. The production of Eumolpus' poem is, as we have also seen, implicated in the discourse of authorship and death, for it seems to have been written in the midst of the deadly storm which overtook Lichas' ship. When we reach the endless end of Eumolpus' *Bellum Civile*, and read its allusion to the endless end of Lucan's *Bellum Civile*, we are reading the lines which almost killed their author by making him oblivious to rescue.

In an essay about literary works in difficulty at their ends, it is difficult not to feel some trepidation when framing a conclusion. To the broad question of how to interpret the *Satyricon* in Neronian culture, I offered a very narrowly defined response: consider the relationship of Eumolpus' and Lucan's poems on the civil war between Caesar and Pompey. In response to the narrow question, what precisely is this relationship, I have tried to show that the *Satyricon*'s *B.C.* participates in a broad Roman discourse of authorship and death. The fictionally 'unfinished' end of Eumolpus' *Bellum Civile* alludes to the real unfinished end of Lucan's Civil War poem and thus might function through the discourse of authorship and death as a reminder for some readers that it was Nero who prevented Lucan's poem from being finished. Whether such a reminder would support or subvert Nero's political and poetic powers, whether it would mock the outrages of or lament the loss of Lucan, must remain, I think, an open question.

The openness of this question can itself contribute to our undertanding of Neronian culture. The representation of a literary artist within a literary work can provide an author with an opportunity to reflect upon his own literary project and its place in his own society. Thus if the Homeric bard Demodocus, for example, can be viewed as a self-conscious representation of the role of the poet in Homeric society, perhaps then Eumolpus too can be interpreted as a self-conscious representation of a poet in a world where literary brilliance could become a dangerous thing. Admittedly, Eumolpus is a less 'heroic' poet than Demodocus, perhaps because his is a less 'heroic' age. Eumolpus' Civil War poem may be read as a narrative of the political events of over a century earlier which shaped the Empire at whose centre Petronius lived, and the *Satyricon*'s account of Eumolpus composing poetry on a sinking ship may in turn reflect the pressures in the increasingly storm-tossed society of Nero's Rome which could end any poet's life and text. On the other hand, it is also possible to imagine, along Sullivan's lines, Nero getting a big laugh out of the *Satyricon*'s representation of a hapless poet of civil war, or even, along Masters' lines, Nero actually enjoying interpreting the *Satyricon*'s engagement in the discourse of authorship and death as a criticism of him.[28]

Perhaps such openness to competing interpretations is just what we should expect from a text produced in the latter part of Nero's reign. Perhaps a discourse open to competing interpretations seemed essential. Suetonius reports in an anecdote from the latter stages of Nero's reign that people engaged in a riddling discourse of subversion: 'at night many people pretending that they were having quarrels with their slaves would call out repeatedly for a protector' (*iam noctibus iurgia cum servis plerique simulantes crebro vindicem poscebant*, Suet. *Nero* 45.2). Thus they could call out in support of Vindex in Gaul while seeming only to seek someone (a *vindex*) to protect them from their slaves. Perhaps the *Satyricon* too is such a riddle.[29]

Notes

1. Rose (1971) thoroughly reviews the problem and argues for the identification of the author of the *Satyricon* with Tacitus' Petronius (*Ann.* 16.18-19). A more sceptical view of the evidence is offered by Smith (1975 pp. xii-xiv, 213-19). The text of the *Satyricon* will be cited from Müller and Ehlers 1983.

2. See George 1974, Slater 1990 pp. 198-9, and Smith 1975 pp. 214-17.

3. Sanford (1931) surveys Roman reactions to Lucan's poem; recently Feeney (1991, pp. 250-301), has done much to demonstrate precisely how revolutionary Lucan is in

his epic of absent gods, arguing that 'the gods' failure to participate is a vacuum which sucks the poem into active discontinuity with its tradition ... ' (p. 301).

4. Connors 1989.

5. *B.C.* 7.473 is adduced by Rose (1971 p. 91), and Baldwin (1911 ad loc.).

6. The Rubicon's etymological connection with the color red (*rubor*) is glossed by Lucan with the adjective *puniceus* (red) at *B.C.* 1.214. Elements of the 'Rubicon' motif appears repeatedly in Lucan's poem: the Tiber is described as a swollen river of blood running into the sea in the aftermath of Sulla's proscriptions at *B.C.* 2.214-8; and the image of blood-red water reappears at 2.713 in a description of a skirmish when two of Pompey's ships ran aground during his escape from Italy: *hic primum rubuit civili sanguine Nereus* (Here the sea first reddened with the blood of civil war); Caesar's crossing of the Sicoris (*B.C.* 4.130-52) has been read as a re-iteration of the Rubicon crossing, cf. Masters 1992 p. 66.

7. Hardie 1989.

8. It was Caesar himself who said this: so Suet. *Jul.* 36; Plut. *Pomp.* 65.8, *Caes.* 39.4-8; Appian *b.c.* 2.9.62; cf. Lucan *B.C.* 6.296-313 and Caes. *Bell. Civ.* 3.70.1.

9. For another etymological pun on *damnum/Epidamnus* see Plaut. Men. 263-4 and cf. Plin. *Nat. Hist.* 3.23.145. I explore Vergilian allusions in the mention of the walls of Epidamnus in Connors 1989 pp. 149-52.

10. Rose 1971 p. 94 (placed at the end of an appendix, these are the last words of Rose's posthumously published book).

11. Sullivan (1968 pp. 165-86), concentrates on formal issues and argues that 'Petronius intended a sketch of how Lucan should do it' (p. 181); at Sullivan 1985 pp. 153-79 he argues for a more overt political agenda on the part of Petronius.

12. See Griffin 1984 pp. 155-9 with references.

13. There is a similar figure of speech in Sen. *Epist.* 66.48, in an account of the death of Epicurus.

14. e.g. Cic. *Cael.* 65 (in a comparison to dramatic performances); Suet. *Aug.* 99.1 (Augustus recites the end of a Greek play on his deathbed); Cic. *de Orat.* 2.240 (of the punch-line of a joke); Cic. *Fam.* 2.4.2, Phil. 13.47, Sen. *Epist.* 11.8 (of the end of a letter).

15. See, e.g., Cic. *de Orat.* 3.191-3, and the accessible summary at OCD^2 s.v. prose-rhythm §16.

16. See Boym 1991 pp. 102-74 ('The suicide tactic: writing in the language of the other') for ways in which suicide notes can operate as oppositional or subversive texts.

17. On Seneca's death and Thrasea's re-enactment of it, signalled especially because Thrasea repeats Seneca's libation of water from the bath to '*Iovi liberatori*,' with a libation of his own blood, see Griffin 1976 pp. 369-72. On the ways in which Cato's suicide was used as an exemplar, see Griffin 1986a and 1986b. For details of Thrasea's death as a re-enactment of Cato's re-enactment of Socrates' death see Geiger 1979 pp. 62-7. Cicero interpreted Cato's death as a re-enactment of the Socratic paradigm: see *Tusc. Disp.* 1.74 and compare his ironic remarks at *Scaur.* 4-5.

18. Burnet 1911 on 117b.

19. Tac. *Ann.* 15.70. Lucan *B.C.* 3.635-46, a description of a soldier bleeding to death, has been suggested as an appropriate passage; see Furneaux 1907^2 on Tac. *Ann.* 15.70.

20. Tac. *Ann.* 16.19. This gesture of closure prevents a document under his name from being used to harm someone else (as has happened in the immediately preceding chapter [*Ann.* 16.17] in which Tacitus recounts the death of Lucan's father Annaeus Mela) and protects the integrity of his will.

21. Here it is tempting to compare Trimalchio's stipulation that the inscription on his tomb conclude its list of his accomplishments with the phrase *nec umquam philosophum audivit* (nor did he ever listen to a philosopher, *Sat.* 71.12.).

22. Examples of the ship of poetry in Roman literature include: Verg. *Georg.* 2.39-45, 4.116-17; Prop. 3.3.22-4; Juv. 1.149, with the note *ad loc.* of Courtney (1980); and compare Quint. *Inst.* 12.10.37. The figure is especially frequent in Ovid: see, e.g., *Ars* 3.26, *Fast.* 1.4, and other instances collected at Kenney 1958 p. 206. When we learn that Eumolpus' poem deals with civil strife, the figure of the ship of state also comes into play (cf. *Sat.* 123.233-7).

23. Indeed *laborat* can be used of a foundering ship: see Cic. *N.D.* 3.89, Caes. *Bell. Civ.* 2.6.5, Ov. *Pont.* 2.6.22.

24. This observation has been made in passing at, e.g., H. Stubbe 1933 pp. 68-9, Rose 1966 p. 298.

25. See Suetonius/Donatus *Vit. Virg.* 35-42, *Servius Vita* 27-42; *Vita Probiana* 22-8 and Grisart 1959.

26. This is the most important element of the argument that Lucan's poem is not unfinished made by Haffter (1957).

27. My reading of Lucan here is guided by Henderson (1988 pp. 132-3) and Masters (1992 pp. 247-59).

28. Sullivan 1985 pp. 171-2; for Masters see above, p. 171.

29. I would like to thank Alain Gowing, S. E. Hinds and James I. Porter for their helpful comments.

Bibliography

Baldwin, F.T. (1911), *The Bellum Civile of Petronius*, New York.
Boym, S. (1991), *Death in quotation marks: cultural myths of the modern poet*, Cambridge, Mass. and London.
Burnet, J. (1911), *Plato's Phaedo*, edited with introduction and notes, Oxford.
Chambers, R. (1991), *Room for maneuver: reading (the) oppositional (in) narrative*, Chicago and London.
Connors, C.M. (1989), *Petronius' Bellum Civile and the poetics of discord*, diss., Michigan.
Courtney, E. (1980), *A commentary on the satires of Juvenal*, London.
Feeney, D.C. (1991), *The gods in epic: poets and critics of the classical tradition*, Oxford.
Furneaux, H. (1907²), *The Annals of Tacitus* vol. 2, second edition revised by H.F. Pelham and C.D. Fisher, Oxford.
Geiger, J. (1979), 'Munatius Rufus and Thrasea Paetus on Cato the Younger', *Athenaeum* 57 pp. 48-72.
George, P.A. (1974), 'Petronius and Lucan, De Bello Civili', *C.Q.* 24 pp. 119-33.
Griffin, M.T. (1976), *Seneca: a philosopher in politics*, Oxford.
——— (1984), *Nero: the end of a dynasty*, London.
——— (1986a), 'Philosophy, Cato, and Roman suicide: I', *G & R* 33 pp. 64-77.
——— (1986b), 'Philosophy, Cato, and Roman suicide: II', *G & R* 33 pp. 192-202.
Haffter, H. (1957), 'Dem schwanken Zünglein lauschend wachte Cäsar dort', *Museum Helveticum* 14 pp. 118-26.
Hardie, P. (1989), 'Flavian epicists on Virgil's epic technique', *Ramus* 18 pp. 3-20.
Henderson, J.G.W. (1988), 'Lucan / The word at war', *Ramus* 16 pp. 122-64.
Kenney, E.J. (1958), 'Nequitiae Poeta', in N.I. Herescu, ed. *Ovidiana*, Paris, pp. 201-9.
Masters, J. (1992), *Poetry and civil war in Lucan's 'Bellum Civile'*, Cambridge.
Müller, K. and Ehelers, W. (1983), *Satyrica*, München.
Rose, K.F.C. (1966), 'The Petronian inquisition: an auto-da-fé', *Arion* 5 pp. 275-301.
——— (1971), *The date and author of the Satyricon*, Mnemosyne Supplement no. 16, Leiden.
Slater, N.W. (1990), *Reading Petronius*, Baltimore and London.

Smith, M.S. (1975), *Petronius Cena Trimalchionis*, Oxford.
Stubbe, H. (1933), *Die Verseinlagen im Petron*, Philologus Supplement 25, Leipzig.
Sullivan, J.P. (1968), *The Satyricon of Petronius*, London.
——— (1985), *Literature and politics in the age of Nero*, Ithaca and London.

Index

actors, 83-6
Agrippina, assassination of, 39-40, 55, 58, 92-3, 178-80
Alexander the Great, 104, 108 n. 24
Augustus, building programme of, 114-15, 117; carries off sacred images from Greece, 100-1; death of, 93; as example for Nero, 133; mildness of, 170, 184-5; ruthlessness of, 185

banquets, imperial: 'public', 69-71; 'private', 71-2
Bolton, Edmund, 34
Britannicus, assassination of, 55, 92, 138
Bruni, Leonardo, 30f
buildings, 112-24; on coins, 115, 120, 123

Caligula, 53-5, 60 n. 40, 61 n. 53; buildings of, 87, 116-17
Calpurnius Siculus, 131-2, 144-5
Carolano, Gerolamo, 33
censorship, literary, 132, 170-1
Cicero, 51, 53; *Pro Cluentio*, 56; *Rhetor*, 220
civil war, as an unpopular theme, 169, 225; *see also* Lucan; Petronius
Claudius, death of, 52, 55; buildings of, 119
comets, 190
Corbulo, Domitius, 40
Corinth, canal at, 99, 101-3
court politics, 3-5
credibility in history, 1-3
Cremutius Cordus, 169-70

death, and texts, 227; suicide, 228
decadence, 5, 38-9, 115-19, 196
decocta Neronis, 72-3, 131, 133, 137, 139
Domitia, death of, 134
Domitius Ahenobarbus, L., in Lucan, 163-7; as Nero's ancestor, 174 n. 51
Domus Aurea, 112, 117-22

Elizabeth I, 34-5
enargeia (vivid description), 50-1

epic, objectivity of, 159, 161-2

fama (fame), 159-60
Ficino, Marsilio, 32-3
fire of Rome, the great, 55, 189-91
fire, and love, 189, 199

Gibbon, Edward, 41-2, 46 n. 72
Golden Age, in the *Octavia*, 181; and Nero, 136
Greece, 98-107; liberation of, 99, 103-4; enslavement of, 103-4; Greek response to Nero, 106-7
growth, metaphor of, 135ff
Guicciardini, 31-2, 43 n. 13

haste, metaphor of, 131, 133ff
heat, metaphor of, 135, 137-8
Herodes Atticus, 101
invective, 50, 52; *see also* Lucian

Juvenal, 88

libertas, 170; in Lucan, 157; Renaissance attitudes to, 31; in Tacitus, 37, 40, 45 n. 48
Lucan, *Bellum Civile*: abrupt end of, 226-7, 231; Brutus in, 165-6; and Caesar's *De Bello Civili*, 156, 164, 167, 231; as eyewitness account, 161-2; historical accuracy of, 151; historical distortions in, 153-4, 163-8; and Homer, 164-5; obscurity of, 153, 155; and Petronius' Civil War poem, 225-7; politics of, 151-72; and Vergil, 112, 131, 155-6
Lucan, career of, 170-1; death of, 229; and Nero, 171
Lucian, and invective, 55-6

Machiavelli, 31; Machiavellianism, 42 n. 7
matricide, *see* parricide
metaphor, 220-1; *see also* Seneca, *Moral Epistles*; growth; heat; haste; precocity

Nero, and acting, 52, 83, 86-91; and

238 Index

Agrippina, 52, 212; buildings of, 113-14, 119-22, 136-7, 230; and charioteering, 52; childishness of, 134; in cinema, 11-24; competes in festivals, 89, 98-9, 100, 104-5; and the *damnatio memoriae*, 107; debauchery of, 53f; early youth of, 52, 212; education of, 212-13; and Fascists, 17-18; and gluttony, 67-79; and heralds, 52; his History of Rome, 140; horoscope of, 51; image in the Middle Ages, 29, 32; image in the Renaissance, 29ff; irreligion of, 53, 99; and music, 52, 98, 132, 212; Neronian decadence, 38-9; opposed to Augustus, 1, 106, 184-5; as persecutor of Christians, 12, 14; physical appearance of, 57; as popular emperor, 76-9; putting aristocrats on stage, 51, 86; response to Galba's revolt, 72-3; roaming streets in disguise, 77-8, 91; suicide of, 51, 93, 131, 139, 230; as sun-king, 131-2; as symbol in 1950s America, 11; tolerance of, 132, 171; transfers cult images, 101; as tyrant, 35-6, 180, 182-5; vices of, 1-2, 29, 37, 51-3, 68, 180-1

Neronian age: self-fashioning, 6; degenerate, 5; literary climate, 170-1

Neronis Encomium, by Cardano, 33

Neros, false, 197

objectivity, 48f; *see also* epic; Suetonius

Octavia, 136; execution of, 55

Octavia (play), authorship and date, 180; divided chorus in, 188; Nero in, 182-8; and Ovid, 178; as a political commentary on principate, 112-13; Seneca in, 180-7; Stoicism in, 180-91.

Ovid, *Metamorphoses*, 231; *Tristia*, 178, 231

panegyric, 50

parricide and matricide, 55-6, 179-80

Persius, 131-2, 139-45; and Horace, 140; and Lucan, 141; name, 140-1; speakers in *Sat.* 3, 142-4; Suetonian life, 140

Petronius, *Satyricon*: Civil War poem, 225-7; abrupt ending of, 225, 229-31; dating of, 225-7; and Lucan, 225-7; Eumolpus, 227, 229-30, 232; Trimalchio, 229

Petronius, as character in *Quo Vadis*, 13-14, 23; death of, 229

philosopher as artist, 217

physiognomics, *see* Polemo of Laodicea

Poggio Bracciolini, 31ff

Polemo of Laodicea, 56-8

Poppaea, 136; in the *Octavia*, 186-7

precocity, metaphor of, 135

principate, ancient debate on, 112-13; imperial self-definition, 87, 114-15, 123

propaganda, 115, 152-3, 158, 161-3, 168-9, 171-2

Quinquennium Neronis, 124 n. 5

Quintilian, 50-1, 139, 220

Quo Vadis, 1951 film, 11, 22-4; novel 11-14; early cinematic adaptations, 14-17; *see also The Sign of the Cross*

rhetoric, 48ff; history as, 30; lies in, 51, 58; use of buildings in, 116-19

rivers of blood, 226

Rome, Julio-Claudian building programmes in, 112; as a Neronian stage set, 91; *see also* Augustus; Caligula; Claudius; Nero; Tiberius; Vespasian

Savile, Henry, 34

Seneca, on actors, 83-4; career of, 211-12; death of, 228; hypocrisy of, 213, 215; on peace of mind, 220; as speechwriter, 212; on suicide, 227-8; in Tacitus, 39; on teaching, 213ff

Seneca, *Apocolocyntosis*, 5, 55, 113, 181, 212

Sececa, *De Clementia*, 56, 113, 182, 184

Seneca, *Moral Epistles*, 211-22, 227-8; addressee in, 215-16; as fiction, 215; metaphor in, 219-21

Seneca, *Thyestes*: Atreus in, 196, 203-7; and Euripides, 199; and frenzy (*furor*), 199; metadramatic reflection in, 197f, 202-3, 205; and *nefas* (evil), 198, 200, 204, 207; and repetition, 202; and silence, 204; and Stoicism, 199, 203; Tantalus in, 197, 203-4, 206-7; Thyestes in, 206-7

The Sign of the Cross, 1932 film, 19-22

Socrates, death of, 228

soul as text, 218-19

Stoicism, in Seneca, 214, 220-1; in Renaissance, 32-3; *see also* Octavia; Seneca, *Thyestes*

stormy seas, literary tradition of, 178; and poetic struggle, 229-30

Suetonius, 48-58, 212; detail in, 50-1; divisions in Lives, 52; irony in, 52; objectivity in, 52; as rhetorician, 58; as *scholasticus*, 48, 50; sources of, 59

Sulla, impiety of, 101

Tacitism, 30-2; and Machiavellianism, 30, 34
Tacitus, 35ff; *Agricola*, 38; *Annals*, 36-7, 39, 228-9; and ancient historiography, 36; in Middle Ages, 30; in modern readings, 41-2; and political thought, 30f; in Renaissance, 30ff; as rhetorician, 35; Syme on, 29, 41
Thrasea Paetus, 40

Tiberius, buildings of, 114-15; irreligion of, 53; and sex, 54; vices of, 51

Vergil, end of *Aeneid*, 231; and Lucan, 112, 155-6
Vespasian, buildings of, 123; enslavement of Greece, 103-4

word and deed (in philosophy), 214, 217-19, 221-2